PERFORMS IN TEMPERATURES DOWN TO -22°C EVEN WHEN THE CARTRIDGE IS GETTING EMPTY

PRIMUS® WINTER GAS

WINTER GAS

Fast, easy, clean – and no need to preheat

SWE **PRIMUS**

www.primus.eu

THE
ALPINE JOURNAL
2015

Nico Favresse on *Shepton's Shove* (E6 6b, 5.12a, 1000m), Walker Citadel, east coast of Baffin Island. The route continues up the pillar, with the hardest pitches at the top. *(Oli Favresse)*

THE
ALPINE JOURNAL
2015

The Journal of the Alpine Club

A record of mountain adventure
and scientific observation

Editors: Susan Jensen & Ed Douglas

Production Editor: Bernard Newman

Volume 119

Number 363

Supported by the
MOUNT EVEREST FOUNDATION

Published by
THE ALPINE CLUB

THE ALPINE JOURNAL 2015
Volume 119 No 363

www.alpine-club.org.uk

Address all editorial communication to the Hon Editor:
Alpine Club, 55 Charlotte Rd, London, EC2A 3QF
email: journal.editor@alpine-club.org.uk

Address all sales and distribution communications to:
Cordee, 11 Jacknell Rd, Dodwells Bridge Ind Est, Hinckley, LE10 3BS

Back numbers:
Apply to the Alpine Club, 55 Charlotte Rd, London, EC2A 3QF or, for
1969 to date, apply to Cordee, as above.

First published in 2015 by The Alpine Club
Typeset by Bernard Newman
Photo production by Tom Prentice
Printed and bound by Novoprint SA, Barcelona

A CIP catalogue record for this book is available from The British Library

ISBN 978-0-9569309-4-1

Front cover: Andy Inglis on the first pitch of *Teufel Grooves* (IX,9), Ben Nevis, during the first winter ascent. *(Iain Small)*

Endpapers
Front: The Matterhorn from Cervinia. *(Bernard Newman)*
Back: Stephen Skelton on the first pitch of *The Little Hard Climb* (I, 22) on the Petit Dur, Central Darrans, New Zealand, during the first ascent. Te Puoho Glacier terminal lake is below. *(Kester Brown)*

Foreword

The shock of the earthquake that struck Nepal on 25 April, killing around 9000 people, is still very fresh in our minds. The country holds a special place in the hearts of AC members, something highlighted by the immediate offers of help by so many of them. Several former presidents have made appeals for support, not least Doug Scott, whose charity Community Action Nepal has been working on development projects in Nepal for many years. Other members, including current vice-president Victor Saunders, were in Nepal when the earthquake struck, and gave up their climbing ambitions in order to help the extraordinary grass-roots relief effort that quickly got underway, organised and financed by ordinary Nepalis as well as foreign friends.

The media's obsession with Everest and the negative impacts of tourism can leave the public with the impression that all climbers are selfish egomaniacs with no regard for the people they hire to help them achieve their seemingly pointless ambitions. No doubt a few of them are guilty as charged, but the wholehearted support from so many climbing friends of Nepal suggests that the vast majority have a deep and well-meaning respect for the country and its people.

The urgent requests from many directions for tourists to continue coming to Nepal shows how important mountain tourism is to one of the poorest countries in Asia. The impact migrant labour is having on the social fabric of Nepal is well documented – and so are the costs, as breadwinners leave their families for long periods of time to take on sometimes dangerous work in the Gulf States and elsewhere. There are undoubtedly dangers for those working in Nepal's trekking and climbing industries, and there always will be, but it remains a valuable – and valid – business for local people to exploit so they can share in a little of our prosperity.

Trekking and climbing businesses working in Nepal are only too aware of the problems ineffective regulation and outright corruption can cause. The aftermath of this terrible disaster is the right moment to think about what the future of mountain tourism in Nepal should look like. Those who work in the industry should be properly protected, and insurance schemes are beginning to improve; there have been some effective training initiatives to improve local guides. But it is often the case that the best companies, who do much more than is required of them to care for their workers, are undermined by those that cut corners – something that can have dire consequences in the mountains.

The travails of Nepal's mountain tourism would come as no surprise to members of the Alpine Club in the late nineteenth century. As Koen van Loocke explains in his review of the embryonic guiding profession on page 273, the Club was intimately involved in developing standards for guides and protecting the interests of alpinists against growing commercialism. This year's 150 anniversary of the first ascent of the Matterhorn – reflected on in a special section starting on page 159 – is a reminder of the transformation the fashion for mountains wrought on the sleepy hamlet of Zermatt. A similar if not identical process is now underway in the Himalaya; we must hope that the best climbing ethical standards are respected by those in a position of authority.

It is fair to say there are still parts of the world that haven't had the stamp of tourism marked on the landscape. Tom Nakamura and Evelio Echevarría describe unexplored areas in Tibet and Peru; Raja Mukherjee follows well-documented footsteps through the Indian Himalaya and still finds blanks on the map. Exploration continues, but with the internet and Google Earth, as described by George Cave's article, are we on the last stretch of untouched areas?

Mountainous parts of the world fall in and out of fashion. Kyrgyzstan, with its relatively easy access and logistics and with lots of interesting mountains that aren't thin-air high, is definitely popular; this volume has two expedition articles and several entries in the MEF report summaries. The Alps aren't quite as high on the list of places for exploratory mountaineering these days, but Simon Richardson's article on 20 years of new routing and exploration in the Val Ferret shows that even in the Mont Blanc massif there are overlooked lines.

Sometimes how you get to the mountains can be more interesting – or harder – than the climbing itself, as described in the By Sea section. The Reverend Shepton takes his band of climbers and *Dodo's Delight* back to Greenland, and Crag Jones and Bjørn Riis-Johannessen sail to South Georgia in two separate articles.

Many thanks go to the authors of the articles, area notes and obituaries, and in particular to Catherine Moorehead who has been kept very busy compiling the obituaries this year. Thanks also to Bernard Newman, our tireless production editor, to Margot Blyth, whose proofreading keeps us consistent, and everyone else who makes the *Alpine Journal* possible.

Ed Douglas and Susan Jensen

Contents

HIGH ASIA

First Ascent of Gasherbrum V   *Chi-Young Ahn & Peter Jensen-Choi*   3
The Climb   *Malcolm Bass*   10
Hagshu North-east Face   *Mick Fowler*   18
North-eastern Spiti   *Derek Buckle*   32
On Finding Peaks and Pushing Limits   *Aleksey Zholobenko*   39
No Sleep till Bishkek   *Timothy Elson*   47
In The Tracks of The Snow Leopard   *Adrian Dye*   57

SURVEYS

Blue Sky Expedition   *Tom Nakamura*   69
South Simvu   *Anindya Mukherjee*   75
Zumthul Phuk   *Anindya Mukherjee*   84
Undiscovered Granite   *Paul Knott*   91
Cordillera Chaupijanca, Peru   *Evelio Echevarría*   101

BY SEA

Greenland and Baffin Island   *Rev Bob Shepton*   113
The Last Leviathan   *Caradog (Crag) Jones*   125
The Shackleton Traverse   *Bjørn Riis-Johannessen*   136

ALPS

The Lonely Pillar   *Simon Richardson*   147

MATTERHORN 150

14 July 1865   *Ian Smith*   161
Letters From The Matterhorn   *Roger Birnstingl*   168
Made For Television   *John Cleare*   177

LITERATURE

My Gypsy Self   *Karen Stockham*   189
One Hundred Mountains of Japan   *Martin Hood*   199

SCIENCE & NATURE

Digital Expedition Planning   *George Cave*   209
A New Proposal for Reducing AMS   *Victor Saunders*   215
Slippery When Wet   *Allan Pentecost*   218

ART & PHOTOGRAPHY

Stereo Views	*Peter Blair*	227
Alfred Williams of Salisbury	*Simon Pierse*	234
Life in a Carousel	*Dennis Gray*	245

HISTORY

'Machiavellian Bastardy?'	*Mick Conefrey*	257
Sacking the Editor	*Peter Foster & Gareth Jones*	266
The Shaping of Nineteenth Century Guiding	*Koen Van Loocke*	273
One Hundred Years Ago	*C A Russell*	284

AREA NOTES

Alps & Dolomites 2014	*Lindsay Griffin*	291
Scottish Winter 2014-15	*Simon Richardson*	301
China & Tibet 2014	*Bruce Normand*	310
Indian Himalaya 2013	*Rajesh Gadgil*	323
Nepal 2014	*Ian Wall*	332
Argentina 2014	*Marcelo Scanu*	338
New Zealand 2014	*Kester Brown*	345
MEF Reports	*Summarised by Glyn Hughes*	350

REVIEWS

REVIEWS	365

IN MEMORIAM

IN MEMORIAM	400

ALPINE CLUB NOTES

ALPINE CLUB NOTES		443
Early Drawings of the Matterhorn	*Robin Campbell*	443
Robin Collomb: An Appreciation	*John Cleare*	445
Kekoo Naoroji Award	*Tony Smythe*	448
Lines of Ascent: William Heaton Cooper	*Terry Gifford*	449
First Female Ascent of Monviso	*Adele Long and Livio Perotti*	451
AC Library Annual Report 2014	*Hywel Lloyd*	454
Contributors		457

Index	464

NOTES FOR CONTRIBUTORS

The *Alpine Journal* records all aspects of mountains and mountaineering, including expeditions, adventure, art, literature, geography, history, geology, medicine, ethics and the mountain environment.

Articles Contributions in English are invited. They should be sent to the Hon Editor *The Alpine Journal*, Alpine Club, 55 Charlotte Road, London EC2A 3QF, UK. (**journal.editor@alpine-club.org.uk**) Articles, including images, should be sent on a disk or memory stick (with accompanying hard copy as appropriate, e.g. sketch maps) or as an email attachment. With files created in Microsoft Word please confine any extra formatting to italics and bold and set the language to English UK. Length should not exceed 3000 words without prior approval of the editor **and may be edited or shortened at their discretion**. It is regretted that the *Alpine Journal* is unable to offer a fee for articles published, but authors who are not AC members receive a complimentary copy of the issue of the *Journal* in which their article appears.

Preferably, articles and book reviews should not have been published in substantially the same form by any other publication.

Maps and diagrams These should be well researched, accurate, and show the most important place-names mentioned in the text. It is the author's responsibility to get their maps redrawn if necessary. If submitted electronically, maps and route diagrams should be originated as CMYK .eps files in Adobe Illustrator, Freehand or similar ensuring any embedded images are at 300dpi resolution and CMYK. Hard copy should be scanned as a Photoshop compatible 300dpi tiff at A4 finished size. This can be arranged through the production editor if required.

Photographs Colour transparencies should be originals (not copies) in 35mm format or larger. Prints (any size) should be numbered (in pencil) on the back and accompanied by a separate list of captions (see below). Pre-scanned images should be **300dpi** Greyscale or RGB, tiffs or Maximum Quality jpegs at A4 final size or larger. **Images from digital cameras** should be submitted at the largest file size (quality) the camera can produce, e.g. 'Large' jpegs, tiffs or RAW files. Image files should have **short**, unique names/serial numbers **that correspond to the list of captions** appended to your article, as a separate word processing document, or in an email. Captions should be reasonably detailed and include the photographer's name. Captions must be provided for all images, including any slides and prints.

Copyright It is the author's responsibility to obtain copyright clearance for text, photographs, digital images and maps, to pay any fees involved and to ensure that acknowledgements are in the form required by the copyright owner.

Summaries A brief summary, listing dates, team members, objectives attempted and/or achieved, should be included at the end of articles where appropriate.

Biographies Authors are asked to provide a short biography, in about 50 words, listing the most noteworthy items in their climbing career and anything else they wish to mention.

Deadline Copy and photographs should reach the editor by 1 February of the year of publication.

High Asia

The Matterhorn from Winkelmatten. Hans Conrad Escher von der Linth. 14th August 1806. Watercolour. 24.2 x 22.4cm.
(Zentralbibliothek Zürich, Department of Prints and Drawings/ Photo Archive)

The section frontispiece images for this year's Journal feature early artistic interpretations of the Matterhorn, in celebration of the 150th anniversary of the first ascent. Robin Campbell's introduction to these images can be found in the AC Notes, p443.

CHI-YOUNG AHN & PETER JENSEN-CHOI

First Ascent of Gasherbrum V

South Face of Gasherbrum V
showing the line of the Ahn-Choi
route. *(All photos: Chi-young Ahn
and Nak-jong Seong)*

Bare and insignificant against the blinding white backdrop of Gasher-brum V's south face, our silhouettes stand perched on an opposing hill with the full view of its prominent glacier field and snow wall propped up before us like a perfect mural. The complex characteristics of the glacier remind me of the snake scales of a dragon's tail leading up to the jagged bergschrund that rests at the base of this massive wall looming over us. We have spotted an S-shaped line through the glacier and possible weak points along crevasse-like, corniced lines of the middle section and to the rightmost side of the wall in the upper mixed section, finishing off with a straightforward enough line to the summit.

We never thought of a route here until after being denied passage up GV's east face where we trudged through thigh-deep snow to position ourselves for camp one. The face, covered in crumbly ice and snow, was nearly impossible to protect. We raced between radio signals to climb each time an avalanche cleared. The constantly falling ice and snow shower debris pouring down from above posed the greatest threats. We finally had no choice but to evacuate from our high point of 6400m.

The unsuccessful attempt had killed any desire to climb. As the leader, the troublesome quandaries of a second attempt weighed heavily on my conscience. Our problems weren't just our already physically weakened state and shot confidence, but mid-July was passing us by as snows laid siege to the camps once again. The dilemma of the hard work and extra time required to relocate base camp with our small team also seemed less than appealing.

Ahn navigating crevasses on the approach.

I realised finally that the summit counted for far less than I had thought. Only our truly best efforts could prevail over any failures; this would act as our holy grail and device to keep from quitting at even our weakest moments through the remainder. And with the consensus of my team, I decided we would try one more time, up the south face; we mobilised base camp.

We knew that unlocking the intricacies of the long glacial approach would be critical to saving strength for the actual climb. We gambled by not roping up to each other to minimise time and conserve energy. Navigating our way through the complex terrain, though far harder than we had anticipated, we reached the plateau two hours faster than planned and we were at the bergschrund (5720m) near 10am.

Traces of avalanched snow chunks and debris filled the vicinity of the bergschrund and headwall entry point. We quickly gathered ourselves beneath a rock to shelter from the cornices resting far above us. I tied in first and started our climb with Nak-jong following and we remained connected by our two 7mm ropes throughout the day.

The surrounding walls that day felt like the imaginary arena of an ancient coliseum, as we wielded our axes, parrying and dodging our way up. The

Bivvy at c6550m on Gasherbrum V.

hot sun beating off the worthless, crust-fried snow scorched our faces. The scree-like snow sapped our strength with every step, requiring two or three hard swings to set our picks. We instantly huddled into the wall each time exploding avalanches boomed off the mid section, followed by frequent snow showers.

To avoid the enormous, roughly 300m wide cornice looming from above, we continuously moved to the left for higher ground. As time passed, gradually my calves and thighs began to scream and I resorted to side-stepping to relieve the fatigue. Leaving the bergschrund at roughly 11 that morning, we had expected to be at our intended bivvy site by 5pm, but we had progressed slowly and were only two-thirds of the way up to our bivvy; it was to be an ice cave this time. By dusk, our one-litre bottles were dry. The effects of dehydration quickly took their toll on us and at around 10pm, after realizing the ice cave was farther than it appeared, we rested quickly to boil and drink some water. After warming our bodies and coming back to life, we finally reached the bivvy site at midnight.

Our thirst was unquenchable while I chopped and cut away at the ice floor to pitch our tent. The site was worse than I had expected, with irregular formations of soft snow, oddly-angled ice and hard mini crevasses all over. After struggling to flatten out a platform, our less-than-two-man-sized tent sat unevenly with its left corner sagging out into the air of a gaping hole.

There was no argument that we desperately needed water, so as we crouched in our tiny tent we diligently melted ice to stave off the freezing

5

Seong leading above the first bivvy during the first ascent of Gasherbrum V.

cold and relax our hypothermic shivers. Too exhausted and parched to chew, we added thin amounts of porridge to drink in our water. We had been on the move since 5am from base camp and had advanced roughly 1800m in altitude. We fixed the tent and tied ourselves back into our rope before finally bedding down. Our cramped and tired bodies lay unaffected by the mountainside's deep, fissure-cracking groans as the temperatures dropped even further into the night.

The following afternoon, while we sipped tea, a palm-sized stone gashed the left tent wall, landing on the mattress. I shrieked as Nak-jong just stared at me, bewildered; a smaller stone had penetrated the tent and badly bruised my knee. We re-situated our tent and stayed there a while, to alleviate my bruised knee and regain our strength. We were out climbing again by 3am, 25 July.

That early there was no rockfall, and climbing conditions were prime. We advanced up along the slanted, gash-like, edgy feature, traversed to the right roughly 200m below the seemingly un-crossable, very long and wide bergschrund-like feature until we discovered an ice column no more than waist-sized in girth. Formed by the melt-off, this column connected us up and beyond to the technically hardest stage of the climb, a roughly 300-400m chossy rock section. The amount of rockfall encountered kept us speechless, and a tremendous and tedious amount of care and effort was made to place gear and keep the falling rock clear of the belayer. With just the slightest grasp, the loose rock wanted out, and clearing for something better seemed useless but we somehow managed to get some protection.

Relieved to be transitioning out of the mixed terrain, the final roughly 300m snow wall section posed a new set of less than welcome challenges. There were no rocky outcrops up here and my heart raced in fear over the avalanche danger. The snow wall was crusty and lacked any real integrity; we continually re-stepped to regain our sliding foot positions, both while climbing and resting at the belay.

It was growing late and we still could not see how much further there was to go. Concerns about another late night of climbing crept in to my thoughts. Gasherbrum VI's summit finally came into view off in the

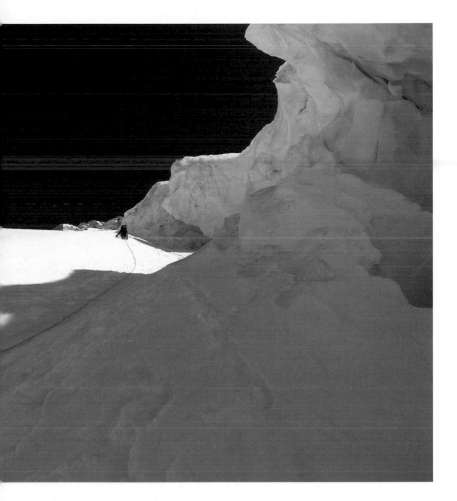

distance. I knew we were near, but a dark grey gloom of clouds filled and hung in the westerly skies. Mist built up and was rising toward the summit I prayed for the good weather to persist for just a little bit longer, knowing it would likely change for the worse very soon. Snow stake and ice screw anchors were unquestionably weak, and would be unlikely to brake the slightest of slips. I fretted over the obvious and Nak-jong replied with nothing more than a look and nod. The tedious snow slowed our pace. Step after each slow step we pushed our bodies up to Gasherbrum V's summit by 7.20pm. The summit was not hard, nor solid, but comprised an extended series of very precarious cornices on the verge of collapse. We stood as high as we could safely go, just off the highest corniced section.

To the north and east were glimmers of Gasherbrums I and II veiled in the mist. Sensing the urgency, we quickly snapped shots and promptly started down climbing to economise our gear, retracing our footsteps back to the chossy section. A more direct abseil through the overhangs, muddled

Chi-young Ahn leading near the top of the upper section of poor rock c6800m.

rock and ice runnels seemed to make the most sense due to the numerous awkward diagonal and outcropping sections of rock on our way up. We took one of many ravines to the right and, once committed, shifting the direction of the rappel would be unfathomable, especially in our wasted condition. Sticking tightly together but slightly offset, we were particularly careful to not accidentally pitch loose rock onto each other.

The further we descended without any trace of our climb up and, despite the numerous V-threads, our quickly diminishing gear continued to up the ante on our survival. We made countless raps, not caring to keep track anymore, and still we had no sign of our route up. Our sense of direction seemed to have disappeared in the surrounding darkness of night. We were completely lost and an indescribable reality of fear such as I have never experienced sank deeply into my scattered, futile and trivial thoughts.

The surrounding walls seemed to wrap themselves around us the further down we progressed. Our bodies were so very exhausted and we had maybe only a snow stake and ice screw left to use, I cannot recollect exactly. Fear and stress were having their ways with us until a loud bellow of relief reached me from below at about midnight: 'I've spotted our foot-prints…above the cornice!'

Right: A final section of poor snow leads to the summit.

Below: Chi-young Ahn and Nak-jong Seong on the summit of Gasherbrum V.

I sighed with relief as I hung roughly 150m above our site. I had earlier spotted an angled corner we could have huddled in if things got desperate, but now as the breadth of our minds slowly returned, I folded such desperate thoughts out. We returned to our bivvy site at roughly 4am. We had climbed for over 24 hours straight and collapsed into our squishy, ripped tent. Not much gas was left in the canister, so we melted only enough ice to share and drink. We hadn't drunk water since late afternoon and our bodies were hypothermic. We melted just a little more and let sleep take over.

We remained tied in until the last snow wall section, then downclimbed at last the roughly 300m to the bergschrund. Much of the glacier field had transformed since what seemed to be so long ago. We were safely back to the foot of the glacier by 6pm that evening and back at base camp an hour later as the sun settled down beyond Mustagh Tower. I was so eager to be finished with our descent, and worried about how repairs for our stone ripped tent might go – how glad I was to be worrying over such a trivial matter! The sun slid into the night. Without a nudge, base camp came to life with the relief of laughter.

Summary

An account of the first ascent of Gasherbrum V (7147m) via the southeast face (*Korean Direct*, WI4-5, M4), by Chi-young Ahn and Nak-jong Seong (Korea). The ascent was done in alpine style, 23-26 July 2014.

MALCOLM BASS

The Climb

Malcolm Bass traversing towards the bivvy site on day one. *(Simon Yearsley)*

They say that which doesn't kill you makes you stronger; this doesn't seem to me to be true of rock fall. The solitary rock arcing out of a clear blue sky to crumple my partner on our third day on a huge, half rotten face, and, years before, the cowering for hours beneath a relentless fusillade of rock and ice on a mountain not two miles from here: these have reduced rather than strengthened me. They have left me with all too clear a view of our vulnerability.

We were vulnerable now, Simon Yearsley and I, as we crossed the bergschrund beneath the south-west buttress of Janahut. Two little lights poking around ice chasms and fragile bridges at the foot of a great mountain in the dark, a kilometre and a half of terrain above us, an unknown depth of ice beneath. We were vulnerable and felt it. Midnight gave way to those early hours when we all want warmth and bed, not cold and fear. We were vulnerable to the drop, to what might drop on us, to our fears of both, and more besides. So much loomed above that we couldn't see and had no way of knowing.

Two roped pitches saw us over the bergschrund; a tiny impression made. A foothold established in the couloir that would hopefully take us up the lower part of the face, we relaxed slightly; Simon coiled the rope, we had a drink and ate a gel. 'Let's get this done.' Turning in to the slope and planting our shafts higher, just then it came: first a whirring sound then the impact one metre to my left. Huge, not properly seen, smashing into the snow, then spinning, tumbling, out and off again. We pressed ourselves into the slope, held our breath, and listened: only the diminishing rattle below and adrenaline pushed pulses. The moment passed. I let out a stream of obscenities about west faces, Gangotri, that specific rock, rocks in general, mountains, my fated ill luck, and just how lucky we had been. Then we started climbing.

With dawn the morning became much more fun. Snow conditions were good and we had no need of the rope. It was the best of alpine climbing, moving smoothly over moderate terrain in a magnificent setting. To the south the Maiandi glacier merged with the massive Gangotri and a long view down past Kharchakund to the Kedar peaks; to our north were the head of the Maiandi and the south side of Swachand peak. I had been this way before: in 2004 I had climbed this same ground with Paul Figg and Andy Brown. We had come to a halt on a snowy night a little further up. On the same night our Kiwi friend Pat Deavoll had been suffering the miseries of altitude sickness hundreds of metres above at 6400m on the south ridge, having reached the ridge via the big couloir in the west face with her partner Marty Beare. They too had to descend. Since then American Bryan Hylenski and various partners including Anindya Mukherjee had made two attempts from the east side of the mountain (and then onto the south ridge), the second reaching around 6500m.

My fear had gone now, replaced with the breathless curiosity of finding the route. A little gully of little promise neatly outflanked a wall for the price of a few steep moves; we reached the 2004 high point under another steep wall. Out right under this wall to a shattered col as the late morning sun hit the upper face and, now twelve hours on with 700m in the bag, we began to look for somewhere to bivouac. The route ahead lay up a big couloir which nipped into a tight throat just above us, and we had to decide whether to press on up hoping to reach some sort of sanctuary before the sun sent rocks flying down the couloir, or to stop a little early under an overhanging wall just to the right of the fall line. Mindful of history we chose the overhang. It didn't take long to widen the natural ledge and, as the sun reached us, we were able to savour the joys of warmth and safety from the comfort of our tent as the stove purred for tea.

The next morning was far from comfortable as we climbed up through the gully throat and into a broadening couloir in the dark. We and the face were both well frozen; we weren't silenced though and kept up our babble, the ritual incantations of inanity that we have spoken from Glen Coe to

Malcolm Bass on the easier angled snow arête, approaching The Castle and, opposite, engaged in the steep initial crux. *(Simon Yearsley)*

Garhwal, from the '80s till now. Their function is social, but not communicative; the honks of migrating geese may carry more meaning. We managed to talk sense long enough to agree to put the rope on and place runners as Simon led over windslab into the upper couloir. The dawn light revealed a fine series of rock spires adorning the right bank, then a well-chosen double back took us off the south-west face and up into the sun. We were very glad of its warmth and felt an urge to luxuriate. Finding nowhere suitable we belayed and I started up a scrappy, loose mixed pitch on the ridge crest. Keen to sit down in the sun I rushed the climbing, finding myself quite unexpectedly making hard moves, but that same impatience pushed me up them at a decent pace to the pleasures of a sitting belay.

After another couple of pitches the ridge reared up in a pitch of steep, hard ice. It was my lead, I was tiring, and I really didn't fancy it. I set off in a spirit of resignation. An early screw to protect the belay, the sense of front points barely buried, then the insidious and inevitable onset of burning calves. The ridge was clearly very corniced over the west face, but the cornice was made of such deliciously soft stuff, and Simon so well belayed on the east side that the temptation was just too much: I edged over on to the unsupported snow and scuttled up it till the rope ran out.

The ridge didn't offer many obvious tent sites, so when we came across a slightly flatter section behind an impressive gendarme at about 6500m we took our chance and began to dig. Digging soon gave way to chipping, and chipping to standing around nursing our backs and panting. Two hours later we finally pitched the tent. It was a magnificent campsite and we

enjoyed our time there. Clouds bubbled up from the wild rainforest gorges beyond the Chaukhambas and were lit up by the warm colours of evening. We could see down to Meade's col where we had camped 19 years before. We leavened the aesthetics and nostalgia by making a video of ourselves interviewing one another about the day. It's not much to look at as the lens was totally steamed up (we're better in audio anyway), and we don't make much sense, but one quote stands out: 'The summit looks pretty close, but that's probably an illusion...'

Next morning we left the tent pitched and set out for the summit. Short sections of technical climbing around gendarmes alternated with long sections of narrow horizontal ridge and moderate ice slopes. From time to time we stopped to warm toes and fingers. As morning turned to afternoon a brisk breeze began to blow and it grew colder. A long section of icy ridge led to The Castle, a steep rock step around 80m high that seemed to be the last major obstacle before the summit. After a quick scout around its defences we decided on a frontal assault. A steep chimney succumbed to Cairngorm style climbing, each series of harder moves heralding a major fit of gasping. Despite the oxygen debt it was exhilarating to be bridging, hooking, jamming and torqueing up a pitch like this so high on an unclimbed mountain. When I thought it was finished I sat smugly on top in the late afternoon sun belaying Simon. He came up, took the rack and vanished over the crest. The rope ran out smoothly for a while, then came familiar staccato pulls and pauses: hard climbing ahead. It turned out to be another chimney, steep and smooth sided, redeemed only by helpful chock stones. I don't think my breathing has ever been faster.

We now stood on a sharp rock crest. A smooth slab covered in a foot or more of soft snow barred the way forward. We had both tried it. We both felt very cold. The high point we had been aiming for all day revealed itself from here to be a false summit. The wind was rising and the night was coming. We were very tired and guessed that we didn't have much left. And there was something else, something sensed rather than known. There wasn't much discussion. Simon set the first abseil anchor. Two days and one dramatic night later we were back on the glacier.

What to make of it all? Human minds love to categorise and judge. They are especially keen on binary judgements. Success or failure? Good trip or bad trip? Worthwhile or waste? Win or lose?

Yet this trip just won't cohere for me. It won't resolve neatly, insists on remaining a series of almost unrelated experiences and emotions. Frustration at being so close, only 140m below the untrodden summit, when such chances are so very rare. Pride and amazement at our climbing so high in such vast solitude. The beauty of cramponning into the dawn on our acclimatisation on the east flank of Kedar. The human warmth in the camaraderie of our little team. The sadness in the wind on our last dusk walks around base camp, neither of us young anymore. Still climbing hard at 6600m. And then that decision: what of that decision?

I still want it badly. The summit, the personal sense of achievement and, although I wish I didn't, I do still want some glory. So it matters to me to make sense of our decision to retreat. It matters even though the direct experience of our great mountain journey lies beyond such judgements. From the comfort of home, my mind still insists on asking whether we made the right call. Should we have pressed on into the darkness? We have climbed on into many dark nights. Could we have found a way round the snowed up slabs? After a rest and a gel could we have summoned enough

Simon Yearsley following the initial crux. *(Malcolm Bass)*

energy to go on to the new summit? But what I am beginning to understand now is that our bodies and the more primitive parts of our minds knew the score. They knew what was happening inside and out, and knew what was going to happen next. They sent us the best signals they could. We did well to hear them.

Back to the first night of the descent, and there is no shelter on the open ice slope. The wind relentless; vastness, darkness, cold and stars as if in space. Technique, technology, and two cold-numbed brains maintain a slowly descending circle of light and life from V-thread to V-thread. The wind strengthens. We reach a rock buttress, try to cram ourselves in a cleft for shelter, but the rift funnels the wind straight onto us. Gasping now with cold, our good kit and continued movement are our salvation. A jammed rope, delay and shivering. Eighteen hours on the go. Sluggish thoughts. Another rope length down. Everything slowing. Then finally the tent. We crawl in fully kitted and just lie there. All we can do is lie there.

Details of The Expedition

Janahut was our third-choice objective for the trip. We had originally sought permission for Rimo III, but the Indian Army refused. Our secondary objective was Chaukhamba IV and the Indian Mountaineering Foundation pulled out all the stops to provide us with this permit at short notice. However once we were in the field it became clear that in prevailing snow conditions all routes up Chaukhamba IV were unsafe, so we obtained permission from our Liaison Officer, Subedar Dan Singh of the Indian Army, to attempt Janahut.

Other permanent team members were: Ming Temba Sherpa (high altitude porter), Chewang Gyalson (high altitude porter), Santbir Sherpa (cook), Danesh Rai (assistant cook).

The strain of Himalayan climbing: Bass and Yearsley at their high point. *(Simon Yearsley)*

Base camp was established at Sunderban (4600m) on 31 May. There was still a lot of snow there. On 2 and 3 June Malcolm and Simon acclimatised on the normal route on Kedar Dome, camping at 5100m and ascending to 6000m.

On 6 June Malcolm, Simon, Dan, Ming Temba, and Chewang left base camp carrying food, gas and climbing equipment for Malcolm and Simon to attempt Janahut. We all camped near the foot of the Swachand glacier, about halfway to Janahut. There was quite a lot of snow on the glacier and the moraine and this made for easy travel. On 7 June all five carried loads up to the foot of the Maiandi glacier. Dan, Ming Temba, and Chewang then returned to base camp, whilst Malcolm and Simon stayed on and began the attempt described above on the night of 9 June. The attempt took the south-west buttress of Janahut to the south ridge. The high point of the attempt was above the Castle at 6660m on 12 June. After the cold night descent from the high point back to the tent at 6300m we descended the east side of the mountain to a high glacial bowl, and from there back to the start point at the junction

Bass/Yearsley line on the South-west Buttress of Janahut. *(Simon Yearsley)*

between the Maiandi and Gangotri glaciers. After a night's rest we plodded the 20 km back to base camp. Glacial streams proved difficult to cross on the way back down. Malcolm and Simon's loads didn't quite make it all the way back to base camp, so on 17 June Chewang and Ming Temba went back to the end of the moraine to collect them. We left base camp on 20 June and arrived back at Gangotri on 21 June.

Summary

An account of an attempt on the unclimbed Janahut (6805m) via the south-west buttress to the south ridge, 9-15 June 2014, by Malcolm Bass and Simon Yearsley. This peak is at the head of the Gangotri glacier and has defied four previous attempts.

Acknowledgements

The expedition was supported by generous grants from the Mount Everest Foundation, the British Mountaineering Council and the Alpine Club. The Alpine Club grant is part sponsored by First Ascent. These grants are the envy of alpinists from other nations. Malcolm and Simon are sponsored by Montane and Lyon Outdoor (Petzl and La Sportiva). We are very grateful for their excellent support and superb kit.

MICK FOWLER

Hagshu North-east Face

The bear kept visiting base camp every evening and just wouldn't go away. No one in our party had ever seen a Himalayan brown bear before, so initially this was very exciting. After several days, though, it became clear that Rinku, our Liaison Officer, was tiring of the situation. The standard tips he had been given for dealing with bears – shout, chase it away, light a fire, etc. – were not having the desired effect and he, our cook Prittam and the kitchen boy Kapil were getting a bit weary of staying up most of the night to protect our food supplies.

'I think it best that we finish the expedition early,' Rinku announced.

Over the years I have experienced an interesting array of non-climbing

Mick Fowler, day three, first ascent of Hagshu North-east Face, looking north across the Hagshu glacier. *(All photos: Mick Fowler/Paul Ramsden*

Himalayan challenges but this was a new one on me.

As it happened, though, the members of the British Hagshu Expedition 2014 were lying contented in their tents, letting retrospective pleasure flow over them. Steve Burns and Ian Cartwright had all but climbed an unclimbed and un-named 6000m peak, and Paul Ramsden and I had managed a week long traverse of Hagshu, the Matterhorn of Zanskar.

Fresh snow lay on the ground, the sky was grey and there was no particular reason to hang around. Getting back to home and work a few days early always goes down well and we were happy to go along with Rinku's suggestion.

It had been an unusual trip. Hagshu first appeared on my radar 25 years ago; I spotted its distinctive outline when climbing in Kishtwar in 1989. Unbeknownst to me it was climbed for the first time that year, firstly by a Polish team up the south-east ridge and then, days later, by a British team via the east face. I saw it again when I returned to Kishtwar in 1993, and again when climbing in the area with Paul in 2012 and 2013. By late 2013 Paul and I decided that it had risen to the top of our list of exciting objectives. Steve Burns and Ian Cartwright were keen to join us and so the British Hagshu Expedition 2014 came into being.

Mountaineering in India is strictly controlled by a permit system and by January 2014 we had booked the north face of Hagshu for the post-monsoon season. Bureaucracy can be a major hurdle in Himalayan mountaineering and we were pleased to feel that, ascents in the meantime aside, we would have the opportunity to attempt the first ascent in September. How wrong could we be? A week or two before our departure the Indian authorities issued two further permits for the same face at the same time as our expedition. An American team had other aspirations but this still meant that a Slovenian team comprising three of the world's best alpinists,

Marko Prezelj, Luca Lindic and Ales Cesen, had been granted a permit for 'our' objective. And they would be getting there a week ahead of us. We were not best pleased.

An attraction of Hagshu for us was that we would approach through Ladakh and Zanskar which were areas that we had not been to before. Much as I was aware that the climate in Ladakh is very different to that of Kishtwar I wasn't quite prepared to see sand dunes as we flew into Leh. Equally I was not prepared for the proudly advertised 'Leh Beautification Project' which appeared intent on carrying out every aspect of 'beautification' at the same time. The network of deep trenches on the sides of the streets was such that access to many of the shops was only possible by crossing dubi-

North side of Hagshu from base camp.

ously balanced planks with significant drops below. Overall, though, Leh was more touristy than I expected with a vast array of cultural artefacts for sale. As one shop truthfully advertised: 'more junk upstairs.'

Being keen as ever to save time and get to base camp quickly we left Leh immediately to drive along the 200 kilometres or so of tarmac to the town of Kargil, close to the Pakistani border. Unfortunately the roads were such that I missed most of the stunning scenery as I spent much of the journey calling for our driver to stop so I could be sick.

I had heard many rude comments about Kargil but initial impressions were pleasing in that the delightfully inappropriately named Hotel Greenland had hot water taps that ran with hot water. This was a near first for me on climbing trips to India. That aside, the atmosphere was decidedly tense with caged army trucks, complete with security guards, in use as school buses. In September the temperature was comfortable but Rinku told us that winters were ferocious; the coldest temperature ever recorded in India, -45°C, was at the town of Dras just a few kilometres down the road.

The second day of our drive took us past the remote monastery of Rangdum. An armed guard at a checkpoint outside seemed ludicrously unnecessary until Rinku explained that the monastery had been attacked by terrorists in 2000 and several monks, along with a German hitch-hiker, were killed. To us it seemed the most tranquil, remote and unlikely target; it was a sharp reminder that this is a far from peaceful part of the world.

North-east face of Hagshu on left with Fowler/Ramsden (solid) line; snowy
north face on right with Slovenian line (dashed).

The road continued over the 4400m Pensi La pass and dropped into
Zanskar. As the only motorable route into Zanskar we were reliant on this
pass still being open on our return journey in mid-October. Nicki, my wife,
once had to spend a whole winter stranded in a Ladakh valley so I was
acutely aware of this risk, not to mention that we were now near where that
record low temperature had been recorded.

The village of Akshu was small and friendly and one of the first we
reached in Zanskar. Prittam and Kapil had already arrived and had
arranged for yaks to take us to base camp the next day. I like yaks and
never cease to be amazed by them. These had wooden rings through their
noses and their owners pulled hard on them to make the beasts comply.
Their noses stretched a lot and it looked uncomfortable to say the least, but
they seemed not to mind.

Getting to base camp was reportedly a two-day walk. In reality that
meant that we had to pay for two days but everyone recognised that it
would be done in one, if we went the right way. Research had revealed that
a team back in the 1990s had spent an entire day walking up the nearside
of the river only to decide that they couldn't cross to where they wanted

to be. The river did look to be a significant challenge. A couple of yaks chose to cross via a rickety bridge but most clearly relished the refreshing challenge of deep, fast flowing glacial water. With loads of perhaps 100kg plus a yak driver on top, I could hardly believe when the water level rose to over halfway up the loads, yet they kept going at a steady pace, stopping for an occasional drink of the silt-laden water. I never did quite work out how they avoided being swept downstream. Impressive beasts, these yaks.

Our base camp, situated in the ablation valley on the true left bank of the Hagshu glacier, was idyllic. The Slovenians and Americans were camping close together some five minutes higher; the next day we wandered up to say hello. The three Americans were enthusiastic about their intended line on Barnaj and from the Slovenian team we met Luca who had stayed back with a stomach upset but told us that Marko and Ales were undertaking a reconnaissance of the west face of Hagshu. We made suitably encouraging noises and set about our own plans.

Steve and Ian were planning exploration of unclimbed 6000m peaks to the south of base camp whereas Paul and I were focused exclusively on the north face of Hagshu. First we needed to acclimatise and so all four of us set out together to spend a few nights on a c5700m peak to the north-west of Hagshu. This, we reasoned, should satisfy all our needs; Paul and I would get a good, close-up view of our intended route and Steve and Ian would be able to enjoy a panoramic view of the approach to the peaks they were interested in.

Above: Mick Fowler and friend. Opposite page: Fowler leading mixed ground on day two.

After three days of heavy breathing the four of us were camped in a wind scoop at about 5500m. It seemed a lovely, calm spot when we arrived but by midway through the night I was bracing myself against the side-wall as each gust roared through. Uncomfortably I recalled the last time I experienced this kind of situation. That was in east Tibet back in 2007 and then Paul had eventually asked me to climb on top of him to stop the wind lifting his side of the tent. On this occasion he snored ('breathing heavily' he calls it) contentedly, blissfully unaware of my exertions.

By morning all was calm and he was disparagingly disbelieving of my night-time efforts. But the skies had cleared and we were treated to a wonderful panorama of the Kishtwar peaks to the south. It was amazing to think that those valleys were lush and well populated whereas the Zanskar valley through which we had approached was harsh, dry and unpopulated. It was a stark contrast over such a short distance.

Sleeping arrangements. Above: Ramsden at the sitting bivouac site after day 3.
Below: Better – the 'wonderful' site of the second bivvy.

We moved the tent a little higher to a better position, climbed to the top of the peak and returned to relax and read in the tent. The next day Steve and Ian decreed themselves sufficiently acclimatised for their plans and headed off down to base camp whereas Paul and I decided to spend another day sucking in thin air before caching our equipment below the north face and heading down. On the way down we left a note in the Slovenians' advance base camp tent indicating the line that we planned to take and saying we hoped the west face was to their liking and we would see their footprints on the top.

The next day we were back at base camp and Paul was peering through binoculars at the north face.

'They are on 'our' line.'

Sure enough there were prominent tracks in the snow cone at the foot, heading straight for the line that we had dreamed of for nine months and intended to start out for the next day. We were disappointed but there was no way either of us wanted to follow in their footsteps.

It was time to refocus. Building enthusiasm when one's heart has been set on a specific objective is always difficult, but on the bright side the northern end of Hagshu was not short of inspirational ground. A day of discussion, deliberation and binocular gazing ensued before we decided to go for a prominent slanting line on the north-east face. Actually it was more the eastern side of the north face but it seemed more straightforward to describe it as the north-east face.

Acclimatised now we comfortably reached the foot of the face in a day with enough time for Paul to retrieve our cache of equipment from beneath the north face while I put up the tent. The good weather spell showed every sign of continuing; as we settled down for the night, excitement levels were rising. After 25 years we were finally about to try to climb it.

'There we are. Our bergschrund for the year crossed.'

Paul and I are both family men with full-time jobs; this has become a regular and true annual comment of mine.

From a distance the initial slopes had looked to be good snow, but were glassy ice with just a dusting of snow. Soon we were climbing one at a time, easing the calf muscles gently back into the joys of Himalayan ice slopes.

Paul and I have developed our own routine over 13 years of climbing together in the Himalaya. One thing we like to do is stop early, soak up our surroundings and just generally enjoy being up high in the mountains. On a normal day we will start looking for a bivouac spot at around 3pm. And so it was with much pleasure that, at just about exactly our 'start search in earnest' time, we came across a perfectly horizontal projecting prow of rock with a covering of snow just thick enough to smooth out and pitch the tent on. It hardly seemed necessary but we belayed the tent and ourselves before settling down to catch up on a little reading. Leisure reading is something I never seem to find time for at home. I do more on my annual Himalayan trip than in the whole of the rest of the year.

It was perhaps inevitable that a good night's sleep should lead to a leisurely

Fowler traverses beneath the summit buttress to join the Slovenian tracks.

start. Thus far the way had been obvious but now the weakness we were following reared up into a series of steep walls festooned with hanging icicles. A Scottish-style gully cleaved the lower section but that was regularly flushed by waves of spindrift and ended in an overhanging amphitheatre. The best option looked to be steep ground right of the gully. That was safe from spindrift avalanches but it did look like it might offer hard mixed climbing. Fortunately that's the kind of climbing Paul and I like.

The day progressed in the way of my ideal Himalayan climbing day. Cloudless skies, difficult pitches with much heavy breathing, relaxing sessions of belaying and a generous amount of time marvelling at our surroundings from a position completely safe from objective dangers. And we unexpectedly came across a perfect, near flat, wind blown snow ledge at just the right time. For the second night in a row the tent was pitched perfectly. It felt almost too good to be true.

The obvious way forward was to move left into an area where snow was blasted up under overhangs. I'm always wary when I see this as it almost inevitably means that heavy waves of spindrift pour down when there is the slightest snowfall. Today luck was with us, the weather was calm, the sky clear and tricky mixed pitches led on to hard ice slopes towards the summit buttress.

Our plan had been to climb this direct but now we were here the obvious way was to move right and climb the right hand side. The ice slope we would have to cross looked as glassy and brittle as that we had just climbed; it wasn't far but climbing really hard ice is exhausting and I was tired. A quick foray confirmed fears that we might not have enough daylight to make it to possible bivouac sites on the far side. Progress was faltering and 30 metres below us the snow/ice fluting we were standing on eased to a

short horizontal section. That might provide a third night of campsite type comfort.

I lowered and Paul abseiled. Together we then stood attached to an ice screw and contemplated. The sharp snow crest wasn't horizontal at all and turned to ice at a depth of a few centimetres.

'This is crap.'

Paul was right. But to either side were ice slopes with no chance of cutting even a reasonable bum ledge. We would just have to make do. At this point we seemed to lose co-ordination. I hacked away with the optimistic intention of getting the poles in and draping the tent over the crest while Paul hacked away working towards a sitting width ledge. After a bit we took

Looking along the summit ridge to the main summit of Hagshu. Ramsden and Slovenian tracks in foreground.

a break to marvel at our conflicting handiwork. It wasn't looking good. In fact it was bad, very bad. It had become clear that the ice was so hard that all we could do was cut into the crest and make a triangular ledge about 50 centimetres wide at its widest point. We ended up with a sitting side-by-side arrangement using the tent as a bivouac sack. That would have been all very nice on a linear ledge but didn't work at all well on a triangular one, particularly after my side collapsed. Tetchiness soon prevailed.

Over the years that Paul and I have climbed together he has increasingly complained about my fidgeting, as I have about his snoring. It used to be that I fell asleep readily on such bivouacs but the tables have definitely turned. Soon Paul was 'breathing heavily' while I upset his sleeping by experimenting with numerous different hanging positions (Paul would call it 'fidgeting'). At length we settled down to me hanging deep inside the fabric while Paul sat upright with his head out the top, soaking in the perfect night.

'There's a lot of activity down there.'

I squirmed upright and looked at my watch. It was 3am. I peered down towards base camp but without my contact lenses in I didn't stand a hope in hell of seeing anything.

'Lights all over the place at base camp and on the south side of Barnaj, too,' enlarged Paul.

This gave us a subject to chat about and pass the time. We knew the Americans were trying the north side of Barnaj and concluded that they must have succeeded and for some reason chosen to descend the south side through the night. The base camp lights were more of a mystery and gave rise to many theories. We never guessed that a bear was showing great interest in our food store and resisting all attempts to frighten it off. And that the Americans had retreated from the north side of Barnaj and were making a determined attempt from the south which had to be done partially at night because they had such little time left before they were due to leave.

At this level the traverse towards the right edge of the summit buttress looked more amenable than it had the day before. The slopes formed the top of the north face and it was still early in the morning when we joined the Slovenians' tracks exiting from the face to a fine bivouac spot. If we had pressed on rather than spent so much time cutting a small, uncomfortable triangular ledge we could have enjoyed a luxury camping spot. Hindsight is a wonderful thing.

Ahead there were tracks to follow, which was a new Himalayan experience for the two of us. Somehow it made everything feel more familiar and less adventurous. We followed them up to steep, sunny and pleasant rock climbing and then on towards the previously unclimbed north summit. Just before the north summit we were surprised to find an extensive flat area which just called out to be camped on.

From the views we had seen, our best guess was that the ridge between here and the main summit would be long, narrow and devoid of easy bivouac places. In any event, the weather was so good that it seemed a shame not to use this place to enjoy a good night's sleep. The wind was light and there was no need to belay. We wandered around unroped, marvelled at our position, felt very lucky to be able to get to such a place and generally relaxed.

Much as we don't bother with altimeters and suchlike we were obviously gaining height well as we could increasingly see over the top of the nearby

Paul Ramsden and Mick Fowler on the summit of Hagshu.

6000m peaks. Beyond them interesting potential objectives increasingly reared their heads for closer study later.

The north summit was just five minutes above us and it was something of a surprise to gain it the next morning and see that the way ahead was much more straightforward than we had expected. I wasn't quite sure whether to be disappointed or not. Easy walking led to a saddle followed by a beautiful, if exhausting, few hours along the ridge to the summit that we had been dreaming of for so long.

For the last few years it has been a ritual for Paul and I to take summit selfies, to relive summit moments and chart our ageing process. Summit formalities over we continued the traverse with a descent of the south-east ridge, the route taken by the Polish first ascentionists back in 1989. We knew that there had been unsuccessful attempts to repeat this line and were uncomfortably aware that we had not been able to get a decent view of it before starting the traverse. The Slovenian tracks continued inexorably onwards; we passed their comfortable looking bivouac spot just below the summit and continued along a sharper ridge until abseiling became neces-

Ramsden descending to the huge snowy expanse of the upper Hagshu glacier.

sary. Soon we were hanging free on big abseils down rock pillars wondering exactly where the Polish team had climbed back in 1989. Wherever they went it was certainly a fine effort.

Clouds were at last appearing on the horizon and after a final bivouac below the difficulties we were down on the enormous snowfields of the upper Hagshu glacier. Heavy snow began and a white-out made the tracks difficult to follow but by that afternoon, seven days after leaving, we were back at base camp. Steve and Ian had arrived the day before, having completed all but the final overhanging five metres of their peak.

By next day our perfect weather window seemed to be over. It had snowed heavily overnight, the bear was making life difficult and Rinku was keen to leave. It was time to return to our other lives.

It had been a great outing but three teams at the same base camp did not appeal to my sense of adventure. I'll be checking my objectives file very carefully for next year. Maybe areas protected by difficult access issues have a lot going for them after all.

Summary

An account of the first ascent of the *North-east Face* of Hagshu, Zanskar (India), 1 - 6 October 2014, by Mick Fowler and Paul Ramsden.

DEREK BUCKLE

North-eastern Spiti

Exploring The Canyonlands of Himachal Pradesh[1]

Exiting the ravine on route to camp four. *(Derek Buckle)*

In answer to the perennial question of where to explore, in 2014 we eventually homed in on the region surrounding the Spiti valley in India's
Himachal Pradesh. This area was especially attractive as Harish Kapadia
had previously suggested that we might like to attempt Kamen Gyalmo,
an unclimbed 6531m peak to the north-east of the Lingti nala. Adding to
our interest was the fact that, being close to the border with Tibet, this area
was for many years closed to non-Indian nationals, and as such had been
rarely visited. Indeed, the only climbing teams known to have penetrated
the area were those led by Harish in 1983 and 1987 when they successfully
climbed Sibu (5700m) and Lagma (5786m)[1,2]. By contrast, the mountains
to the west of the Lingti nala have attracted considerably more attention.

Following discussions with Harish Kapadia it was known at the outset that simply getting to Kamen Gyalmo might be a major challenge as the region is crossed by deep, impenetrable gorges and access lies against the grain of the Himalaya. Having studied the available terrestrial maps and Google satellite images, our preferred option was to approach our objective from the east by way of the Giu nala, but because of its proximity to Tibet we felt that obtaining permission from the Indian authorities for this route might be problematic. Eventually we settled on entry from the west via the Lingti nala, even though this would involve a longer, more circuitous route.

As the date for our departure approached we waited with some trepidation for our permit to arrive from India. After a flurry of correspondence it eventually did, but with one major omission: Hamish, a late addition to the team, was not included. Unfortunately this meant that he was only able to get a tourist visa, rather than the obligatory X-visa required by the Indian Mountaineering Foundation. As a consequence he was not authorised to climb above base camp. Having largely anticipated this response Hamish had stoically planned an alter-native schedule during the period that we were actively climbing.

With arrangements made, we flew from the UK to Delhi on 27 August 2014 to begin the long drive to Shimla where we obtained Inner Line Permits before continuing on to Sarahan, Kalpa and Tabo to Lingti. At Lingti we joined our porters and support team before making the short drive to the roadhead at Lalung (3737m) from where we began our trek.

The trek to and from base camp (see map)

After discussions with the villagers at Lalung we were strongly discour-aged from following the Lingti gorge and took their suggestion to use the higher route over the Tuthi Pass (4515m, Zingtu Top[4]). A steep descent from this pass led to the Zingzung nala from where a brief climb and diffi-cult descent led to the Lingti nala and camp one at 3775m, situated a little before the deserted hamlet of Kebri*. This was the first of two long, hard days during which several porters struggled to manoeuvre their loads over the difficult terrain.

Beyond Kebri, a steep 1300m climb on a well-defined track led to the Goldem pass (5085m),[5] with its extensive views, before descending steeply to a small plateau overlooking the Sisbang nala. This plateau was especially

During the first ascent of Fossil Gully. *(Geoff Cohen)*

interesting as it was our first opportunity to find the numerous belemnites and other fossils that are extensively exposed in this area. The Lingti shales are famous for their Jurassic fossils, and an extensive collection gathered by Dr Richard Hey and Peter Holmes in 1955 is housed at the Sedgwick Museum in Cambridge, UK[6]. Further on, a break in the cliffs bordering the Sisbang nala led via yet another steep descent on uneven ground to the river itself. We were able to bivouac here (camp two) at 4520m in a shallow cave some 15-20m above the water. Because of the difficult terrain we were once again well ahead of the porters and several only arrived well after dark, having dropped their loads as far back as the Goldem pass.

The next day was comparatively short so after retrieving the dropped loads we continued over the Sisbang pass (4812m) to camp three situated on scrubby grass at 4801m, close to the Sabu Spring. With little idea where to establish base camp we chose to spend a day at the spring while the climbing team and high altitude porters explored possible options. Although poor visibility hampered these forays somewhat, a suitable base camp site was eventually found beside one of the Sheru nala tributaries at 5130m and we relocated there on 7 September. At this point Hamish left with our Sirdar and the porters. Hoping to get back to Lalung more quickly than the four days taken in ascent they chose to descend directly to the Lingti nala and then follow the river down. In spite of eight or more forced

The high cirque from Chota Sgurr. *(Derek Buckle)*

river crossings this alternative could be accomplished in one hard day and it was the route by which the remaining team descended when we eventually returned to Lalung in two separate parties on 24 and 25 September.

Exploration and ascents east of the Lingti nala

With the base camp established, we now had sixteen days in which to explore the area and, hopefully, to establish a viable route to Kamen Gyalmo at the head of the Talung nala. It was clear from initial explorations that we were still some way from our objective and that we needed to ascend the broad Lagma plateau in order to improve our understanding of the local topography. Once again we were faced with several options. One of these was to climb a north-facing ice gully (WI2, *Fossil Gully*[7]), which Dave, Mike and I successfully managed on 9 September. By continuing up the exit snowfield then we then made the first ascent of a subsidiary top (Peak 5782) before traversing eastwards to where Geoff and one of the high altitude porters had located an advanced base camp (ABC) at 5807m adjacent to the Tangmor snowfield. Two days later we occupied this camp from where Dave, Geoff and I continued south-south-east across the easy-angled snowfield to complete the first ascent of Tangmor (5920m). Mike repeated this ascent the following day when he too relocated to ABC while the ever active Dave traversed the broad scree plateau to make the second

The awkward descent to the Lingti. *(Mike Cocker)*

ascent of what we now know to be Lagma (5796m). Glacial recession has had a marked impact on this plateau, since the dangerous cornices that caused Harish Kapadia to abort his attempt on Tangmor in 1983[2] no longer exist and the area of snowfield shown on older maps is significantly diminished and replaced by fine, unconsolidated scree.

Beyond Tangmor, the Lagma plateau extends southwards to terminate in a rocky outlier, Peak 5927, which we climbed on 13 September via its straightforward north ridge and for which we suggest the name Taklu[8]. While not a memorable first ascent, this summit did offer fantastic views of Kamen Gyalmo and the high mountains to the east, although deep gorges prevented access from here.

Returning to base camp we subsequently crossed the Sheru nala to establish camp four on a grassy area close to a small spring at 4485m. From here two additional camps, camp five (5008m) and camp six (5476m) were later established. Both of these higher camps were on previously occupied sites which were presumed to be those used by Harish Kapadia during his ascent of Lagma in 1983[2]. The higher camp was adjacent to the ice band bordering the northern slopes of Lagma, which was unequivocally identified by Dave as the peak that he had climbed, and marked with a cairn, a week before. Had we appreciated the puzzling topography, and realised the existence of the ice band as a source of water, we could have accessed this same area relatively easily from ABC.

With our interest focused on Kamen Gyalmo and the high cirque of mountains heading the Talung nala, on 19 September we traversed the northern slopes of Lagma on easy scree before reaching a broad ridge which dropped to a col separating the Talung and Tabo nalas. Easy scree

Mike Cocker with Tangmor (5920m) (right), PK 5927 (centre) and Manirang (6500m) behind. *(Derek Buckle)*

slopes (no longer glaciated as shown on the map) then led to the broken, rocky north ridge of the eastern part of the cirque which culminated in a pleasant snow crest. Soloing this ridge and crest we made the first ascent of the compact, rocky 5924m summit which we tentatively called Chota Sgurr[9]. Panoramic views extended in all directions from this summit, but were particularly impressive towards the cirque itself.

It was abundantly clear that we now had insufficient time to progress further along the ridge towards Kamen Gyalmo and these higher unclimbed peaks and that we would have to content ourselves with Peak 5924 as a consolation prize. Still wanting to achieve as much as possible while we were here, on 20 September Mike and I also climbed Lagma, while Dave and Geoff returned directly to camp five. Although it was an uninspiring climb up the unstable boulder-field south-west of camp six, it was relatively short-lived and soon we reached the broad scree ridge that led south to the 5796m summit. The compensation was, of course, the extensive views that this fairly innocuous summit gave. Now that we had a much better understanding of the local geography it was possible to pick out, if not necessarily identify, many of the major peaks that characterise north-eastern Spiti and to appreciate that there is still much left to do here given sufficient time, energy and motivation.

All that remained now was to rejoin Dave and Geoff at camp five before returning to base camp and subsequently to the road-head at Lalung where the expedition officially ended.

Sisbang (5668m) from the north. *(Derek Buckle)*

Summary

In September 2014 a five-man British team, Derek Buckle (leader), Dave Broadhead, Mike Cocker, Geoff Cohen and Hamish Irvine (non-climber), explored the mountains to the east of the Lingti nala in the north-eastern Spiti region of Himachal Pradesh, close to the border with Tibet. Team members made first ascents of several of the subsidiary tops on the Lagma plateau, including: Peak 5782 via a WI2 gully (*Fossil Gully*, 9 September) on its north face, Tangmor (5920m, 11 September), and the second ascent of Lagma (5796m) itself on 12 September. They also made the first ascents of Peak 5927 (Taklu), 13 September and Peak 5924 (Chota Sgurr), 19 September, both by their north ridges.

Acknowledgements

The team gratefully acknowledges the financial support of the Mount Everest Foundation, the Alpine Club Climbing Fund and the Austrian Alpine Club. We are also grateful to Rimo Expeditions for organising the in-country logistics and for the unstinting support provided by our base camp staff and three high altitude porters.

References and Notes

1. For a full expedition report see DR Buckle, 2014 British Spiti Expedition, *Mount Everest Foundation Report*, 2014
2. H Kapadia, *Himalayan Journal*, **40**, 96-107, 1983
3. H Kapadia, *Himalayan Journal*, **44**, 96-101, 1987
4. H Kapadia, *Spiti*, Published by India Publications, Delhi
5. Name given to this pass by the Lalung villagers.
6. Not currently on display but held in store at the museum.
7. A name chosen to reflect the numerous fossils found around base camp and elsewhere and the mature ages of the first ascent party!
8. The Indian transliteration of the English word 'Baldy' in reference to the lack of snow on and around the summit.
9. Derived from the Indian word Chota and the Scottish word Sgurr (meaning small pointed peak).
*Place names in the Spiti valley have a variety of different spellings, possibly reflecting the local Spitan and other dialects. Thus, Kebri is sometimes written as Kibri. Some other names have even more variants. The names used herein are primarily those used by the Survey of India except where noted. Apart from Sibu, all the heights recorded here are the result of GPS measurements.

ALEKSEY ZHOLOBENKO

On Finding Peaks and Pushing Limits

The north face of Patrasi. X marks high point, prospective route line dashed.
(Aleksey Zholobenko)

Occasionally I have one of those days when I wake up bright and early and proceed to curse everything and anything under the sun. It's generally when, at 6am, my alarm loudly declares that it's time to go work, and every fibre of my being rallies outside my cerebral cortex in protest. Then I get a headache and start cursing all of creation. Naturally, all of creation doesn't appreciate being cursed, and spends the rest of the day trying to give me a good reason to curse it. Sometimes it succeeds, and I spend the rest of the day trapped in a vicious circle, like a hamster in its wheel, cursing the foundations upon which my life is built, while the foundations curse me back. It makes me wonder whether hamsters face the same problem.

That's roughly how I felt when I woke up at 6am tied into a tree. My climbing partner was in no way attached to me; Bradley was tied into another tree a few paces below me. Himalayan expeditions are funny like that: you think you're going to wake up on an icy ledge half way up a shadowy face, but there you are, supported by a tangle of birches that grow almost sideways in a seemingly endless gorge. I turned my head to the left. The cleft in the slope just ahead barred our retreat and necessitated uphill. Tree climbing. Certainly, I realised, I would be cursing all of crea-

39

Swimming the glacier to the base of Patrasi. *(Aleksey Zholobenko)*

tion today, not least because I had never been very good at tree climbing.

Yesterday we were convinced that this stretch of unpleasant terrain was only a temporary inconvenience. We were correct in the sense that we only went through the 'Groundhog Day'-like loop five times, and in the end escaped the Chyangdayng Khola with most of our possessions and a portion of our sanity intact. Clearly we had misplaced our confidence, both in the choice of descent route and, more globally, in our own abilities. Despite, or perhaps on account of, the belief that we had planned everything perfectly, all those mousy little errors had worked their way into our expedition and had eventually gnawed away those tenuous strings that anchored our lofty hopes to reality.

You could say that it started with an overly optimistic email. To my surprise, the offending communication was from Bradley. We had been discussing the possibility of another expedition for a while, but so far nothing had materialised – I was finally enjoying my work and Bradley was skint. Now the situation had apparently changed and he wanted my opinion on the feasibility of a 20-day expedition. I rubbed my eyes, throwing myself against the backrest and looking at the plain, sterile ceiling, even duller than the October sky. It was a bold proposal. Too bold, even. Three weeks, on the other hand... Under the sway of alpine enthusiasm, which is so overpowering to the untested mountaineer, I sent a reply that was as flowery and over-optimistic as the original query. With the appropriate artificial acclimatisation, Herculean training, the proper doping regime, a virgin sacrifice, and a lifetime allowance of good luck, a three week expedition up a remote Himalayan six-thousander might just succeed. In any case, the dialogue had began, and as it went on, three weeks turned to four, four weeks became five, and five weeks spilled over onto nearby Mondays and Fridays. The fate of my yearly leave and Bradley's admittedly shallow financial reserves were sealed.

It hadn't taken us very long to find our target. With the power of satellite imagery at our fingertips, we had soon gone through most Himalayan north faces, though figuring out what was suitable and accessible was a little harder. In a moment of decadent genius, Bradley suggested criteria both strict and sensible: the base camp should be on a grassy meadow, ideally next to a clear mountain lake. Those criteria would almost entirely eliminate the burdensome element of choice. A certain patch of glaciation in the Kanjiroba Himal that was surrounded by a sea of brown and green caught my eye. This small patch of white was the kilometre and a half high face of Kande Huinchuli and the adjoining glacier. As it turned out, it was true that this patch of scree-covered ice didn't extend more than a couple of kilometres away from the face in any direction, but when the mountain was submerged in bottomless powder, it felt anything but small. In any case, our target had been decided. Of course I was not deaf to the voice of doubt and the closer we came to our departure day, the louder its whispers. Its message? That any self-respecting Himalayan north face would eat us alive.

And then it really did begin to come apart. You could say that the first sign came when I balked at the weight of plastics and the price of overboots. I had read about one of Dyhrenfurth's expeditions, where the writer scoffed at the super-heavy boots the expedition leader had proposed and had instead got by with an extra pair of socks. Modern mctereological science gave us one chance to put everything right: checking the weather forecast a few days before departure, I hoped that the mirror on the wall would declare me the fairest of them all and confirm that the gamble of heading off into the Kanjiroba Himal, deep in post-monsoon season, would pay off. Instead my magic mirror showed me nothing but the prospects of the snow-white future I wanted to avoid, in the form of the tropical storm which would later claim the lives of dozens of porters and trekkers in the Annapurna region. Unlike a certain wicked stepmother, I took no heed of my magic mirror and with the words 'It'll be grand!' the fate of our expedition was sealed.

We completed our preparations as planned. Our equipment was light, functional and in good repair. In light of bitter experience, we resolved to abstain from local cuisine and Bradley even armed himself with a bottle of hand sanitiser. Our menu, synthesised from the experiences of two generations of mountaineers from two different mountaineering traditions, was the best we had eaten in the outdoors by a margin which even Jamie Oliver would envy. Our permits, porters, transport and accommodation had all been sorted and we just had to take off, land, turn our back on the civilised world and walk away. Since we lacked previous Himalayan experience, we had no idea how well our preparations would fare in the face of reality, but when we stepped, sweaty palmed, off the Twin Otter at Jumla and faced the mountains, we still looked at the future of the expedition through the prism of optimism.

Our target mountain goes by several different names – Kande Huinchuli, Sisne and Patrasi. To compound the issue a couple of other mountains nearby also go by the names of Sisne and Patrasi. This makes asking the locals for directions pointless at best. The mountain itself had first been mapped in the 1930s, but the first ascent had to wait until a Japanese expedition succeeded in climbing its south ridge. Since then there had been two more ascents – one of the same ridge by a different Japanese expedition and one of the north-west ridge of a sub-peak (Sisne) by a Swiss expedition. There were then a number of other attempts, all which ended in different degrees of failure. One intriguing trend that emerged, for no reason apparent to us, was the absolute, systematic inability of small, alpine style expeditions to make it to the top. The Japanese expeditions approached from the south, while the Swiss expedition, in whose footsteps we were following, approached from the south and then, having traversed a high pass, descended into the cirque of the mountain's impressive north face. It was specifically this north face, untried and unclimbed, that we had come to attempt.

With the exception of an unexpectedly snowy 4942m pass, which was crossed without porters, the approach to base camp was smooth and pleasant (and yes, we had a meadow and a mountain 'lake'). After a couple of days of lazing around base camp, partly to watch the build-up of another half metre of snow, we packed our bags with gear and eight days of rations and set off up the glacier. The plan was to climb just under a kilometre, from the grassy valley at 4200 metres, to the glacial cirque at between 4900 and 5100 metres. The mountain threw down its second challenge. The way up to the glacier consisted of scree, scree disguised by unconsolidated snow, and more deep, soft, yet paradoxically stable, snow. Then we encountered a short (but somehow very, very long), narrow, shady gully, which in the end could only be overcome when Bradley, exasperated, stopped and, holding out a demanding hand, uttered the one word.

'Shovel.'

That word marked the end of the transition from the gentle fantasy inspired by the soft walk-in and our preconceptions of the word 'post-monsoon', to the reality that called for a shovel. We had been ascending a gentle snow gully that might pass as a Scottish I when Bradley finally had enough of sinking lower and lower for every step uphill he took. It took us the rest of the day to dig our way up the gully, and then a bivvy platform. We had been battling with the snow since we had parted ways with our porters, but up to now, as we passed the high col that separated the mountain's north face from Jumla and the south-west face, the snow had been bearable. It was either shallow as we ascended the col or it was on the downhill, and snow on the downhill usually makes life easier. Here, on the

Spindrift Rainbow: Alek on the easy snow slope at the base of the north face.
(Bradley Morrell)

other hand, it was deep, and more importantly it was on the uphill and as consolidated as the sanity of anyone who was about to climb it. One more realisation came to us in this shadowed gully: this frustrating white powder was most likely to haunt us all the way to the summit. We chose to ignore this epiphany and continue until our eight days of provisions ran out.

It was at the first bivvy that I first had a faint impression that my boots might not be warm enough a kilometre higher up. The impression got stronger the next day, when I sat down facing the sun and spent a good ten minutes massaging a pair of feet that simply refused to warm up on their own, even with the rest of me breaking a sweat. Despite these small

Shovel Grade Gully: Bradley, digging us out of a dead end and into trouble.
(Aleksey Zholobenko)

setbacks, we spent the rest of the day clambering and lumbering over the lateral moraine of a dying glacier and by sunset we were tucked into our bivvy bags. At that point the problem of waking up with cold feet in the morning came under the scrutiny of my clearly insufficient intellect. The best I could come up with was tucking my still be-booted feet into a dry bag before tucking myself into the sleeping bag.

In the morning, I had toasty feet and thought about perhaps writing a UKClimbing article on methods of keeping one's feet warm when your boots just don't cut it. My jubilant mood was short lived, as half an hour later the boots had acquired the material properties of plastic and my feet were once again on the chilly side. I was concerned. As we explored the area, sizing up the face, I suggested we pick a line that gets at least a little sunlight. Unfortunately the best line was quite naturally tucked into the darkest, coldest corner of the face. And what a line! It looked like 400m of thick, 80° ice, or at worst dirty névé followed by easier terrain, which culminated in either a struggle up a vertical rock face (which would have been impossible for us), or an ever steepening ramp up to the ridge. We admired this line for a while, wishing that our boots were just that little bit warmer and didn't freeze early in the morning. Then reason prevailed and we picked a more sensible line; it had a couple hours of sunlight in the afternoon and can be summarised as a meandering route over dodgy-looking mixed, followed by steep, dodgy-looking mixed, followed by a long, steep snow slope. It did not inspire in the same way, but perhaps the short window of sunlight would make it bearable.

This last day of our three day approach was particularly humbling. Our 'advance camp' was separated from the face and our chosen route by two kilometres of rather tame, glaciated terrain. This meant that two kilometres of quicksand which pretended to be snow separated us from the base of our route. These two kilometres took us most of the day. I can swim that distance faster, significantly faster. Despite feeling like a couple of fugitives who had escaped from a gulag only to find ourselves surrounded by a wintry tundra, we did eventually reach a series of crevasses which marked the bottom of the route. Here the glacier reared up to the start of the mixed climbing. Here, in a fit of Scottish madness, we constructed a snowhole. After a poor night's sleep, punctuated by periodically digging Bradley out of a snowy coffin, we started the climb.

I say we started the climb, but actually, as an expedition, we had something of a threshold moment. It's like when you stand on a pier in early May in your swimming trunks and battle the fear of jumping into icy water, or when you stand on a tiny ledge under a crux with poor gear below you. Then there is a moment when it is all decided, and you either commit to the challenge or slink away. We packed the bags and debated, throwing hesitant glances up the face. On the one hand, we would have liked nothing better than to descend to our grassy base camp, regroup, and make another attempt. At the same time we were quite aware that if we went down now, we probably wouldn't have the will left to get to the start of the route a second time. We committed. Since we had come this far, we would keep going. We would push our limits and see this glacier from above.

Thus hours and spindrift flew past and I found myself sat on a snowy ledge, untying my shoelaces. The suspicious sensation of bunched up socks that had been following me all morning turned out to have a more sinister cause. We had spent five hours front-pointing, post-holing, and swimming up the slope, all as a powdery spindrift flowed down to meet us. In those five hours I had gained some wonderfully colourful blotches on my toes. I tapped them. They were quite wooden. It was over. We had plodded, post-holed and swum through ever deeper snow on and off for the past week and a half, and just as we had reached the interesting bit, those limits that we had intended to push had begun to push back. It appeared that our limits didn't take kindly to it.

From this highpoint at c5450m, though who knows what the actual height was, it took us 12 hours to limp back to base camp. The descent had an element of surreal lightness to it: perhaps because Bradley had volunteered to lighten my rucksack. Or perhaps because the weight of ambition and uncertainty had been taken off my shoulders and only the single-minded goal of preserving my toes remained. The fact that it was all downhill did help.

After we had mulled the situation over for a few days and it became

And then there were trees: Not quite a nice easy, downhill retreat along the Chyangdayan Khola. *(Aleksey Zholobenko)*

apparent that the much-maligned digits had no intention of falling off, we decided on a bold move. Instead of hobbling back to Jumla the way we had come, we would take the long, low road, the road that no other expedition had used before. We imagined that if we could at least report a wonderful, alternative route up the valley, it would all be worth it and the sense of purpose could be salvaged.

There's a lot left unsaid, but in brief, that is the story of how I woke up tied into a tree. Just walking, walking, more walking and not a scrap of duelling – just us and the laws of physics on that overhanging chessboard. And in the end I seem to have learned the wrong lesson. If, today, a passer-by were to stop me and instead of asking for directions (don't ask me for directions, I'm not from around here), were to put on a solemn expression and ask whether I'd go there again, to those very ordinary mountains, I would think about the limits that I can't seem to overcome, those limits of will, common sense and experience beyond which lies the promise of the extraordinary. And I would still answer with a pensive 'yes'.

Summary

A yarn about the attempt on the unclimbed north face of Patrasi/Sisne/Huinchuli in the Kanjiroba Himal of western Nepal, by Bradley Morrell and Aleksey Zholobenko in October-November 2014.

Acknowledgements

This expedition was supported by the British Mountaineering Council and the Alpine Club. It was also supported by Vlad, who provided most of the cheese, and a few other items, consumed on this venture.

TIMOTHY ELSON

No Sleep till Bishkek

Eyeing-up the line of *Open Misère*, Peak Vinton-Boot, during our reconnaissance. *(Reg Measures)*

What defines success? In this case we defined it as making the first ascent of Djanghorn by the south ridge and traversing the rest of the summits on the ridge to the highest peak in the range, Peak After-You, in alpine style.

Strictly speaking we failed: the aim was the traverse of *all* the summits; we didn't climb Peak After-You.

We were a team of six from the UK and New Zealand, and arrived in Bishkek at the beginning of August. We spent a day buying food and meeting the other AC team from Bristol with whom we were sharing transport to basecamp. The next morning started early, with a six-hour minibus to Karakol before a swap into a Soviet all-terrain vehicle that travelled the same speed whatever the surface or angle. It was ideal, as the only road to

Maida-Adyr, our day's destination, was largely a bulldozed track which went over a 3600m col. We arrived just as it was getting dark; Maida-Adyr is the starting point for flights into Khan Tengri and Peak Pobeda, two famous 'Snow Leopard' peaks. The next morning we caught a helicopter going in the opposite direction – west – towards the Djangart range.

The Djangart is in the Tien Shan and has eight main glacier systems that lead south from the Djangart River to the Chinese border. The first successful expedition into the Djangart was a Russian team in 2008, and there have been expeditions visiting every summer since. Both the Bristol team and us had the same primary objective of making the first ascent of the highest peak in the range – Peak 5318. This was scuppered at the start when we were informed that it had been climbed by an American team two weeks prior to our arrival, who had named it Peak After-You.

The helicopter dropped us off, and after it had left we discovered that we were about 12km away from, and in a different valley than, our intended location; our basecamp ended up situated next to the Djangart river between the ends of the N1 and N2 glaciers.

There was a friendly rivalry between the two teams which intensified at the end of the first week when the Bristol team made the first ascent of Peak 5025; our team had spent the week exploring Chulaktor, Akoguz, N2 and N1 glacier systems for suitable objectives. When there was a break in the weather at the beginning of our second week, all six of our team headed up the N2 glacier. Max, Reg and I started off with the first ascent of Peak MacMillan (5051m) via the Frima (north-west) face at D-, which was reminiscent of the north face of Lyskamm and required 700m of front pointing mostly at 50°, then up the west ridge to the summit cornice. We descended the west ridge and south-west face.

Two days later we made the first ascent of Peak Vinton-Boot (5168m) via a stunning north-west facing ice gully which we called *Open Misère* (TD) and involved nine pitches up to Scottish Grade V followed by endless simul-climbing to the summit. Following all this with the tricky descent of a broken glacier made for one very long day.

Tom, Hugh and Neil in the meantime had made the first ascents of Peak Fotheringham (4871m) by going up the east ridge and down the west; this was followed by Point Andrea (4566m), and then two days later by Peak Kinmundy (4950m), all from the N2 glacier. On 19 August Max, Reg and I had made our first attempt on our main aim of the trip, traversing from the unclimbed Djanghorn (5274m) to Peak After-You (5318m) via three other 5000m peaks. This was ended at the start by a substantial rockfall that hit us on the approach slopes; we were very lucky to sustain only minor injuries. The next week was spent sitting out bad weather in basecamp, before Max, Reg and I made the long trek round to the Sauktor glacier. We attempted to climb Pt 5112 (climbed by an AC team in 2014), but abandoned the attempt due to poor weather. Meanwhile, Tom, Neil and Hugh had a scary experience attempting to cross the Djangart River. Neil was almost washed away which put a stop to their plans. This left us with two

The first pitched section of the south ridge of the Djanghorn. *(Reg Measures)*

days of good weather at the end of our trip. We vainly tried to re-arrange the helicopter pick up date, but didn't receive any confirmation. We still had a burning desire to get back on the Djanghorn.

Liberation

In *Nausea*, Sartre's character Antoine struggles with the existential doubt created by the realisation of radical freedom. Nausea is the giddy feeling of knowing you can do whatever you want while contemplating the inherent insecurity of the consequences of your actions. In alpine climbing, nausea is the feeling you get at the bivvy the night before the climb and approaching the bergschrund in the dark; it is the fear and doubt of the outcome of the climb bubbling to the surface. There is an ultimate feeling of liberation once committed on an alpine climb; your struggle with doubt is suspended once you have made the choice to commit.

The mighty unclimbed Dawn Wall (east face) of the Djanghorn (left) to Peak After-You Ridge (right) from the N2 Glacier. *(Hugh Thomas)*

The feeling of liberation comes when, once committed, you have lost your freedom and given yourself purpose; you must get up and back down the mountain. Either consciously or accidentally, and usually based on a deluded sense of reality, a decision to go up has been made to commit. Questions like 'what's the point?' and 'will we succeed?' leave your mind; this is the essence of the loss of doubt and the feeling of liberation.

Djanghorn

Climbing through the same rockfall zone that ended things on our first attempt, this time we are earlier and climbing faster, but there is real doubt and fear about our ability to get up this mountain. Reg forces the pace up open snowfields that we hope link to the col at the base of the ridge. It is dark and everything is uncertain, the doubt in this project is building to a crescendo that I hope will end in liberation at dawn.

As the col is gained, the darkness fades; in light the uncertainty remains.

Above we are greeted by overhanging, loose granite; all options look bad, but at least there are some to choose from. At this point doubt is deafening and defining. The shaded rock of the Tien Shan at dawn is painfully cold to touch. Max steps up; he has the team's pair of rock boots. The introduction is loose, cold and severe, and Reg falls seconding when what he is climbing parts company with the mountain.

Pitch two is the turning point. A loose overhanging groove is the only way; doubt is building; we will fail at this point...I don't want to descend the rockfall zone... does this even lead anywhere? I can just see more over-hangs above...

Yet that is the whole reason we are here: uncertainty, the unknown; over-coming this is the point. Affirmation of existence can only occur because

of uncertainty. Liberation is the temporary loss of uncertainty achieved by limiting its domain: narrowing your focus to an alpine climb.

Max tries to free the groove; it is freezing and he is climbing in bare hands; a flake snaps off.

'*...Do....do my work...do my dirty work scapegoat...*'[1] is ringing in my head as he aids up on expanding flakes, and a steady stream of rocks and potential holds falls past us. How can something so steep be this loose? Max makes it to a belay; this was the turning point though we didn't realise it at the time. After he had led something so horrible we couldn't back down.

'How does it look?'

'Er... it's just an overhang above me.'

This is the point of liberation; doubt has gone. I am liberated by commitment; my ropemate has got us through this section, so we have to succeed, I need to equal his belief.

Liberation is not accompanied by a feeling of lightness; I am just certain I can get to the top. The scope of life has narrowed to the domain of the Djanghorn.

Max climbs the next overhangs. We find a sneaky traverse around a

Timothy Elson and Reg Measures on the summit of the Djanghorn. Peak After-You in background. *(Max Folkett)*

1. *Sad But True*, Metallica

The west face of the Djanghorn (right) to Peak After-You Ridge (left); the south ridge of the Djanghorn is on the right and the col just before Peak After-You is where the team descended. *(Hugh Thomas)*

bottomless off-width. I climb an icy, mixed pitch with an awful, loose exit. Pitches and moving together blur into one long, loosely bonded memory after the scapegoat pitch. After each difficult step we vainly hope it is the last. Disappointment accompanies every realisation that there is always more to go. At all times during this section to the summit I am accompanied by a certainly: I will get to the top.

The altitude starts to bite and Reg plods on in the lead; somehow several more hours have passed; the ridge is foreshortened. Surely it cannot take long to reach the cornice up there? Ten paces and rest, repeat. I can't make out what Reg shouts when he gets over the cornice, but by its deflated tone of disappointment I don't think this is the top. It's not. Ten paces and rest, repeat. There is another cornice further ahead, surely it can't take long to reach it? Ten paces and rest, repeat. After another eternity the second cornice is reached, and finally the top.

Then the three of us are standing on the summit of the Djanghorn. I have no sense of elation; there is still 2.5km of unknown ridge to go over with another three summits before the first opportunity for descent.

Alpine climbing is easy: you make a hopelessly optimistic plan and then carry on regardless. We left our high camp at 1am with light day packs, the intention being to reach this summit at the latest by midday. Looking at our watches it is 5.45pm. It gets dark in two hours and our bivvy kit consists of

belay jackets, a two-man bothy bag and a Jetboil.

We are very alone, on top of a committing mountain in the middle of the Tien Shan with some teammates a day or so away at base camp. I have been liberated by commitment and not even darkness can impinge on my certain self.

We make a quick brew just down from the summit then try to get as far along the ridge as possible before darkness. I end up on top of a pinnacle looking down a 30m drop, but can't find anything to abseil from; we have to go back and descend around the pinnacles.

Two abseils and some down-climbing lead to darkness. At this point liberation is lost and doubt has set in. I stop. 'We're bivying here – I'm f**ked.' The three of us squeeze into our two-man bothy bag and we light the stove. An argument ensues and I quite rightly lose:

1. In the 30 minutes we sit there the temperature plummets. We have all our clothes on and we're all shivering; Max can't feel his toes.

2. It's the end of our trip and the helicopter might be coming to pick us up from base camp at 8am tomorrow morning.

Moving upwards towards the ridge again feels like a superhuman effort. Every time I stop I start to drift off; it is only momentary, but feels like I am falling – while knowing I am climbing – and I jolt awake. The other two drag me along; liberation is lost as no thoughts exist now, only tiredness and cold; the wind picks up as we climb, continuing to wear every stitch of clothing. Two more summits pass by and we reach the 'needle col' below

The top section of the Scapegoat pitch. (*Reg Measures*)

Peak After-You. We don't even discuss heading up, we've been on the move for over 24 hours and down is all we can manage.

Well past the middle of the night we reach our high camp. I argue for sleep, but the others reiterate our need to get down to base camp – we have no confirmation of the change to the helicopter date and they don't want to be left alone in the middle of nowhere.

In the disorientated waking dream of the descent from our high camp, I can hear a voice I recognise, but don't know from where, singing just out of earshot. I try to stop and listen yet automatically my legs move anyway, and I can't make out the song or voice. In front Reg stops then Max too: a stream, a sip of water. I have moved past the point of falling asleep when I stop; I feel nothing in particular; my knees hurt. The effort of continuing is fading. I think I can keep walking indefinitely now; there is no pressure, no pending darkness, only endless moraine.

Eventually all moraine ends

On arrival at base camp I am speechless and incapable of coherent thought for a while – I just have a feeling of contentment, of having achieved something. Momentarily freeing oneself of doubt and completing the climb led to liberation of other sorts. So what is the achievement – Liberation? No. The first ascent? No. It is getting back down having lived through the experience.

Leaving the summit of Pk 5207 part way along the traverse. *(Reg Measures)*

The team with Soviet era Kyrgyz Army helicopter: Neil Thomas, Timothy Elson, Reg Measures, Max Folkett, Hugh Thomas and Tom Bell. *(Timothy Elson)*

Postscript

We arrived at base camp 10 minutes before the pick up time; the helicopter arrived the next day. At times it felt like we would not get to sleep until we were returned safely to Bishkek. Thirty-one hours on the climb wiped us out, and the satisfaction lasted for weeks.

The helicopter picked us up the day we had re-arranged it for and dropped us off back at Maida-Adyr. Strangely, they wouldn't let us take any of our bags out of the helicopter and there appeared to be quite a bit of military about. We eventually understood that we were to wait by the landing strip. At this point we were starting to get quite concerned as none of us had any idea what was going on, but everyone seemed to be being quite friendly so hopefully that boded well.

After a while some other climbers and trekkers turned up; one team was a group of Czechs who could speak English and they explained that the road was shut. That didn't seem surprising, though we thought it must be major if the all-terrain Soviet vehicle could not cope with it. After some more chatting they started mentioning the 'exclusion zone' which at first we thought might just be a mistranslation – but it turned out to be a bubonic plague exclusion zone.

In fact this helicopter was the last one flying out, which was why we had no confirmation of the change to the date of our helicopter. Tien Shan Travel (who facilitated our trip) had been busy organising the evacuation of all the teams and their staff in the area. Eventually we flew out to Karkara on the Kazak boarder where we were seamlessly met by a mini-bus that took us back to Bishkek.

Summary

An account of the first ascent of the south ridge of the Djanghorn (5274m), (ED, HVS A2, Scottish IV, 750m) and the traverse of Pk 5207 (FA), Pk Buddyness and Pk Betelgeuse (2.5km), Djangart region, Tien Shan; 31 July to 27 August 2013.

Team members: Tom Bell, Hugh Thomas, Neil Thomas, Max Folkett, Richard 'Reg' Measures and Timothy Elson.

Routes and peaks: Frima face (D-, 45-70°, Scottish III, 900m), Peak Macmillan (5051m FA) – Reg Measures, Max Folkett and Timothy Elson 14/08/13).

Open Misère (TD, 90°, Scottish V, 500m) on Pk Vinton-Boot (5162m FA) – Reg Measures, Max Folkett and Timothy Elson 16 Aug 2013.

South ridge and traverse (ED, HVS, A2, Scottish IV 750m + 2.5km of ridge) Djanghorn (5274m, FA), and Pik 5207m (FA), Pk Buddyness (5172m, 2nd ascent), and Pk Betelgeuse (5100m, 2nd ascent) – Reg Measures, Max Folkett and Timothy Elson, 27 Aug 2013.

East Ridge (AD, 400m, FA) of Pk Fotheringham (4871m), – Tom Bell, Hugh Thomas and Neil Thomas 15 Aug 2013.

Pk Kinmundy (4950m), (PD, 400m FA) – Tom Bell, Hugh Thomas and Neil Thomas 18 Aug 2013.

Point Andrea (4566m), (F 200m, FA) – Tom Bell, Hugh Thomas and Neil Thomas 16 Aug 2013).

Acknowledgements

We would like to thank the Alpine Club, the Mount Everest Foundation and the Austrian Alpine Club for financial assistance on the expedition; Tien Shan Travel for facilitating our trip, and Facewest.co.uk for their assistance with gear.

ADRIAN DYE

In The Tracks of The Snow Leopard

The author walking in to the Little Poobah (5481m). *(Rob Middleton)*

The 2012 Alpine Club symposium on the states of the former Soviet Union provided many inspiring areas and objectives in the space of a few hours, rather than the usual weeks of research. One country clearly stood out as having inspiration combined with simple logistics and bureaucracy: Kyrgyzstan. The capital, Bishkek, is a fairly nondescript former Soviet city, with few cultural highlights to alleviate the challenges of amassing supplies in the stifling heat of August 2014. Finishing our shopping in Osh's bazaar and the city's more modern supermarkets, we loaded our supplies onto the mighty six-wheel-drive KAMAZ truck, glad to be heading south into the cooler climes of the Tien Shan.

As we rolled onwards and upwards the temperatures became more comfortable, tarmac became rarer and the yurts and horses of the nomadic

Pik Donstanski (4780m) with the Western Couloir (D, 600m) rising up to the summit. *(Adrian Dye)*

people increasingly dominated the landscape. After a pleasant night in a homestay in Naryn, the remoteness of our surroundings increased until the border posts seemed to mark the edge of civilisation. Beyond them the nomadic population became even more sparse, and old Soviet-constructed dirt roads disintegrated and reminded me of the Russian quote: 'We built poor quality roads to test our trucks on.'

Thankfully the truck and driver Sergei, who provided rolling maintenance, were more than up to the challenge, negotiating us through glacial meltwater rivers and periglacial block fields to our ideal drop-off point at 4100m. Crucially, this meant that our approach to base camp was greatly assisted by gravity, so walking fully laden downhill to our base camp at about 3400m (near the Sarychat river), followed by an unladen return journey to 4100m, proved to be good acclimatisation over the three days of load carrying.

Base camp was established in a pleasant meadow full of marmots and was next to the only reliable non-glacial stream in the valley for drinking water. We settled in just in time for the first day of bad weather and a much appreciated rest day. The approach had afforded us excellent views of a wide range of peaks up to 5982m, consisting of varieties of rock from the finest granite through to material that doesn't really deserve to be called rock. The team enthusiastically began eyeing up objectives in the surrounding mountains of the Sarychat and Fersmana glaciers. The ever eager team of Ian and Rob were quick off the mark with the first ascent of *A Grand Tour of Africa* (HVS 4c, 20m) on a granite crag near base camp, whilst Hannah patiently assisted Scott (the quartermaster) in organising the food we had carried in for the duration of the trip.

Looking around, it seemed that accessing our objectives through recently de-glaciated terrain could well prove the crux for the whole expedition. The snout of the Fersmana glacier proved to be a formidable challenge, with its bungalow sized granite boulders delicately perched on loose, hummocky moraine that seemed to go on forever. 'Moraine camp' was established at the north edge of this moraine, once we had made our way up the valley and navigated the unstable scree slopes of the glacial meltwater rivers. Rob, Hannah and Ian pressed through this boulder maze early on the morning of 14 August and were then able to make a swift ascent of the first unclimbed summit of the expedition: Peak 4645. Whilst they were enjoying the virgin summit experience, I had negotiated the maze and pressed on up to the Sarychat glacier snout to recce a route up to our next objective before depositing some gear and returning to the moraine camp. Scott returned from his recce of the Fersmana glacier with good news of a terrace that provided easy going along the west margin, before terminating in unstable, steep moraine slopes above a chaotic and crevassed glacier; that would have to wait until later in the trip.

The morning of 15 August dawned bright and clear, by which time Rob, Scott and I were several kilometres up the Sarychat glacier and nearing the base of our objective. Peak 4780 had an enticing gully line between ribs of rotten rock leading directly up to the summit. Despite cloud increasingly looming up from the Chinese side, a hard frost had left the delicate snow bridges strong enough for us to safely cross three bergschrunds guarding the gully above. Early progress was good as we moved together despite dinner plating ice, and it seemed as though I was living the childhood dream of reaching an unclimbed summit via an attractive snow line.

Rob had taken the lead and the gradually rising temperatures took their toll on the ribs of dark material either side of the gully. Early skirmishes of pebble sized rocks developed into an onslaught of microwave sized blocks that saw us rapidly veering to the shelter of the right hand side of the gully. This was steeper and the ice was harder and more brittle, and I became increasingly aware of having to hang from my axes as a steepening (75°) led us into the relative safety of the upper gully. On reaching the summit at 12:30pm, we were greeted with thunder and the dream of reaching my first unclimbed summit had been replaced by the stark reality of being in a serious situation. Scott and I agreed to name it Pik Donstanski (4780m) after my cousin Donald and his father Stanley, who both lost battles with cancer.

Both Rob and I realised that our initial plan of descending snow slopes to the south would put us into further danger of rockfall and deeper into

Huw looking towards peak 4849m. *(Ian Peachey)*

the bad weather. Instead, it seemed far more appealing to traverse the ridge to the north and take in two more unclimbed summits that would lead us to Peak 4645, which we knew would provide a suitable descent route even if it was over five miles away. We radioed base camp and informed Hannah of our plan, in which we then became engrossed and totally forgot about the rest of the team. The weather seemed to swallow us up as wet snow began to fall and cloud reduced visibility of the unknown ground we still had to cover. This proved to consist of rock that was best dealt with in crampons as the spikes seemed to hold it together better. There were sections of gendarmes made of coherent rock, and one of those provided the fine summit of The Castle (4601m) at around 3pm. By this time my thoughts had turned to finding a suitable descent route despite the thick cloud; benightment in the wet snow on an exposed ridge did not seem particularly appealing, regardless of how many unclimbed summits we had reached.

Thankfully, as darkness approached the cloud retreated and enabled Rob to find an excellent descent route with thoroughly enjoyable scree running, leading us down to our camp below the Sarychat glacier. A pot full of Yorkshire tea seemed to be a suitable celebration for reaching the tent just before darkness and further snowfall. It continued to snow through the

The summits on the ridge in the foreground are around 5000m and most likely unclimbed. *(Ian Peachey)*

night and into the next day, so Rob quit his damp bivvy bag and descended to moraine camp to discover that Hannah had valiantly carried our spare sleeping bags and supplies up in case we reached it the night before. We all safely reached a now-snowy base camp that afternoon and were pleased to leave the rumble of avalanches behind.

Despite the inclement weather, Ian and Huw were keen to make the most of a drier interlude with a reconnaissance of the unexplored glacier and unclimbed peaks to the east of our base camp. The rest of the team admired their efforts from the comfort of their tents, which I am sure Ian and Huw would have fully appreciated during the ensuing 'character building' bivouac high on the mountain. They returned the next day with valuable photos of yet more excellent, unclimbed objectives just under 5000m, and with a lot of wet gear. As the weather seemed intent on continuing with the wet theme, we remained in tents and I began to worry about tent fever setting in.

Thankfully the next day dawned cold with fresh snow down to below base camp, and not a cloud in the sky. Rob and Hannah climbed an impressive route of 350m at HVS 4b on the limestone buttress 'El Naranjo' behind base camp, made more exciting by the melting snow and ice that had to be crossed in rock shoes at the top of the climb. Meanwhile, the rest of the team continued to dry out gear, enjoy the sunshine and negotiate with violently protesting digestive systems that seemed intent on disrupting any further mountaineering plans.

Internal workings seemed to settle down the next day and the weather continued its settled form so Hannah, Huw and Ian made the cold, early morning crossing of the Sarychat river to the previously unexplored glacier affectionately known as 'Alf'; Rob and I returned to the debris covered maze of the Fersmana. Spurred on by clear skies, increased nutritional intake and good early progress along the western terrace of Scott's reconnaissance, our spirits were high. Progressing onto the Fersmana proved 'challenging', and moving out into the jumbled mess was spurned in favour of running frantically along the lateral moraine slopes as they moved underneath us. Progress became much slower and almost came to a halt as we saw two sets of footprints going up the glacier in the fresh snow. Were other people already on our unclimbed mountain? Could we overtake them? Perhaps it was just border guards patrolling the area.

Eventually we made it on to the knee-deep, fresh snow on the glacier, which confirmed my fears about the quality of the snow pack and disproved our various human footprint theories; they were actually hoof prints (possibly ibex) that went up to at least 4000m. High spirits returned and we made our way to below our unclimbed objective, the Little Poobah (5481m), where we established the single skin tent before going any deeper into the snow pack. The unconsolidated snow at least provided a plentiful supply for melting water. That night on the Fersmana we had a hard frost: our boots froze despite having been between our sleeping bags, the gas refused to work and the inside of the tent had a generous decoration of ice crystals. Unfortunately, the previous day's temperatures had not risen sufficiently to melt the snow pack so that it could solidify overnight, and first steps from the tent went through the windslab crust up to our knees in poorly consolidated graupel and powder, lying over wet glacier ice. This was our moment, our chance to climb an impressive virgin summit in great weather and atrocious snow pack conditions... Valiantly Rob did most of the trail breaking up to the bottom of our intended route, but progress was slow and the snowpack showed no signs of encouraging us up a southwest facing couloir of questionable stability. The Dye digestive system had regained some functionality and my gut instinct suggested that a painful retreat to the single skin tent was in order; so too did my seriously cold feet. The snowpack showed no signs of settling down that day and time was running short before we had to complete the carry out to our pick-up point, so we regretfully turned our backs on the mountain and returned to base camp.

In the meantime Hannah, Huw and Ian were having much more success on the Alf glacier, with the first ascent of Peak 4753 in snow conditions that did little to assist progress across crevasses. After successfully getting themselves (and eventually all their belongings) off the glacier by midday, an attractive looking peak to the south caught their eye. Again snow conditions were less than ideal, but the team made a successful ascent of Peak 4849 via the west face to give 700m of climbing around AD. Once again a relatively early descent paid dividends, and even then snow conditions

El Naranjo. Left: More Cheese Vicar? (HVS 4c) 460m, (Middleton, Dye 23.8.14), right: Where Vultures Dare (HVS 4b) 350m, (Middleton, Moulton 19.8.14) *(Adrian Dye)*

Ranimal Point. 1. *Ranimal Point* (HVS 4c) 370m, (Middleton, Moulton 24.8.14), 2. *The Garlic Fische* (E1 5a) 360m, (Goodall, Peachey 24.8.14), 3. *Love and Marriage* (VS 4b) 240m, (Dye, Gillespie 24.8.14). *(Adrian Dye)*

were deteriorating and team members began to disappear ever deeper into crevasses.

With the team all safely back in base camp, time was running short for further mountaineering in the surrounding area. El Naranjo was an obvious cragging objective and Rob was psyched for a more direct line than the previous route. The lower sections provided some delightful, sparsely protected technical slab climbing over good limestone. The quality of rock gradually deteriorated and reliable protection became even more sparse. Getting halfway up a pitch that was memorable for all the wrong reasons had left me feeling unusually uninspired. Rob ignored me and pressed on to discover more good pitches above, on improving rock, to top out of 460m of HVS 4c climbing. The following day was filled with more quality trad climbing on the buttress to the north of base camp, with the whole team operating as three pairs to climb routes around 300m long and ranging between VS 4b and E1 5a. We all topped out at similar times and made our way northwards to deposit the climbing gear near our mid-way camp for the carry out, and even saw some other people for the first time in 18 days.

The carry out proved to be fairly character building as we had to carry everything from 3400m, over a 4300m hill in low visibility with wet snow. Thankfully Sergei had arrived early to collect a tired and happy team from a very successful expedition of exploratory mountaineering in the Western Kokshaal Too.

Summary

An account of an expedition to the Sarychat and Fersmana glaciers in the Western Kokshaal Too region of Kyrgyzstan, 3-30 August 2014. The team was: Alpine Club members Adrian Dye (leader), Rob Middleton and Hannah Moulton; and non Alpine Club members Ian Peachey, Scott Gillespie and Huw Goodall. First ascents of: Pk Donstanski (4780m) via the western couloir (600m, D, 70°); Pk 4545, Pik 4606 (both PD); Pk 4645 (F); Pk 4753 (PD-) and Pk 4849 via the west face (AD). Three of the team explored the glacier basin descending from unclimbed peak 4849. The team also climbed five new alpine rock routes up to 460m long and up to HVS 5a.

Acknowledgements

The 2014 Little Poobah expedition would like to thank the Mount Everest Foundation and the Alpine Club for helping to fund the expedition, the 2012 Alpine Club Symposium for its inspiration, ITMC for providing logistics support and Sergei (the driver), and Alpkit for loan of two tents during the expedition.

Surveys

The Matterhorn from the Zen Stecken Bridge (now Upper Zermatt). Johann Jakob Sperli the Younger. Date unknown. Watercolour. 7 x 10cm. After an engraving by Johann-Jakob Meyer, Helvetische Almanach für 1820.
(Alpine Club Collection HE059P)

TOM NAKAMURA

Blue Sky Expedition

A Journey in South Tibet

Holy mountain Yalaxianbo: main peak (left) and south peak (north-west face).
(All photos: Tom Nakamura)

Once again, Tom was the 'Man of Blue Sky'. Clear, blue skies warmly welcomed us in every key point of our journey except for one, at the Goikarla Rigyu range.

The original plan of our expedition was to begin with the exploration of the unfrequented Goikarla Rigyu. This range has several veiled peaks over 6000m and extends some 250km from east of Lhasa to Bayizhen of Nyinchi Prefecture, between the Sichuan-Tibet Highway (north) and the Yarlung Tsangpo river (south). For efficiency in our investigations, we made full use of a Toyota Landcruiser, rather than camping and horse caravans; unfortunately this met with poor results. The 6000m peaks were elusive; complex valleys and ridges hindered views of our objective peaks. We had insufficient harvest in this mountain range.

Our second objective was to approach as closely as possible to the McMahon Line in south Tibet. Here, however, the difficulty came in the

Above: holy mountain Yalaxianbo, south-east face. Below: the route.

South of the Tsangpo–McMahon Line. 6151m peak, north face, on south bank of Yarlung Tsangpo west.

Goikarla Rigyu: holy mountain Worde Konggye (5725m), west face.

North face of Goikarla Rigyu (6060m) seen from Bahozhen, Sichuan-Tibet Highway.

Kulha Kangri and West: (from left) Karengjian north 6824m, main 7221m; Kulha Kangri (from left): north 7381m, central 7418m, main peak 7538m

Nyainqentanglha West and Nam Tso: Kyizi (6206m) south-east face

Nyainqentanglha West and Nam Tso: Golden Dragon (6614m) south-east face.

Samdain Kangsang 6590m (left end) and 6000m peaks, west faces.

form of strict and frequent checks and controls by Public Security Bureau and police. All counties adjacent to borders with Bhutan and India are totally closed to foreigners. Unsurprisingly, we met no foreigners en route. We were luckier in our harvest this time, owing to our capable Tibetan guide who had the sense to carefully detour checkpoints, which contain Public Security, police and army. A compete profile of the east face of Tarlha Ri (6777m) massif, peaks ranging south to the Bhutan border and every side of the massif of the holy mountain Yalaxianbo were photographed.

We were lucky to reach a heavenly lake called Puma Yumco (4980m), which is now closed to foreigners. From there, a grand panorama of Kulha Kangri (7538m) massif and the mountains ranging to south-west on the Bhutan border overwhelmingly inspired us. The north face of the world's highest unclimbed peak, Gangkar Puensum (7570m), was glimpsed to south.

We also made a two-day excursion to Nyainqentanglha West: the first day to Qungmo Kangri (7048m) and following day to the north bank of the holy lake Nam Tso at 4718m.

Summary

A brief account of the exploration of unclimbed mountainous regions in south Tibet by Tom Nakamura (79), Tsuyoshi Nagai (82) and, at 70, the baby of the group, Tadao Shintani, 11-25 Oct 2014. The trip involved some 4500km of driving from Bayizhen to Lhasa and several days of perfect weather: Oct 14: South of Nang Xian (Peak Bobonng 6152m south of Yarlung Tsangpo), Oct 16: Yalaxianbo 6635m and access to south toward McMahon Line, Oct 17: Tarlha Ri 6777m and peaks close to Bhutan border, Oct 20: Puma Yumco, Kulha Kangri massif, Gangkar Puensum and further west, Oct 24: Nyainqentanglha West and Nam Tso.

ANINDYA MUKHERJEE

South Simvu

Secrets of the Great South Ridge of Kangchenjunga, Part One

Siniolchu over the 5215m unnamed col, from our high point on Peak 6130. The rock needles on the watershed between Passauram and Zumthul Phuk glaciers are visible immediately right of col. *(All photos: Anindya Mukherjee)*

Maps, if caviare [sic] to the general, are, as Louis Stevenson has insisted, very suggestive to persons with proper imagination.
Douglas Freshfield, *Round Kangchenjunga* (1903)

For the last few years I have been exploring the valleys and glaciers of the south-eastern flanks of Kangchenjunga. To be more specific, my explorations have focused on the little – or completely – unknown glaciers of Talung, Tongshyong, South Simvu, Passauram and Zumthul Phuk, and their respective valley systems. In this article and its companion, which follows in this volume, I cover my recent (2014) explorations of South

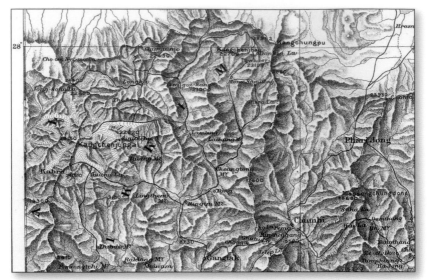

Above: John Claude White's map of Sikkim and Bhutan (RGS 1910) shows Talung, Tongshyong and Passauram glaciers. (*Geographical Journal 1910*). Below: Prof EJ Garwood's map shows Talung, Tongshyong, Passauram and Zumtu (Zumthul Phuk) glaciers but no South Simvu.

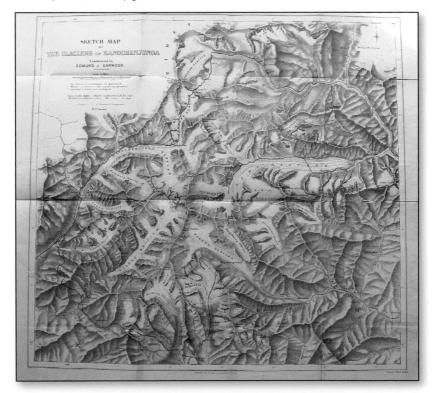

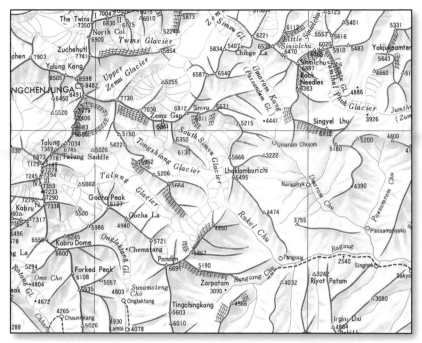

A section of Tadashi Toyoshima's map of 1977.

Simvu and Zumthul Phuk[1] glaciers only; my explorations of the Talung and Tongshyong glaciers are described in the *Alpine Journal*, vol. **116**[2].

The Great East Ridge

From the south summit of Kangchenjunga (8476m) a high ridge extends east. This ridge stretches all the way towards the Teesta valley and ends at the twin peak of Lama Angden[3] (5868m). This 'Great East Ridge' separates the Zemu glacier valley to the north from the complex, multi-glacier valley system to the south. The prominent peaks and features on the Great East Ridge are, from west to east: Zemu Peak (7730m), Unnamed Peak (7038m), Zemu Gap (5861m), Simvu Twins (6812m and 6811m), Siniolchu (6887m), Kishong la (4785m) and Lama Angden. The glaciers due south of the Great East Ridge (from west to east) are Talung, Tongshyong, South Simvu, Passauram and Zumthul Phuk.

While Talung, Tongshyong and South Simvu are clustered together and form the head of the Talung Basin, Passauram and Zumthul Phuk are located a bit further to the east and have their respective valley systems. These eventually join and contribute to the Rongyoung[4] Chu, meeting Teesta near Sanklang, below the busy town of Mangan. Although explorers had visited Talung, Tongshyong and Passauram glaciers before (Talung, for the first time in 1890 by John Claude White, Tongshyong in 1920 by Harold Raeburn, Passauram in 1937 by Paul Bauer's party), one glacier remained completely unknown: the South Simvu glacier.

The junction of Talung and Tongshyong Chu. Base camp tents are visible. Pandim's north face is in the background.

The Invisible Glacier

How an entire glacier in the close vicinity of the mighty Kangchenjunga stood unnoticed for this long is intriguing. The lack of a detailed and authentic map has always been a major hindrance for the exploring kind, especially in the Indian Himalaya. But in the curious case of South Simvu glacier, the glacier itself did not seem to exist. Colonel Waugh's map of 1848 and Sir Joseph Hooker's map of 1849 (and subsequently of 1854) did not have any detail of the Talung valley since no one had yet ventured there. John Claude White's crossing of the Guicha la and his subsequent journey down the Talung Chu gorge in 1890 resulted in another map which noted the Talung and Tongshyong glaciers for the first time.

The most significant cartographic work for this area was done as part of Douglas Freshfield's 'high level tour' of the Kangchenjunga in 1899. Freshfield's party included cartographer Professor EJ Garwood.

Garwood's map was very close to being perfect with reference to the other glaciers in the same valley, namely the Talung, Tongshyong, and even Passauram[5] glaciers. But once again there was no sign of South Simvu on his map. The invisibility of the glacier is easier to understand today, when one reads Garwood's comments on drawing this particular section: ' ...in the case of heads of the glens under Si-imvovonchum and Siniolchum[6], from sketches made by Mr Freshfield from above Gantok.[7]' Any map of jagged terrain of Himalayan scale, drawn from observations made from as far away and as low as Gangtok surely cannot be without errors.

Simvu twins on the right and Kangchenjunga on the left. The ridge in centre foreground is the Lhokamburichi ridge that guards the South Simvu glacier.

The glacier did not appear in the knowledge base until relatively recent mappings done by the Swiss, with the help of the Survey of India, which produced the Sikkim Himalaya map of 1951. This was later incorporated into the American Army Corps of Engineers' map of 1955. However, the very clear depiction of Upper Talung region, especially of South Simvu, that drew my attention most was Tadashi Toyoshima's map of 1977. In all my expeditions in the Sikkim Himalaya so far, I have used Toyoshima's map for preliminary planning and found it to be very accurate, despite not being topographical.

The Protagonists

White's journey through the Talung gorge and Freshfield's epic tour around Kangchenjunga opened doors for exploratory mountaineers. In the era from Harold Raeburn (1920) to H W Tilman (1938), the visitors of upper Talung valley had distinct yet limited objectives. Mount Pandim (6691m), the Zemu Gap (5861m) and Kangchenjunga remained their centre of attraction. Everything else was overshadowed. Once they were done with their efforts and attempts, they did not have enough time or energy to stay back and look around in this inhospitable part of remote Sikkim. The only significant exploration in the Raeburn-Tilman era was done by a small team from Paul Bauer's expedition in 1931. They crossed the Great East Ridge from the north (Zemu glacier) and entered the middle Talung valley via a col[8] located at the head of Passauram glacier[9]. During

Lhokamburichi as seen from the South Simvu glacier.

Peak 6130m on the left and Simvu west 6812m on the right.

this crossing in October 1931, in all probability they could not have noticed the existence of South Simvu glacier, as 'their' col didn't give them the necessary elevation to have a sneaky peek of what lay immediately south of the Simvu twins.

This era was followed by a complete absence of exploratory action in this valley until 1975, when a second phase of exploration began[10]. This second phase concentrated on what their predecessors left unfinished, with a series of onslaughts on Zemu Gap. Thus, in spite of being visible on maps since the 1950s, the glacier of South Simvu remained unnoticed until our visit in May 2014. As a mountain explorer, I looked at this blank in the map as a lodestone sending out strong vibrations of invitation.

Expedition

In April-May 2014 I was part of an expedition, led by Alberto Peruffo, which aimed to further explore the Tongshyong glacier and Talung glaciers. While my colleagues were happily occupied with the prospect of countless new routes all around us, I decided to head off in the direction of the last unexplored glacier of the Talung Valley: the South Simvu.

Our base camp was near the confluence of Talung and Tongshyong streams, almost in the same camping ground as our Zemu Gap expedition of December 2011. From the observations made during my three expeditions in 2011, I had formed a fair idea how to approach the South Simvu glacier, which like Tongshyong lay completely out of sight from the Talung gorge. Signs such as old, settled terminal and lateral moraine ridges and a powerful, braided outwash stream coming from the direction of Mount Simvu, gave strong suggestion of a glacier as indicated by the map. But the glacier itself was not visible. We assumed it had withdrawn to a higher shelf and had become a hanging glacier, possibly leaving a cirque. The question of how and when this happened can only be diagnosed by a glaciologist; my thought was that as a climbing problem, would a cirque or hanging glacier not offer a greater challenge than that of a valley glacier? What will this one throw at us?

On 3 May 2014, along with Thendup Sherpa and Lakpa Sherpa, I left base camp and followed the steep, right lateral moraine coming down from the direction of South Simvu. After a continuous steep hike and scramble of five hours we reached a big, slightly overhanging rock cliff. During all of April-May 2014, the whole of upper Talung valley was engulfed daily in thick fog from as early as 9am. This pattern of early white-out lasted for nearly four weeks of our stay inside the gorge, including that first day of exploration, allowing us no chance for better visibility. Later in the day, we took shelter below the overhanging cliff.

For the next two days we did reconnaissance trips further up the valley, hoping for clearer weather. Finally one morning, before the clouds came rushing up, we saw the outline of an icefall that announced South Simvu's presence. To our delight, we also saw the twin summits of Simvu rising above the icefall. This re-affirmed our motivation and on 6 May 2014,

View of Siniolchu from our high camp in the South Simvu glacier.

Thendup Sherpa and I left our overhang shelter, hoping to cross the first icefall obstacle and set up a high camp. An easy snow gully to the true right of the icefall gave us access to the upper plateau of the glacier. Due to poor visibility and bad snow conditions it took us nearly seven hours to reach névé on the glacier itself. We pushed on and camped at around 5300m.

An Attempt on Peak 6130m

From the Swiss contour map, I was aware of the existence of two unnamed 6000m peaks somewhere nearby. Peak 6350m and Peak 6130m are located on the ridge running south-east that divides Tongshyong and South Simvu glaciers. Now that we had entered the South Simvu, my immediate attention was drawn towards those unclimbed peaks. But, due to poor visibility, we got no bearings on our position that entire day (6 May 2014) and waited patiently for the early hours of the next morning, when we hoped to be able to orient ourselves.

On 7 May 2014 we woke up with great expectations; today we would see and document a glacier that had never been seen before. We felt fortunate and a bit proud to be the first and were not disappointed with the view that morning. To our north the Simvu twins (6812m West and 6811m East) looked gigantesque and dominated the skyline. To our north-north-east, after a stretch of a snowfield full of crescentric crevasses, we could clearly see a col (5215m) a bit lower than our campsite sharply dropping to the Passauram[11] side. Above and beyond that col rose Siniolchu (6887m) in all its grandeur. To our east, right across the glacier to the south of a 5215m col, rock peaks (5666m) and Lhokamburichi (5495m) formed the boundary wall between South Simvu and Passauram glaciers. Looking at the unmistakable, thumb-like feature of Lhokamburichi, I realised that this is the ridge one can see from the lower Talung valley while looking at Simvu. This is what completely hides South Simvu glacier from its east and south-east and the reason it never came out in the sketches made by Freshfield from above Gangtok. Lhokamburichi blocked the view.

To our south we could see Narsing (5825m), the Jopuno (5936m) group of peaks, Pandim (6691m) and to our immediate north-west stood the two unnamed peaks: 6350m and 6130m respectively. Thendup and I roped up and started towards the objective nearest our campsite, Peak 6130m.

Within the next four hours we climbed through a narrow gully to the east of Peak 6130m and reached the base of the summit rock pyramid. It did not take us long to decide that we were not bagging any peaks that day. To climb the rock pyramid we would need protection, which neither of us carried in our lightweight push. When we left base camp the best we were hoping to achieve was to find and reach the right glacier, and when we reached the glacier, we took our ambition a level higher: to bag an unclimbed 6000m peak. Such is human nature.

We stopped close to 6000m and our high point was the perfect vantage position for exploratory photo documentation and so I told myself to be happy with what we achieved, and then to retreat. From here we could photograph extraordinary views of the head of South Simvu glacier, the Simvu twins, Siniolchu and its rock needles rising across and above the Passauram valley. It was nearly midday, and snow conditions became worse. Thendup and I have been climbing together nearly a decade now, and trust was important in these conditions. We reached camp in a complete whiteout, packed up the next morning and started down towards base camp with heavy backpacks but happy minds. South Simvu glacier is not invisible anymore.

Summary

An account of exploration of the South Simvu glacier and an attempt on Peak 6130m, in April-May 2014. The expedition members were Anindya Mukherjee, Thendup Sherpa, Lakpa Sherpa.

Notes

1. Also spelled Jumthul Phuk or Zumtu glacier in some maps.
2. Zemu Gap from the South, *Alpine Journal* 2012.
3. Also spelled Lama Ongden, Lamo Angdang and Lamo Anden.
4. Also referred to as Talung Chu.
5. Also spelled Passanram.
6. Traditional Lepcha names for peaks Simvu and Siniolchu.
7. Freshfield, *Round Kangchenjunga*, p304.
8. Simvu Saddle.
9. *Himalayan Journal* 05, p58.
10. For a history of exploration in the upper Talung valley see *Alpine Journal*, vol. 116, p118.
11. Also referred to as 'Umaram Kang' on some maps.

ANINDYA MUKHERJEE

Zumthul Phuk

Secrets of the Great South Ridge of Kangchenjunga, Part Two

Siniolchu south-east and east faces, from base camp in Zumthul Phuk valley.
(All photos: Anindya Mukherjee)

The second of two articles describing exploration of the glaciers on the south-eastern flanks of Kangchenjunga recalls the exploration of the Zumthul Phuk glacier and its legendary Rock Needles.

Background

John Claude White, the first British political officer to Sikkim, was also the first person to express an interest in exploring Zumthul Phuk glacier. He never mentioned the name or existence of a glacier but he did give the name of the river emanating from it, calling it Zamtu Chu. In July 1891, on his way to Lhonak valley, White took the Tholung Gompa-Kishong La-Thiu La route[1]. During his journey he made the following observation:

Whilst on the first day's march I discovered that a large stream, the Zamtu-Chu, takes its rise on the eastern slopes of Siniolchu and joins the Rimpi[2] on its right bank, thus proving the survey maps to be wrong in showing it, as they have hitherto done, running to the south.

I was much tempted to follow up this stream, as Siniolchu is the most lovely peak of Sikhim, and the views at the head of the valley must be magnificent, but it would probably have taken me over a week and I could not spare the time, as I wanted to go north across several snow ranges and so reach a drier climate.[3]

White was not able to return to fulfill his desire. Forty years later, in October 1931, after their daring attempt on climbing Kangchenjunga[4],

Siniolchu Needles (5712m) on the left, Zumthul Phuk glacier and lake in centre, Siniolchu in backdrop.

Dr Eugen Allwein and Pircher[5] crossed the Simvu Saddle from the Zemu glacier side into the Passauram valley. While entering the valley they were struck by a prominent mountain feature. Quoting Allwein:

On a ridge radiating south-eastwards is set a mountain strangely contrasting in character to the mass of Siniolchu, a kind of Dent du Geant, but vastly larger in scale, with a mountain character one would scarcely expect to meet among the icy giants of the Himalaya.[6]

This appears to be the first documented sighting of the Rock Needles of Siniolchu. Another German expedition followed in 1937, led by Dr Paul Bauer. During their expedition to climb Siniolchu from the Zemu glacier side, they also did some exploration in the Zumthul Phuk Valley[7]. They were able to cross a col from near their base camp in the Zemu glacier valley and enter the Zumthul Phuk glacier. They then crossed the water-

Rock Needles (5712m) and Brothers Tees Col (5250m) as seen from ABC 2.
Below: Rock Needles, in close-up.

shed between Passauram and Zumthul Phuk glaciers and reached a pass-like feature to the south-east of Rock Needles (or Siniolchu Needles). They named it 'Kukur La'. I quote Dr Karl Wein:

> *After crossing the Zemu glacier we climbed, on the 23rd August, a pass 5,300m. (17,387 feet) high to the south-east of our base camp. From there, when there was a gap in the clouds, we looked upon a rugged mountainous country traversed by glaciers of unexpected beauty. From the precipitous south-east flank of Siniolchu hanging glaciers plunged down to feed the Zumtu glacier, which, like the Zemu glaciers, was completely covered with debris. To the south of this glacier stood some rocky mountains of incredible steepness. They ranged even higher than the continuation of the south ridge of Siniolchu. The loftiest point was the Siniolchu Needle, about 20,000 feet high. Undiscovered land lay before us, for no one had previously set foot in this valley. Unfortunately we only caught a fleeting view of it in the morning; the rest of the time it poured in torrents.*[8]

From that time, no party had gone near, much less attempted to go into Zumthul Phuk valley to have close look at the Rock Needles, these Needles of Siniolchu. In 2006, I went with Zamyong Lepcha, a boy from Lingzya village, up the Zamtu Chu (Zumthul Chu) gorge and reached above the tree lines, to the terminal moraines of the Zumthul Phuk glacier. Bad weather prevented us from getting any view of the mountains. In 2009, Thendup Sherpa and I partially entered the Zumthul Chu gorge and caught a clear view of the Rock Needles[9]. We could see how, starting with the German explorers of 1931 and 1937, the Needles with their distinct and unique features have become objects of fascination. They certainly were for us.

Expedition

In October-November 2014, led by Alan Tees, a past president of Mountaineering Ireland, our party became the first team to complete the traverse of the Zumthul Phuk Chu gorge as envisioned by White in 1891, and successfully reach the Zumthul Phuk glacier. The team was a group of seven, ranging in age from 45 to 75, and in experience from expedition rookies to veterans. We had a variety of aspirations, whose realisation depended on the entirely unknown terrain that lay ahead of us.

We arrived at the village of Be on 29 October. November tends to be settled in Sikkim but there was cloud on our approach, although it saved the rain until we started our trek in from Be. Three short days took us to Tolung[10] via Tholung monastery, where we shared the campsite with a herd of yak. The main trail goes over the Kishong La, but we headed up the Zumthul valley towards Siniolchu, and into the unknown. Several of our porters were sent ahead to blaze a trail with machetes through the dense rhododendron, and two days of hard work by everybody brought us to a level area at about 3800m above the worst of the vegetation, ideal for a base camp. The porters left to go down.

Above: Panorama looking west from 'One Hand Peak'.

Next morning was lovely. The clear skies and our wonderful location left us euphoric as we contemplated a rest day, with some local exploration and lots of sunshine. Half an hour above base camp was a big and beautiful lake[11] with the Zumthul Phuk Glacier calving lumps of ice into the far side, and the snowy ramparts of Siniolchu dominating the valley behind. To the left were the Rock Needles, their upper slopes still partly shrouded but then there was nothing, as cloud rose from the valleys below. It snowed in the afternoon, but some of us climbed a gully above base camp to pass the day.

The following morning was again lovely, and we set off to carry gear and find an advanced base camp (ABC). This took us around the lake and up onto the glacier, to the base of a big buttress at the bottom of the first needle. We were surrounded by steep and spectacular peaks, all unexplored and with their still-hidden route possibilities. By the time we had returned to base camp it had clouded in, and soon it was snowing.

The remaining group moved to ABC where they spent two days. One of these days was used to search for a route to a high camp on the shoulder of the Rock Needles. Their eventual line led up a gully of Scottish III or IV on thin ice and névé, giving access to easier angled slopes; high camp was established at 4740m. The following day, three hours of hard labour led to the col above (5250m), which we named 'Brothers Tees Col', from where there were magnificent views of the Upper Talung Valley and western Sikkim peaks. We were standing on a watershed between Passauram and Zumthul Phuk glaciers. Most prominent were Pandim (6691m), Kabru,

Below: Panorama of unnamed northerly glacier valleys of Zumthul Phuk.

Talung, Kangchenjunga, and Simvu. We could also see the Tongshyong glacier and section of the South Simvu glacier. There were snow leopard tracks on the col.

We returned down the newly named Thendup and Tenzing Gully to ABC. The following day ABC was moved to the other side of the moraine, as a better base from which to explore the northern side of the Zumthul valley. Next day some tents were packed, and we followed a moraine to a junction of two higher, unknown glaciers, and a second high camp (ABC2) was established beside a shallow lake at 4768m. This upper valley is much wider than was indicated on the map. Weather continued to be unsettled with sporadic rain and snow. Thursday 13 November dawned with another covering of snow, but we managed to climb a col at 5046m (named Mari Col), which was a narrow opening on a sharp ridge. From there we discovered a new, massive glacier stretching intact up to the Siniolchu ridge, with a series of unclimbed peaks at the end of it. A small peak at 5100m was ascended and named 'One Hand Peak' before descent to ABC2 and ABC. This was the hottest day so far, and clouds were starting to build again at lower altitudes.

The next day ABC was packed up and retreat made to base camp via the shores of the Zumthul Lake. This required a tricky crossing of the river but avoided exposure to the stonefall problem of the south bank. The weather was cloudy and miserable again at base camp, but our fantastic porters arrived on schedule for the walk out the following day. A tough seven-hour

Martin Bonar on One Hand Peak, with Peak 6020m and an unnamed glacier in the background.

walk through the mist and rhododendron brought us and porters to the Forest Department's[12] hut at Tolung (Temrong).

Summary

An account of exploration of the Zumthul Phuk glacier in October-November 2014, with first ascents of the col between the Passauram and Zumthul Phuk glaciers, and of One Hand Peak (5100m) overlooking unknown glaciers and endless unclimbed peaks. Team members were Jack Bergin, Martin Boner, Kevin Higgins, Ursula McPherson, Keith Monaghan, Anindya Mukherjee, Thendup Sherpa, Alan Tees (Leader) and Jimmy Tees.

Notes
1. Kishong La is also known as Yumtso La.
2. Ringi Chu.
3. *Sikhim and Bhutan: Twenty One Years on the North-East Frontier 1887-1908*, J Claude White p67.
4. Under the leadership of Paul Bauer.
5. Along with three Sherpa companions.
6. The Passauram and Talung Valleys, Sikkim, Dr. Eugen Allwein, *Himalayan Journal* Vol.5, p-58-64).
7. Zumthul Phuk Valley, spelled differently as Zamtu or Zumtu by different authors.
8. The 1937 German party were the first to see and photograph these unnamed glaciers as they were looking for a passage on the watershed of Zumthul Phuk and Passauram glaciers. They found their passage (Kukur La), but could not complete the journey, and retraced their steps back to Zemu glacier. Source: Himalayan Journal Vols **5, 7**.
9. The Rock Needles or Siniolchu Needles are also marked as Singyel Lhu, 5712m in some maps.
10. Known as Temrong nowadays.
11. Interestingly, the German party that had entered Zumthul glacier from north in 1937 and ascended Kukur La did not mention a lake. Perhaps a sign of global warming speeding up in the last decades? It is difficult to pinpoint the exact timeframe in which this lake was created.
12. Kangchenjunga National Park.

PAUL KNOTT

Undiscovered Granite

In the Alaskan Fairweathers

South side of Pk 8290ft from the high bowl overlooking the Johns Hopkins glacier. We reached the summit pyramid via the extended south-east ridge on the right skyline, and on the granite top climbed the arête dividing light and shade. *(Paul Knott)*

In April-May 2014, Kieran Parsons and I were fortunate to make the first ascents of three summits between Mt Abbe and Mt Bertha in south-east Alaska's Fairweather range. The most exciting of these was Peak 8290ft (2527m), whose top sports a tantalising pyramid of clean granite. Peak 8290, like many summits in this area, is unnamed other than its spot height on USGS maps. The quality of the granite we climbed augurs well for the potential of steeper pillars on this and adjoining summits.

As is often the case with fickle coastal climbing, Peak 8290 was not our original plan. Base camp was 20km away by the east ridge of Mt Crillon (3879m) – a longstanding challenge Bradford Washburn first put forward back in 1941. Mt Crillon dominates Glacier Bay's West Arm peninsula, and its east ridge presents a very exposed 10km-long route. Route of this

Part of the corniced ridge beyond Pt 6706ft. The ridge contains numerous hidden steps. *(Paul Knott)*

type are not for everyone, as they involve many days' climbing with loaded packs in uncertain and unforgiving weather. Luckily, Kieran was fresh from an active period in New Zealand's Southern Alps, whose rigours breed the necessary fitness and stamina as well as judgment and humility. Thus, I had the reassurance I needed to return to the Alaskan coast after an unfortunate epic the year before (*Alpine Journal* 2013).

We reached base camp the same day we arrived in Haines, 21 April, thanks to the skilful judgement of our ski plane pilot, Paul Swanstrom. But when we tried to approach Mt Crillon, poor visibility hampered our efforts.

wo views of the west side of Peak 8290ft, April 2011: above from near the summit of Pk
7400ft *(Paul Knott)*

The top granite pyramid of Pk 8290ft. We climbed close to the arête throughout.
(Paul Knott)

The forecast was for continued unreliable weather, and we concluded this
was not conducive to such a long and serious route. Instead, we made a
20km traverse on the Brady Icefield to the area north of Mt Bertha, with
the idea to explore unclimbed peaks in the Mt Abbe group. Although

low in altitude, the Abbe peaks are still large by many standards and present a vertiginous profile as they consist largely of granite (unlike much else in south-east Alaska).

After eight hours of snow-shoeing and pulling sleds, we made a camp at 1230m on the glacier north-east of Mt Bertha. Unfortunately, this was our high point on this attempt. Over the next four days, poor weather confined us to the tent and put down 150cm of snow. In the midst of the storm, we had to dig out the buried tent and drag it to the new surface. For a while, we found ourselves scrunched uncomfortably on a stepped floor. Luckily, that evening the weather cleared enough for us to make a firmer platform and regain some dignity. In the main, the storm was not much hardship: we had food, good books, and the right equipment including a strong single-skin tent and up-to-date sleeping bags with proofed outers. In lulls, the powerful XGK stove quickly topped up our water.

What was to test our mettle somewhat, though, was the 20km return to base camp. We broke through half-formed crust so badly that after the first two and a half hours we had moved only 614m. We stopped early that day in the hope of improving conditions, but felt under pressure given that we had only two more days' supplies. Fortunately, the snow was firmer the following day as I had hoped, and by late afternoon we were within reach of base camp. We camped close

Above and below: Kieran Parsons starting pitch 2 on the summit pyramid of Pk 8290ft. *(Paul Knott)*

to a curious patch of snow that must have been the roost for a migrating flock of geese. That night, high wind buffeted the tent. We had done our best to build snow walls, but they melted to nothing. High up, huge plumes of snow blew from the plateau below Mt Crillon. After four hours of plodding, we arrived at base camp to find the tent almost completely buried in dense, wind-blown snow.

The weather update told us nearby Yakutat had recorded a record warm temperature for the date. The good news was that the strong winds were from building high pressure. We were keen to make the most of this, but concerned about conditions for Mt Crillon. Our route involved a potentially threatened south-facing slope followed by similarly exposed east-facing slopes below the upper ridge. Given the recent heavy snow and high winds, and no sign of a reliable freeze, one or both of these seemed prohibitively risky.

Hence, after just one full day's rest, we set off with renewed determination for the Abbe peaks. We set off at 3am under clear skies, and with the surface transformed, in six hours we were already above our previous high camp. Early next morning, we stashed our snowshoes and poles as best we could before climbing the obviously avalanche-prone slope to a col at 1887m. This col was the key to a high bowl overlooking the Johns Hopkins glacier. We could see everything from Mt Bertha and the north ridge of Mt Crillon, right up to the Mt Fairweather massif at the opposite end of the range. In front of us was the south face of Peak 8290ft with its tantalising granite top. Beneath our feet, the sun glinted off the snow. The crust supported our weight intermittently and there was no substance underneath. This energy-sapping combination tried our patience as we crossed to the south side of the bowl for our first objectives.

Early on 6 May, we set off up the snowy northern arête of Peak 7507ft (2288m). We made fast progress on this, and hence after descending from the summit we moved directly to the adjacent Peak 7274ft (2217m) via its north-west spur and west ridge. The view from these peaks convinced us that the most direct approach to the granite top of Peak 8290ft, the snowy south-east face, was not viable because an ice cliff across its middle was too threatening and the face ran with wet slides each afternoon. Instead, early on 7 May we set off on the 2km-long south-east ridge from a camp by the 1887m col. We had noted the potential for time-consuming difficulties along this ridge, and beyond the small foresummit 6706ft (2044m) we found ourselves tackling a series of knife-edge corniced mushrooms and towers. As expected, the rock here was sedimentary and loose. It took us nearly three hours to negotiate a few hundred metres of ridge. Above, an easier snow arête took us to the base of the granite pyramid. The only way up this was on steep rock, but the granite was superb, providing secure climbing with juggy holds and plentiful protection. We climbed close to the crest, in three pitches of about Hard Severe – which made for pleasant climbing with our single half-rope, rigid boots and light rack.

From the summit, we could see how much untapped potential exists

Kieran Parsons on our return along the corniced ridge to Pt 6706ft. The ridge contains numerous hidden steps. *(Paul Knott)*

for harder and more sustained granite climbing. I had noticed some of this rock on previous visits in 2009 and 2011, but the quality of what we had just climbed highlighted just how exciting the possibilities could be. Only two teams have climbed in the Abbe group. In 1977, the team of Alan Givler, Dusan Jagersky, Steve Marts and James Wickwire (who, like us, originally set out to approach Mt Crillon) most notably climbed a steep mixed route on the south-west face of Peak 8440ft (2573m). In 1991, a determined Walter Gove and Bill Pilling climbed Mt Abbe from the north-

South face of peak 8410ft (right), April 2011. The pinnacle to the left is peak 7260ft on the western side of Mt Abbe. *(Paul Knott)*

east side, directly from the sea. These ascents leave the main granite pillars untouched. The western side of Peak 8290ft sports a continuous 450m pillar. But the most striking rock lies nearer Mt Abbe. Peak 8410ft (2563m) immediately to its south has monolithic pillars up to 750m in height on its western and southern sides. Mt Abbe itself presents several clean granite walls overlooking the Clark glacier and on its western outlier Peak 7260ft (2213m). Peak 8440ft looks more mixed and alpine, but still looks to have the same rock as we had just climbed.

Access to these pillars need not be difficult. While the 1977 party made a circuitous approach from the Brady glacier, one could nowadays land by ski plane on the west shoulder of Mt Abbe. This was the key to my 2009 and 2011 climbs elsewhere in the Johns Hopkins basin (which itself remains otherwise untouched by climbers). A landing higher up, directly below Peak 8440ft, might also be possible. Bergschrunds could be one remaining problem, as was my experience in the upper bowl in 2011, along with a striking frigidity in the shade of the steep walls.

By the time we had taken in the view from the summit and arranged four abseils back to the snow shoulder, it was already after midday. As we picked our way down in the afternoon warmth, we found the difficulties on the approach ridge transformed from mostly snow to mostly rock. Collapsing cornices, sodden snow and disintegrating rock concentrated our minds and forced us to make two awkward diagonal abseils. At one point, a cornice 150cm wide and 8m long detached beside me and fell down the steep northern face. One of my ice tools dangled down the face by its umbilical. Equally, it was hard to ignore the ominous clouds gathering

South-west face of peak 8440ft, April 2011. *(Paul Knott)*

over the ocean south of us.

We finally ploughed our way to the tent in mist and light snow at 6:30pm. We were pleased with our climb, and relieved to reach relative safety where we could rest and rehydrate. But our position was still exposed. Any oncoming storm would load the avalanche-prone slopes we still had to descend. I was especially mindful of the epic I had experienced on Mt Eaton the year before, and we were both ready to continue descending that evening despite the risk of wet slides. Importantly, we had the physical capacity to do so. After a phone conversation with pilot Paul, we nevertheless decided to wait overnight for a freeze, as high pressure was due to hold the storm offshore.

Early next morning, in intermittent visibility, we post-holed down from the col, finding our footprints obliterated by wet slides. Towards the bottom of the slope, we noticed a cone of ice blocks from a huge serac collapse extending out over the glacier, and realised that our stashed snowshoes lay just within the cone. This made the 20km walk back to base camp a distinctly unappealing prospect that could well have been a repeat of our post-storm trenching the week before. Luckily, by the afternoon the cloud had cleared and pilot Paul was able to pick us up directly.

Fly-in, fly-out climbs involve dramatic transitions. After spending almost three weeks in a world of snow, we dismounted from the plane to powerful spring fragrance, green shoots, and birdsong. We spent a few days in Haines amongst this paradise, a fitting way to cool down after such a vivid high mountain experience. The whole adventure left me with a renewed sense of how majestic and elevating the climbing here can be – given, of course, a strong party and a bit of luck with the weather.

Aerial views, April 2011 of above: twin summits of Mt Abbe from the west; the walls on the left overlook the Clark Glacier, the face at the far right is on Peak 7260ft. and below: Peak 8410ft from the north-west. The wall on the far left is on Peak 7260ft. On the right are Peak 8440ft and Peak 8290ft. *(Paul Knott)*

Summary

An account of the first ascent of three peaks south of Mt Abbe, over-looking the Johns Hopkins glacier in south-east Alaska's Fairweather range. The team of Paul Knott and Kieran Parsons climbed from 21 April to 8 May 2014 on what was Paul's ninth trip to the area. A highlight was finding perfect mountain granite.

Acknowledgements

We are grateful for financial support for this trip from the Mount Everest Foundation and the Canterbury Mountaineering Club.

EVELIO ECHEVARRÍA

Cordillera Chaupijanca, Peru

The Huaraz – Pachapaqui – Huallanca road, with the ridge of the Tancán peaks in the background. *(All photos: Evelio Echevarría)*

Its former name was Cordillera Huallanca and thus it appeared in the reports of the first expeditions between 1969 and 1972. That name disappeared in 1974 when the Instituto Geográfico Militar of Peru launched its definitive Carta Nacional and the range began to display its original and true native name, Cordillera Chaupijanca; Chaupi in Quichua means 'middle' and janca, 'heights'. An accurate name, since the Chaupijanca is compressed between the two giant ranges of northern Peru, the Cordillera Blanca and the Cordillera Huayhuash. Indeed the Incas knew best how to name their mountains.

The Chaupijanca may well be the smallest of the 26 cordilleras known to exist in Peru, but what matters is what it has to offer visiting mountaineers. It runs north-north-west to south-south-east for some 35 to 40 kilometres. It averages some seven kilometres wide, except at the tract near the village of Aquia, where its width must be about 14 kilometres. This is due to the fact that its highest point, Nevado Pampash (5338m) sits somewhat apart and to the west. The entire range is bound in the north by the Pativilca river

The winding Pachapaqui – Yanashalla pass, with the NW side of the Burro massif in background.

valley, which separates it from the Cordillera Blanca and in the south, by the Yanacocha moors, separating it from the Cordillera Huayhuash.

The Chaupijanca is mining country in its northern third, with agriculture and cattle raising (sheep and llamas) in the other two thirds. There is little population and few settlements. The village of Pachapaqui (3963m; about 900 people) is the best place to access the northern half of the range. The town of Aquia (3300m) could yield access to the western and southern half, while the mining town of Huallanca could perhaps do so into the unknown eastern slopes.

Nature is disappointing. Animals, even birds, are rarely seen. In the lower valleys grow small clusters of blue lupins and yellow senecios. In the higher meadows, scattered groves of queñua (*Polylepis sp.*), a red bark tree that may reach to around 4500m are found. The one attraction in this respect is the puya (*Puya raimondii*), a striking broad plant with a flowering spike that can reach 2m high. It has been declared under the protection of the government of Peru but in the highlands, shepherds, mostly young boys, for warmth, burn their leaves and flanks. In the valley of Rodeo I counted about 160 such plants, with some 70 already burnt.

The mountaineering season runs in the tropical winter between May and September, and the weather is usually dry and pleasant. There is clear water in lagoons as well as in fountains and trickles draining down from the hills.

The whole northern and western Chaupijanca district is serviced by a

The valley and road leading to the Gara mine, access to the Burro massif.

vehicular road that starts at the city of Huaraz in the north, heads south to Aquia, then east and through the Yanashalla pass (4680m), to the towns of Huallanca and La Unión. A Huaraz bus company offers a daily service for this route.

There remains the purpose of this brief presentation: what kind of mountaineering could this small range offer? Since most of the Cordillera Chaupijanca is still in the epoch of exploratory mountaineering, what matters most is first ascents. The one pertinent sheet of the National Chart (1:100,000) shows 17 mountain peaks between 4900m and 5000m and 34 between 5000m and, plus the 5338m of Nevado Pampash, the highest. Of these 51 peaks, 16 are known to have registered ascents. The majority of them, at least on maps, are still unnamed. Many have been fixed with accurate heights.

Points of access and their main groups of peaks are:

1. For the northern extreme of the range, that is, north and south of the Yanashalla pass (4680m), one can use, I dare say comfortably, the daily rural bus and get off wherever one may wish, then hike, camp and climb. There are about 10 bold peaks, mostly rock, between 4950m to 5200m.

2. For the heavily glaciated district of the Burro massif, arrive in Pachapaqui by bus, then march along the vehicular road to the Gara mine or enlist a ride with a lorry taking miners to the same place. Mountain peaks are the nevados Huallanca or western Burro (5269m), Cumbre de los Burros (5268m) and a few others accessible from the Gara mine. The easternmost

Unclimbed Condorhuayín ridge (5000m?).

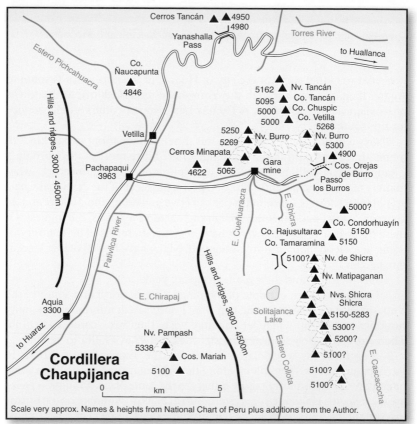

Cerros Tancán ▲ ▲4950
4980

Yanashalla
Pass

Torres River

to Huallanca

Estero Pichcahuacra

Co.
Ñaucapunta
▲
4846

Nv. Tancán
5162 ▲
5095 ▲ Co. Tancán
5000 ▲ Co. Chuspic
5000 ▲ Co. Vetilla
5268

Hills and ridges, 3000 - 4500m

Vetilla ■

5250 ▲ Nv. Burro
5269

Nv. Burro
▲ 5300
▲4900

Cerros Minapata

Co. Orejas
de Burro

Pachapaqui
3963 ■

4622 ▲ 5065

Gara
mine ■

Passo
los Burros

E. Cueñuaracra

E. Shicra

▲5000?

Co. Condorhuayín
Co. Rajusultarac   5150
Co. Tamaramina ▲ 5150

Pativilca River

) (5100?▲ Nv. de Shicra

Nv. Matipaganan

Hills and ridges, 3800 - 4500m

E. Chirapaj

Solitajanca
Lake

Nvs. Shicra
Shicra
▲ ▲5150-5283
▲ 5300?
▲ 5200?

Aquia
3300 ■

to Huaraz

Nv. Pampash

5338 ▲
▲ Cos. Mariah
5100 ▲

Estero Collota

▲ 5100?

E. Cascacocha

Cordillera
Chaupijanca

5100? ▲
5100? ▲

0   km   5

Scale very approx. Names & heights from National Chart of Peru plus additions from the Author.

Shicra valley with unclimbed rock peaks Rajusultarac and Tamaramina (5100m?). Puya plants in foreground.
(Evelio Echevarría)

peak of the Burro massif, mapped at 5300m, is in my opinion no higher than 5150m, but still an imposing objective.

Incidentally, why are those impressive heights prosaically called the Burro peaks? Simply by extension, since they dominate the Paso de los Burros (Pass of the Donkeys). When I visited the area I heard that the lower rock peaks by the pass were labelled Orejas de Burro (Donkey's Ears).

3. For the central group, reach Pachapaqui and hire some *arriero* (herdsman) with a horse or donkey to carry loads up the Quebrada (valley) de Shicra and camp wherever water is at hand. After a gap in the area is crossed, then descend south into the valleys of the southern ridge of ice peaks. This central section is collectively called Shicra Shicra and it rises from 5100 to 5283m. According to a Spanish guidebook by JJ Tomé this group could also be approached from the town of Huallanca, on the eastern slopes.

4. The little known southern half of the Chaupijanca has to my knowledge not entered climbing reports. I assume it can be accessed from the village of Aquia. The National Chart shows several contour-lined nevados at 5200-5300m. Finally the southernmost Azul Cuncush 5000ers bring the range to an end.

The climbing history of Cordillera Chaupijanca is short but shows that rather large expeditions were attracted by this small mountain range. In 1969 a Brazilian expedition of eight, under D Giobbi, ascended the two Burro peaks (5269 and 5268m) as well as Minapata (5065m) and an unlocated Tunacancha.

In 1971 a team of four led by Hugh Clark, all Anglo-Saxon surnames, climbed three of the Shicra Shicra nevados (5150, 5190 and 5283m) and two of the Tancán peaks in the north side (5095 and 5165m). A month

The rather artistic indigenous landmark of the Paso de los Burros (Pass of the Donkeys), 4700m.

Part of the Gara glacier with the south-west face of the south-east peak of the Burro massif (5150m?).

Part of the Shicra Shicra ridge (5150 - 5283m) from the north-north-west.

later, an Italian party of 10, under Sergio Macció, probably reclimbed Clark's Nevado (5190m).

In 1972 another Italian party, six members under G Mainini, climbed Nevado de Shicra (5150m?), Condoraju (5115m) and Matipaganán (5170m). And in 1984 one Peruvian and two Americans reascended Nevado Pampash or Huamánhuequi (5338m), which had been won by three Peruvians in 1967.

Finally our own experiences: in June 2003 the well known Spanish Cordillera Blanca experts Antonio Gómez and wife Consuelo, plus myself, camped in the upper Quebrada de Shicra. My two companions opened a new route on the icy west face of Nevado de Shicra (5150m?). In June 2005 I reconnoitred alone the valleys of Vetilla, Queñuaracra and Gara, reaching to the Paso de los Burros (4700m). And in 2008, in a short side trip from Huaraz, the Spaniards Antonio Gómez and Txomín Uriarte made the first ascent of the sharp rock peaks of Ñaucapunta (4846m), north-west of the Vetilla valley.

In conclusion, besides the opening of new routes—something nearly unknown in the Cordillera Chaupijanca—the mountains located in the northern and southern ends of this range will represent the main attractions for future pioneer work.

Nowadays, when even humble 5000ers in the giant ranges of Asia are sought by climbers, other equally small, more accessible and less costly mountain ranges like the Chaupijanca could well offer better choices.

Bibliography

Since the New National Chart of Peru did not appear until 1974, nearly every report below quotes the old name Cordillera Huallanca, now in disuse.

R Beretta, '28 giorni in Peru,' *Rivista Mensile* 92, 500-508, 1973

Hugh Clark, 'Nevados Shicra Shicra and other peaks, Cordillera Huallanca,' in *American Alpine Journal* 18, 168-170, 1972

_____, 'La Cordillera de Huallanca,' *Revista Peruana de Andinismo* 10, 60-63, 1973

Evelio Echevarría, 'Chaupijanca: Perú y su cordillera escondida,' *Pyrenaica* 222, 34-39, 2006

D Giobbi, 'Cordillera Huallanca,' *American Alpine Journal* 16, 426-428, 1969

S Macció, 'Il Margaroli Raju,' in *Rivista Mensile* 93, 9-15, 1974.

G Mainini, 'La spedizione Citta de Maceratta alla Cordillera de Huallanca,' in *Rivista Mensile* 92, 495-499, 1973.

JJ Tomé, *Guía de las Cordilleras Huayhuash y Huallanca.* Madrid: Empograf, 2004.

Maps

Instituto Geográfico Nacional (formerly Instituto Geográfico Militar) of Peru: Carta Nacional (National Chart) 1:100.000, 1974, *hoja* (sheet) 20-j La Unión.

By Sea

Mont-Cervin. Zermatt and the Matterhorn. Drawn by H. Meyer, engraved by Salathé. 1829. Coloured aquatint. 14.5 x 20.8cm. From M. Sauvan. *Le Rhône: description historique et pittoresque de son cours.* Paris 1829. *(Alpine Club Collection HE021P)*

BOB SHEPTON

Greenland and Baffin Island

Big Walls Expedition 2014

Ikerasak's iconic mountain. Left and right ridges of left main face were climbed by the team. *(Bob Shepton)*

It turned out to be a tough expedition, mainly because of the remote and uncompromising nature of the terrain, the weather – the conditions generally, especially in Baffin. It was another Tilman-type expedition of sailing, and climbing from, my Westerly 33ft sloop *Dodo's Delight,* in two distinct phases, joined by a sea passage across Baffin Bay.

Greenland

The crew and climbers, the 'Wild Bunch' from our 2010 expedition, were Nico and Oli Favresse, Sean Villaneuva, and Ben Ditto. They joined the boat in Aasiaat, west Greenland, in early July and we sailed soon afterwards for Uummannaq to the north. We knew some climbing had been done in this area but there seemed to be a lot more to do. We also knew that there was a danger of loose rock and indeed the team rejected possibilities on the first reconnaissance in the fjörd, to the south of the settlement of Iserasak and west of Uummannaq, on those grounds. Instead they established two new routes on the peak overlooking the settlement, on the east and west arêtes of the main face. These were *Married Men's Way* (E3 5c, 5.10, 400m), taking the left ridge, likely to become a classic Alpine style ridge climb. The second was more exacting; *Crocodiles have Teeth* (E5 6a, 5.11b/c, 400m) gave consistently steep climbing, finishing up two pitches of an overhanging crack. Ikcrasak also gave good bouldering, an important training feature for the team between the big face climbs.

Dodo's Delight looking for climbers on Funky Tower. *(Nico Favresse)*

Next was a big wall on the south-east corner of Qaquglugssuit, to the north of Iserasak, and two climbs were made on the buttress on the east side. We named this buttress Goliath – it was big, bold, brazen and blocky. *Standard Deviation* (E4 6a, 5.11) took the left side of it; a black band of rather loose rock soon after the start did concentrate the mind somewhat. Goliath was also defeated by *Slingshot* (E3 5c, 5.10) to the right; both routes are 500m in length. The four climbers descended by walking along the ridge some distance and down to the boat which was anchored rather precariously off the shore, waiting for them.

We next traversed round to the north side of this island to what became known to us as Windy Gulch, with strong and unpredictable katabatic winds which forced us to put a line ashore and a kedge anchor astern, in addition to the usual main anchor. Here we discovered walls with tremendous potential for long, serious, medium grade routes on what appeared to be mainly good rock, but the team did not consider they were quite steep or serious enough. Instead much bouldering was done nearby whilst we waited for the winds to sort themselves out, which they proved reluctant to do. We left in a gale.

Eventually one further route was pioneered in this area, on a wall of Drygalskis Halvo that the team named Funky Tower. It was *No Place for People,* aka *Sunshine and Roses* (E6 6b, 5.12a, 500m). This was sustained, varied, technical, formidable, and with a lot of loose rock reported, especially by our American team member who did not like it at all. There was good bouldering and excellent fishing in the cove to the north-east where the boat was anchored by an abandoned Inuit tent, with suitable abandoned tools and detritus lying around.

The formidable-looking Goliath Buttress. *(Bob Shepton)*

All this time we had been waiting for the ice to clear from the east coast of Baffin. We were receiving ice reports by email from 'my man in Scotland' but they showed the pack ice sticking stubbornly to the Baffin coast in the area round the settlement of Clyde River. Meantime, much bouldering was done at the west bay of Uummannaq where we were now anchored, waiting. We met up with two other boats who called in to this excellent anchorage. They were not climbing, but they did enjoy the musical jam

More arctic bouldering, Baffin Island. *(Nico Favresse)*

sessions provided by the Wild Bunch; the music is such an integral part of their climbing and lifestyle.

At last it looked as if the ice on Baffin was beginning to move. There was a last minute purchase of stores in the 'town' of Uummannaq and we set sail – or rather we motored since there was no wind. We anchored for the night on a hidden bank by a stream outlet near the village of Niaqornat towards the end of this huge peninsula of Nuugssuaq, and set out for Baffin next morning; spontaneity and manoeuvrability are the great advantages of climbing from a boat. We motored at first, then the wind came in and gradually increased. I kept too much sail up that first night but then we settled down to a lively but uneventful three-day passage across to Baffin. Uneventful, that is, except for the last stretch when, seventy miles out from the coast and early on a misty morning, we suddenly came to a huge field of pack ice. Obviously that stubborn shore ice was at last moving out, and fortunately the wind and swell had now broken the pack up sufficiently for us to weave our way through. We made our way into Clyde River to check into Canada, sighting eight polar bears and cubs on the ice floes along the way.

Baffin Island

The next day we were on our way towards Sam Ford Fjörd. The first route in Sam Ford was perhaps more wine induced than wisely planned, after a pleasant evening aboard another boat which had come round to

Above: Oli Favresse leading on *Shepton's Shove*, Walker Citadel. *(Nico Favresse)*
Below: Nico Favresse – 'The cracks just kept on coming. . .' *(Oli Favresse)*

see us. It found the climbers *Up The Creek Without a Paddle* (E5 6a, 5.11+, 500m) – a paddle was lost while landing in the dinghy from the boat. The paddle fortunately reappeared, floating back on the tidal current when the team were three pitches up. After seven pitches on the route, Sean and Ben were surprised to come across bolts and a lot of smart gear; they collected the gear and finished the climb completely free, without using any of it. As it turned out, Mike Libecki had climbed that way in the previous winter or spring; he generously allowed us to keep the gear. Sean and Ben climbed the wall so quickly that they had a 15-hour bivvy under a boulder in a gully, in the mist and rain, while waiting for the boat to come and collect them.

Nico and Oli, meantime, had attempted the south-east pillar of the Walker Citadel but were defeated by the bad weather that had set in. Another attempt was also aborted but finally a third attempt, in fine sunshine over two days, with a snow shower in between, gave the first ascent of this arête in a 24-hour push: *Shepton's Shove* (E6 6b, 5.12a, 1000m). I did get

Anyone for BASE jumping? View from the top of the Turret.
(*Oli Favresse*)

into trouble for not telling them that the forecast had indicated some precipitation; I hadn't really taken note of it very seriously as it was clear and sunny. And if I had, why spoil morale, knowing that they had aborted twice already? Meantime, Sean and Ben had made the first free ascent of SuperUnknown Tower, by *Imaginary Line* (E3 5c, 5.10+, 1000m), abseiling back down the sheer wall of the original aid route and using some of the bolts left from 20 years before.

Nico and Oli added another quality route, where 'the cracks kept on coming'. It was the first route on the east face of the Turret, *Life on the Kedge* (E6 6b, sustained in the 5.11/5.12 range, 900m). Picking them up next day from the dinghy in gusts of 30 knots of wind was a bit too 'exciting'. Sean and Ben were not so lucky with their route; after nine pitches up a dihedral on the east side of Big Cross Wall and an involuntary peel by Sean, they decided the rock really was too loose and came back down. They had then to wait for two days as wind and waves were just too strong and vicious to let us pick them up. Fortunately the team had a tent and food at the bottom of the wall.

We took the boat round to Gibbs Fjörd. This is another remote land of stupendous rock sculptures with clear, undisturbed evidence of how the glaciers have receded over the years. Initially, the rock here also looked rather loose. We had made an inspection of the Ship's Prow and the west face of Scott Island, but the logistics of landing climbers on the sheer walls and, even more important, picking them up again afterwards if the weather worsened made us cautious. So we went further into Gibbs Fjörd, where another quality first ascent was climbed here by Nico and Sean, on a north face arête: *Walking The Plank* (E4 6a, 5.11+, 900m, on excellent rock). Again 'the cracks kept coming', though some sections were also covered in snow.

Getting dark now, but no let up at night: *Walking The Plank*. *(Nico Favresse)*

Whilst Nico and Sean were climbing this route, Ben and Oli walked up the hill above the boat's anchorage, thinking they didn't really need to take the rifle. At the top they admired the view, and had just started down when a polar bear suddenly appeared from behind a boulder '15 metres away'. They froze, but fortunately it was the polar bear that turned and ran away; they returned to the boat suitably chastened.

A big-wall style climb with portaledges had been staked out in Sam Ford Fjörd but the weather never co-operated. It is perhaps important to point out that all the new routes done by this team in Sam Ford Fjörd and Gibbs Fjörd (as well as in the Uummannaq region) were climbed on sight and completely free, in an area where nearly all previous climbs had been done with aid. To be fair this was partly because the previous climbs were usually done earlier in the year, going in by skidoo over the ice. But that did mean that all the big wall climbs on this trip were completed by long, Alpine style pushes and completely free, which is rather harder and more stressful than conventional big-wall tactics.

There was again good bouldering at the anchorages in the inlet by Walker Citadel (Sam Ford Fjörd) and at Refuge Harbour (Gibbs Fjörd), as we waited for the weather. We ran out of fresh water on the return sea passage but there was an iceberg nearby with bits broken off in the water which we could hook on board, so we were saved. On the final rock-strewn approach to Sisimiut we encountered 40-44 knot winds; a fitting finale to a tough expedition.

Sean *Walking The Plank. (Nico Favresse)*

Acknowledgements

We are very grateful to the Gino Watkins Memorial Fund for their generous support of this expedition.

Summary of Climbs

Where given, co-ordinates are taken from the sea opposite the routes.

Uummannaq Area: Ikerasak Peak

Married Men's Way (E3 5c, 5.10, 400m). Takes the left ridge of this peak. FA: Oli Favresse, Ben Ditto 13 July 2014.
Crocodiles Have Teeth (E5 6a, 5.11b/c, 400m). The right hand edge of the

Fantastic rock sculpture, Sam Ford Fjörd, Baffin Island. *(Oli Favresse)*

main face, moving right at the top to finish by an overhanging crack. FA: Nico Favresse, Sean Villaneuva 13 July 2014.

Qaqugdlugssuit: Goliath Butress (70°41'N 51°13'W)
Standard Deviation (E4 6a, 5.11, 500m). Follows lines on left of this buttress, some loose rock especially in the basalt band. FA: Nico Favresse, Ben Ditto 17 July 2014.
Slingshot (E3 5c, 5.10, 500m). Follows lines on right side of the buttress. FA: Oli Favresse, Sean Villaneuva 17 July 2014

Drygalskis Halvo: Funky Tower (70°35'N 51°16'W)
No Place For People, a.k.a. *Sunshine and Roses* (E6 6b, 5.12a, 500m). A steep, varied, technical line towards the left side of this face. Reports of much loose rock, especially on the sloping terrace leading to the summit ridge. FA: Sean Villaneuva, Ben Ditto 24 July 2014.

Baffin Island: east coast

Sam Ford Fjörd: Lurking Tower (Mike Libecki's name) 70°35'N 71°17'W)
Up The Creek Without a Paddle (E5 6a, 5.11+, 500m). Starts up the dihedral on the right and follows crack lines, turning a roof, to the top. Libecki's aid route was followed after 7 pitches but without using any of the aid. FFA: Sean Villaneuva, Ben Ditto over 12 hours on 15-16 August 2014

Super Unknown Tower
Imaginary Line (E3 5c, 5.10+, 1000m). Takes the obvious red groove and crack leading almost to the top on the right of the Tower. The hardest pitches were after the groove at the top, especially as it was wet and snowy.

This was the first free ascent of the SuperUnknown. A rappel to remember straight down the original sheer aid route completed the night. FA: Sean Villaneuva, Ben Ditto 21-22 August 2014

Walker Citadel: South-east Pillar (Drunken Pillar) (70° 50'N 71° 43'W)
Shepton's Shove (E6 6b, 5.12a, 1000m). The obvious arête leading to the top of the pillar. The hardest pitches were at the top. FA: Nico Favresse, Oli Favresse 23-24 August 2014

The Turret
Life on The Kedge (E6 6b, 5.12, 900m). The first route on the east face of the Turret: a quality climb. Takes the buttress just right of the chimney crack that splits the Turret from top to bottom, and follows the obvious, clean cut crack on the left hand side. 'The cracks just kept on coming'. Sustained pitches in 5.11/5.12 range. FA: Nico Favresse, Oli Favresse 28-29 August 2014

Gibbs Fjörd: Plank Wall (70° 50'N 71° 43'W)
Walking the Plank (E4 6a, 5.11+, 900m). Keeps to the steep arête. Another quality climb, on excellent rock but north facing, with little sun. Sections of the climbing were covered in snow. FA: Nico Favresse, Sean Villaneuva 4-5 September 2014

Notes: All the climbs both at Uummannaq and Baffin were done on sight and free without the use of aid; there was no use of pitons or bolts.

A curious place to play your music. *(Oli Favresse)*

CARADOG JONES

The Last Leviathan

'Ere comes the boat, only 'alf afloat. No, it's not the 'Last Boat to Cairo', but it's the last we'll see of *Pelagic Australis* for 10 days after being dropped off at the snout of the Nordenskjöld glacier. *(Richard Spillett)*

'It's unclimbed,' Tim Carr told me. 'Criquet said so himself.' I could hardly believe my ears. It was 2007 and Tim had just revealed that Nordenskjöld Peak, at 2355m the second-highest peak in South Georgia sitting slap bang in the middle of the island, had yet to receive its first ascent. 'I've been keeping that under my belt, in case I had the chance, like, but I'll be off soon. If anyone deserves to know, you do.'

Tim and Pauline Carr were shortly to leave South Georgia, one of the few couples ever to have lived there for a long period of time. This jewel of information was his generous parting gift. It had long been assumed that

125

Trying to scout a way through the icefall for the sledges. *(Crag Jones)*

the scientist and explorer Christian de Marliave – known as 'Criquet' – had made the first and only ascent in 1988. Christian's bold and determined solo effort had seen him get high on the mountain but not, it now turned out, to the summit. The cat was out of the bag and into my pocket – for the time being at least.

I made an attempt with Skip Novak and Julian Freeman-Attwood in November 2009, after which certain elements of the opposition grew suspicious of my eccentric interest. Stephen Venables had recently been spotted stalking its approaches making sinister comments along the lines that all was fair in love and war. Make no mistake, that charming exterior conceals a predatory competitor. Why should he be scrapping around for leftovers if one of the great beasts remained available?

So I returned to South Georgia in November 2011 for my ninth visit, counting various work and play trips over the years. It is a place I have come to know well. The island, whilst amazingly beautiful, is also prone to ferocious weather. The inspiration offered by the former has therefore to be tempered with consideration for the latter.

I first worked there in 1990 as the sole civilian living with the military garrison. My role was to re-establish civilian management of shipping and fisheries. I have returned many times for research and management work but also increasingly on private mountaineering expeditions, often in the company of the American Skip Novak on his specialist Antarctic sailing vessels *Pelagic* and *Pelagic Australis*. We were again transported and supported by the *Pelagic* team, now also comprising Miles and Laura West as captain and first mate with Dave Roberts as second mate.

My teammate for this venture was Richard Spillett, an old climbing friend whose calm exterior masks a determined and adventurous soul. While I masquerade as a househusband, Richard's daytime job is as a derivatives trader turned risk manager in a sort of poacher turned gamekeeper role. As usual with Richard, I fully expected to improve my education on the finer points of capitalism while he would undoubtedly benefit from broadsides of my unreconstructed Marxism. It was the sort of well-balanced team that might never leave the tent.

'All those thieving so-and-sos should be shot.'

'You were happy to accept the credit when the going was good. It's the juice that oils the wheels of industry. '

Ten minutes of this and I'm howling at the moon while Richard is laughing his socks off. Yet as unlikely as it seems, the more of this cussedness the better when it comes to climbing mountains, especially in South Georgia. Madness also helps.

We joined *Pelagic Australis* in Stanley in the Falkland Islands for the 800-mile journey east – four days downwind but a few more on our return. The plan was to drop us at the head of Cumberland Bay East, where the glacier reaches the sea. It would take us about three days to ski with sledges to the foot of the mountain before we started the technical climbing proper.

Wind and weather looked good for a quick departure from the Falklands so there was little time to catch up with old friends. We were so busy making sure we had everything: checking gear, buying food and stowing everything aboard. We cast off on the evening of 13 November.

The rest of the crew were the Stephen brothers, Jim and Bob, from Chicago, Julian Fox from London and Marcelo Telles from Bahia, Brazil, a ship's pilot who was looking forward to his first sight of snow. Jim and Bob ran a family business, the Weber Grill

A snow petrel comes to nibble at my skis. *(Crag Jones)*

Co, suppliers of fancy cooking platforms to the barbecue world. They have a passion for form and function, being to a seared steak what Steve Jobs was to the computer. Even so, they couldn't spot a British wind-up. Back on the Falklands we had Bob and Jim on the run from 'dangerous' feral sheep.

'ALWAYS maintain eye contact, it's essential.'

'You sure about that?'

Richard Spillett, intractable economist.
(Crag Jones)

Crag Jones, the mad polemicist.
(Richard Spillett)

'Believe me, I'm an expert – don't EVER let them get the upper hand, psychologically speaking, so to speak.'

'Christ, it's bad enough with all these landmines. Skip never said anything about this.'

We had steady sailing in calm conditions, by Southern Ocean standards, with winds no more than 35 knots. On the afternoon of 16 November we passed the magnificent Shag Rocks towering out of a misty sea. In the past we have sailed between them but not this time. I remembered battling past on a dark and stormy night going in the opposite direction, back to Stanley as the sole 'escort' on a Russian long-liner, the *Maksheevo*. We had arrested the crew for poaching. The patrol ship followed behind but I was not the most welcome of passengers. Fortunately their sense of fate preserved me; the filleting knife under my pillow proved an unnecessary precaution.

After four days we closed on South Georgia, expecting to reach Bird Sound by mid-morning. The weather was forecast to hold fair up to the moment we planned to be dropped off. Then it would turn foul for three days. It seemed best though to get ashore at the earliest opportunity. It is fatal to cling to the comfort of the boat. As evening closed in, a bitter wind swept off the Nordenskjöld glacier. Miles calmly nosed the boat through icebergs to the head of Cumberland Bay East to give Dave as short a run as possible to get us ashore in the dinghy. He looked askance at all our kit.

'Don't worry, Dave,' I told him. 'We'll thin it out tomorrow and stash the barrels behind the beach.'

'We're sick of packing,' Richard said. 'We can't be arsed to do it tonight.'

The vast majority of yachtsmen and women have a primal aversion to being parted from their boats. They looked pityingly at us as we voluntarily forsook *Pelagic*'s warm delights for a grim and barren shore. We bid everyone a wistful farewell.

'See you in ten days,' Miles said. 'We'll have two more for leeway if the sea is too rough for a pick-up then or the ice blows in.'

Boot Camp. *(Richard Spillett)*

Then we staggered across the boulder beach avoiding grumbling seals and irritated penguins towards a rock bluff that offered shelter in its lee behind a ten-foot whale vertebrae. (Smaller ones made nice stools.) As it grew dark Richard wrestled the tent into shape while I ferried loads up from the landing spot. Time is tight on a one-month charter. Unless you have the boat on continuous standby, the only option is to go heavy and keep moving up in bad weather with enough kit, food and fuel to sit out any bad periods. Hopefully we would be in a position to take immediate advantage of any good days without becoming extended.

Two years before, we skied from the beach but now there was much less snow. The first day was spent thinning loads to two heavy packs apiece. These we ferried up on to the glacier where we could start using sledges, though not the skis which had to be added to the loads. Next day we started our approach. The icefall was almost 'dry' this year, hard ice with all crevasses visible and open. It meant very torturous and slow progress navigating the sledges through this labyrinth.

The glacier itself appeared to breaking down with large new depressions and major inward collapse, giving us a surreal passage. One cannot but help draw parallels with the decimation of the whale stocks in the last century. It is the next stage of change wrought by man, this time on the physical fabric of our surroundings. As the glaciers spew their entrails, we are witnessing the murder of the last leviathans. Places I carried loads to over a week, ten years ago, can now be sailed to in open water. No one will ever see again the fabled filling and flushing of the huge and mysterious

Richard Spillett finishes the hard pull to the top of the icefield to gain the upper glacier. *(Crag Jones)*

Lake Gulbransen. The Neumayer glacier has receded four kilometres in the last ten years.

We crested the icefall and found the first skiable ribbon of snow, a 'yellow brick road' heading gently downwards into another broad collapsing basin about half a mile across. Richard had not used mountaineering skis for a while and complained they were turning outwards. 'Keep your knees together and think of England,' I told him. My flippancy was short-lived. I soon discovered the heel of my expensive Italian boots had come unstuck and was flapping uselessly.

This could scupper the entire expedition and my brain started racing. There was Skip's pair under the forward bunk on the boat and the crew had been invited on board a cruise ship the day before. A skinful of booze meant it likely they had not yet left Cumberland Bay. A frantic call on our satellite phone confirmed this scenario. The boots were on their way. Dave Roberts on *Pelagic Australis* was not the sort of man to be deterred by crashing surf laden with ice blocks. He was up to his neck in freezing seawater but got the boots ashore.

Back down I went, through the belly of the beast. I took a more circuitous route, avoiding soft snow and bridged crevasses. Everything went smoothly and I was at the beach by midday, marvelling at Skip's multicoloured footwear. These would give me sex appeal. After a quick refuel on some stashed chocolate I set off back uphill, racing to beat advancing fog to the lip of the glacier. In the end I had to stop to deal with the inevitable blisters but took solace at the sheer beauty of these boots. One has to suffer for art, especially someone else's.

Next day we made an early start pulling sledges in crampons and found a way through a lateral moraine leading to the toe of the ridge extending northwards from Sheridan Peak. This gave a steep climb just on the limit of what is possible with skins and we were soon over the lip and on to the third section of the Nordenskjöld, a broad snow-covered valley leading up alongside the western slopes of Sheridan Peak.

Roped up again, we marvelled at how skis and sledges crossed crevasse after crevasse without any breaking through, even in hot soft conditions. I knew from previous experience that terrain like this would be murderous if we were on foot. By early afternoon we were near our high camp from two years previously. This time we camped out on the glacier flat away from the avalanche danger and snow dumps that had done for us on that occasion.

I was determined to establish an advanced camp at the foot of the technical climbing rather than begin our climb from here. Next morning we loaded our rucksacks and climbed the long steep snowfield to the upper stage of the Nordenskjöld glacier. It took two carries to get the gear up. Returning to dump the second load was a test of Richard's GPS skills but he navigated perfectly in a whiteout. All that practise on Clapham Common with his daughter Lottie was paying off. It was only a few kilometres further to the site of our final camp and I wanted to press on. Richard was having none of it. We were soaked and tired and in the whiteout we might site the final camp in a poor spot and have to move it again. We were soon ensconced in our sleeping bags, making dinner.

Next morning we set a location on the GPS so we could navigate in the continuing whiteout. Occasional breaks in the cloud allowed me to remember the lay of the land. As we pulled onto the final flat, a brief clearing gave us our bearings and we chose a good spot to camp, anchoring the tent with guy-lines attached to sections of buried engine hose. The following day was my birthday and we stayed in bed. My daughter Laura had packed me a special candle, which we ceremoniously placed in a mini Christmas pudding. Having triangulated various weather forecasts, we decided tomorrow was the day. Timings had worked out well for once.

We rose at 2am on 26 November, finally getting away at around 4am after the ritual faffing. The right-hand side of the north face is threatened by seracs but by skirting the rocks on the left we avoided them. There was much less snow and ice cover than on our previous attempt but the line was still there. A convenient spindrift avalanche cone bridged the bergschrund and we were soon on the face, moving together up and right, aiming for the foot of a steep gully that broke through the rocks.

After 150m the growing void became uncomfortable. On this kind of

terrain, a mixture of rotten ice and powdery snow, it's essential to have a clear instinct for every crumbling step. You also have to trust each other and concentrate on not making a single error. To move fast you cannot afford the luxury of belaying and climbing in stages. The rope is only out to be deployed quickly when needed. As I reached the start of the gully I placed our first ice screw but we kept moving together, only stopping when all the ice screws had been used up and swapping them back to the leader. Emerging from the gully it was a relief to find the ice was slightly softer than on our previous attempt.

That had been a harrowing night, descending hard ice under spindrift avalanches. Now we made quick progress and by 8am we were where we'd been at 5pm first time around. We crossed rubble chutes and broken terrain and finally reached the crest of the east ridge. The rock is hilariously rotten. In high winds chunks are simply blown off. All those years Richard and I spent climbing on Devon's shale were paying dividends. After Tintagel, this tottering heap of Weetabix wasn't so frightening.

The boiling cloud-broth thickened. Soon all I could see was a thin shard of dark shale soaring skyward. Eventually even this ran out leaving us with white on white. The angle was not extreme but the north side fell

Our top camp, at last. *(Richard Spillett)*

away very steeply. I crawled forward on my belly in the strong wind and poked my head over the south side – another impressive drop. The ice was glassy along the crest but a ribbon of wind-blown snow was glued to it like a rooster comb.

If I chose my spot carefully and drove down hard enough I could get the shaft of my left axe in to the hilt. Meanwhile I could use the pick of my right axe in the hard ice and make progress like some sort of demented crab. We shortened the rope and kept at least one ice screw between us. When the wind dropped we could stand up and balance along our precarious banister rail.

Every now and then the snow comb would develop into a proper cornice. I was also haunted by the thought that progress was only possible if the winds remained low. Richard was becoming increasingly demented as downward pointing ribs of snow kept snagging slack rope. Each time this happened, he had to make a horrible descent off the banister onto the hard ice in order to free the rope. I looked on in bemused horror.

After a while we reached a more level section where we could walk. The mist cleared briefly and revealed bulbous overhanging ice pillars disappearing into the southern depths in a grotesque fantasy. If Gaudi designed mountains, this would be one of his. Then things got steeper again. We surmised we were on top of 'the knob' – a distinctive lump visible from afar high on the summit ridge. Creeping over the top, we climbed down a steep pitch of pure crystal to reach a saddle beyond.

It was the sort of place where you make the final commitment to go for the top. We felt like we were space-walking now, out on a limb. Visibility got worse but we knew we must be getting close and prayed there would not be a horrible obstacle at the last. Richard's bank of instrumentation – altimeters and GPS – was registering summit proximity. What appeared to be a long 'S' in the ridge seemed significant but the mist was playing tricks and we passed it quickly.

Gradually, the angle eased. After 1200m of height gain and almost double that in actual climbing, what looked like a typical South Georgia summit

Surreal progress on the very crest – except you can't see it. *(Richard Spillett)*
Below: Tippety-top, summit joy for Richard Spillett. *(Crag Jones)*

took shape: a flat platform crested by a three-metre rounded bollard with a slightly higher whaleback a little to the right. All was plastered in hoar frost. Everything fell away in all directions. It was high noon. I waited and peered through breaks in the broth to make sure there was nothing higher nearby. It was the top. We logged the point on Richard's GPS.

The same thing was on both our minds: 'Right, we're halfway there. Let's get our arses off of here in one piece.' We stepped down on to the platform and called the research station at King Edward Point on our VHF radio. We had hoped they might have seen us on the summit. We offered to do a highland jig. They suggested setting fire to some bushes. We turned tail for the long haul home.

The steep sections on the upper icy ridge were demanding. Crampons balled up even with a little snow, then skidded on the polished ice. I had to keep going fast enough along the snowy banister to stop the rope tangling but not so fast as to pull Richard off. I felt the toes of one foot waving in space long enough not to step down further. I had almost gone over the lip of a huge void plunging into the great unknown of the south-east face. When the shale crest appeared below out of the blank white we felt relief at just seeing something.

The clag ended at the same altitude we'd entered it, on the shoulder. This allowed us to pick the right line back across the middle of the face. I carried on first to find the route and set up any belays. Richard had the unenviable task of coming second. No comfort of a rope from above for him. A 150m diagonal descent across the ice led to rocks. I started traversing back and forth, failing to find the upper entry to the gully. Too far west and we'd be under the seracs. Too far east and we'd end up on collapsing rock with no safe place to secure the rope. Worse still, I could not find any good ice to place an ice screw to protect Richard as he descended.

Finally I made a decision, committing to what I thought might be the right place. I crossed a thin scab of ice lying on a blank slab. In the mush on the other side I dug down a metre until I hit hard ice, drilled in a good ice screw and set off down the steep gully with Richard following. I doubled up two poor ice screws at the bottom exit and traversed left onto a rotten rock pillar. All snow and ice was now just about useless for belays but I finally constructed a reliable piton belay after some desperate hammering. Richard hove into view in the last of the light.

We fished out our headtorches and I re-racked the gear and resumed our descent. The last 200m felt steep and unreliable, that infuriating consistency that was too soft for ice screws but too hard for the shafts of our axes. Digging down to the depths of my armpits, I found revealed a morass of soft crystals, like demerara. We were so tired but had to find reliable belays or something terrible could go wrong. From the depths of my memory a solution wafted towards the surface.

Perhaps if I buried my axes deep enough in a 'T' shape, the horizontal bar of the T would brace the vertical leg to make a strong and secure anchor, even in this shit. I dug like hell and eventually my axes were lashed into a T and sunk in the hole. We could hang a bloody herd of elephants off this set up.

'OK, Richard. You can fall as far as you like!' He joined me at my proud belay. 'Look at this, man. You can breathe easy now.' We carried on down, pitch after pitch, diagonally to our right, searching for the one point we could cross the bergschrund that would not involve an overhanging abseil. Finally I spotted it and gently eased across the spindrift cone without it collapsing.

Almost drunk with fatigue, I staggered down the last of the slope in the halo of my headtorch to join Richard on the flat glacier. I wanted to sink to my knees and kiss the beautiful horizontal. Aided by Richard's GPS, we finally found camp and collapsed into the tent at 2am. As we drifted into oblivion yesterday's alarm went off. We laughed wearily. This had definitely been a 24-hour round-trip. Then we slept.

Summary
An account of the first ascent of Nordenskjöld Peak (2355m) in the Allardyce Range of South Georgia. Approaching from Cumberland Bay East, Caradog (Crag) Jones and Richard Spillett were on the mountain on 26-27 November 2014.

Acknowledgements
With special thanks to DMM International, High Latitudes for our satellite phone, Terra Nova for a bombproof tent and solargadgetstore.co.uk for their Power Monkey Extreme solar charger, Ieuenctid Cambria Youth for spot trackers and blogging services and *Pelagic Australis*, the boat guaranteed to reach places other boats cannot reach.

BJØRN RIIS-JOHANNESSEN

The Shackleton Traverse

King Haakon Bay with Murray Icefield and the Shackleton Gap at the end of the Bay. *(All photos: Bjørn Riis-Johannessen)*

On 10 May 1916, nearly one hundred years ago, Ernest Shackleton and five of his crew arrived at King Haakon Bay on the south coast of South Georgia. They had sailed 700 stormy nautical miles from Elephant Island across the Scotia Sea, in the 22ft *James Caird*, to get help. There were 22 crew remaining at Elephant Island, following the wreck of the *Endurance* in the ice of the Weddell Sea six months earlier.

After a few days of rest, Shackleton and two of his men set off across the island to reach Husvik whaling station and rescue. The trip across South Georgia, from King Haakon Bay to Stromness (where they ended up, rather than Husvik) is now known as the Shackleton Traverse and is recognised as one of many epic Antarctic journeys. In October 2014 a team of three Alpine Club and two Swiss Alpine Club members (including the author, who is both), set out on this traverse under the leadership of Phil Wickens. It did not take long for our admiration of Shackleton's achievement to reach new heights.

Even today, getting to South Georgia is not simple. There is no airport or regular connection by ship. A number of expedition cruise ships visit the island during summer, but they do not take passengers who wish to remain on the island for any length of time. If you are the member of one of a handful of expeditions that go to South Georgia every year, you are generally left with a sailing trip from the Falkland Islands as the only alternative.

And then it is not just a question of chartering a yacht and setting off. Permission to land must be applied for, backed by a detailed plan laying out expedition objectives, members' experience and – last but not least – a plan for emergencies, such as escape routes, in case the traverse has to be aborted.

For our team, the traverse was to be made on skis, and relatively late in the season. We decided not to follow slavishly in Shackleton's footsteps, and for parts of the traverse a higher route was picked, hoping for a better chance of good snow. In his traverse, Shackleton had to turn back at several attempts to cross mountain ranges. Not being purists, we saw no need to repeat these attempts, and some of his descents were unsuitable for sledges so we skipped those, too.

The team (less photographer), from the left: Benoit Duplay, Phil Wickens, Sylwia Duda, Dan Harwood.

With all preparations well in place, including a generous supply of sea sickness pills, we put to sea at Port Stanley, on the *Icebird*. *Icebird* is a 10 berth, 61ft expedition yacht, specially equipped for high latitude operation. The sea crossing typically takes 5-6 days and there are good chances of an exciting trip. Skipper Cath Hew, a pleasant and blunt-speaking Australian and veteran Antarctic sailor, assured us that conditions were mild. 'Mild' conditions means 30 knots of wind and 4-5m waves. Not so mild for most land lubbers, but good for losing a couple of pounds.

After some five days in the open sea, we noticed signs of approaching land. Shallower water makes for sharper waves, and coastal sea birds started to appear. Soon we had the entry to King Haakon Bay ahead, as it must have appeared to Shackleton and his men almost 100 years ago. On their first attempt to land, they were blown off in a gale, but managed eventually to enter the bay where they landed at Cave Cove. We sailed on, into the eastern end of the bay to anchor in lee of the Vincent Islands, with the first leg of the traverse in view: the Murray Snowfield with the Shackleton Gap.

Following a day of rest and generous protein intake in the form of barbequed Argentine beef, we ferried all the equipment onto the beach, carried the gear a couple of kilometres up to the glacier, and set off. We were

The three-day storm finally over and time to dig out the tents.

equipped for 10 days: four days planned for the traverse, two to three days for some extra-curricular ski touring on the way, plus a bit of reserve. The load amounted to about 30kg per person, split roughly 50/50 between rucksacks and haul loads. The route included both traverses and long descents so we were using 'dry bags' for hauling, rather than pulks or sledges. On a traverse the dry bags just slide downhill below you and are far easier to handle than a pulk.

Day two started with reasonable weather, but before long we were in a complete whiteout. The South Georgia map is 1:200,000 scale so there isn't an overabundance of details. Combined with Google Earth satellite images, where you can take GPS waypoints from the online images, we were able to establish a pretty good route before we left. The imagery dates may not be very current, but they show important key features, such as heavily crevassed areas one may want to navigate around.

Progress in a total whiteout tends to resemble a drunkard's walk, and we used the 'right' – 'left' calls from down the line to navigate; Shackleton and his team were in similar conditions and used the same method but with a 'port' and 'starboard' touch. Our modern team had the added advantage of the occasional GPS check and we succeeded in a bull's-eye hit on the planned location for camp 2, on a small pass below the Trident.

Day three started with a brief view of the surroundings, but conditions again went from bad to pretty awful. We were now heading for the highest point on the route, the Zig-Zag pass, at about 1100m. The terrain was fairly easy but conditions continued to worsen, with increasing wind and a bit of freezing fog thrown in for good measure. We were clearly experiencing 'weather; highly variable and harsh' as it says in the description of the island's climate. With goggles iced up, and even worse visibility without them, we proceeded with caution along the ridge of a monstrous wind scoop just below the pass. It must have been close to 100m across and just as deep, with almost vertical walls. A pretty scary sight it was, at least what we could see. Conditions were distinctly unfavourable, but after a quick review of the options we decided to carry on over the pass and hope for better conditions on the other side.

Safely through the Zig-Zag pass, we descended on to the Kohl-Larsen Plateau where we pitched our third camp. With the tents anchored in all 24 points, snow valances well covered and substantial lee walls in place, we crawled into our sleeping bags, hoping the worst had passed.

That was definitely not to be the case. A couple of hours later we woke to wind gusting at 100 knots. Getting slightly worried as this carried on through the night, we had bivvy bags at the ready in case something should rip. The tents, all Helsport Fjellheimen X-Trem, stood up to the beating and made it through the night without problem.

Day four. The wind dropped, but was still blowing at a steady 50 knots and now with a heavy snowfall, so any departure was completely out of the question. The wind was no longer the main worry as far as the tents were concerned but we had to keep digging to prevent them from getting buried and collapsing under the weight of the snow.

Day five. Slight improvement, but still blowing at 40-50 knots. Dig – eat – dig – sleep – dig – read – dig, dig, dig; and so it went on.

Day six. Still no significant improvement. Getting bored. iPhone and Kindle batteries starting to run out.

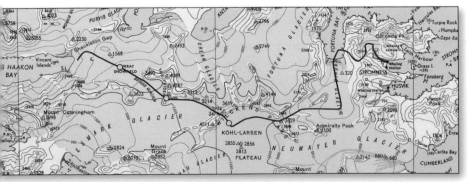

The route: King Haakon Bay to Stromness.
(South Georgia (1958) published by the Directorate of Ordnance Surveys)

Approaching the window leading onto the König Glacier.

Day seven. Completely still. Clouds drifted away and a spectacular view appeared as we dug ourselves out of the tents. High up on the Kohl-Larsen Plateau, we were surrounded by the Wilkens Peaks to the north and start of the Allardyce Range in the south. For the first time we could actually see where we wanted to go – to a small window at the east end of the Wilkens Peaks that we would hopefully get through, then down on to the König Glacier and on to Fortuna Bay. And what a day it was: sun, no wind and great snow. We made it through the window and a 15m scramble put us down on the glacier where we enjoyed a 10km descent that dropped us 900m down to Fortuna Bay.

King penguins in Fortuna Bay.

Reunited with the *Icebird*, we spent the night onboard the boat. After a day hauling our equipment back across the 4km long König Glacier end moraine, we set off on the last leg of the traverse: Fortuna Bay to Stromness Harbour. Not a lot of snow there, but no need for over-

Descending the König Glacier to Fortuna Bay.

night equipment, so the crossing was made as a pleasant day of spring skiing over the Stromness-Fortuna pass and down the Shackleton Valley.

Looking down on Stromness from the pass, it is difficult to imagine how Shackleton and his men must have felt at that point. They sailed out of Grytviken on the *Endurance* on 5 December 1914. During the subsequent 18 months, the *Endurance* eventually sank after being stuck in the ice and suffering a slow death by crushing. After abandoning the ship, the crew spent six months on the ice with the ship's three lifeboats, drifting northwards. They eventually made it across open water to Elephant Island and from there Shackleton and five of his crew set off in the largest of the lifeboats, the *James Caird*, to sail the 700 nautical miles to South Georgia. On arrival, three of them legged it across the island in 36 hours, to reach Stromness on 20 May, 1916.

Shackleton's possibly apocryphal advertisement for crew on that expedition read:

Men Wanted for Hazardous Journey
Small wages, bitter cold, long months of complete darkness, constant danger, safe return doubtful. Honour and recognition in case of success.
– Ernest Shackleton

The advert, real or fabricated, was correct in its description, and yet the whole *Endurance* crew made it home – one of the really big achievements in Antarctic history.

Above: the Shackleton Valley with Stromness harbour in the background.
Below: *Icebird* in St Andrew's Bay, home to some 750,000 king penguins.

A typical yacht-based expedition to South Georgia lasts four to five weeks. Having completed the traverse, we still had a week or so to travel the coast and experience this amazing place. Not without reason, Tim and Pauline Carr named it an 'Antarctic Oasis' in their splendid book about the five years they spent at the island, based in their 100-year-old, 28ft cutter *Curlew*.

Following a couple of day ski tours and visits to some of the spectacular wildlife sites, such as St Andrews Bay with its half-a-million-plus king penguins, the last item on the agenda was to experience some of the historical sites from the whaling days. Most of the sites are closed for access due to asbestos danger and buildings falling down, but Grytviken has been restored, with access and an excellent museum and souvenir shop, open during the southern summer months.

Shackleton is buried at the Grytviken cemetery, and it is customary to drink a toast in honour of 'The Boss' when you visit the grave. He died in 1922 at South Georgia, and considering the life he had led, his heart failure seems insufficiently dramatic.

After a few days of good weather and with the storms a distant memory, we set off for a last anchorage at Rosita Bay before the return crossing. Great plans for a farewell party were quickly squashed when all hell broke loose again, as South Georgia had not yet finished with us. Wind of 70-80 knots – that's well into Beaufort force 12, hurricane – blew us off the anchorage and out of the bay three times before we gave up, put out to sea and headed back to the Falklands to a late celebratory pint in the Globe, the battle hardened watering hole in Port Stanley harbour.

Summary

A team of five (Phil Wickens, Bjørn Riis-Johannessen, Dan Harwood, Sylwia Duda, Benoit Duplay) repeated the Shackleton Traverse on South Georgia, from King Haakon Bay to Stromness, on 11 to 19 October 2014. While this might be a bit longer than the 36 hours of the first team's crossing, we did have the added burden of Kindles to carry, and needed the poor weather days in which to use them. The expedition, from Stanley to Stanley, ran from 5-31 October 2014.

Antarctic storm.

Alps

The Matterhorn from the Italian side of the Theodule Pass. Probably John Antony Cramer (1793-1848). Date unknown. Pen and ink wash. 27 x 23cm. Catalogued as by James D. Forbes, but noted on the verso as 'Dessiné par le Revd. Antoine Cramer, chef d'un des collèges d'Oxford': the author of this attribution and of the geological notes on the recto and verso is unknown.
(Alpine Club Collection HE085P)

SIMON RICHARDSON

The Lonely Pillar

The East Face of Mont Greuvetta from Pointe 2810m, Mont Vert de Gruevetta.
(Tom Prentice)

Few climbers seem to have heard of Mont Greuvetta. At first this seems rather surprising, as at 3684m it is a significant peak in the Mont Blanc Range, but there again it's a retiring mountain: the summit is difficult to see from the valley and is only really visible from the alpine pastures high above Val Ferret. Or perhaps it is so little known because nobody can figure out exactly how to spell its name? Gruetta, Greuvetta, Greuvettaz are all used in various publications with the latter being the latest 'official' spelling. I prefer 'Greuvetta', as the peak is named in Gino Buscaini's Vallot guidebook to the Grandes Jorasses area of the Mont Blanc range. I have a bookcase full of guidebooks, but this carefully written and beautifully illustrated labour of love is one of my favourites. It was an expensive purchase for an impecunious student back in 1982, but it has inspired many adventures over the years and still fuels new dreams.

When I first opened the hard green cover all those years ago I was immediately struck by a beautiful pen and ink drawing of the east face of Mont Greuvetta. It was steep, remote and little frequented, and I was intrigued. A couple of years later I met the celebrated French climber André Contamine in Chamonix, and soon I was quizzing him about the Greuvetta. I think he was rather surprised that a young British climber was so curious about such a remote corner of the Mont Blanc range, so he took me into the hallowed grounds of ENSA, and in their impressive library we found an article in an Italian magazine detailing recent activity on Greuvetta's east face. One of these routes, *Il Pilastro del Sorriso* (TD+) by the great Italian climber Ugo Manera in 1982, caught my eye and I resolved to attempt it at the next opportunity.

Numerous obligatory Alpine classics and trips to the greater ranges intervened, but eventually ten years later, in July 1994, Chris Cartwright and I headed up to the Comino Hut to attempt the route. This small bivouac was built in 1981 in memory of Gianni Comino who formed a productive

partnership with the legendary Giancarlo Grassi in the late 1970s. They climbed a series of groundbreaking ice routes including *The Hypercouloir* on the south side of the Grandes Jorasses, but unfortunately Gianni was killed whilst attempting a direct route through the seracs to the right of The Pear on the Brenva Face. The hut has considerably eased access to the Greuvetta Glacier that previously was one of the most difficult to reach places in the range. Before the new hut path from the Triolet moraines, climbers accessed the hanging valley below the glacier by following a steep stream-bed, and battling up large rock steps covered in vegetation. The hut is delightfully situated overlooking Val Ferret, but it is a long way from the chaotic Greuvetta glacier that guards access to the east face.

Chris Cartwright, first free ascent of *Pilastro del Sorriso* (TD+), East Face of Mont Greuvetta, July 1994. *(Simon Richardson)*

After a reconnaissance the day before, Chris and I carefully picked our way through a succession of moraines and negotiated the steep and crevassed glacier to gain the foot of the route at daybreak. Fortunately, heavy snowfall the previous spring rendered the crevasses passable,

Simon Richardson, first ascent of *South-West Ridge* (TD), Pointe 2810m, Mont Vert de Greuvetta. *(Tom Prentice)*

although the huge gaping bergschrund gave Chris an interesting mixed pitch. Once established on the wall, the climbing was sustained and enjoyable, although the route finding kept us guessing all the way to the top. We couldn't find the correct line above a terrace at one-third height so we climbed a variation that avoided the aid moves on the roof above, and in doing so made the first free ascent of the route.

The 500m-high east face of Mont Greuvetta is one of the finest rock walls in the Mont Blanc Range. The rock is beautiful, light-coloured, fine-grained granite, and was first climbed via its left edge in 1942, a remarkable tour de force that is currently graded TD+. It now sports half a dozen bolt-protected routes that were (mainly) put up in the early 1980s. Only two routes run the full height of the wall and most parties abseil off below the

The tiny Comino Bivouac hut perched below the Mont Vert de Greuvetta. *(Simon Richardson)*

The vast southern aspect of Mont Greuvetta. *(Tom Prentice)*

upper section where the rock quality deteriorates.

Whilst we were climbing the *Pilastro del Sorriso* I was struck by a distinctive pillar abutting the wall between Petit Mont Greuvetta and the main summit. A few months later, *Mountain* magazine published a photograph that picked out the line of the pillar in the sun. High and isolated, it had a singular and enigmatic charm. I christened it 'the Lonely Pillar' in my mind and in July 1998 Dore Green and I decided to attempt it. In the Comino Hut, however, we came across a written description (in Italian) of the Grassi-Lang-Meneghin 1982 route, and I interpreted this – incorrectly as it turned out – to be an ascent of the Lonely Pillar. So instead, Dore and I switched from exploratory climbing to bolt-clipping mode and made an ascent of *La Roue de la Fortune* (ED) on the main east face of the Greuvetta. Our disappointment at finding that our line had already been climbed was quickly dispelled by the excellent quality of climbing on this modern classic.

The story now steps forward 13 years to 2011 when Tom Prentice and I made an enjoyable trip to the Dolomites. We had a busy week climbing

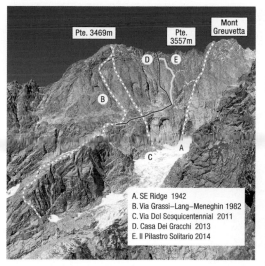

A. SE Ridge 1942
B. Via Grassi–Lang–Meneghin 1982
C. Via Del Scsquicentennial 2011
D. Casa Dei Gracchi 2013
E. Il Pilastro Solitario 2014

Mont Greuvetta routes.
(Tom Prentice)

medium-grade classics in the Sella Pass area, but all the while we were attracted to other features on the surrounding peaks, often wondering whether they had been climbed. This rekindled an old ambition to visit the Mont Blanc range and specifically target new routes. During previous visits to the massif I had noted several possibilities, so Tom and I decided to give them a try in September 2012. The plan was to climb three new routes, all south-facing buttresses that looked objectively safe and would clear fast after poor weather. The concept was simple – climb in rock boots and descend the same line by abseil.

The starting point of our campaign was Mont Vert de Greuvetta, which lies at the end of the long south-east ridge of the main peak. It is situated directly behind the Comino Hut and was first climbed, via the south ridge of Pointe 2810m, by Richard Goedeke and Tim Bartelds in July 1995. They descended by traversing the other two summits of Mont Vert de Greuvetta and climbing down close to the Greuvetta glacier. I was aware that a bolt-protected route had been climbed on Pointe 2810m (*Carletto,* 2010), but as far as I knew there were no independent routes on the other two summits. In particular, from distant photos

Simon Richardson bivouacking below the Petit Mont Greuvetta. The *Grassi-Lang-Meneghin* follows the left-slanting groove left of the prominent heart shaped feature. The *Direct Start* climbs the wall to the left. *(Tom Prentice)*

taken across Val Ferret I had seen on the internet, there appeared to be an attractive looking spur running up the south-west face of Pointe 2873m.

Tom and I arrived in Chamonix to be greeted by the first autumnal storm. It was raining hard, snow was down to 1600m, and it was bitterly cold. The weather was still poor the following morning, but we decided to drive through the Mont Blanc Tunnel and take a walk up Val Ferret to have a look at our proposed route on Pointe 2873m. The Greuvetta cirque appeared to be clear of snow, so we made an immediate change of plan and headed up to the Comino Hut with food and fuel for a couple of nights. There was even time that evening to scout out Pointe 2873m, and sure enough, there was an attractive line of ramps and grooves running up the south-west spur.

Tom Prentice, first ascent of the *South-west Ridge* (TD) of Pointe 2810m, Mont Vert de Greuvetta. *(Simon Richardson)*

Next day we had a leisurely start (by alpine standards) to allow the rock to warm up, and were climbing by 8:30am. The initial pitches went smoothly, and as planned, we entered the great groove cleaving the right side of the face. One pitch up we encountered a huge capping roof, and the hoped-for crack on the right wall was just a black streak. The pleasures of new routeing! It was decision time, so we followed our instincts along a break on the left, and where it faded we climbed a steep 5c pitch through an impending wall to a finely positioned arête above. Two more rope lengths and we were on top of the nine-pitch *South-West Spur* (D). We descended the gully system to the west and spent a leisurely night in the hut before descending the next day to Val Ferret.

Our next objective was on the south-west face of Pointe de la Fouly (3608m) at the head of the Argentière Basin. This was a bigger, more serious affair, but on 7 September we climbed the complex, pinnacled ridge that descends west-south-west from the highest point. This is left of, and parallel to, the *Charlet-Ratheaux Route*. The route had 19 pitches up to 6a, and although it climbed some easy ground, we felt it merited an overall grade of TD. The next day we made a long and complex descent of the south-west face back to the Argentière Glacier. For a bit of fun, we decided to call it the *Scottish Route*.

Tom Prentice on a reconnaissance of the east face of Mont Greuvetta in July 2014. (Simon Richardson)

We had time for a quick, modern, bolted route in the Aiguilles Rouges before the next big storm rolled in from the north-west in the middle of our second week. Once again it deposited snow to low levels, but this time it was followed by a bitterly cold north-east wind. This put paid to our third objective on the Aiguille du Chardonnet, so it was a natural decision to head back to Mont Vert de Greuvetta and climb a direct line up the previously unclimbed *South-West Ridge*. Entry to this is barred by a steep rock wall, which provided a difficult five-pitch start to the 300m TD route. The spectacular skyline ridge in the middle part of the climb was surprisingly straightforward and we gained the summit ridge just left of the *Carletto* route on the south face. We completed this climb (after reconnaissance the previous day) on 15 September, and then indulged in the luxury of a bolt-equipped descent of the *Carletto*. The weather was superb, and looking across into the main Greuvetta cirque, we were struck by a prominent slanting groove-line cutting through the vertical east face of Petit Mont Greuvetta.

We spent our last evening back in the hut before descending to Val Ferret and driving straight to Geneva to catch our flight. It had been a very successful trip. In 17 days away from home we had spent 13 days in the mountains and climbed three new routes, but in many ways the job felt unfinished. The route on the Chardonnet was unclimbed and we had spotted a compelling new line on the east face of Mont Greuvetta. We would have to return the following summer!

We made the groove on Petit Mont Greuvetta our first objective in August 2013. It is a compelling feature, but from afar it was impossible to judge the steepness of the groove. We had spent all winter studying photos and fretting about the potential difficulty, but after a long approach involving a bivouac we started up the route (with some trepidation) on 12 August. We climbed four pitches up a subsidiary groove to the left until we were sucked into the main groove-line. Here, horror of horrors, we found an old abseil sling and then a peg – clearly someone had been there before us. We continued for another seven pitches up the upper part of the groove, followed by a ramp that led to the summit ridge; we then descended our line by abseil, making another bivouac on the way. It turned out that this line was in fact the Grassi-Lang-Meneghin 1982 route and we had added a four-pitch direct start. Our initial disappointment turned to excitement, when we realised that this meant that the Lonely Pillar was unclimbed after all!

Our next objective, however, was a prominent rock pillar on the south side of the Aiguille du Chardonnet. Countless skiers must have passed underneath this attractive feature on their way to the Col du Chardonnet when doing the Haute Route, but as far as we knew it was unclimbed. Our approach to the col in summer conditions of unstable moraine and receding glaciers was a long and gruelling affair (which involved yet another bivouac), but we managed to squeeze in our 350m TD route before the weather broke. Nine varied pitches led to the summit crest of Pointe Alphonse Couttet (3660m), and once again we abseiled our line of ascent, just making the glacier by nightfall and reaching our bivouac site at midnight.

By the time the bad weather had cleared there was time for just one more route. It was now late August and the glaciers were beginning to break up, so we decided to return to the Greuvetta and attempt the Lonely Pillar. Our plan was to climb the crest of the pillar, but we were soon sucked into the prominent line of corners defining its left edge. This provided us with the best route of the trip; an excellent 11-pitch TD+ involving bivouacs on both the approach and descent. We were completely alone for three days, only accompanied by choughs (who had a nest under a great chockstone halfway up the route), so *Casa Dei Gracchi* (House of the Choughs) seemed an appropriate route name to capture the savage location. Once again, the descent was a race against time and we arrived on the Greuvetta glacier to crashes of thunder and bolts of lightning with flash floods in the valleys below. *Casa Dei Gracchi* (TD+, 6b) turned out to be an excellent climb following a very strong line, but it didn't follow the crest of the pillar that lay just out of reach to our right. We knew that we would have to return.

Tom Prentice on the first ascent of *Casa Dei Gracchi* (TD+) on the East Face of Mont Greuvetta. *(Simon Richardson)*

So the Lonely Pillar became the key objective for 2014. Unfortunately the weather was very poor during the last two weeks of July and we were confined to low-level routes around the Envers Hut and in the Aiguilles Rouges. At the beginning of the trip we made a reconnaissance of the Greuvetta, but there was too much snow on the approach and we ended up making an early repeat of the *Via Carletto* (TD, 6b) on Mont Vert de Greuvetta. Luckily at the end of our second week, the weather forecast magically

Simon Richardson on the first ascent of *Il Pilastro Solitario* TD+, east face of Mont Greuvetta. *(Tom Prentice)*

changed and a three-day weather window emerged. The previous year, *Casa Dei Gracchi* had taken a full three days (one day each for the ascent, climb and descent), so we planned on a similar period for the pillar.

We walked up to the Comino Hut in the rain, and set off in deep fog early in the morning of 31 July. Fortunately the cloud lifted resulting in a glorious day. Unlike 2013, when our approach to a bivouac at the foot of the pillar took a full day, we were so familiar with the approach that we reached a similar point in half the time, so just after midday we set off up the pillar itself.

The route links the two hanging ramps to join the crest of the upper pillar. From directly below, these looked undercut and very steep, and overall the route was very intimidating. But luck was on our side, because as soon as we started the technical climbing the rock quality became superb with many hidden incut holds and chicken heads on otherwise blank sections. The climbing up the ramps was sustained 6a with Tom leading a memorable 6a+ section up a thin finger crack. Where the second ramp faded, there was a long intricate pitch weaving through hanging slabs leading to the easier upper crest. These pitches were amongst the best alpine rock climbing we had ever done, and certainly justified the long approach. The upper pillar led naturally up the crest and then left on to the top section of *Casa Dei Gracchi* that leads to the south-south-east ridge of Mont Greuvetta. We abseiled down the 2013 route to reach a cramped bivouac at the foot of the pillar by nightfall.

The foot of the pillar is one of the most serious places I've visited in the Alps. Abseiling down to the glacier was not possible as the ground below is undercut by a huge arch, and the only way out is to downclimb the long,

Tom Prentice on the first ascent of *Il Pilastro Solitario* (TD+) on the east face of Mont Greuvetta. *(Simon Richardson)*

ascending approach traverse. The situation felt more committing than climbing on the south side of Mont Blanc and was reminiscent of the east face of the Grandes Jorasses. The next day was forecast to be good, but it soon clouded in and rained all day. Fully committed, we had no option but to very slowly and carefully reverse our approach in the wet. We reached Val Ferret early in the evening. Our three-day good weather window had shrunk to a single day, and if we had known this at the outset we wouldn't have even considered the attempt. We called our route *Il Pilastro Solitario* (The Lonely Pillar) and graded it similar to *Casa Dei Gracchi*, TD+.

Our ascent of the Lonely Pillar concluded a 20-year quest on the east side of the Greuvetta massif. During this time I have been lucky enough to climb eight routes (six with Tom), and four of these have been first ascents. But *Il Pilastro Solitario* is the finest climb of all, taking a marvellous feature. Many thanks to Tom for sharing the adventure.

Summary

An account of several visits to the beautiful granite of the Greuvetta massif on the south side of the Mont Blanc Range, over the course of 20 years. These culminated in first ascents of *Casa Dei Gracchi* (House of the Choughs), 500m, TD+ 6b, 22-23 August 2013 and *Il Pilastro Solitario* (The Lonely Pillar), 500m, TD+ 6a+, 31 July 2014. During the course of the exploration, new routes were also added to Mont Vert de Greuvetta, Aiguille du Chardonnet and Pointe de la Fouly. Topos and descriptions for these routes can be found in 2013 and 2014 *Alpine Journal* Area Notes to the Alps and Dolomites.

Matterhorn 150

The Cervin from the North East. The Matterhorn from the Stafelalp. Drawn by John Ruskin, 1849, engraved by J C Armytage. 1856. Engraving. 13 x 11cm. From *Modern Painters. Volume IV*, Part 5 – Of Mountain Beauty. Smith Elder 1856.

Materiana 150

IAN SMITH

14 July 1865

The Matterhorn, with the Hörnli Ridge toward the camera. *(Alex Messenger)*

'The first ascent of the Matterhorn might have been a brilliant success.'

By the time Edward Whymper wrote those words, in an article published at the end of his life,[1] the events of 14 July 1865 had taken on a dominant place in Whymper's consciousness. Over the last 20 years of his life he was regularly in Zermatt, and told the story in public lectures on hundreds of occasions. In the journals he now habitually kept, the date of 14 July is usually underlined.

Whymper knew it was the Matterhorn for which he was famous, but privately he was prouder of his ascent of the Aiguille Verte, just two weeks earlier. He had put ten years of his life into his magnificent book describing the mountains of Ecuador, and he always enjoyed telling tales of his

1. Edward Whymper, 'Mountaineering tragedies,' *Strand Magazine* **37** (January 1909), 55.

travels in Greenland, but as he got older it was the Matterhorn that came
to dominate his life. Staying in Zermatt, Thomas Hardy remembered his
first meeting with Whymper, 'when he gave us such a vivid description
of the catastrophe,' and Hardy was sufficiently impressed with the story
that he wrote a sonnet about the climb.[2] There are many such accounts of
Whymper telling acquaintances the story of that pivotal day in his life, and
invariably they followed the same pattern, dwelling on Hadow's inexperience and Hudson's crass over-confidence in bringing his young protégé;
but Whymper would often lose himself in the story, as if he were back on
the vertiginous slope of the Matterhorn's north side as his life flashed past
him. 'The veteran re-told us the story of the Matterhorn accident,' remembered one young climber who met him in Zermatt. 'I shall never forget the
old man's almost uncanny, convulsive grip on the corner of the table, and
the fierce flash in his eyes as speech suddenly failed.'[3]

Whymper knew nothing of mountains when he first saw the Matterhorn, but refused to be overawed. The following year he came marching
up the valley 'en route for the Matterhorn' (as he signed himself in the
Valtournanche inn visitors' book), just 21 years of age, but now thinking
he knew everything about mountaineering after an ascent of the Pelvoux,
in the Dauphiné. With an inexperienced porter he spent a memorable night
on the Col de Lion, and made a first creditable attempt at the Italian ridge.
One year later, now a member of the Alpine Club, he left his mark on
the south-west ridge, climbing, alone, higher than anyone before him, and
feeling that he had some personal ownership of the mountain.

In 1863 Whymper had only two weeks away from work and a single
attempt on the Matterhorn's south-east ridge was stopped by the weather.
The following year Whymper's mountaineering horizons were widened
when he attached himself to Adolphus Moore and Horace Walker, making
the first ascent of the Barre des Écrins, then with Adams Reilly a fine series
of climbs in the Mont Blanc range. But despite success right across the
Alps, work cut short Whymper's summer and the Matterhorn was left
untouched in 1864.

In 1865, still only 25 years old, Whymper became a member of the Royal
Geographic Society and was already thinking of travel and exploration
beyond the Alps. He wrote to Adams Reilly of making one final campaign
in the Alps and clearly wanted to finish with the Matterhorn. After his
dramatic summer of 1862, during which he did not keep a journal, in 1863
Whymper started recording his Alpine excursions in a small notebook
(now in the Scott Polar Research Institute in Cambridge) which he used
until the winter of 1868. The entries for 1865 begin on Saturday 10 June:

> '*Started from Charing Cross by tidal train, at Paris at 6.45pm. Off again by
> express to Bale at 8.05pm.*'[4]

2. Richard Little Purdy and Michael Millgate, eds., *The collected letters of Thomas Hardy: volume two – 1893-1901*
(Oxford: Clarendon Press, 1980), 168-9. *Thomas Hardy, Poems of the past and present* (London: Harper and Brothers,
1902).
3. George Abraham, 'Recollections of a great mountaineer and his mountains,' *Fell and Rock Climbing Club Journal* 4,
no. 3 (1918): 168-9.
4. Edward Whymper, '*Notes of an Alpine tour in 1865*' 10 June, SPRI MS 822/2; BJ.

Whymper managed to record the events of the hectic three weeks which followed, and often gave a good idea of what was going on in his mind and what he thought of his companions – principally Croz, Biener and Almer. After climbing the Grand Cornier and the Dent Blanche, on 21 June a remarkably ambitious (or foolhardy) attempt was made on the south face of the Matterhorn. On 24 June the Grandes Jorasses was climbed for the first time; two days later they crossed the Col Dolent, mountaineering a generation ahead of its time; on 29 June Whymper, Biener and Almer made the first ascent of the Aiguille Verte. Whymper's diary entry for that day ends with his arrival in Chamonix and the astonished congratulations of friends:

> *Arrive at 8.15pm. Meet Baxter, meet 'Vicar of Bradford'. Guns. Heaps of friends. Kennedy, Glover. Champagne. Perrn, a row brewing. Retire to bed with a dancing head. Warm bath prepared.*

The following day contains the penultimate entry in his notebook for 1865, which begins:

> *30 June. At Chamonix. These days are mixed up in my head in an inextricable jumble. I know that I had my watch mended, my hair cut and that innumerable people talked endless rubbish to me. I know that the weather was abominable and that I was very like the weather.*

Late on Sunday 2 July, Whymper walked up to 'Montanvert', and the next day, still with Biener and Almer, made a new crossing to Courmayeur. The last journal entry for the summer describes the start of the day:

> *An infernal dream ended by Couttet knocking at the door, woke me up an hour after time... The guides were difficult to rouse and we did not get off till 4am. The others (Girdlestone and Co) started a few minutes before. We followed and caught them at the 'Ponts.'*

Over the next few days, via a new pass and the first ascent of the Ruinette, the party of three made their way to Breuil, whence Almer and Biener departed for Zermatt. Whymper spent the best part of a week kicking about the Valtournanche but made no attempt to catch up with his diary. After the last entry quoted above there are several blank pages, then a sketch of Lucy Walker with the note: 'Miss Walker as leaving Hotel at Breuil. July 1865.'

Over his life, when keeping a diary or travel journal, Whymper did not make it a regular habit to record each day's events before retiring to bed. His teenage diary, kept from the age of 14 to 19, was often filled in several days at a time, but it is clear that more personal or significant events invariably caused Whymper to dry up. His commission to illustrate Samuel Smiles's life of George Stephenson, for John Murray, sent him to Liverpool, Newcastle and Derby but this two-week break from life in London is one of the few blanks in diary. Another blank follows the entry for 23 March 1859:

> *'I have just managed to get myself into rather a queer position, as follows.'*

This queer position involved a Miss Wilson, but all the reader finds is a column left tantalisingly blank.

Edward Whymper in his late 50s – a studio portrait taken in Chamonix.

When Whymper first travelled to Greenland, two years after the Matterhorn ascent, and later in Ecuador, he determined to do what a good explorer, a fellow of the Royal Geographical Society, should do – keep a regular authoritative journal. He designed for himself official notebooks with pre-printed spaces for the meteorological conditions, but in fact in Greenland he kept a personal diary – now in the Alpine Club archives – as well as this explorer's journal, now with most of his Greenland material in the Scott Polar Research Institute. These two records are interchangeable and both contain accounts of his daily activities, socialising, and comments, mostly unfavourable, on his travelling companions Brown and Tegner. However, when it comes to the defining moment of the whole expedition, the attempt to make a sledging journey into the interior, Whymper is unable to describe their failure, and says nothing of their brief sortie with the sledges – even though space is given to the howling of the dogs, the difficulties of cooking, and the shitting habits of the Greenlanders.

Thirteen years later, Whymper's two pre-printed journals recording his exploration of Ecuador give a fascinating account of the practicalities, his own thoughts and feelings, his difficult relationship to the two Carrels, and are complete but for one blank day, 4 January 1880, when he and the Carrels made the first ascent of the highest mountain then known to have been climbed, Chimborazo. Whymper clearly intended to write up the events of the day in his journal, but never did, although the following day, spent lying in the tent, has a long entry which records 'passed greater part of day in writing up notes.'[5] Their second ascent of Chimborazo, six months later, is fully described.

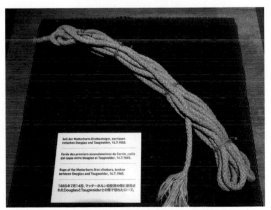

The thin line used to join Lord Francis Douglas and the older Peter Taugwalder. Whymper and Hudson had discussed using this rope as a fixed line on descent but somehow it ended up as a climbing rope. *(Ed Douglas)*

Why did Whymper record nothing in his journal after leaving 'Montanvert' on 3 July 1865? The sketch of Lucy Walker (whose father and brother, on 15 July, the day that Whymper returned in tears to Zermatt, were in the party making the first ascent of the Brenva Spur) rather indicates that Whymper was happy to sit about passing the time with acquaintances, but he does not bother to mention the ascent of the Ruinette, or his confused dealings with Carrel over these days. Although his first meeting with Girdlestone on 2 July is described, and Girdlestone

5. Edward Whymper, *'Journal and general notes in Ecuador, 1879-80,'* 5 January 1880, SPRI MS 822/7/1; BJ. A page is left blank for 4 January.

then played a significant part in the events leading up to the Matterhorn ascent, walking over the Théodule Pass with Whymper and Douglas on 12 July, he is not mentioned again. Whymper was still quite casual about keeping a journal, and probably in 1865 had no thought of writing a book on his mountaineering. (He always intended to write a book about Greenland, but this came to nothing.) Perhaps he thought he was going to climb the Matterhorn with Carrel, and full of confidence after such a triumphant summer so far, was waiting to tell a story of resounding success.

His letter to the president of the Swiss Alpine Club, sent from Interlaken on 25 July, is his first written account of the Matterhorn ascent. Two weeks later, back at his father's house in Haslemere, Whymper wrote a long letter to *The Times* describing in a matter-of-fact way the first ascent of the Matterhorn, the accident and the subsequent events in Zermatt.[6] Once he had written this long piece, it became established as Whymper's account, and re-appeared six years later, with minor changes, in *Scrambles amongst the Alps*.

Twelve months later, now well into his preparations for the exploration of Greenland, he returned to the Alps to investigate in situ the formation of glaciers. There were many places he could have done this, but the location he chose was the Col de Valpelline, an easily reached pass giving a splendid panorama of the Dent d'Hérens and the Matterhorn. Whymper pitched his tent part way up the path from Zermatt, directly opposite the north face of the Matterhorn, from where he could supervise his workmen, braving the cold and wind on the col to dig a hole in the ice. He could not have chosen a better, or more imposing, place to dwell on the events of the year before. Taking up again his mountaineering notebook, this time he leaves a full account of his struggles in poor weather to sample the depth of the glacier, the agonies of snow blindness, the lack of enthusiasm of his workmen, and the companionship he received from the Seilers (particularly Katharina), but makes no direct comment on the Matterhorn, although it hangs like an unspoken presence over the entries.

Croz's grave in the Zermatt cemetary.
(Ed Douglas)

Whymper was briefly in Breuil and Zermatt in 1869, checking details for his book and then returned with a camera in 1874, this time to make his second ascent of the Matterhorn. With Carrel and Bich, who had both stood on the summit three days after Whymper in 1865, and Lochmatter,

6. Edward Whymper, 'The Matterhorn accident,' *Times*, 8 August 1865.

Whymper climbed again the Hörnli Ridge, spending two nights in the rather squalid cabin now established a couple of thousand feet higher than their 1865 campsite. Whymper kept some pencil notes of this climb on a piece of paper, as eloquent as much for what they do not say as for what they do. Returning from the summit, he sat outside the hut watching the sunset casting its lavender colours over Monte Rosa, inevitably musing on what ought to have happened nine years earlier. Whymper returned two years later to his camping site of 1865, but then work, the Andes and his great book on Ecuador intervened, and it was not until 1892 that he saw the Matterhorn again. He took Franz Biener and his sons up to the 1865 camping site, where they cleared away the rubble and Whymper re-carved the initials he had so exultantly scratched 27 years earlier.

Starting the following year Whymper earned a reasonable income lecturing regularly on his mountaineering with his glass lanternslides, retelling the story of the Matterhorn according to his established narrative. After more than 20 years trying to move on, the Matterhorn now came back to haunt him, and for the last 20 of his life he was regularly in Zermatt. A young Guido Rey, later to write his own book on the Matterhorn, had this experience;

I was descending from the Theodul. Half-way between the Col and the Jomein I saw coming slowly up towards me a fine, tall old man… As I passed him I took off my hat to him, as is the polite custom of those who meet in the mountains. He returned my bow and passed on. My guide had stopped to talk to his. When he rejoined me he whispered, 'Do you know who that is?' I answered that I did not. 'Monsieur Whymper!' And he pronounced the name in a tone of respect. I was as much moved as if I were in the presence of a ghost. I had never seen Whymper except in photographs. I at once turned round to look at him. He had stopped too and was looking at the Matterhorn, whose aspect was one of marvellous grandeur from this point.

I cannot describe how much I was impressed by that meeting in that spot… They were there, the Matterhorn and Whymper, the two great rivals, and the sight of them in each other's presence brought home to one the superiority of the tiny conqueror to the conquered giant. He had come back after thirty years to see once more the mountain that had made him famous.

I would fain have made some sign, have shown him some act of reverence, some proof of my sympathetic interest; have told him that I had read his book again and again … [7]

After the euphoria of reaching untrodden snow on one of the finest days imaginable, to look down on his defeated rivals, Whymper would be haunted for the rest of his life by the aftermath, and the experience of those few seconds before the rope snapped never would leave him.

• Ian Smith's definitive biography of Edward Whymper, *Shadow of the Matterhorn*, is published by Carreg, £25.

7. Guido Rey, *The Matterhorn*, trans. J. Eaton, rev. R.L.G. Irving (Oxford: Blackwell, 1946), 153-4.

ROGER BIRNSTINGL

Letters From The Matterhorn

In the early 1860s the statesman Quintino Sella was finance minister in the government of Italy during the *Risorgimento*. He was a mineralogist, geologist and dedicated alpinist who agreed wholeheartedly with the president Camillo Cavour when he said: 'we have created Italy, now we must create Italians.' For Sella, an essential part of this process was to make first ascents of the great mountains on the Italian frontier. Already Monviso, so obvious from Italy's then capital Turin where Sella was a professor, had been lost in 1860 to William Mathews and with a Chamonix guide, not an Italian one. The remaining and crowning glory was the Matterhorn; it was obvious to Sella that Italians must climb it, and from the Italian side.

In 1980, the Fondazione Sella was established to collect together material relating to the Sella family, so many of whom had been mountaineers or closely associated with mountains, like Guido Rey, Quintino's nephew, the great alpinist and writer, and Vittorio Sella, another of Quintino's nephews and a renowned mountain photographer. In the archive of the Fondazione Sella, among the personal correspondence of Quintino, some letters have recently been unearthed shedding new light on Whymper's account of the first ascent. This cache has been made available to the AC through the generosity of the president of the Sella Foundation, Ludovico Sella, scion of the famous family, and Pietro Crivellaro. Some of these letters must have been seen by Guido Rey for his well researched book *Il Monte Cervino* (1907) but some are new to us.

It is clear Whymper can have had no idea what was going on behind the scenes when he said he had been 'bamboozled and humbugged' by his Breuil (Cervinia) guide Jean-Antoine Carrel. Whymper's account describes how he had engaged Carrel for this, his seventh attempt on the Matterhorn. Yet only a couple of days before the proposed ascent, Carrel told him he could not come because he was committed to a prior engagement with 'a family of distinction'. Whymper was furious but had to accept that he had lost his favourite guide whom he had described as 'the greatest rock climber I have ever encountered.'

On waking next day he learnt that a large party had already left that morning intent on the Matterhorn and led by Jean-Antoine Carrel. Having found binoculars, Whymper could see the group on the lower slopes of the mountain. This then was the 'family of distinction'. Whymper then hurried over to Zermatt to join forces with Charles Hudson and others, led by the Chamonix guide Michel Croz with whom he had made many previous first ascents including the Barre des Écrins, Aiguille d'Argentière, Grandes Jorasses and Mont Dolent. The story of this, the most famous first

Quintino Sella by Giuseppe Venanzio Sella, 1860. *(Fondazione Sella)*

ascent made in the Alps and the tragic deaths of three English climbers and Michel Croz, hardly needs retelling here. There is strong reason to suppose that had Whymper climbed in 1865 with Carrel, the ascent would have been a triumph rather than a tragedy caused by an oversized party that included one very inexperienced member – Douglas Hadow.

One needs also to know the name Felice Giordano who had studied at the school of mining in Paris together with Quintino Sella. They became

Jean Antoine Carrel, unknown photographer, published in the CAI journal 1868. *(Fondazione Sella)*

lifelong friends and both were passionate about mountaineering. Sella, as finance minister in the government, had obligations which curtailed his freedom but did not prevent him from helping found the Italian Alpine Club (CAI) in 1863, inspired by the example of the Alpine Club six years earlier.

Jean-Antoine Carrel is the most important man in this story. He was a *bersagliere*, the elite regiment of alpine soldiers who wear black feathers in their hats; Carrel had fought in battles against the Austrians, in particular the *Risorgimento* victory at Solferino in 1859, whose horrors led directly to the Geneva Conventions and the founding of the International Red Cross. He also fought in the Crimean War. He was therefore a great patriot but as a mountain guide with a considerable family to support, he was obliged to work very often with foreign climbers and in particular with climbers from the British Isles.

Felice Giordano wrote to Quintino that he considered Carrel a very fine climber but somewhat venal and indeed the evidence tends to suggest that Carrel on several occasions persuaded his clients to abandon attempts even when the summit was within striking distance. This happened in 1862 to John Tyndall after getting to the south-west shoulder peak, now called Pic Tyndall and to Whymper in 1863. Could it be that he thought the Matterhorn, once climbed, would be less attractive to his prospective clients and that it was in his interest to keep it virgin? It is significant that only three days after Whymper's success he reached the peak from the Italian side with a four-man party. Giordano had wished to be in that group but Carrel refused to let him come saying he could not cope with a 'tourist'. Perhaps Giordano should have offered him a better fee but instead he remained in Breuil desperately disappointed. On their return, when the entire village was *en fête,* a miserable Giordano left Breuil and descended the valley.

It would be interesting to know whether Carrel was held responsible for missing opportunities of getting to the summit of the Matterhorn *per l'Italia.* From perusing the letters I do not get the impression that he was, although in 1877 when the guide Giuseppe Maquignaz was climbing with the Sella family, he spoke of the climb on the Italian side when Whymper was making his attempt from Zermatt. He told how he had been putting in pitons (actually nails) and fixing ropes on the Grande Tour below Pic Tyndall which involved carrying some 25kg on his back. He wanted to dump the sack and get on faster. There was an animated discussion and much loss of time. Apparently Carrel was so convinced that Whymper had no hope of success from Zermatt that he simply was not hurried.

Some of the letters passed between Giordano and Sella during those vital days in 1865 make things clear. On 7 July Giordano wrote to Sella from Turin:

I leave for the noted destination heavily loaded. [Author's note: he doesn't mention Breuil.] The day before yesterday I sent up a tent, 300m of rope and various metal hooks together with provisions, an oil-stove to heat water, etc. All this stuff weighs about 100kg and as it must go on a cart from Ivrea to Châtillon it won't arrive until this evening or tomorrow. Also I am sending 200 lire to Carrel so that he can transport it all to Val Tournanche or Breuil. I should be there tomorrow in order to supervise the matter. I will take another tent and barometers including your own. When I am there I shall write to you. Only think about yourself, which means bringing a good overcoat, two or three blankets, good cigars and wine and don't forget the cash because I can't carry more than 300 lire. Let's get on and attack this devil mountain and let us succeed if only Whymper does not get there first!

The next letter is dated 11 July when Giordano, having now arrived in Breuil, wrote to Sella:

I sent letters, ropes and other equipment to Carrel on the fifth hoping to find him in Châtillon [in the Aosta valley] but he wasn't there as letters are taking an incredible time to get to the Val Tournanche (they only arrived on 9 [July]). So on the eighth I found the ropes and other provisions in Châtillon and sent them up with mules. At midday I was in Val Tournanche and found Carrel just returned from an exploration on the mountain but had given up in bad weather. Whymper, who had already been there for some days, engaged Carrel who had not received my letters. Fortunately the weather was bad and Whymper was unable to make this attempt. Carrel cancelled his engagement and came with me with five men amongst the best in the valley.

A preliminary expedition was organised straightaway with these men and Carrel in control. We got the ropes and other stuff out of sight by taking them up the moun-tain to a hut, which serves as a base camp. From here two men climbed and fixed ropes whilst two acted as porters. I won't write more details for the moment and am established at Breuil at 2000 metres.

The weather (our terrible god on which all depends) is very variable. Yesterday morning it was again snowing on the Cervino but by the evening had cleared up. On the night of 10-11 July six men left with tents etc and I hope at this moment are high up on the mountain. The weather is changing again and the mountain is in cloud but I hope for clear passages.

Weather permitting, ie good, I hope in three to four days to have good news. Carrel told me not to climb with him and to await news. Naturally he wants to be assured about the last problems of the climb. Looking at them from here I don't feel they are insurmountable but before we can say anything definite we need to 'touch' them which means finding a bivouac site higher than Whymper's highest.

So as soon as I know something definite I will send an express message to St Vincent from where a telegram will be sent to you. Then you must come immediately because the atmosphere here changes from hour to hour [literally from six hours to six hours in the Italian] and it's a desperate situation. When you receive this be kind enough to send me a couple of lines. My greatest worry is the weather, the excessive expenses (each man must be paid 20 lire per day of work plus his food), and Whymper.

I have tried to keep everything secret but this individual whose very life seems to depend on the Cervino is prying into everything. I have taken away all the capable men but nevertheless he could still try to get others or at least make a great scene. He is here in the hotel but I try everything not to talk to him. So in short I am doing everything to help us succeed. That the Greek gods should help us!

I won't write more hoping soon to be able to give you good news. Even so I hope at least that these Alpine matters get your mind off ministerial and Turin business.

Your affectionate Giordano.

What is interesting about these two letters is that they make it quite clear the original plan was for the two friends, Quintino Sella and Felice Giordano, to make an almost 1920s Himalayan-style attack on the mountain. Carrel and other guides would achieve the first ascent and having equipped it suitably with fixed ropes and pitons the friends would make a second ascent. This is why Giordano did not go with the party that left on 11 July.

Whymper writes in *Scrambles in the Alps* that having descended the Val Tournanche on 9 July to see a sick Englishman, he meets 'a foreign gentleman' together with Carrel and others. This must have been Giordano but the meeting is not referred to in the latter's letter of 11 July. On 14 July Giordano writes:

Dear Quintino,

Today at 2pm with good binoculars I saw Carrel and company on the extreme summit of the Cervino. There were several people with me and thus one can say that the success seems certain in spite of all the snow that fell the day before yesterday. Whymper left to try from the other side but I think in vain. The trouble is that I don't know where you are and have had no news for more than eight days. If you don't come or telegraph me before tomorrow I shall have to ascend the mountain myself and plant the Italian flag on the summit as is very necessary. However I would rather wait so that you can be with me.

This is Giordano on the following day and in a very different mood:

Felice Giordano, photographed by Vittorio Besso in 1864. *(Fondazione Sella)*

Dear Quintino,

Yesterday was an awful one; Whymper made it against the unhappy Carrel. Whymper in desperation and seeing Carrel starting up the mountain made this attack from Zermatt. Everyone thought it impossible from that side including Carrel and therefore was unconcerned. On 11 July Carrel climbed to a fair height but that night and the whole of the twelfth were horrible with snow. The thirteenth was better and 14 July fine. On the thirteenth some work was done (ie fixing ropes) and on the fourteenth Carrel could have been on the summit but at about 2pm he saw Whymper and six others had arrived. Whymper must have promised a fortune to the various Swiss guides to pull him up and with the luck of the weather he was successful.

I tried to get a message through to Carrel that Whymper was also making an attempt and that he should make all haste and not waste any time. This did not get to him and in any case Carrel did not think it possible from the north.

Poor Carrel when he saw he had been preceded did not have the courage to continue and descended with armi e bagagli *[arms and baggage]. He arrived here this morning so I send this express to stop you from coming.*

You see in spite of all our efforts this is a lost battle and I am desolate in the extreme.

Perhaps there is one way to avenge this. Someone must climb the mountain from our side, which will show that it is indeed possible, as Carrel believes. I am just a bit angry with him for having brought all the equipment back down which had been taken up with so much fatigue to about 200m below the summit. He will put the blame on the whole group which was so discouraged and feared that I wouldn't come up with more cash.

However I don't want to put blame on anyone. What is important, as I said, is to plant the flag up there. I shall try to organise another expedition but apart from Carrel and one other, there is no cuore *[heart] for another attempt. Without that, there is not a lot of hope.*

Still, I am trying to organise another bash and hope to keep it as economical as possible. Again I won't get the satisfaction of climbing myself as Carrel has said that it is better to go without 'tourists'. The weather is still very variable. What tribulations!

Yesterday the entire valley was en fête thinking 'our men' had made it and today comes the disillusion. Poor Carrel so much believed it impossible to succeed from the north that he had not been in enough haste.

The expenses have been really tough and I must implore you to help me out a bit. Your F G

On a scrap of paper he added:

In spite of everything that has happened you still could make the ascent yourself if you can find the time but until now Carrel has not been able to really assure me of the feasibility of the last part of the climb.

Giordano wrote again on 16 July having now heard of the terrible tragedy of Whymper's descent, during which the famous Chamonix guide

Michel Croz and 'three tourists' fell to their deaths. He believes Whymper had cut the rope that attached him to the others. Because of this accident he wrote that at least tourists would be put off from trying again from Zermatt.

He laments that Carrel turned back when he was so close to the summit, which means that it all has to be done again. Then he says that by getting sufficiently angry he had managed to organise a party, which had left that very morning. He couldn't get everyone from the first attempt to go this time but was pleased to have procured the Abbé Gorret, godson of Jean-Antoine Carrel, who was reputed to be as good as any guide. (He certainly proved a godsend as a climber and what is more, persuaded the others on the party not to accept a fee and climb for the honour of their country. This must have been good news for Giordano.) He goes on to say that all this has made him ill and he has no appetite. He intends to go to Turin at the first opportunity but needs to have the result of this last try for the summit.

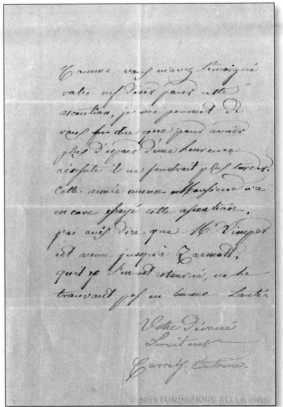

The next letter we have is indeed from Turin, dated 20 July, saying that he had left Breuil the previous day in hopeless weather and had come to Turin hoping to find Quintino but had heard that he had left for Florence. (Sella was trying

The second page of a letter from Carrel to Quintino sent in 1864, the year before the first ascent, telling him that the mountain was in prime condition for an attempt. *(Fondazione Sella)*

to keep the capital of Italy in Turin but in vain; it was moved to Florence and to Rome in 1873.)

He writes: 'I wanted to tell you that if you still wish, it is not too late to climb the Cervino with the <u>honour</u> of being the first <u>Monsieur</u> to have done it...' After lamenting that he had to remain in the valley while the new attempt was made, he writes how the caravan left on 16 July and at 2pm 'our flag was on the summit. Apparently the difficulties near the top were not too bad but Carrel wants to fit some climbing aids to make it easier before he takes any tourists up. That same evening the weather turned really bad with sleet and snow so I decided to come down to Turin.' He again says how disappointed he is not to have put his feet on the summit and has to content himself with a piece of rock, some sort of yellow mica, which Carrel had brought down. 'Val Tournanche is really *en fête* again with music and dancing; even a song has been composed with the words: *C'est un monsieur Italien / Qui a vaincu le Mont Cervin.*'

No more attempts were made that year. The previous year, Quintino Sella, who lived in Biella, which was not such a distance from Val Tournanche, had asked Carrel to go there in person. It is not clear what passed at that meeting but shortly afterwards, on 7 August, Carrel wrote to Sella saying that the mountain could not be in better conditions for a summit attempt and that Sella should come to Breuil as quickly as possible. He also mentions that 'Vimper' had returned to London. (This was because Whymper's mother had died).

Unfortunately Sella was unable to go, being involved with state matters and suffering from some sort of infection in his leg that kept him in bed. It could be argued that the battle was lost then in 1864 with the great Sella *hors du combat*. It was he who so much wanted this conquest for the honour of the *Nuova Italia* and in a way is an illustration of the growth in importance of competitive sport between nations, which became so important from the end of the nineteenth century.

Quintino Sella's own ambitions for the mountain were not realised until some twelve years later when, for his fiftieth year, he finally made the ascent with his two sons, a nephew, Jean-Antoine Carrel and no less than three other renowned guides. Giordano, who was not a state minister and had more time, attempted it again in 1866 but was blocked 'for several days' at Pic Tyndall before having to descend. Returning in 1867 he was beaten by the weather. It was not until 1868 that he finally achieved his ambition. His friend Quintino was delighted and popularised the geological studies that Giordano had made on the structure of the Matterhorn. After the disappointment of it not being an Italian making the first ascent, he hoped at least it could be Italy at the forefront of Alpine geological research.

Elsewhere in the archive are plenty of letters from later years including ones of jubilation when Sella climbed the Monviso and indeed the Matterhorn and correspondence relating to the invitation of King Vittorio Emanuele, himself a great lover of the mountains, to accept the presidency of the CAI – and a gift to him of Whymper's books. There is plenty of scope here for future research.

JOHN CLEARE

Made For Television

The Matterhorn Centenary

The centenary of the Matterhorn's first ascent in 1965 was, the Swiss declared, to be 'The Year of the Alps'; marked by frolics, fun and festivities throughout the country. Radio Geneva's input was to be nothing less than a televised ascent of the Matterhorn on 14 July on the very day, even the very hour, of the anniversary that would be transmitted around the world.

Ambition is one thing, practicality another. The Swiss had little experience of this kind of thing so the BBC, with its live outside broadcast expertise, was invited to assist. Fifty years ago there was no colour television, let alone digital imaging, and live 'OBs' were still a fraught art, demanding very different treatment from film or even video recording. Knowing the size of the mountain and the fickleness of the weather, the project seems foolhardy in retrospect. But nothing ventured, nothing gained. Hamish MacInnes and I were drafted in to handle the task.

Actually, there were four of us, since each portable radio-camera required a two-man team. The camera itself was cabled to a large metal pack on the cameraman's back, whence more cables linked to another heavy transmission box carried by the second man, and onwards to an aerial. Our respective assistants, or 'tweakers', expected to hold the ropes, man the radios and tune in the transmitter, were our respective climbing partners, Davy Crabbe and Rusty Baillie.

Spring was late in 1965 and the Matterhorn hadn't yet been climbed that year. Up at the Hörnli Hut the snow was deep, soggy and uneven. Pandemonium reigned at the Belvedere Inn, temporarily turned into a television control-room, where engineers, technicians, directors, producers and celebrities were shouting in their own languages at no one in particular. It was clear few of them had been on a mountain before and many were suffering from altitude. Not surprisingly we had already decided to camp and we pitched our tents in falling snow among boulders a little way above the hut.

Snow fell for several days while we were briefed on our tasks; as the nature of the enterprise became clear, we realised how impractical the arrangements were to carry it out. There would be two large static TV cameras with telephoto lenses, one on a railway flatcar at the Gornergrat some five miles from the mountain, and another, airlifted in, close by the hut but still four thousand feet below the summit and a mile distant. The detail of the climb itself, the personalities, their commentary, the chat and the close-ups, would depend entirely on our two cameras sending back radio pictures to the control-room, though it was uncertain that this was possible at the distances necessary. Six 25-minute transmission slots had already been scheduled throughout 14 July. Come what may, we must be on-air. But the transmission times bore little relation to the mountaineering involved.

Together with Alan Chivers, the inspirational BBC supremo, Hamish and I worked out a fresh plan of campaign. Once the straightforward first transmission – leaving the hut at dawn – was off-air, we would dismantle the gear, overtake the celebrities and leapfrog our respective teams up the mountain. I would handle the second transmission at a suitable location commensurate with the allotted time while Hamish continued upwards to locate the next likely site and be tuned in, ready for when the celebrities arrived for the next.

Meanwhile I'd dismantle and move through, overtaking the celebrities again to select the next photogenic site. And so on. It ought to work, but it meant that only one camera would be covering each 25-minute slot – supplemented of course by the long lenses from far below. We could only trust that the timing would allow us to locate reasonably photogenic locations and that the celebrities could keep up.

We'd need to move fast and logistics were a serious concern. Obviously the heaps of television and radio equipment, besides the normal gear needed by climbers on a major Alpine peak, made crucifying loads and so local porters had been booked. However, this was The Year of the Alps, and the best men were otherwise occupied.

Management held a press conference down at Schwarzsee. Besides the celebrities who were to climb the Hörnli Ridge, and the notable Swiss alpinists who were concurrently to attempt the North Face, the four of us who were to do the hard work were also presented to the European press. 'Who were we?' they asked. 'Were we real alpinists?'

MacInnes admitted to some remarkable Caucasus adventures while Rusty confessed to the Eigerwand with Haston two years previously. And then it was Davy's turn:

'And vot ist your best climb, Herr Crabbe?'

There was a pause before Davy answered.

'The first winter traverse of the Cuillin,' he finally told them.

'*Bitte*, vere is Das Cuillin, Herr Crabbe?' said a puzzled reporter. 'In Patagonia, *nein*?'

'Nay mon, 'tis in God's own country,' Davy countered rather testily.

'But pleez Herr Crabbe,' replied the puzzled German, still anxious for his quote, 'vot about ze Alps?'

'Ach, mon, 'tis good training for Scotland in winter.'

After a short but meteoric Alpine career and some considerable achievements on Scottish ice, I heard later that Davy had eschewed climbing and taken up ski instructing.

The plan called for us to make a reconnaissance on 12 July to transmit summit pictures but with no concern about timing. On 13 July there would

Rusty Baillie supports the author, busy concentrating on transmitting a steady picture with his radio-camera, in an exposed position at the 1865 accident site – the final transmission of the Matterhorn Centenary Live Outside Broadcast, 14 July 1965. Note the cables, aerials, electronic boxes, climbing ropes and associated gear. *(John Cleare/Mountain Camera Picture Library)*

be a full rehearsal with the entire programme recorded on videotape against the possibility – probability? – of bad weather or even disaster on the anniversary itself. But the Matterhorn was still inviolate and conditions were downright dangerous, with knee-deep slush lying on ice. Nevertheless we fought our way to the Solvay where the cameras wouldn't work and the stroppy local porters did nothing to inspire confidence. It was near dusk

when we returned to the hut after a long day, dejected and frustrated.

Alan Chivers was not discouraged. A Battle of Britain fighter ace, 'Chiv' oozed confidence, whatever he must have thought privately about the situation. Ever alert to our concerns, he'd sent an assistant through the Zermatt streets that day, contract forms in hand, and recruited two likely looking English climbers as 'sherpas' to augment the uncooperative local porters. We were relieved to have Barry Whybrow and his chum join us; these were fellows we could trust.

Next day the full rehearsal started well. For the second transmission,

A Radio Geneva cameraman checks focus on a static camera positioned a few yards above the Hörnli Hut, prior to the live TV broadcast. This was the closest any conventional TV camera got to the action. *(John Cleare/Mountain Camera Picture Library)*

there was time to select a good camera position below the rock tower at the Whymper bivouac site at 3817m and, when he arrived, work out stage directions with Ian McNaught-Davis, the lead celebrity. 'Mac' had taken Chris Brasher's place as commentator after Chris developed piles, and was climbing with Heini Taugwalder, Zermatt's chief guide and a direct descendent of Wymper's guides on the fateful ascent. Then we were on-air. Chiv's steady voice crackled over my headphones: 'Okay John, we're on you now. Nice picture. Zoom in a bit. Hold that.'

Silhouetted against the distant Mischabel, Heini and Mac picked their way along the ridge crest and scrambled towards me. Panting a little and sweating below his white 'flat 'at', Mac started to explain that although the climbing appeared easy, this was a big serious mountain and a hundred years ago Mr Whymper had bivouacked here on the eve of his successful ascent. Now close in front of me, I held Mac's face full frame as he went on to describe another tragedy that had occurred right here. I zoomed slowly out, intending to show a bronze plaque explaining how four men had died in a storm in 1890 to which Mac was now pointing.

I zoomed out to find in frame four healthy-looking fellows sitting beside the plaque and munching sandwiches. A burst of puzzled indignation filled my headphones.

'Cut! What the hell's all this?'

I yelled at Rusty who scrambled off across the snow and started gesticulating. The four fellows were rather piqued, being Italian celebrities who'd avoided the briefing, knew nothing of the scenario and had missed breakfast. Thankfully they accepted our explanations in good grace and the transmission was able to proceed. Luckily we were only on tape.

But the mountain was still dangerous. Despite knowing the summit sequence was scheduled for 3pm next day, the local porters refused to continue upwards after mid-morning. Despite the efforts of our new sherpas, the exercise seized up. Jabbering voices filled the airwaves, evidence of a shambles down at base also. Finally Chiv, remarkably sounding calm through the crackling chaos, ordered a retreat.

Back at the hut the well-lubricated debriefing session proved a fraught affair, but we were reassured to learn Chiv was now in complete charge. It turned out the local big chief had suffered a nervous breakdown. Then a hush fell. Approaching barefoot through the snow under a large rucksack came Mary Stewart.

'Who's that?' a BBC engineer whispered to Davy.

'A Glasgee mither o' five,' he answered loudly.

Close behind this redheaded Amazon plodded four more of our chums: Ian 'Jock' Martin, Johnnie Wright, Kris Paterson and complete with celebrated grin, Eric Beard, the Leeds fell-runner known as the 'Alpine Clown' in Rock and Ice circles.

'Sherpas, Chiv! Grab 'em,' shouted Hamish. 'Sign 'em up quick!'

Morale soared.

And so, on the day, although we were continuously extemporising, transmission followed transmission without a hitch until my camera died after the Shoulder slot, and we entered cloud. Now time was tight, for the next transmission was scheduled from the summit at 3pm and the fixed ropes were congested with struggling celebrities and their guides. But with our lusty sherpas we barged through, set up the single camera on the summit crest – considerably beyond its designed operating range – and endeavoured to 'net in'. A few moments before we were due on-air, Chiv came over the radio to say he had pictures and they were good.

After all that, the summit broadcast was something of an anti-climax. The celebrities plodded into view, arriving over the convex curve that concealed the north face, and there was much backslapping and handshaking. Hamish covered the transmission. It was a gruelling task and before it was over the sherpas had actually to hold him up. But for me the crux was still to come. The final transmission in some forty minutes time was mine, supposedly at the place where the 1865 accident had occurred.

No longer able to leapfrog, the moment Hamish was off-air we dismantled the gear and set off downwards with large packs at speed but a caravan of celebrities and guides of several nations were still occupying the fixed ropes. There were angry scenes as we tried to pass. Rusty even exchanged blows with one obdurate guide. But we located the site, set up and netted in just in time.

The two BBC radio-camera teams, l – r: John Cleare, Hamish MacInnes, Davy Crabbe and Rusty Baillie (on radio). *(John Cleare/Mountain Camera Picture Library)*

With Heini behind him on a short rope, picking his way gingerly down a stretch of unpleasant, rather loose and very exposed ground, Mac was explaining that this was where Douglas Hadow had slipped, dragging his companions to their death, exactly a century ago. Suddenly his feet shot from beneath him. He stumbled and fell. And was held easily after a few feet by Heini. It was entirely unexpected and the tension was incredible.

Ever the performer, Mac claimed afterwards that this fall had not been intentional, but whether it was or not, Chiv was soon on the radio with a special request from London; was I prepared to over-run for ten more minutes? We were all very tired and the camera was getting very heavy, but buttressed by Rusty I managed to shoot the other celebrity ropes as they crossed the awkward ground back to the Shoulder.

At long last Chiv came on again:

'We're off you now John. Thank you, my boy. Over and out.'

I let the camera fall on its strap and collapsed against the rope. With a rumble the big boulder on which I had been propped tumbled away to go plunging down the north face. Rusty pulled me back into balance and a sherpa put a mug of fresh-brewed tea into my hand. It was done. But there was still a mountain to descend and the weather was breaking. It was late afternoon, snow was falling, thunder rolled and we feared verglas, so we dumped most of the equipment in the Solvay Hut and continued the descent more easily and safely.

A guide leads one of the celebrities onto the summit past Hamish MacInnes driving his radio camera. Now in poor visibility, the whole show depends on the BBC team. *(John Cleare/Mountain Camera Picture Library)*

Mac claimed that during the descent he saw a local porter swing off his rucksack – heavily loaded with BBC spare batteries – to remove his crampons. But they must have pierced the sack and picked up a charge, for he received a hefty electric shock. With, Mac said, a cry of 'Himmel! The BBC has bewitched me,' he hurled the sack and its expensive contents into the void of the north face. Mac was unable to confirm the story.

At camp we gathered ourselves together and hurried on down to Schwarzee where the cable car was running especially late. Of course it was the culminating day of the celebrations and Zermatt was making merry when we arrived; the bars were crowded and the restaurants were full. We had just put the Matterhorn on worldwide television but now, tired, hungry, dishevelled and impecunious, we wandered down the street feeling rather out of place.

Striding up the street came Chris Brasher. 'Disgraceful!' he cried. 'After what you've done!' And he led us into the best restaurant in town, introduced us to the management, had a table cleared and treated us to the best evening that Zermatt and the BBC could provide. In the early hours, replete and well satisfied, we crept away to crash out in the cave behind the station. It had been a hard day.

There was a sequel. Aware that official gratitude had been lacking, Constant Cashin, the Zermatt Kurdirektor, kindly invited Hamish and me back to Zermatt the following year, expenses paid, to attempt a film on the north face of the Matterhorn. But that's another story.

Literature

Le Mont-Cervin vu de Riffelberg. Drawn by Gabriel Loppé, lithography by
Tirpenne, printed Lemercier, Paris. c1860. Colour lithograph. 13.5 x 10cm.
From *Souvenirs de la Suisse*, edited by Becherat.
(Courtesy of Tony Astill – www. mountaineeringbooks.org)

KAREN STOCKHAM

My Gypsy Self

Dorothy Pilley and Women's Mountaineering

Dorothy Pilley, Glacier National Park, 1930s. *(Alpine Club Photo Library)*

This year marks the eightieth anniversary of the publication of an enduring classic of mountaineering literature, Dorothy Pilley's *Climbing Days*. Little is known about this remarkable woman beyond these memoirs of her formative mountaineering years, and an appraisal of her achievements and wider contributions to the development of women's mountaineering in the twentieth century is long overdue.

Dorothy Eleanor Pilley was born in Camberwell, London, in 1894, the oldest of four children born to Annie Maria Young and John Pilley, an industrial chemist. Known to her mountaineering contemporaries as 'Pilley', Dorothy's upbringing was solidly Victorian and middle-class. Regular church attendance, a girls' boarding school in Eastbourne from the age of twelve, a year in Germany 'for the culture' and a subsequent year spent in domestic education, was a typical life-course for young women of Pilley's background.

From an early age the Pilley children were expected to keep a daily diary, not unusual in turn-of-the century England when many of the moral precepts of the Victorian age continued, including the belief that writing a diary instilled mental discipline, regular habits and improved children's writing skills. For Pilley, as with so many women, writing a diary came to mean much more than a laborious noting down of the day's events. While she sometimes viewed maintaining her diary as a chore, and in her entry on 5 June 1921 revealed how she and her siblings were 'bribed weekly by Father to keep up a regular account of our doings', her diaries became confidantes and friends and she consigned to them her hopes, fears, tribulations and triumphs beginning as a young girl until her death in 1986.

Her marriage and mountaineering partnership with Ivor Armstrong Richards – the 'IAR' of *Climbing Days* – opened doors not just into the world of mountaineering but meant she would rub shoulders with some of the literary and philosophical giants of the twentieth century, among them William Empson and T S Eliot. Her diaries from those encounters yield riches far beyond the world of mountaineering, encompassing horizons ranging across twentieth-century literature. But they also open a window on women's mountaineering, the growth in women's mountaineering literature and a life of travel and adventure spanning Europe, Asia and North America.

At 18, Pilley set her heart on a career in horticulture, inspired by pottering in the family's garden in Camberwell. In the early twentieth century, horticulture was one of the few respectable professions open for middle-class girls, made so by doughty women's colleges like Swanley in Kent and Waterperry in Oxford. Yet Pilley's father refused to countenance such training. Pilley grimly noted in her diary entry of 13 September 1912: 'it is so hard to decide definitely for the gardening with everybody against you.' Bowing to parental pressure, she enrolled for a year's course in domestic science in 1913 and despite her antipathy to domestic work became good at it, both from skill and necessity, given that her mother was an ineffective and unwilling domestic manager, conceding in her diary on 6 December 1913: 'I did think that it was a useful course and not a waste of time.'

A carefully-written, descriptive account of the Alps in one of the 12-year-old Dorothy's schoolbooks bore no signs of the passion for mountaineering which was to develop from 1914 onwards: 'The Alps are the great mass of mountains,' she gravely explained, 'reaching from the Gulf of Genoa, round the mouth of Italy to the west of the Adriatic Sea. They're in France, Switzerland, Italy and Austria. These mountains are the grandest in Europe. Mont Blanc is one of the highest mountains in Europe.' Little did the young Dorothy imagine that 22 years later in July 1928, she and 'IAR', with the Georges brothers, would make the first ascent of the north ridge of one of the highest peak in the Alps, Dent Blanche – an adventure she relates in the last chapter of *Climbing Days* with great verve and humour.

Pilley had to wait until September 1914 for the experience which was to alter her entire future and lay down the bedrock for a life of mountaineering and adventure. To celebrate her twentieth birthday, Dorothy's Aunt Clara issued her with an invitation to join herself and her cousin, Elsie, for a week's holiday in a cottage in Snowdonia. Pilley harboured no illusions that her father would grant her permission to go. She tried to keep her excitement in check, writing gloomily in her diary on 9 September: 'feel sure I will be disappointed as Father will almost certainly say no.' Yet to her unrestrained delight and surprise, her father consented; this was an unprecedented departure from family holidays by the sea on the Isle of Wight.

Pilley was to write about this Snowdonia interlude in the opening pages of *Climbing Days,* describing it as a magical experience. 'In place of the pleasant family holidays by the sea... came the grey village street, the tawny blotches of the bracken, the reeds swaying in the breeze round the shores of Llyn Dinas, the smell of the moss and the peat.'

Everything about the holiday in Snowdonia was a novelty to her, including the long railway journey from London to North Wales. Writing in her diary on 11 September 1914, Pilley noted that the countryside was 'wonderful, with cold grey sea on one side and mountains on the other.' She found their accommodation a delight, writing that 'the cottage has splendid views of a giant mountain with a torrential stream running down its face, and always, it seems, a glowing welcoming fire.' Declaring in *Climbing Days,* 'what did it matter that we went up Craig-y-Llan in long skirts and in what the boot-sellers regard as feminine boots,' this sojourn into the mountains of North Wales was, she explained, 'like waking up from a half sleep with the senses cleared, the self released.'

On the day of Pilley's birthday, the three women undertook a trip to Snowdon. According to her diary they enjoyed a 'long drive up to Snowden [*sic*] behind weary steed' and ate 'sodden sandwiches seated in puddles with utmost relish! Sea amidst glow of brass and copper and Pen y Pass Hotel.' The high spirits of Pilley and her cousin, Elsie, are captured in Pilley's diary through sketches contributed by Elsie, as seen in Figure 1. Although hampered by long skirts and 'feminine boots', the girls made the most of the freedom to 'wander around' the mountainous landscape, getting caught, as Pilley wrote, 'in the twilight' and having 'to come down the bare rock in the dark' an experience caught with good humour in Elsie's sketches.

Arriving back in London after the Snowdon trip, Pilley felt a terrible

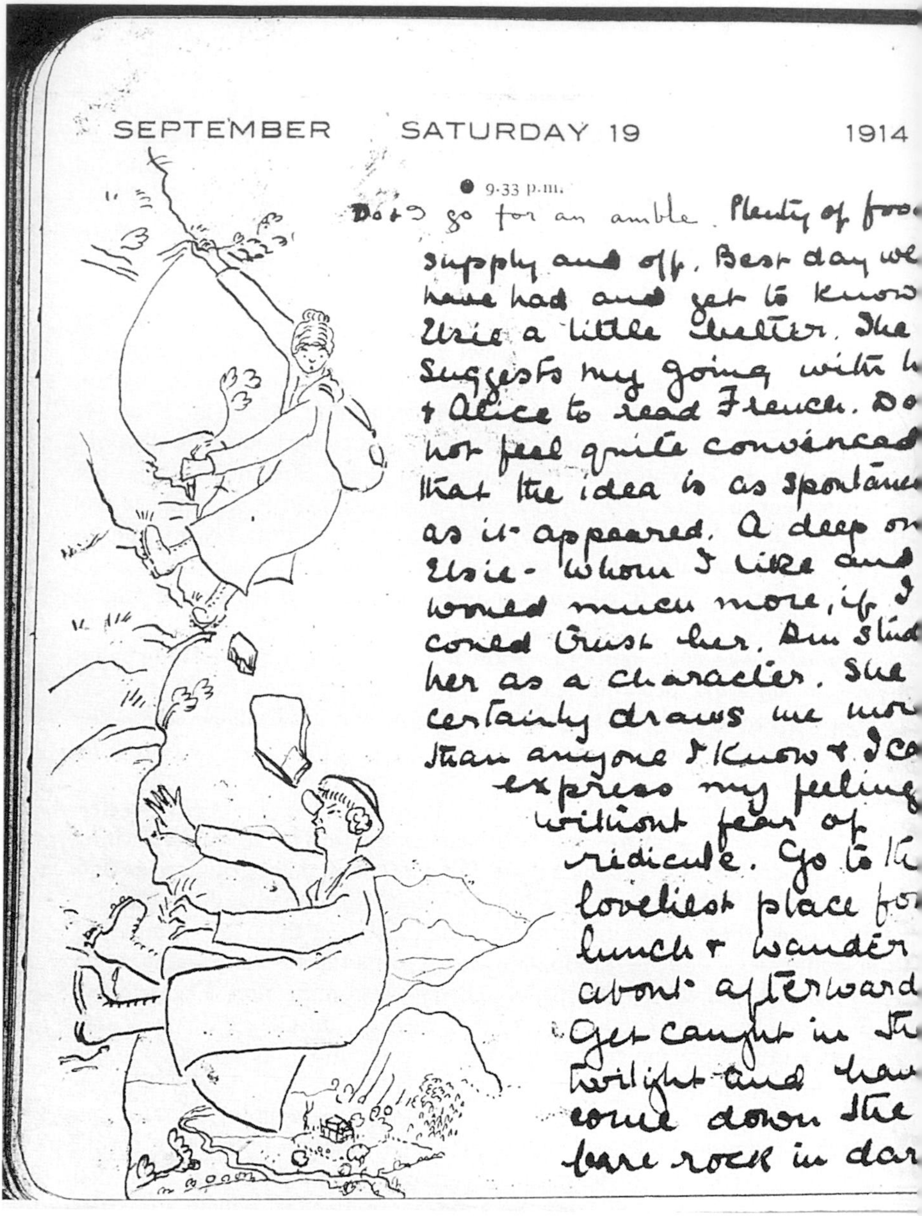

Figure 1: Dorothy Pilley's diary entry for 19 and 20 September 1914, illustrated by Elsie McNaught. (© *Estate of D E and I A Richards*)

anti-climax, contrasting the magic of the mountains of North Wales to the 'drab' existence at home. 'It's dreadful the drab colour existence has here,' she wrote about home on 27 September. For the first time, she had experienced a freedom previously unimagined.

In common with many middle-class women, Pilley spent the years of the Great War engaged in charitable work. After completing her domestic training in the winter of 1913 she took up a voluntary position with the

15th after Trinity.

D. paddled in the river & said "the water was delicious cool! Yo hear h? Ten Kiss mr intent! Good intentions however disappear with appearance of the Sun. The water was <u>deliciously</u> cool; after all, mby matter of comparison in odious thing – it might have been horribly cool but I did not choose to call it so! Elsie, in sudden burst of enthusiasm for the fresh air instead of her usual nap, dragged us over the sick wall and to a place she knew of, to spend an afternoon. Both Auntie Clara & I unbearably peevish. Elsie struggled on manfully through many very wet fields. Suddenly in a blue funk can not find 'the place'. All three toil back very bad humours. Resume good spirits after tea drinking. Walk to Dinas lake, where gloat over yesterdays achievement. Looks really formidable by daylight. Fine sun set glow on lake which looks like molten lead.

Wives of Soldiers' and Sailors' Relief Association. The work gave her, for the first time, glimpses of the desperate circumstances suffered by women forced to seek charity. In 1916 she accepted a secretarial post with the British Women's Patriotic League. 'The League', as Pilley referred to it, was a highly patriotic organisation bringing together like-minded, educated, middle-class and aristocratic women to support the interests of Great Britain through charitable endeavours.

In April 1915, Pilley completed her first real climb with a girlfriend and the mountaineer Herbert Carr. The anticipation and excitement gave her a sleepless night. In *Climbing Days,* she writes of this ascent of Tryfan, which was to become one of her favourite mountains, capturing the 'glorious' experience and concluding that '"mountain madness' had me now for ever in its grasp."

At home, however, all was not well. Her father increasingly disapproved of her mountaineering, particularly un-chaperoned with men who were not family members. It was similar Victorian etiquette that led to mountaineers such as Lucy Walker never climbing without her favoured guide, Melchior Anderegg, and her father or brother. Pilley found her father's insistence that one or other of her brothers should accompany her irksome and her increasing stubbornness and strong character frequently resulted in battles on home turf as she asserted her intention to go mountaineering. She was alone in this, abandoning initial hopes that her mother might speak up in support of her; Annie Pilley was clearly unwilling to consider the needs of her daughter in preference to her own.

After Pilley and Herbert Carr had a mountaineering accident in the summer of 1915, an incident described in *Climbing Days,* her father forbade her to climb again. 'Beddgelert shook its head,' she wrote. 'The lack of all proper perspective shown in such climbing enthusiasm was pointed out to me.' On 1 July 1915 Pilley wrote in her diary that her father 'put his foot down and says it's most indiscreet, lacks judgment and tries to extract a promise that I will never do it again.' It was a demand, as she noted in *Climbing Days,* which was in vain. Pilley continued to defy her parents, taking every opportunity to travel by rail from London to North Wales on Friday evenings in order to climb with friends at the weekend before returning to work on Monday, a dedication she shared with Janet Adam Smith, who recounts similar long journeys from her office in London to her home mountains of Scotland in her own memoirs, *Mountain Holidays.*

1916 was an important mountaineering year for Pilley, a year in which she took every opportunity to develop her skills, confidence and competence in climbing. It was also the year of her introduction to the mountaineer and Cambridge scholar Ivor Armstrong Richards, beginning a friendship and climbing partnership that eventually culminated in their marriage 10 years later.

Throughout 1916, the mountains of North Wales provided Pilley with her mountaineering apprenticeship; Snowdonia became both teacher and mentor. On 17 May 1916 she wrote in her diary that 'the days preceding a journey thither are full of wonders – what shall be learnt, what felt. One is never quite unafraid. So with Wales.' The subject matter of her reading also changed. Instead of novels, works on literary criticism, history and philosophy she was reading as much mountaineering literature she could lay her hands on. Guido Rey's *The Matterhorn,* A F Mummery's *My Climbs in the Alps and Caucasus,* Edward Whymper's *Travels amongst the Great Andes of the Equator* and W P Haskett Smith's *Climbing in the British Isles* are all listed in her 1916 diary. On 19 June 1916 she reflected that 'a mountain is

Dorothy Pilley in action on the Calyn Face, 1930s. *(Alpine Club Photo Library)*

something more than a thing to climb'; mountaineering was already, for her, symbolic of much more than simply scaling a mountain.

Increasingly, she contrasted the excitement of mountaineering with the mundane aspects of home life, turning more and more to her diary to rail against the tedium of activities other women appeared to enjoy. In a description of a shopping trip with her mother in early July 1916, referred to as 'saling', she wrote: 'shoping [*sic*] is decidedly the most tiring form of exercise. It makes your eyes ache and feet ache, it's exhausting, it's patience trying, it's confusing, it's debasing, at least when you fight with other females at a sale.'

Figure 2: 'Do in London' illustration by Elsie
McNaught. (©Estate of D E and I A Richards)

She longed to be away climbing. In late July 1916, Pilley recorded in her diary that: 'Elsie rang up to know if I would come Thursday. What a question. Everything in me cried to be away in the mountains. At home they naturally do not understand. I felt selfish, even thinking of leaving them again... Why should I not have the wonder of the mountains in that extra time? To get away from the world, alone on the heights, is a desire, which hurts, an agony of longing. I have never felt anything like the call of the mountains, it draws me, it carries me, sober me, off my feet.' Declaring in *Climbing Days* that climbing made her feel 'ardently alive', she wrote of the alienation she experienced on returning to London from the mountains, using a term that referenced schizophrenia and the growing interest in psychiatry and psychoanalysis: 'To go back to gloves and high-heeled shoes, pavements and taxicabs. Walking with an umbrella in Piccadilly one felt as though with a little more strain one would become a case of a divided personality.' In her diary, the tension of these two worlds is brilliantly captured by another of Elsie's drawings, captioned 'Do in London', which can be seen in Figure 2.

During the 1920s Pilley completed her first alpine campaigns and became a seasoned mountaineer. Her disapproving father reconciled himself to her mountaineering, his objections crumbling when Pilley's younger sister, Violet (Vi) also caught the climbing bug, as Pilley delightedly observed in her diary of 18 May, 1918: '[Cecil Frederick] Holland seems to have taken my sister on wild exploits, she seems badly bitten and she must have come on amazingly.' (C F Holland, known as Charlie, was on the first ascent of Scafell's *Central Buttress* with Siegfried Herford.) Her diaries record her deep happiness in the mountains, with this comment from 3 April 1920 being typical. 'Enjoyed being among the hills again more than I can say.'

Like mountaineers before her, Pilley learned wider social and life skills through mountaineering, testing herself, as she wrote in *Climbing Days*, 'against some external standard, when to trust myself, with caution, and when not, and to meditate on matters not merely personal. Companionship with men and women of all types, often under conditions of hardship and strain, gave useful lessons in human nature.' An American scholar of mountaineering literature, William A Geiger, agreed, writing in an essay on Pilley and IAR that 'mountaineering for Pilley functioned as a university functioned for others. She learned to trust her ability against an objective referent and scale of values, to trust others and to form important friendships.' She found in mountaineering an answer to life itself.

That Pilley eventually saw the two worlds of home and mountaineering happily reconciled in a 53-year marriage with IAR, came only after years of heart-searching to satisfy herself that marriage need not mean renouncing the freedom she had fought so hard to attain through mountaineering. Marriage was a mutually satisfying conclusion to a long campaign for her own independence, during which she had frequently taken up her pen to assert in her diary: 'I will not be dependent on a man for my travelling, for my experience.' Reflections during a solo sojourn in the Canadian Rockies in 1925, ostensibly to gather material for mountain journalism, together with IAR's persistence, together melted her final objections and they were married in Honolulu on New Year's Eve in 1926.

By the late 1920s the couple had completed many successful alpine campaigns together, which she summarises in the final two chapters of *Climbing Days*. Richards's academic work was to lead them to long residences in Cambridge (Massachusetts), Japan and China, allowing them to travel and explore less-known mountain ranges like the Southern Japanese Alps and the White Mountains of New England. Pilley's articles in the 1933 and 1948 editions of the *Ladies' Alpine Club Year Book*, respectively titled 'Japanese Mountain Impressions' and 'Snowshoeing in the White Mountains of New England' describe some of these experiences.

Pilley's contributions to developments in women's mountaineering in the early decades of the twentieth century, both in the fields of mountaineering endeavour and women's mountaineering literature are significant. Women undertaking guideless – and therefore man-less – climbing was a revolutionary undertaking at the time and in June 1921, she embarked on one of the earliest *cordées féminines* with an ascent of the Egginergrat in Switzerland with two other members of the Pinnacle Club, an experience she described with good humour in *Climbing Days*, recalling the sensation the three women caused at Zermatt train station as they sorted, repacked, then proceeded to carry their own rucksacks off the station.

As secretary of the Ladies' Alpine Club in the 1920s and then president of the Pinnacle Club in the middle and late 1930s, Pilley was instrumental in creating opportunities for women mountaineers to publish their mountaineering experiences. Desperate for a women's mountaineering journal which could hold its head up alongside the *Alpine Journal*, she hoped that a successful journal on women's mountaineering would publicise the ever-increasing achievements of women mountaineers and cement her own journalistic ambitions at the same time. Pilley thus took on the shared editorship of the fledgling *Pinnacle Club Journal* alongside Lillian Bray in the mid-1920s and became a champion of women's mountaineering literature, exhorting and bullying fellow Pinnacle Club members to write about their experiences.

Pilley's legacy to mountaineering literature and the literature of women's mountaineering is assured. In *Climbing Days*, in her wider mountaineering writings and through her diaries she shows with eloquence and energy what women could achieve in the mountains: as individuals; as members of a wider mountaineering community of women and as writers of mountaineering literature. Indomitable in old age and still active, despite an almost fatal car crash in Spain in 1958, she travelled to Skye in January 1986 with her nephew. Skye was, she recorded in her diary on 22 January, 'fiercely cold and icy, but we camped in the mountain hut at Glen Brittle where I climbed joyfully 50 years ago which made me feel like my gypsy self.'

It seems fitting to conclude with a poem, which she penned on the frontispiece of her 1937 diary, titled *Triolet of a Hedonist.*

I climb because I like it;
Individual though it be
I climb (because I like it)
Though it's usual to like it
It means a lot to me;
This climbing – for, you see,
I climb because I like it

Acknowledgements

I gratefully acknowledge the permission of Dr Richard Luckett, Emeritus Pepys Librarian of Magdalene College, University of Cambridge, to quote from Dorothy Pilley Richards's diaries and to reproduce the pages illustrated in Figures 1 and 2.

Bibliography

Geiger, William A (1982) 'Dorothea and I A Richards on Mountaineering'. *Essays on the Literature of Mountaineering* (Ed), Armand E Singer. Morgantown: West Virginia University Press, 81-93.

Pilley, Dorothy (1933) 'Japanese Mountain Impressions'. *Ladies' Alpine Club Year Book* London: Ladies' Alpine Club, 4-13.

– (1935) *Climbing Days*. London: G Bell & Sons Ltd.

– (1948) 'Snowshoeing in the White Mountains of New England'.

– *Ladies' Alpine Club Year Book* London: Ladies' Alpine Club, 13-19.

– Diaries, Magdalene College, University of Cambridge.

Smith, Janet Adam. (1946) *Mountain Holidays*. London: The Travel Book Club.

MARTIN HOOD

One Hundred Mountains of Japan

A Japanese classic in translation sheds light on how
another island people see their native mountains

Shirouma-dake – White-horse mountain. 'The name Shirouma came about
because the snow on one face of the mountain leaves a horse-shaped patch as
it melts. As the horse would appear when farmers started to plough the fields
before planting out the rice seedlings (*nawashirokaki*), the name comes from
shiro, meaning rice nursery, and *uma* for horse.' *(Martin Hood)*

To outsiders, Japan's mountains are a black hole. Until recently, it was
easier to find information, in English at least, about East Greenland or
the remoter Himalaya than the Japanese Alps. One or two hiking guides
existed, a few blogs, and that was about it. But this gap is now partially
filled by a new translation of Fukada Kyuya's *One Hundred Mountains of
Japan*, a book that sums up the mountaineering traditions of its country.

What are these mountains? Open up a hiking map to almost any backcountry area of Japan, and you'll see a select few peaks marked as 'Nihon
Hyakumeizan' – those included on the list of Japan's One Hundred
Mountains. Yet this list has no official standing. Instead it represents the
personal choice of a failed novelist and mountaineer who, half a century
ago, published a series of short magazine articles about his favourite peaks.

In 1964, these articles were gathered into a best-selling book, the *Nihon*

Hyakumeizan – or *One Hundred Mountains of Japan*. In his afterword, Fukada wrote that mountains form the very bedrock of the Japanese soul. That is a sweeping claim, yet readers seemed to endorse it; the book swiftly won a major literary prize and became a bestseller.

Within a few years, Fukada's *One Hundred Mountains* had morphed into a canon. Today, thousands of hikers flock annually to the selected peaks, making it the goal of a few seasons or a lifetime to climb them all. Even foreigners are getting in on the act; a few years ago, an English-whelped border terrier named Hana and her master claimed the first canine round of all one hundred summits.

Fukada himself would have been bemused by this enthusiasm: 'Ultimately, the Hyakumeizan are a personal choice and I make no claims for them beyond that,' he wrote, adding that 'if the book is reprinted, I may well change a mountain or two.' For good or ill, it is too late for that now. Fukada died of a brain haemorrhage on a mountain hike in 1971. Since then, his list of mountains has been enshrined in maps, a raft of spin-off books, and even a TV mini-series.

If Fukada didn't mean to create a kind of national peak-bagging circuit, what is his book really about? A clue is found in the chapter on his own native mountain, the one in whose shadow he grew up. The essay on Hakusan, a dormant 2702m volcano on the Japan Sea coast, opens like this:

> *A mountain watches over the home village of most Japanese people. Tall or short, near or far, some mountain watches over our native village like a tutelary deity. We spend our childhood in the shadow of our mountain and we carry it with us in memory when we grow up and leave the village. And however much our lives may change, the mountain will always be there, just as it always has been, to welcome us back to our home village.*

This paragraph is practically an authorial manifesto. Setting out to show what mountains mean to the Japanese people, Fukada went about his task by weaving together, and with masterly assurance, historical incidents, travelogues, literary quotations, and his own reminiscences – for a mountain could only be included in his book if he had climbed it itself.

Read a few of these essays, and you'll notice that Fukada quotes generously from one source in particular. This is *Sangaku* (*Mountain*), the Japanese Alpine Club's journal, which was launched in 1906 on the model of the original *Alpine Journal* in which you read this. *Sangaku* owed its inspiration to Walter Weston, the English missionary and proud member of the Alpine Club, who roamed far and wide through the Japanese Alps during the early 1890s.

The idea of a Japanese Alpine Club – and its concomitant journal – was

Opposite page: Mt Harinoki above a sea of clouds at dawn, North Alps, Japan.
(Peter Skov)

Tsurugi, Japan's most 'alpine' mountain, is described as a 'tiltyard of alpinism' – a bit like Ben Nevis – in Chapter 48 of *One Hundred Mountains of Japan*. *(Martin Hood)*

first floated on a Saturday afternoon in early 1903, over an afternoon tea between Walter Weston and two young Japanese mountain-lovers. This fateful conversation led in due course to the foundation not just of Japan's but Asia's first mountaineering club.

Sangaku quickly became a hothouse – in fact, for years, the only hothouse – for Japan's first generation of mountain writers. As many of these authors are quoted in *One Hundred Mountains of Japan*, one might say that the book inherited more than a few genes from the original *Alpine Journal* and its rich tradition of mountain writing.

Here and there, Fukada makes a nod towards that tradition. In his chapter on Nantai, a volcanic peak north of Tokyo, he likens the emotions of Shodo, the monk who first climbed the mountain in 781, to those of a famous Alpine Club member on his best-known Himalayan ascent. It is an inspired comparison:

Almost beside himself with joy and grief. How apposite that phrase is. How many mountaineers have experienced that strange mixture of exultation and regret when, after one failed attempt after another, they have at last stepped onto a long-sought summit. As H W Tilman wrote after his ascent of Nanda Devi in the Himalaya: 'After the first joy in victory came a feeling of sadness that the mountain had succumbed, that the proud head of the goddess was bowed.'

In deference to the European precedent, the pioneers of the Japanese Alpine Club even spoke of their own golden age. By this they meant the period of mountain exploration before the Japanese Army surveyors came out with accurate maps, in the mid-teens of the twentieth century. Alas for Japan's alpine pioneers, actual first ascents were hardly possible; all the country's peaks had been climbed centuries before by monks, pilgrims or hunters. Japan's 'golden age' was a period more of rediscovery than true exploration.

Fukada was born a generation too late to experience this era for himself. But when he joined the Japanese Alpine Club in mid-1935, as member 1586, most of the club's founders were still active. In this way, the *Hyakumeizan* author could relive Japan's golden age through the memories and journal accounts of his older colleagues. It was rather as if a present-day editor of the AJ could interview Edward Whymper in person.

It is this institutional memory of the Japanese Alpine Club that accounts for the nostalgia running like a threnody through *Nihon Hyakumeizan*:

It was Kogure himself accompanied by Fujishima Toshio who, in 1919, first forced his arduous way to the top of Sukai, a hitherto virgin peak. In those days, we still had mountains in Japan that nobody knew how to attempt, where you had to find your own way by trial and error, fighting your way through or under the greenery, and so finally winning the summit. In short, we still had mountains where you could taste the true joys of mountaineering.

Although they get their due, the elite of the Japanese Alpine Club are never allowed to crowd others off the page. For *Nihon Hyakumeizan* is the most democratic of books. Everybody is there, from the poets and novelists who wrote about the mountains, to the monks and pilgrims who first climbed them, today's hikers and hard-core alpinists, as well as farmers who timed their spring sowing by watching the telltale snow-patches

Mount Fuji: 'The phrase *hachimen-reirō*, meaning 'graceful in all its aspects', was coined with Fuji in mind. Its form keeps its beauty whether viewed from north or south, east or west. All other mountains have their quirks, from which they draw their individual charm. But Fuji is simply vast and pure.' *(Martin Hood)*

shrink, pioneer botanists who catalogued Japan's alpine plants, and rugged individualists such as the patriot who made it his life's mission to open up the northern island of Hokkaido before the Russians did.

This all-embracing sweep of characters and sources doubtless helped to broaden the book's appeal. *Nihon Hyakumeizan* has been continuously in print for fifty years, often in several different editions simultaneously. Yet none of this fully explains why the book has become a classic. If seeking to answer that question, one might usefully quote the chapter on Ontake, a sacred peak in central Japan still visited by throngs of white-robed pilgrims – and incidentally the very same volcano that erupted last autumn with a grievous loss of life. In Fukada's words:

> *The mountain's inexhaustible treasury of riches is like some endless story-book with its pages uncut. As one follows the rambling plot along, one is always looking forward to reading more. Every page yields things never found in other books. Ontake is that kind of mountain.*

Every page yields things never found in other books; one is always looking forwards to reading more. *Nihon Hyakumeizan* is that kind of book.

• *One Hundred Mountains of Japan* is published by University of Hawaii Press.

Science & Nature

The Matterhorn and Glacier from the Riffel-berg. Edward William Cooke. 18 September 1858. Ink drawing. 18.5 x 26cm. This sketch was used for the engraving in John Tyndall's *Mountaineering* in 1861. Longman Green 1862. *(National Maritime Museum, Greenwich, London (Creative Commons License))*

GEORGE CAVE

Digital Expedition Planning

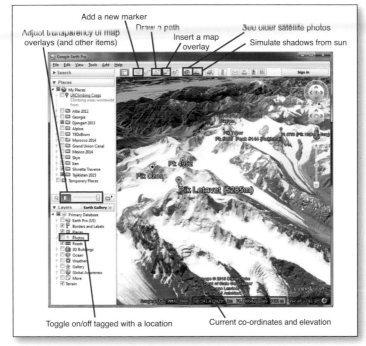

Google Earth cheat sheet (Windows version).

Fundamentally, expedition planning is all about gathering spatially-linked snippets of information from all manner of sources and piecing it together to form a plan. Google provides an incredibly simple tool to achieve this very task and this article is concerned with how best to use the software to your advantage.

Over the last 20 years the internet has served to shrink global distances and permeate the borders and boundaries of the world. Many of you will have strong opinions on the helpful or hindering role that technology can play whilst on expedition, but it is impossible to ignore the incredible wealth of information freely available online to assist with expedition planning. Thanks to an unlikely combination of Google Earth and diligent teams of Soviet cartographers, it is now possible to explore in detail virtually any corner of the world you choose. The following article is intended as an idiot's guide to kick-starting your digital global exploration and is best read with a mouse in one hand and a good drink in the other.

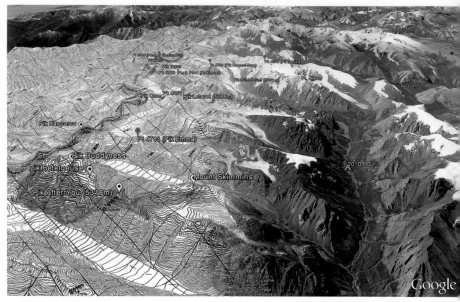

Google Earth with Soviet map overlay.

Which Google?

Google produces two of the best tools for exploring the world: Google Maps and Google Earth. Google Maps was launched in 2005 and can be found by visiting https://www.google.co.uk/maps. You can only access this location when you have an internet connection; the speed with which you can explore the world is limited largely by the capabilities of your web browser (Internet Explorer, Google Chrome, etc.). Google is continually updating the functionality of this website but as of 2015 it was possible to see satellite imagery of the entire world (click on 'Earth' in the bottom left) and pan around this in a semi-3D view (click on the 'Tilt the view' icon). Google Maps also allows you to annotate maps with markers and lines, and to collaborate on your custom maps with others. How to achieve this is beyond the scope of this article, but clicking in the search box and selecting 'My Maps' will start you off.

Google Earth is altogether a different beast. First launched in 2001, it is a separate program downloadable from http://earth.google.com. Prior to 2015 there were two versions – one free and the other a paid-for 'Pro' version but both are now free so you may as well download the best one.

Using Google Earth

It is important to remember that Google Earth combines two separate sets of data: a digital elevation model of the earth and digital satellite imagery taken over a period of many years. Typically a combination of these gives a stunningly accurate representation of the landscape, but at locations of sharp changes in relief (e.g. ridges and summits – points of particular interest to climbers) the resolution is not fine enough to show the contours accurately; a quick look at Crib Goch on Snowdon, or Pinnacle Ridge on Sgurr nan Gillean, will demonstrate this clearly.

To navigate with greatest agility in Google Earth you should acquire a mouse with a middle mouse button. You can then use the left mouse button to spin the globe and hold down the middle mouse button to rotate the view in 3D. It is easy to get lost in an obscure orientation so the 'N' keyboard button is indispensable, as it will rotate the view back to north at the top. I also encourage you to go to Tools>Options (on Google Earth>Preferences on a Mac) and on the Navigation tab select 'Do not automatically tilt while zooming'. Then dive in, start zooming around the world and have a play.

The buttons on the menu at the top allow you to add markers (the 'Add Placemark' drawing pin) and draw on routes (the constellation-looking icon 'Add Path'). Creating a new marker or line will automatically save it into 'My Places' on the left-hand side panel; there is no explicit 'Save' button. As you start marking points of interest you should create folders to save the items into, by right-clicking on 'My Places' and selecting Add>Folder. Double-clicking on an item in the list will zoom the view to that location. Of particular use is the ability to right-click on a path you have drawn and select 'Show Elevation Profile'.

The other options on the top menu are fairly self-explanatory, but two are of particular interest to climbers. The 'Show sunlight across the landscape' icon will visualise the effect of light and shade for a given date and time which can be a helpful guide at unfamiliar latitudes (bearing in mind the caveats stated earlier about the reliability of the data). The 'Show historical imagery' option will present alternative dated satellite images of a location and often give some indication of how the snow cover might vary throughout the year.

Finally, I'd always encourage you to leave the 'Photos' option in the bottom left panel ticked. This will place tiny markers onto the map with geo-tagged images from the web, primarily Panoramio. It is astonishing how after hours of scanning around apparently unvisited ranges a whole host of photographs from a trekking party will suddenly appear on the map.

Sourcing digital maps

In the UK we have some of the most accurate and reliable mapping in the world. In fact, the entire Ordnance Survey 1:25k and 1:50k are available to browse for free on both Bing Maps (http://www.bing.com/maps/) and Streetmap (http://streetmap.co.uk/). The latter website has a relatively old interface but does have the advantage of maps with the horizontal and vertical grid lines perfectly aligned.

The Soviet Union did many things for the world (good and bad), but for mountaineers it was their relentless quest to map the world for which we are most grateful. Their maps come in a variety of scales from 1:50k upwards, depending upon the location, and particularly across much of Asia they will be the most accurate source of topological data available.

Pik Currahee in Djangart, Kyrgyzstan - the missing peak.

You can buy sets of these one country at a time from Mapstor (http://www.mapstor.com/) but there is no need to do that, as huge numbers are available for free online at http://loadmap.net/. This website is arguably the single richest source of information for expedition planning anywhere online.

If you wish to make use of the maps while on expedition it can be worthwhile using a piece of GIS software such as the industry standard ArcGIS (http://www.arcgis.com/) or the free QGIS (http://www.qgis.org/) to overlay the GPS grid; however, the maps are perfectly usable without this.

Importing maps to Google Earth

The ability to annotate maps and collect points of interest makes Google Earth worth the small learning curve, but the real power comes when you are able to import other maps and overlay them. To do this, you need to have your map file (e.g. a GIF image file downloaded from loadmap.net) handy. In Google Earth, navigate to roughly where you want the map to be positioned and click on the 'Add Image Overlay' icon on the menu. Use 'Browse...' to select the map file, wait a few moments and the image will be superimposed onto Google Earth, conforming perfectly to the contours beneath. The first time this happens, it seems almost magical.

To align the map (geo-reference) you have two options. Dragging the green lines at the edge of the map will scale the image across the world and typically achieves a fairly good approximation. If you are attempting to align a hand-drawn sketch map then this is your only real option. You can drag the Transparency slider (see the 'cheat sheet' image to locate that) somewhere between Clear and Opaque to help. The other option is to precisely define the co-ordinates of each of the corners. Right-click on the image and select 'Properties' (or for Mac users, right click on the overlay in 'My Places', then 'Get Info') and then in the Location tab click the 'Convert to LatLonQuad' button. Calculating the correct co-ordinates for an arbitrary map is hard but each download from loadmap.net comes with the information you need. Download and open the .map file (the 'OziExplorer calibration' file – Notepad, TextEdit or Microsoft Word will open it) and you have the co-ordinate information near the bottom in four lines, which reads something like:

MMPLL,1,	72.501143,	38.333031
MMPLL,2,	72.749242,	38.333398
MMPLL,3,	72.748995,	38.167294
MMPLL,4,	72.501461,	38.166945

These four points correspond in turn to the upper left, upper right, lower right and lower left corner in turn. In the pop-up box the order of the points is reversed and in Google Earth the list above refers to the labels '4th corner', '3rd corner', '2nd corner' and '1st corner' respectively. You will also find that the co-ordinates refer to the exact corners of the map and do not take into account the white border in the image so a little stretching and pulling may well be required to get the features perfectly aligned.

Sharing data with others

Google Earth can import other data sets besides image overlays. The common data format used to exchange geospatial information for import/ export is the KML format and there are many sources of such files. If you own a SPOT tracker (or other GPS logging device) they will typically enable you to export the information as a KML file which can then be opened in Google Earth. The popular climbing site UKClimbing.com also provides an export of their entire crags database at http://www.ukclimbing.com/listings/ge.kml.

The biggest challenge for most users of Google Earth is sharing sets of markers with other people. Sadly, there is no efficient way to automatically collaborate on the same map and have changes update live on both individuals' files. However, it is easy to send your information to a friend. Right-click on a marker (or better, a folder of markers) and select 'Save Place As...' , which lets you save a KML file. The option of a KMZ file is also provided. This is a compressed version of the KML file, and is best to use if you wish to include any imported images or map overlays, to ensure the imported graphics are included in the file you share.

A word of warning

Over time you will come to realise that Google Earth is a very simple program, but you must remember that the data should not be taken as gospel and in some cases it can be very wrong. Where data points for the relief model are missing or are incorrectly positioned, entire mountains which are plainly visible in the satellite photography can disappear in the 3D view. One good example is Pik Currahee in the Djangart region of Kyrgyzstan (shown on page 212). Looking down the valley in Google Earth will show the glacier rising to a gentle col on the ridgeline. In reality, the col is topped with a 600m face leading to a 5000m summit. Having tried and failed to climb it in 2013, I can assure you it is very much real.

All of the links and tips discussed in this article can be accessed from the resources on this page: http://www.67hours.co.uk/mountaineering/mapping.

VICTOR SAUNDERS

A New Proposal for Reducing Acute Mountain Sickness

It has been frequently noted that super-fit marathon runners do poorly at high altitude. They suffer more than most from AMS (Acute Mountain Sickness). This is possibly caused by being strong enough to climb high faster than their body will acclimatise, in contrast to unfit climbers, who are too weak to get themselves into trouble.

Although I had noticed this anecdotally, and in statistically insignificant numbers, my occasional climbing colleague Dr Greg Attard, an emergency physician from Malta, said that he'd seen research papers attesting to this result. This observation can be expressed as follows: Athletic Prowess is proportional to the risk of AMS, or to express it formulaically:

AP ~ rAMS

Where AP is Athletic Prowess, '~' means 'proportional to' and rAMS is 'risk of developing AMS', and both terms are theoretically capable of being expressed as positive real numbers. This is Attard's Attestation.

It will be immediately obvious that this direct relationship should be avoidable by the rational expedient of climbing more slowly, but this route to avoiding AMS seems to be difficult for the aforementioned athletes. It has been claimed that highly trained runners have difficulty adjusting the strenuously learned marathon runners' pace to the more leisurely mountaineers' pace.

However, to quote Dr Attard on this: 'To slow down is not rocket science,' which in turn raises the question of intelligence (Intelligence Quotient or IQ). My good friend Mark Cremona, a water engineer also of Malta, notes that if it is not 'rocket science' to slow down, the implication is that the cohort of marathon runners attempting high mountains are blessed with unusually low IQ, the proof of which is that they took up marathon running in the first place.

This is expressed as: IQ is inversely proportional to the risk of AMS, or:

1/IQ ~ rAMS

This is Cremona's Corollary. The Attestation and its Corollary have been combined into a single expression by another colleague, Robert Gatt, an information technologist, again from Malta, into Robert's Rule, where

Altitude lassitude: testing the impact of alcohol on acclimatisation. *(Victor Saunders)*

the ratio of Athletic Prowess to IQ is equal to the risk of AMS:

$$AP/IQ = rAMS$$

We will return to Robert's Rule later, but first we need to look at the effect of alcohol on rAMS. It is usually said that alcohol has a negative effect on climbers, while increasing risk of AMS. We will show this fear to be misplaced.

It can be seen that AC (alcohol consumption) reduces both the numerator and denominator of the left hand side of Robert's Rule. Static or constant rAMS will be maintained if the rate of change of the two terms is proportional for a given quantity of alcohol. This is easily demonstrated.

When zero alcohol has been consumed the quantity of alcohol consumed is 'Q_0'. Now consider (or consume) a quantity of alcohol 'Q_{100}' such that a state of comatose inebriation is attained. At Q_0, AP is 100% of normal, as is IQ. At Q_{100}, the inability to consciously move reduces AP to 0%, while the inability to make any meaningful conversation effectively reduces IQ to 0% too. So we can more or less safely say that

$$(AP+Q_0)/(IQ+Q_0) = (AP+Q_{100})/IQ+Q_{100})$$

and in both cases rAMS will be constant.

We can reasonably assume Robert's Rule follows a linear relationship and so is not violated by AC (alcohol consumption) for any consumed quantity between Q_0 and Q_{100}.

So we can deduce that the consumption of alcohol does not increase the risk of AMS for the climber. This will come as welcome news for many of the climbing fraternity. However, I believe I have even better news for such people.

Returning to Robert's Rule AP/IQ = rAMS, it will be seen that to decrease rAMS, AP must be reduced in relation to IQ. But IQ has proved tantalisingly difficult to raise for marathon runners.

However we propose that a bounce-back effect can be used in the period before exposure to high altitude. It works like this: regular AC (alcohol consumption) reduces both AP and IQ, but if 'AC training', more usually known as 'drinking', is substituted for 'dry (sober) runs' and this is done methodically, the result should be a nicely reduced AP (athletic prowess) over time, with a more or less full recovery of IQ after the 'AC training' sessions, resulting in reduced rAMS.

This idea is expressed in the following formulae:

ACT is Alcohol Consumption Training.

ACR is Alcohol Consumption Recovery.

'->' means 'leads to' and '<' means less than.

(1) represents the initial value

(2) represents the changed – generally lower – value

AP(1)/IQ(1)+ACT -> AP(2)/IQ(2)

AP(2)/IQ(2)+ACR -> AP(2)/IQ(1)

but AP(2)/IQ(1) < AP(1)/IQ(1)

therefore

rAMS [AP(2)/IQ(1)] < rAMS [AP(1)/IQ(1)]

and now rAMS is reduced.

Our team has not yet tested out this proposed method of reducing the risk of AMS, but we believe it has great potential.

ALLAN PENTECOST

Slippery When Wet

The Role of Algae in Mountain Accidents

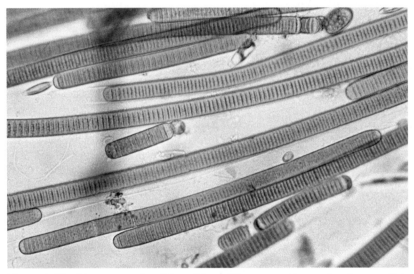

Figure 1: The blue-green alga *Phormidium*. Microscope image showing parallel filaments, magnified about 500x. This alga is common in rocky streams and is very slippery when wet. The filaments are covered in a slimy mucilage and the filaments can also roll over one another.

Hill walkers and mountaineers are particularly vulnerable to slips, a major cause of accidents outside the home. Data obtained from the UK Lake District mountain rescue teams, for example, show that over the past five years, slips of one kind or another accounted for a quarter of all call-outs, with a similar proportion in the Yorkshire Dales. The most common injury was a broken or sprained ankle. Slips are caused by two main processes: 'rolling' on small stones which, if rounded, act like marbles and provide a very unstable surface, and by shear, or the loss of friction between the ground surface and the sole of the walker's boot.

This is caused by particles sliding over one another, usually in a thin 'shear zone'. The latter can take many forms but the best-known example of this is ice, where a thin layer of water develops between the ice and sole of the boot and acts as an efficient lubricant. Flat stones behaving like a pack of cards can also cause slips. Clay or mud behaves in a similar way but here the movement involves millions of minute flake-like mineral particles sliding past each other.

Figure 2: The grey lichen is *Pertusaria corallina*, a common mountain lichen, showing where a boot has slipped on it. This has revealed the green algal layer underneath – the green layer represents a zone of weakness.

A surface layer of algae can also provide a plane of weakness especially if wet, acting like a lubricant between rock and boot, but it's not just rocks and soil that are dangerous. Last year, a small party made its way up the northern slope of Great Borne, a mass of granite towering over Ennerdale Water in the Lake District. The sound of laboured breathing was suddenly punctuated by a loud 'oof' as one of our group slipped on the grass.

Soon we were all down, and hardly able to keep to our feet, as the journey continued with increasing effort and frustration. Upon examination, the grass was found to be covered in patches of green slime, here and there developing into hand-sized gobbets with a jelly-like consistency. It turned out to be the coccoid green alga *Coccomyxa dispar*. Having frequently slipped on grass, I began to question how often algae were responsible for accidents in the hills, and indeed in our towns and cities. Consequently samples from a range of slippery surfaces on rock, stone, wood and grass were examined for their algae.

In all cases examined, similar algae were present: the filamentous blue-greens and the coccoid greens. The former consist of long chains of cells thickly invested in soft mucilage, while the latter either develop into jelly-like clumps visible to the naked eye or consist of microscopic filaments enveloped in mucilage. Algae produce mucilage as a means of retaining moisture during periods of drought and it is this that makes them slippery. The mucilage consists of a complex, highly hydrated polymer, usually a polysaccharide to which may be attached a wide range of lipids and proteins.

When the sole of a boot contacts a rock with a rough surface colonised by a thin layer of algae, local high points touch the sole first and the pressure is normally sufficiently high to force off the algae so that the sole bites onto the rock giving a good grip. But if the rock is smooth, or the algal layer thick, this cannot happen. Locally high pressures do not develop and the algae with their mucilage remain in place causing loss of friction. The polymer molecules slide easily over one another as they do not interact with one another – they are separated from each other by large numbers of water molecules, acting as a lubricant rather like engine oil.

Blue-green algae belonging to the genus *Phormidium* have their long fila-

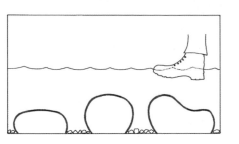

Figure 3: The red colour represents areas of a stream bed covered with cobbles colonised by algae and lichens where a slip will occur if trodden upon.

ments arranged parallel to one another, and aligned with the flow of water. They are particularly treacherous as this arrangement allows them to slip past each other even more easily. They can often be seen as black leathery patches on stones in all kinds of streams and rivers.

Exactly how slippery these surfaces are can be determined experimentally by measuring coefficients of static and dynamic (sliding) friction. The former is the ratio of the force necessary to start the movement of a body on a surface to its weight. The latter is the ratio once the body starts to slide and is generally a little lower than the former. Experiments using Vibram-soled boots on a smooth, algae-covered paving slab give ratios of around 0.2. Because the coefficients tend to be independent of the area of surface in contact with the ground, some simple mechanics allows safety zones to be plotted for non-horizontal surfaces.

How dangerous it is to walk on rounded cobbles submerged in a stream can be judged from Figure 3. Clearly it is very easy to misjudge where to tread and emphasises the danger of crossing rocky rivers. Rocky lake edges are also hazardous although most accidents occur in flowing waters. On the seashore seaweed-covered rocks are dangerous to walk upon for the same reason.

On a recent geology field trip one of our party decided to cross a small innocuous-looking stream no more than a metre wide. Instead of jumping across he placed his foot on an angled outcrop in the middle of the water then slipped sideways and broke his leg in two places. In this case, examination showed that a bloom of diatoms was responsible. These microscopic algae are common in streams and have a silica cell wall covered in a thin layer of mucilage. Accidents such as this must be commonplace

Crags of the Rwenzori
Mountains, Uganda at
c4000m where the rocks often
remain slippery from algae.

but for the most part they
remain unrecorded. With
increasing interest in mountaineering and in the new
sport of canyoning, such
incidents are likely to rise.

Free-living algae tend to
be less common on rocks
that are not wetted for long
periods as most of them
require more or less permanent moisture to survive.
Many lichens however, are
adapted to withstand long
periods of drought and they
are common on all kinds of
exposed surfaces. Lichens
consist of a fungus in close
association with one or more
algae. The algae are mainly
blue-greens or coccoid greens so it should come as no surprise that they
too can cause problems. The crustose lichens in particular make climbing
hazardous in wet weather. They adhere strongly to rock and when dry,
they are reasonably safe to stand upon. However, once they are wetted
by a rain shower, they expand and soften, and the situation becomes very
different. Most lichens are built up of layers rather like a sandwich. The
often brightly covered surface is formed of microscopic fungal cells under-
lain by a layer rich in algae. Beneath this are further layers of fungus. The
algal layer provides a zone of weakness – here there is little fungal material
to supply mechanical strength and it readily shears. The spherical algal
cells are also able to roll over each other. If you are unfortunate enough to
slip on a lichen-covered surface you can often see how the green layer of
algae becomes exposed where your boot has contacted it.

Slips involving lichens can happen at any time of year. Crustose lichens
are perennial, often living for many years, but the free-living algae are
frequently seasonal. In streams, algal growth is often most rapid in spring
when levels of sunlight and dissolved nutrients are high. During summer
and autumn while light levels may remain high, demands for nutrients by
other plants may compete with algae, reducing growth, and in wooded

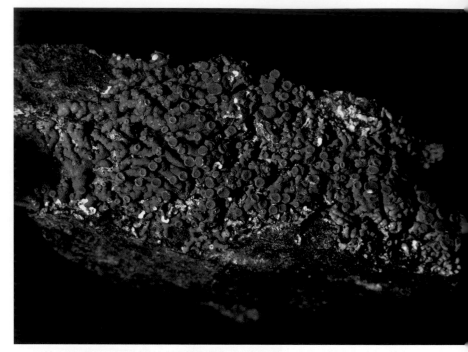

Xanthoria elegans is an orange leafy lichen that grows at high altitudes throughout the world. The yellow colour protects the lichen from damaging UV rays.

streams, light is also reduced by shading. Intense sunlight may in fact be detrimental to algae. A few days of bright sunshine during the spring of 2012 killed most of the algae growing around the shore of Stickle Tarn in Cumbria and the rocks were no longer difficult to walk upon. However it is best to assume that permanently wet rocks are always hazardous.

In the high mountains of the Alps algae and lichens become less troublesome at altitudes exceeding about 3200m. These organisms require a moderate supply of liquid water and in the high mountains this is in short supply. Ultraviolet radiation is also more intense and can damage cells. As a result these plants can be hard to find. It is possible to find small growths of lichen above this altitude and these tend to be on steep, south-facing aspects where snow does not accumulate and solar heating allows liquid water to exist on the surface for short periods. Many of the lichens at this height are often brightly coloured or appear almost black. These are adaptations to screen the delicate algal cells from intense ultraviolet radiation. Generally speaking, the risk of a 'bio-slip' is greater below the snowline. In the East African mountains the rocks are often covered with lichens at altitudes of 4000m or more owing to the elevated snow-line at this low latitude so caution is required at all times.

Old flagstones made of fine-grained sandstones often have a smooth surface. A special group of 'endolithic' algae favour such rocks with their complex microscopic cavities and water-retaining ability. These small algae are able to deeply penetrate minute cavities within the stone where they are protected from strong sunlight and grazing. Once colonisation is complete, the channels, which helped to conduct surface water through the stone, become blocked and these algae begin to grow as a surface film. Extremely dangerous surfaces often result, particularly along shady paths that are little used, even in big cities like London. Again blue-green and coccoid green algae often predominate.

The danger does not stop here. Neglected roads are often colonised by algae and lichens. Once the toxic tarmac surface has been weathered and rendered innocuous, growth begins. Permanent wet patches on roads often occur where there are seepages beneath and a wide range of algae can grow there. These surfaces can be hazardous to cars, pedestrians and particularly to cyclists. If swimming baths are not properly maintained, their surfaces also become extremely slippery from algae, not to mention roofing slates and tiles. The Wimbledon tennis championships of 2012 saw players slipping on the grass and one wonders whether algae played a part there too.

Returning to the countryside, wooden slats or steps are rapidly colonised once any preservative has leached out. Stiles appear to be a particular hazard; mountain rescue teams report several serious slipping accidents each year in Britain. Their flat surfaces reduce water run-off, retaining moisture for long periods, particularly in shady spots. Algae are able to colonise readily as the wood fibres provide a moisture-retaining surface and good adhesion for the cells. Wooden boardwalks can feel as slippery as ice when colonised by green coccoid algae such as the desmid *Mesotaenium*.

We are surrounded by hazardous surfaces for which algae appear to be largely responsible but there are no hard data to determine just how dangerous they are. Slips can certainly occur in their absence, but with warmer and wetter weather predicted for the future, things can only get worse. In fact, mountain algae are probably responsible for more serious accidents than algae responsible for well-publicised shellfish poisoning incidents and toxic water blooms.

Art & Photography

The Matterhorn from the Riffelberg. Drawn by Elijah Walton, lithography by J H Lowes. 1867. Chromolithograph. 35.5 x 25cm. From . Walton & T G Bonney. *Peaks and Valleys of the Alps*. Day & Son, 1867.

PETER BLAIR

Stereo Views

Victorian 3D Photography of The Alps

A rare portrait of William England taken in 1862.

Several years ago, browsing in a junk shop, I came across an intriguing double photograph of the Alps with the title 'Under the Special Patronage of the Alpine Club, Views of Switzerland, Photographed by W England'. As an associate member of the Club, its mention piqued my curiosity. What was this strange double view? Who was W England? What was his special relationship with the Alpine Club?

You may have seen the blockbuster *Avatar* and consider 3D to be a

227

'La Mer de Glace, Montanvert, Chamounix, Savoie' by William England (1863)

modern innovation, but it is much older; 150 years ago virtually every middle-class home had a stereoscope with which to view photographs in 3D. The double view above is a typical example of such an image, known as a 'stereoview'. In the 1860s, these 3D images were the best-selling format of photograph and were popular tourist souvenirs. The stereoscope was the television of its age and provided armchair travel, news and family entertainment – and even erotica.

The scientist and inventor Charles Wheatstone first described the concept of stereoscopic vision in 1832 and he patented a stereoscope based on mirrors in 1838. Initially only simple line drawings of shapes like pyramids or cubes could be reproduced with sufficient accuracy, but the arrival of photography in 1839 opened up huge new potential for the idea. David Brewster used lenses to simplify the design and exhibited his compact stereoscope along with 3D photographs at the Great Exhibition of 1851. Legend relates that Queen Victoria was most definitely amused by the device and a fashion trend was set in motion.

The concept is fairly straightforward. Our two eyes see a slightly different view of the world, which our brain combines into 3D reality. We can reproduce this effect from two-dimensional images by using a camera with two lenses set apart a similar distance to our eyes. The two pictures produced are then recombined using a stereoscope, so that only the left eye sees the left view and the right eye sees the right view. Modern 3D films use an essentially identical approach to obtain the images, but the left and right views are orthogonally polarised, superimposed and then viewed in 3D using suitably polarised glasses in the cinema.

By the 1860s, the London Stereoscopic Company (LSC), on the back of the popularity of 3D views, had become the world's largest photographic enterprise and its principal photographer was William England (1830–1896). England joined the LSC in 1854, the year of its foundation, and became pre-eminent among its in-house photographers.

He visited North America in 1859 and 1860, bringing back a stunning series of views of the east of the United States and Canada. It is claimed that his view of the French acrobat Charles Blondin crossing Niagara Falls on a tightrope sold over 100,000 copies, making it probably the best-selling stereoview of all time. He also made a series of views of Ireland in 1858, Paris in 1860 and was the official photographer for the International Exhibition of 1862 in London.

The LSC did not acknowledge the photographer of its published views. Perhaps William England did not feel he was getting the recognition, or indeed recompense, he deserved for his leading role at the company. In 1862 he invented the focal plane shutter, which allowed greatly increased control over exposure times and consequently an improvement in image quality. Perhaps he felt he could capitalise on his invention because in 1863 he left LSC to form his own photographic enterprise.

His first independent commission was to photograph the Alps on behalf of the Alpine Club. In the summer of 1863 his travels took him to some of the most famous tourist spots: Geneva, Lausanne, Chillon Castle, Sallanches, Chamonix, Gorges du Trient, Martigny, Sion, Zermatt, Interlaken, Grindlewald, Lauterbrunnen, Reichenbach, Rosenlaui, Thun, Berne and Fribourg. The fruits of his labours were published as a series of 130 stereoviews entitled *Views of Switzerland – Under the Special Patronage of the Alpine Club*. Subsequent trips expanded the number of views of the Alps to over one thousand.

Long before the impact of global warming was felt, his stereoviews provide a remarkable photographic record of the Alps at the end of the Little Ice Age with dramatic glaciers reaching valley floors. His images demonstrate a genius for composition and an eye for the picturesque, with people placed in the foreground, usually including his French wife Rosalie, to provide interest and a sense of depth and scale.

In 1863, such a tour of over 500 miles, carrying many kilos of cumbersome and fragile photographic equipment and dangerous chemicals, was a major logistical challenge. Although a new railway had been inaugurated in 1861 linking Geneva, Lausanne and the Rhône valley, the rest of the journey would have been by stagecoach, charabanc, mule or on foot. Roads were poor; for example the coach road to Chamonix wasn't constructed until 1866 and the journey from Geneva still took ten hours. The chemistry of photography remained highly complex; England used the wet collodion process. Each fragile glass negative had to be prepared, coated and sensitised *in situ*. The photograph had to be taken when the plate was still wet and then immediately transferred to a portable darkroom and developed, fixed and washed.

The Alpine Club possesses a small album of photographs by William England from his first tour of Switzerland in 1863. It measures about six inches by eight inches and is bound in red leather. On the front it states: 'By permission, dedicated to the President and members of the Alpine Club. Views of Switzerland and Savoy, photographed by W England.' It contains

A stereoscopic view of the Matterhorn by William England.

24 larger format views (about five inches by four inches) mainly in land-scape format, and 126 smaller format (three inches square) photographs, which are singleton images from a stereoview.

Was this album the commission that allowed him to claim on his stereoviews that they were 'under the special patronage of the Alpine Club'? The minutes of the Alpine Club's committee meeting for 1 March 1864 suggest otherwise:

> *It was brought to the notice of the Committee that Mr England, a Photographer who had received from the Committee, at the suggestion of Mr Longman, permission to dedicate to the Alpine Club a Volume of Photographs, was now superscribing and advertising his Photographs with the notice 'under the special patronage of the Alpine Club'. Mr Longman undertook to make inquiries on the subject before the next meeting.*

Little more than a month later, at the committee meeting of 5 April 1864, Longman had an answer for them:

> *The secretary read some explanations from Mr England the photographer, which had been obtained through Mr Longman. The committee directed the secretary to write to Mr England requesting an undertaking from him not to use the name of the Club in the manner lately complained of.*

Naughty Mr England. The 1850s and 1860s were the golden age of alpinism and the British were at the forefront of the assault on the yet-unconquered peaks. The Alpine Club had an exclusive and exciting profile and England's implied association with them was a canny marketing ploy. He was forced to change the title of his Swiss views to read: 'By permission, dedicated to the Alpine Club.' He later dropped all mention of the Club in his titles. It seems therefore that England's association with the Club was in reality a personal arrangement with William Longman, the publisher. Only three years previously it was Longman who had engaged a young engraver to make his first trip to the Alps. His name was Edward Whymper. His new association with England tells us much about the coming of age of photography. I believe that Longman had the foresight to realise, decades before the printing technology was perfected, that in future it would be the photograph that would enliven the printed page, rather than the sketches and engravings of previous generations.

A contemporary review of England's photographs, contrasting them with the work of prolific Alsace-based stereophotographer, Adolph Braun, appeared in the *Alpine Journal* of 1865-66: '...indeed, Mr. England's work might fairly be judged the best of all; for his pictures excel Braun's both in perfection of workmanship and in artistic grouping.'

Praising the utility of the topographical information in Braun's views taken at altitude, the Journal suggested how England's photos could be of more use to the alpinist for route planning:

We can only express a hope that Mr England will include in his next tour visits to a few scenes which the hoof of the tourist's mule cannot reach. He will find views equally picturesque with those he has already published, and the great mechanical skill displayed by him will be a guarantee for his reproducing accurately the forms and proportions of the mountain scenery.

William England paid no attention to the Alpine Club's exhortations and never ventured far from the tourist's mule track on his at least six tours of the Alps. He left that niche to others, like the Chamonix guide and photographer Joseph Tairraz and the renowned Auguste-Rosalie Bisson, who in 1861 climbed audaciously to the summit of Mont Blanc, with his cameras, glass plates, flasks of wet chemicals and portable darkroom. It is estimated that the 25 guides and porters carried 250kg of photographic materials. It was only the seventy-seventh expedition to reach the summit. On the ascent all the chemicals and solutions froze solid and as no prints from the summit have ever been identified it seems unfortunately that a satisfactory photograph was not obtained.

Bisson was a great photographer, but a lousy businessman and by 1863 he was bankrupt. William England, on the other hand, was a consummate businessman; not for him the costs of dozens of guides or the expense of a posh Paris salon like Bisson's. He understood the market for his photographs. Mass tourism was on the increase, with the growth of the middle class and the advent of cheap and convenient rail travel. Thomas Cook led his first package tour of Switzerland in 1863, following a similar route to England – perhaps they even crossed paths.

Tourists wanted an affordable souvenir of their travels, a memento of where they had been and what they had seen, all in a realistic three-dimensional image. Armchair travellers wanted an attractive view that transported them into the heart of the sublime Alpine scenery. England built up

430 GROUPE DE MOISSONNEURS DANS LA TARENTAISE.

A group of farmworkers, by William England.

a wide network of outlets for his views, such as souvenir shops, stations and mountain huts. It was his business acumen, in addition to his photographic skill, which allowed *Photographic News* to report in 1880 that England was 'probably the largest continental publisher of European views'.

The commercial success of stereoscopy was a prime driver in the development of photography. The small format of stereoviews allowed the use of compact cameras and necessitated shorter exposure times. This led to developments in shutter technology allowing 'instantaneous' views and the first documentary photographs of everyday life. Even the most banal images provide a powerful insight into lost professions and contemporary fashion. Several of William England's most fascinating photographs from his Swiss tours are of this genre.

Although still hampered, until the 1880s, by the wet chemistry required, stereoscopy revolutionised Alpine photography and allowed realistic action shots to be taken at altitude. While Bisson, taking large format photographs, needed 25 porters for his gear, Joseph Tairraz, the Chamonix guide and photographer, could carry all his stereo-photography equipment by himself. Where Bisson seems to have failed to take a satisfactory view from the summit of Mont Blanc, Tairraz succeeded in taking several stereoviews that same summer of 1861.

I find it intriguing that despite being one of the most commercially successful photographers of the mid-nineteenth century, with a lionised artistic talent, William England should have been relegated to a footnote in the history of photography, being virtually unknown today. Even Edward

Whymper, himself a skilled photographer, chose to use at least two of England's views in his famous lantern-slide presentation. Fashions change. In the 1880s, with the simplification of the photographic process and the rise of the amateur photographer, commercial stereoscopy fell out of favour. A new period of rising popularity around 1900 continued into the 1930s, by which time colour film and moving images had created alternative versions of reality.

Raised on the cheap and cheerful 3D images provided by Viewmaster discs, today's photographic historians have possibly viewed the stereoscope as a toy and a gimmick, downplaying its importance in the development of photography and ignoring its prominent photographers. That is sad and misguided. It is more complex to take an artistically satisfactory 3D image than a standard photograph; the skill of the pioneer stereo-photographers should be celebrated.

Early alpine photographs are prominent in the celebrations taking place in Chamonix in the summer of 2015, to commemorate the remarkable summer of 1865, 150 years on from the apogee of the golden age. The stereoviews of William England feature in a 3D exhibition reviewing alpine tourism 150 years ago in the Maison du Village, Argentière from mid May until mid October 2015. They also appear in my book *Chamonix Mont Blanc in 3D*, reviewed in this edition of the Alpine Journal. My website, www. wordpress.3dalps.com contains further examples and information on alpine stereoscopy – and on buying the book.

Bibliography

Alpine Club Committee Meeting Minutes (1864)
Alpine Journal, (Vol II 1865-66, p48) 'Alpine Photographs'
Berg, Peter (2011) *Whymper's Scrambles with a Camera* (Alpine Club, 2011)
Blair, Peter (2014) *William England's Views of Switzerland – a Collector's Catalogue* (www.lulu.com)
– *Chamonix Mont Blanc in 3D*, (Éditions du Belvédère, 2014)
de Hecker Heftler, Sylvaine *Photographier le Mont Blanc* (Guérin, 2001)
Jeffrey, Ian, *An American Journey: The photography of William England* (Prestel, 1999)

SIMON PIERSE

Alfred Williams of Salisbury

Alfred Williams (right) outside his painting hut. Possibly Skye or the Lake District. Sepia toned silver gelatin print mounted on card with photographer's details: 'G P Abraham FRPS, Photo. Keswick.'

One of the main problems in researching the work of Alfred J Williams (1832-1905) is the confusion with another artist of the same name, who died in the same year. Indeed, the 'other' Williams, Alfred Walter Williams (1824-1905) is, arguably, the better known of the two artists and it is his work that more commonly appears on the art market.[1] This has led to a number of instances of miscataloguing at auction, which adds to the confusion. For this reason, the Alpine watercolourist Alfred Williams is often referred to as Alfred Williams of Salisbury, an epithet he himself used on occasion, as when, for example, he signed his name in the visitors' book at Sligachan Hotel in Skye.[2] When Williams was elected a member of the Alpine Club it was for his climbing achievements, and a year or two later he became a founding member of the Swiss Alpine Club and a member of the Scottish Mountaineering Club. But Williams was also a watercolourist of great skill who showed his work alongside Royal Academicians and members of the Royal Watercolour Society at the Alpine Club[3] and was honoured with a memorial exhibition there in 1905.[4]

For most of his life Alfred Williams was not a painter by profession but neither was he an amateur in the way we would use this term today. He had the distinction of showing four paintings at the Royal Academy between 1880 and 1895[5] as well as exhibiting with the Society of British Artists. He included professional artists among his friends, notably Colin Bent Phillip, a member of the Royal Watercolour Society who wrote Williams' obituary, published in the *Alpine Journal*, in which he praised Alfred's artistic ability.[6]

Alfred Williams was born in Newark-on-Trent on 4 May 1832. He was the youngest of three sons born to Congregational minister Reverend Charles Williams (1796-1866) and his wife Mary Smeeton (1791-1871). Alfred grew up in a respectable, scholarly household and was educated first privately and later at University College School in Gower Street, London. We do not know the name of the private academy where he learnt the rudiments of drawing, but he subsequently studied landscape painting under the watercolour artist William Bennett (1811-1871) who lived in Clapham Park, London.

In 1849, as a young man of seventeen, Williams's artistic talent was undeveloped and he honed his skills making drawings of agricultural machinery and livestock, watercolour studies of trees and hedgerow plants. It may have been Bennett who steered the young Williams along the path towards illustration, a career that he pursued until 1856 with commissions from his own family. He illustrated publications of the *Religious Tract Society* (his father was editor of this journal) and provided some of the illustrations to his elder brother Frederick's *Our Iron Roads* (1852).[7] At the same time he continued to develop his skills in watercolour with extended excursions into the countryside lasting several weeks.

In June and July 1852 he went to the Lake District and painted Windermere, Keswick, Bassenthwaite and Derwentwater. In June to August the following year he embarked on a sketching tour of North Wales, visiting Bala, Dolgellau, Beddgelert and Conwy. He worked diligently, dating each sketch and adding notes of his impressions of each scene and how it might be recorded for future reference. Sketching figures on market day at Dolgellau on June 25 1853, Williams noted the type of hats and colour of scarves worn by the local women, and later the same day he stopped to paint a sketch near Llanelltyd: 'an evening effect on a dark cloudy evening after a very wet day.'

The Matterhorn from Zermatt, pencil and watercolour. Inscribed 24 June 1865 on reverse – just three weeks before Edward Whymper's first ascent.

A characteristically rigorous and analytical approach to art was already beginning to develop, even though this ran counter to popular taste. Williams once remarked how different the mountains of the Lake District looked in real life to their portrayal in the fashionable watercolour of the period, suggesting that he would never be a slave to artistic fashion.

In 1854 Williams made an extended walking tour to central and northern Italy and Switzerland. In 1861 he settled in Salisbury where he went into partnership with his brother Charles in a malting business that became known as Williams Brothers Maltings.[8] In the summer months he continued to climb and sketch in the Alps. The earliest dated sketches of Alpine subjects that have so far come to light are 1862 and show a style still as yet unformed where colour is subordinate to strong underlying drawing.

In 1863 Williams married Sarah Gregory, but there were no children. It is probably Sarah who is pictured in a series of photographs taken on holiday with Alfred in Switzerland.[9] The same year Williams became a member of the Swiss Alpine Club, newly founded by its first president Melchior Ulrich (1802-1893), Gottlieb Samuel Studer (1804-1890) and Rudolf Theodor Simler (1833-1873) at an inaugural meeting held in the railway restaurant at Olten.[10] Williams married again in 1866 and with Eliza (née Walker, known as Lillie) he had a daughter and son.

Alfred Williams was one of the pioneers in opening up Zermatt as a holiday resort for the British, staying at the Grand Hotel Gornergrat, Riffel-haus or Monte Rosa Hotel. He climbed with local Swiss mountain guides and became friendly with their families. His favourite guide was Anton Ritz, known as 'Riffelhaus Toni'. In 1865 he was at the Monte Rosa Hotel to paint the Matterhorn and was able to witness the first ascent on 14 July.

Study of Loch Coruisk from the Shoulder, pencil and watercolour, 1888.
Signed on reverse in ink with date and title, 638mm x 958mm.

In 1886, a member of the Alpine Club since 1878, he was able to retire from the malting business and devote his time to climbing and painting. That same year he made what was probably the first of four visits to Skye, staying at the Sligachan Hotel and painting in the landscape on extended fieldtrips. Williams would set up camp to work *en plein air* in relative comfort for periods of a week or more. Visitors relate how even in these remote locations he was able to entertain in some style. The unframed *Study of Loch Coruisk from the Shoulder* (1888) bears all the signs of having been completed entirely on the spot; indeed the location on the north-east side, looking towards the head of the loch, is still identifiable to this day. Other paintings, such as *In Harta Corrie* (perhaps exhibited RA 1888), were most likely studio works intended for exhibition.[11] In 1889 he held an exhibition of his paintings at the Alpine Club.

Williams was unusual in painting on a large scale and, in his later work, there is often the suppression of foreground detail or even of the foreground itself, an element in his style that makes the paintings appear strikingly modern to the contemporary viewer. Whether this was due to Williams' inability to compose to conventional picturesque effect, or whether painting mountains from an advantageous vantage point necessitated climbing up from the valley floor to observe them across a gulf of intervening empty space, is a moot point. In two mid-career paintings of Mont Blanc (both unsigned and undated), it appears that Williams experimented for a time in adding picturesque invented foregrounds to a backdrop of mountain landscape. The shapes of the mountains themselves are near identical in both paintings and might have been traced from a single drawing or even perhaps from a photograph or projected lanternslide. Close inspection of

Mont Blanc de Courmayeur, pencil and watercolour. Perhaps c1879, 690mm x 998mm.

the under-drawing reveals a faint but confidently delineated pencil line that was used as a guide in building up layers of watercolour. The valley floor, by contrast, with its Alpine huts, bridge and stream, are painted in a style at once heavier and sketchier, as if from a sketchbook study or from memory. Moreover, the view of Mont Blanc does not correspond with what is visible from the valley floor near Courmayeur but indicates a much higher vantage point from somewhere on the south-east side of the valley.[12]

The use of photography as an artistic tool was already prevalent in the mid-Victorian period and had been pioneered by John Ruskin (1819-1900) in his own studies of mountain geology. Through his assistant Frederick Crawley, Ruskin had made daguerreotypes of the *Mer de Glace* and *Aiguilles of Chamonix* in 1854 and he encouraged others to make use of his photographs in their work, although remaining skeptical about whether photography had any intrinsic merit.[13] Two photographs taken of Williams outside his makeshift painting huts, one near the Hörnli, the other possibly in Skye or the Lake District, confirms the availability of a camera during these painting expeditions, which might have been used to photograph mountain subjects. But such a hypothesis seems firmly contradicted by the evidence of Colin Bent Phillip who, in Williams's obituary, wrote in some detail about his strenuous *plein air* working methods, describing them as 'a keynote to his character':

He… started soon after daylight, and walked a number of miles, making

Monte Rosa from the Monte Moro, pencil and watercolour heightened with white bodycolour or gouache, with touches of blue and white pastel. No visible date or signature, 717mm x 1054mm.

at the same time a half imperial drawing, rested in the middle of the day, and repeated the performance in the evening; and this day after day.[14]

Undoubtedly, some of Williams's finest watercolours were made in the Alps, painting on the spot and sheltering overnight in the wooden huts he erected on remote and exposed mountainsides in Monte Moro, Pierre à Béranger and south-east of the Italian Val Ferret. This practice aligns Alfred Williams with some of the younger pre-Raphaelite artists working under the influence of John Ruskin such as John William Inchbold (1830-1888) and John Brett (1831-1902). Indeed John Brett was a near contemporary of Alfred Williams and, in his pursuit of 'truth to nature' Brett had gone to the Italian Alps to paint under Ruskin's direction in 1856. But whilst his Alpine subjects (Wetterhorn, Eiger, Glacier of Rosenlaui) are similar to Williams's, Brett's technique is utterly different and his paintings are filled with meticulous foreground detail.[15] Nevertheless, Williams's *Monte Rosa from the Monte Moro*, which depicts the majestic east face of Monte Rosa soaring above the Belvedere Glacier, seen from a rocky vantage point on the Monte Moro pass, does suggest an attempt to represent landscape in terms of the glacial forces that have shaped it. Williams also painted a number of watercolours of glaciers at close range, in which their principal feature is usually the electric blue colour revealed in the icy depths of caves and crevasses. *Blue Ice, Ice Cave* and *A Broken Bridge, Furggen Glacier* are notable examples.

Whatever means Alfred Williams employed to make his paintings, there is no doubt that he struggled both with figures and with foreground detail. In

A Broken Bridge, Furggen Glacier, pencil and watercolour.
Signed and dated July 1895. Dimensions unknown.

a number of paintings that have the appearance of being completed entirely on location, the treatment of foreground rocks and vegetation is noticeably coarser and less confident. From the 1880s onwards, Williams increasingly eliminated the foreground entirely from his compositions to concentrate on the mountains that were his main focus of attention. Some contemporary critics, whilst admiring his careful drawing of mountain form, detail and sense of space, identified 'atmospheric effect' as Williams's Achilles heel and criticized his inability to make 'more picturesque use of his material' by introducing 'more incident and arrangement in his foregrounds'.[16]

November morning at Darjeeling, showing, Jannu, Kabru, Kangchenjanga & Pandim. Pencil, watercolour and bodycolour. Signed on label on reverse of frame, 1900, 762 x 1016mm.

Perhaps the most remarkable achievement of Alfred William's artistic career was the journey he made in 1900 at around seventy years of age to the Sikkim and Kumaon Himalaya. It was an arduous journey for an old man to undertake and although staying at the hill stations of Darjeeling, Mussoorie, Almora and Binsar no doubt offered congenial company and a modicum of comfort, it also meant that the Himalayan peaks invariably remained distant and ethereal objects on the horizon. This made them very difficult to realise in paint but Williams doubled his difficulties by insisting on working *plein air* on large sheets of watercolour paper. He was completely at the mercy of capricious and notoriously changeable weather conditions, and often had to sit for days at a time, 'watching the mists, and hoping against hope that they would clear, in order that he might work.' The snows occasionally 'appeared for a few minutes at a time', wrote Phillip, who considered it 'a marvel that he should have accomplished anything, let alone the drawings he did do.'[17]

Williams's journey eastwards across the Indian Himalaya lasted about a year throughout the early summer, monsoon and autumn months. In November 1900 he was in Darjeeling. Some of the large watercolour paintings he painted in India were a highlight of the Himalayan Exhibition held at the Alpine Club in 1902.[18] They are all quite similar in size (c75cm x 110cm) and were originally gilt-framed behind glass. *November morning at Darjeeling, showing, Jannu, Kabru, Kangchenjanga & Pandim* was painted in

the clear light of mid-morning after the mountain forms had been drawn
out in some considerable detail. Pencil marks are visible on the surface
of the paper where they were painted around in Chinese white or body
colour, creating the forms of the mountains and allowing the surface of the
paper, which has since yellowed somewhat, to show through. A work of
uncertain title, but possibly *The Mists of Early Summer at Binsar*, is a most
subtle painting – an infinitely soft and somewhat indistinct panorama of
the Himalaya near Almora, in which the vast intervening space is treated
as waves of colour, enabling the eyes (as one critic of the time noted) 'to do
what the eyes of the traveller do – fasten at once on the centre and object of
his design, the mystic mountain range.'[19]

When they were first exhibited, the Himalayan paintings were described
as 'all admirably faithful and effective reproductions of the marvellous
landscape that is from time to time revealed to the dwellers on the heights
of Darjeeling – a town in a situation comparable to the top of Monte
Generoso.'[20] The reviewer of the exhibition conceded that 'the ordinary

The Mists of Early Summer at Binsar (?); pencil and watercolour. No visible signature or date but probably 1900, 747mm x 1102mm. Back of frame is inscribed 'Moonrise and Afterglow at the Schwarzsee' suggesting that the frame was reused at some point.

conventional treatment of land-scape is ill adapted to the huge spaces the Himalayas display when seen from a distance', yet, while noting how the sense of space and grandeur 'in the portrayal of a snowy range' was generally admired, he concluded that 'to do full justice to the effects of the Himalaya would require a greater than Turner.' [21] The veiled criticism implied in the last remark over-looks the fact that Alfred Williams was more interested in faithfully depicting the shape of particular mountains in space than he was in 'picture making'. Experience had taught him not to exaggerate or falsify for pictorial effect; he was simply at his best with a kind of sublime topography.

Following the death of his wife in 1892, Alfred Williams devoted his time to painting and travel. Some of the last works he completed were painted at Saas-Fee and Lake Maggiore. He died on 19 March 1905 at the Grand Hotel, St Maxime-sur-Mer, Var, and was buried in the south of France. His achievements were celebrated at the end of that year with a memorial exhibition at the Alpine Club (5-23 December 1905). The reviewer in the *Alpine Journal* concluded that Williams was an artist of conviction who had made the necessary sacrifice of one pictorial quality for another. He was both a 'delineator' and an 'interpreter' of the mountain landscape – 'a delineator in so far as he faithfully used the forms and local conditions of his model, an interpreter in that he strove to convey his own strong convictions, even at the cost of some marked characteristic of his subject. [22]

'He was so impressed by the majestic size of the Alps and other great mountains, and their atmospheric quality, that he sacrificed the extreme brilliance of the sunlit snow against the deep blue of the sky; indeed it is doubtful whether it is possible to convey in art, at one and the same time, the size and the light of an Alpine peak under the effect of brilliant sunshine.'[23]

In his obituary, Williams's appreciation of the beauty of mountain form and atmosphere was again remarked upon. His realization of the size of the mountains that he painted and 'the utter absence of tricks in his works', is what most impressed Colin Bent Phillip in 1905, and it is this same simplicity that continues to make his work so impressive and enduring.

Afterword

In Alfred Williams's paintings there is something precise in the delineation of ridge and peak that denotes the eye of a climber. Perhaps this is why his paintings are most admired by other mountaineers and those who love mountains. The Alpine Club has four watercolours by Alfred Williams in its collection[24] and my hope is that this article may reveal the whereabouts of other Alfred Williams paintings that perhaps are now in the private collections of AC members. With a view to curating an exhibition, I would be particularly interested to know the location of any of the Himalayan paintings that I have so far been unable to trace. Please contact me either at the Alpine Club or by email: srp@aber.ac.uk.

Notes

1. Alfred Walter Williams was from a family of artists sometimes referred to as the Barnes School. He painted mainly in oil, and specialised in picturesque landscapes in a style that is quite different to Williams of Salisbury. Apart from the name the artists have little in common.
2. See Sligachan Hotel visitors' book July 1886; May 1887.
3. *Winter Exhibition of Pictures of Mountain Scenery*, Alpine Club, December 1900. The Royal Academician exhibiting in this show was Alfred Parsons RA (1847-1920). Also exhibiting was Colin Bent Phillip RWS (1855-1932).
4. See *Catalogue of an Exhibition of Water Colour drawings of Mountain Scenery by the late Alfred Williams*, Alpine Club, 5-23 December 1905.
5. *In the Alps, buttresses of the Grandes Jorasses*, exh1880 (cat 841); *Harta Corrie, Skye*, exh 1888 (cat 1336); *Glencoe Crags*, exh 1890 (cat 1264); *Snow on the Cuchullins, Isle of Skye*, exh 1895 (cat 907)
6. Colin Bent Phillip, 'Alfred Williams, In Memoriam', *Alpine Journal*, Vol. XXII, May 1905, pp457-458.
7. Williams, Frederick S, *Our Iron Roads: their History, Construction, and Social Influences* (London: Ingram, Cooke & Co., 1852 and later).
8. See Rosemary Harris, *The Williams Brothers, maltsters at The Maltings, Salisbury*, Salisbury Civic Society Quarterly Magazine, September 2013, pp4, 12-14. I am very grateful to Rosemary Harris for helping me in my research on the life and work of her great grandfather.
9. The occasion was most likely a family holiday but may have been the couple's honeymoon. The album of photographs is still in the family's possession but what became of Alfred's first wife remains a mystery.
10. See Claire Engel, *A History of Mountaineering in the Alps*, (London: Allen and Unwin),1950 (and later), p147. This is according to the artist's great granddaughter Rosemary Harris.
11. Perhaps exhibited RA cat 1336 as *Harta Corrie, Skye*. Harta Corrie is an easy walk from the Sligachan Hotel.
12. I am very grateful to Elizabeth Norton, great granddaughter of the artist, for sharing with me a photograph that she took at a campsite at Plampincieux, near Courmayeur to prove this point, and also for so generously helping me with my research into the life and work of Alfred Williams.
13. See Allen Staley, Christopher Newall et al, *Pre-Raphaelite Vision: Truth to Nature* (London: Tate Publishing, 2004) p149.
14. Colin Bent Phillip, 'Alfred Williams, In Memoriam', *Alpine Journal*, Vol. XXII, May 1905, pp457-458.
15. Allen Staley, Christopher Newall et al, *Pre-Raphaelite Vision: Truth to Nature* (London: Tate Publishing, 2004) pp138-141,151-153.
16. 'The Himalayan Exhibition at the Alpine Club', *Alpine Journal*, Vol. XXI, February 1903, p327.
17. *Alpine Journal*, Vol. XXII, May 1905, p.458.
18. See exhibition review: 'The Himalayan Exhibition at the Alpine Club', *Alpine Journal*, Vol XXI, February 1903, pp326-328.
19. *Alpine Journal*, Vol XXI, February 1903, p327.
20. *Alpine Journal*, Vol XXI, February 1903, p327.
21. *Alpine Journal*, Vol XXI, February 1903, p328.
22. *Alpine Journal*, Vol XXIII, February 1906, pp58-60.
23. *Alpine Journal*, Vol XXIII, February 1906, pp58-60.
24. *Grand Jorasses* (1879); *Alpine Scene* (1890); *The Eiger from Mettenberg* (1885); *The Himalayas from Almora* (1900). Thanks to Peter Mallalieu for this information, and to John Fairley, Keeper of the pictures for allowing me to view these works.

DENNIS GRAY

Life in a Carousel

Climbing Lectures from Whymper to Kirkpatrick

'We do not court publicity, but we do know how to use it.' John Harlin

Today's climbing lecturers, projecting digital images prepared in Keynote or Powerpoint, are far removed from the origins of such entertainment. The magic lantern, essentially a box with a light source, a concave lens and a glass plate with a painting on it, as developed by Christiaan Huygens in the mid 1650s, predated photography by some two hundred years; the combination of the vital new art form of photography with a well-developed form of entertainment benefitting from bright new electric lights was of great public interest.

Mountaineering was no exception, as Peter Berg reveals in *Whymper's Scrambles with a Camera*, published by the Alpine Club in 2011. Berg's book shows Whymper to have been a determinedly commercial professional mountaineer in an age of lofty amateurism, but he was not the first. That accolade must go to Albert Smith. An original member of the Alpine Club, Smith is disparaged in the foreword to Berg's book, written by Stephen Venables, who dismisses Smith as a flashy entertainer with virtually no climbing experience, a charlatan peddling a travesty of the real thing. I am afraid I beg to differ, and so did Whymper who in May 1858 at the age of 18 was inspired after attending Smith's celebrated lecture about his ascent of Mont Blanc.

Given the success of Smith's show – it ran for six years and 200,000 people saw it in its first two seasons alone – Smith must have been one of the most entertaining climbing lecturers to have graced a stage. It certainly made him rich.

The son of a surgeon, he studied medicine in Paris and in 1835, at the age of 19, visited Chamonix, attempting to tag along with a party to ascend Mont Blanc. With no funds – a regular experience for Smith – he was rebuffed, but the seed had been sown. Returning to Britain to practice medicine, Smith discovered a talent for entertaining, and he started writing pieces for *Punch*, eventually publishing sketches, plays, novels and even a pantomime. This led Smith to a new form of entertainment; he travelled to Turkey and Egypt and developed a stage show based on his experiences. Its success led him back to his early obsession to climb Mont Blanc, which he managed to ascend in August 1851, accompanied by three Oxford undergraduates and a number of guides.

It was admittedly merely the fortieth ascent, and he did not find it easy,

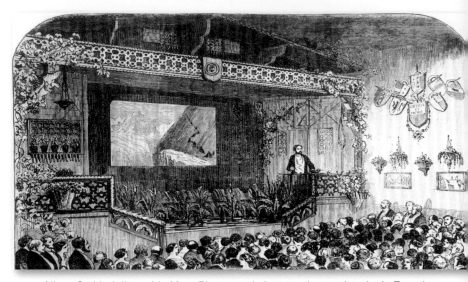

Albert Smith delivers his Mont Blanc magic lantern show at London's Egyptian Hall in 1852. *(Alpine Club Photo Library)*

but Smith exploited this experience brilliantly to concoct an entertainment *The Ascent of Mont Blanc*. He hired the Egyptian Hall in Piccadilly, opening in March 1852, and in the first two years he made £17,000, making Smith a millionaire in today's money. Subsequent historians, like Venables, have been unkind to Smith. But as a lecturer he was at the cutting edge for his era, using dioramas to illustrate the scenery and the climb.

These were the invention, in 1822, of Louis Daguerre, who in 1839 would co-develop the dagueurreotype, the first widely used method of photography.

Staged in a specially adapted theatre, each scene was hand-painted on linen, which was made transparent in selected areas. Depending on the direction and intensity of the lighting, the scene would appear to change. The effect was so subtle and finely rendered that both critics and the public were astounded, believing they were looking at a natural scene. Mont Blanc was the grandest application for this technology.

Smith overlaid his dioramas not just with an account of the climb but with songs and jokes. He even employed showgirls from West End theatres to dress up as Alpine maidens who paraded around with a large St Bernard. Whymper, writing about the performance forty years later, was still in thrall to the experience. 'Albert Smith invented a new treatment. In his hands the whole thing was light-hearted, a piece of sport. He made merry over his troubles; jested at the funny persons he met and laughed at everything. His entertainment took the world by storm, and became the most popular of its kind ever known.'

It may have been mountaineering as music hall, and Smith a Barnum-type figure – the two were friends and Smith borrowed from Barnum – but after him everyone knew about the Alps, not just readers of Shelley, and this must have been a signal event in the development of alpinism. Thousands were inspired as they heard his description of a sunset seen from the Grands Mulets. 'Absorbed by its brilliancy, I saw far more than the most gorgeous vision that opium or hashish could evoke.'

Whymper was the first to produce a popular show about genuine mountaineering accomplishment. In his short Alpine career he made some spectacular first ascents, including perhaps the most written about event in climbing history, the first ascent in 1865 of the Matterhorn and its tragic aftermath. As a talented woodblock engraver, like his father before him, Whymper was sent to make a series of Alpine sketches for the publisher Longman in the period immediately before books and newspapers began reproducing photographs. It was an era of immense public interest in exploration, and Whymper worked with some of the greatest travellers of the age. But after that first trip in 1860 he became one of them, striding around the Alps bagging peak after peak, always with guides, until the Matterhorn. After its terrible outcome he became a nationally known figure aged only 25 and developed a new career as a writer, lecturer and photographer.

Sir David Brewster had taken the first picture using a pinhole camera in 1850. Henry Fox Talbot had produced paper-based calotype negatives in 1841, and in 1884 George Eastman developed dry gel on paper or film to replace the photographic plate. From that date on, a photographer no longer needed to carry boxes of plates and toxic chemicals around. These developments took Whymper away from woodblock engraving and he became something of a pioneer mountain photographer, helping to perfect the dry plate. This interest complemented Whymper's life as a more sober scientific explorer post-Matterhorn.

His lecture tours set the style for many future professionals like Frank Smythe and Chris Bonington. For example, in 1897, criss-crossing the UK, Frank delivered 23 public lectures in six weeks; he also undertook tours in the USA and Switzerland. (Although he was often at odds with other members of the Alpine Club over his commercialism and his ability for self-promotion, he did on occasion lecture to the AC. One of his talks was titled 'Alpine camping skills'.) By the end of the nineteenth century, developments such as the half-tone process and mechanical typesetting allowed photographically illustrated books to be mass-produced. Whymper, like today's stars, used to autograph and sell books and photographs at his talks. Like Smith before him he made a fortune from such activities.

The early Everest expeditions were photographically well covered with large format cameras for panoramas and landscapes and, by that era, some action shots using smaller pocket cameras. Yet while George Mallory and others gave lectures on the expeditions in 1921 and 1922, these were not professional entertainments in the same way. The Mount Everest Committee didn't much care for such things. John Noel invested heavily in producing a film of the 1924 expedition but his attempts to add colour to the final product by having Tibetan lamas dancing on stage caused an

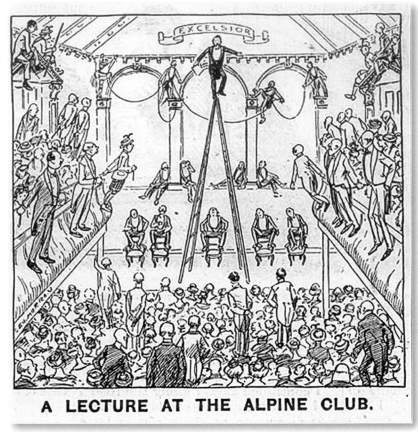

A LECTURE AT THE ALPINE CLUB.

Cartoon of a lecture at the Alpine Club, accurate save the absence of anyone asleep. *(Alpine Club Photo Library)*

international incident. The film was a commercial flop, although thanks to the British Film Institute it has recently been successfully reissued and widely admired.

The true inheritor of Whymper's mantle was Frank Smythe, who emerged a few years later to set a career path many others have followed. Like several other notable mountaineers he made several false starts in developing a career, but was fortunate to come from a wealthy background. He originally trained as an electrical engineer, studying in Yorkshire and Switzerland, by which time the mountain bug had bitten him. He developed into a fine Alpine mountaineer, pioneering with Graham Brown the two most important new routes by British climbers in the Alps during the inter-war period, the *Red Sentinel* in 1927 and *Route Major* a year later, both on the Brenva Face of Mont Blanc.

After spells of service in the RAF and working with Kodak he developed into an outstanding photographer and expedition climber, taking part in an international expedition to Kangchenjunga in 1930 and leading a successful climb of Kamet in 1931 before moving on to Everest in 1933, 1936, and 1938. He also climbed in the Garhwal and the Canadian Rockies. Like Whymper before him, it was said he had a tendency to irascibility that some of his contemporaries noted decreased with altitude. As with Whymper, and to some extent Bonington, some objected to his unashamed self-promotion.

During Smythe's lifetime, photography developed swiftly and became available to a mass market. Leica introduced the 35mm format in 1926, and shortly afterwards enlargers appeared for general use. Before this date, prints were made by contact and so the print would be exactly the size of the print. If you wanted large prints, you needed a large camera. Smythe, despite turning his back on his early electrical engineering career, must have been helped by this background in understanding these technical innovations. In 1935 Kodachrome appeared, and in 1936 Agfacolour. (The breakthrough in developing colour film for general use was made by two classically trained musicians working at Kodak's research laboratories, Leopold Mannes and Leopold Godowsky, who married George and Ira Gershwin's sister.)

Smythe published 27 books, many of them volumes of his mountain photographs. He anticipated later mountain photographers such as Walter Poucher and Ben Humble, who also developed a large market for their books amongst the general public. Smythe, however, like Whymper before him, was a public lecturer, with a professional agent to promote his tours. When I started climbing as a boy in 1947, there were still climbers around the West Yorkshire area who had attended his lectures. The consensus was that these were memorable occasions for the quality of the pictures. The recently published biography of Frank Smythe by his son Tony (*My Father, Frank*) is an outstanding work and helps us understand this driven man, who died in his late forties of cerebral malaria in 1949.

The successful 1953 Everest expedition members embarked on one of the most extensive lecture tours ever undertaken. I attended one of these as a 17-year-old, given by Alf Gregory, the expedition's official photographer, and Wilf Noyce. Although the thought of climbing in the Himalaya was not on my radar, it was truly inspirational. No mention was made that the Swiss had already pioneered the route up to and beyond the South Col the year before. But profits from the lectures and the official book of the expedition set up the Mount Everest Foundation, an act of serendipity and generosity for my, and subsequent, generations.

In 1961 I made my own journey to the Himalaya, and began to give lectures to climbing clubs, often free or for little gain. Lecturing then was a different game from today's high tech formats; you turned up clutching your box of slides, and hoped the organiser of your talk had arranged a suitable projector and screen. My worst experience took place at the Co-operative Hall in Nottingham, an expedition fund-raising event for that city's climbing club, organised by Doug Scott. Shortly after starting, each of my projected slides disappeared in a puff of smoke as soon as they appeared.

The volunteer projectionist cried out he was burning his hands. Then the ancient projector burst into flames. Without waiting, I vaulted off the stage, picked up what was left of my box of transparencies, and exited the hall, to be followed by the audience. Shortly afterwards the fire brigade arrived and, as the flames had spread, decided that the hall must stay closed. As I left the scene some of the audience, standing out on the pavement, were buttonholing Doug and demanding their money back.

That experience prompted me to buy my own projector, first an Aldis, a straight tray slide model, and in 1966 a Kodak Carousel, which revolutionised the way slide projectors worked. In the winter of 1962 I organised and promoted my first large public lecture in Derby, where I then worked in fine-art printing. This was for Chris Bonington and Ian Clough, talking about their first British ascent of the Eigerwand. It was an unqualified success, with a large audience and a successful financial outcome. It illustrated particularly to Chris that there was a real demand both among the climbing community and the general public.

From then on, Bonington became a determined professional like Whymper and Smythe before him, with a gift for communicating about our sport to a wider public, and he developed into the nationally known figure he remains today. Within a few years Chris was able to fill big venues, as I discovered shortly after returning from Gauri Sankar in 1964. One of the staples for professional lecturers was a series of talks each winter organised around the country by public libraries and I was invited to Preston to give one about our recent climb.

I was rather pleased with myself when the librarian kept phoning saying he'd moved me to a bigger venue. Finally, he booked the Guildhall, seating 2000. I was even more impressed when I arrived in Preston to find a pre-talk reception committee headed by the mayor. Alas it transpired the lecture had originally been booked for Chris Bonington, and publicity for the event had gone out with his name as the speaker. Due to a mix-up with his schedule he was unable to appear and so I was his replacement.

As a climbing lecturer I quickly learnt you had to gauge your audience; you couldn't use the same patter at the English Speaking Union as you could at a local climbing club. Jargon and expletives were a no-no, even for some climbers. The secretary of a club in Liverpool phoned me ahead of a lecture to warn me I was not to include any smut in my talk. 'Our members do not like smut.' Was I getting a reputation as a 'blue' speaker?

At the British Mountaineering Council, I conceived the idea of a National Mountaineering Conference, partly as a fund-raiser. There was no money in the coffers to buy essential office and other equipment. The first event was held in 1974 and then every two years until I left, by which time we'd held eight of these jamborees in Buxton's Opera House. They were immediately successful, with Kurt Diemberger and Cesare Maestri as the leading overseas speakers. The names of some of those who appeared at Buxton were among the most important in the history of our sport: Anderl Heckmair, Walter Bonatti, Warren Harding, Don Whillans, Bill Tilman,

John Gill, Catherine Destivelle, Tom Frost, Reinhold Messner, Jeff Lowe and many others.

Over many years of organising lectures two stand out and both included impressive survival stories. The first was by Ivan Waller about his life, and included a story about testing a Blackburn experimental flying boat over the River Clyde during the war. The engines failed and he and the four other crew members bailed out. Ivan's parachute caught on the tail of the aircraft dragging him down into the icy waters. Somehow he managed to crawl along the fuselage as it sank, and with a pocket knife cut himself free. He was in the freezing water for so long before he was rescued that the doctor who treated him believed his survival to be a miracle. He was the only member of the crew to survive. The four others drowned. His description of this escape had the audience on the edge of their seats, myself included. Perhaps his previous mountaineering experiences helped him survive.

George Mallory on a lecture tour of the USA in early 1923. While British lectures were sold out, Mallory received a lukewarm public response in America. *(Alpine Club Photo Library)*

The other memorable lecture was by Tony Barley and included another survival story. Tony was pioneering a new route on the steep 2000ft wall of Mount Superior in the Hex River Mountains of South Africa. He had led a little over halfway up when a ledge he was standing on collapsed and he fell over 200ft, suffering severe head injuries including a fractured skull. Unconscious, his partner somehow lowered him over a long period of time and then with the help of some other climbers in the area managed to summon a helicopter, which flew him to the Groote Schuur hospital in Cape Town, famous as the site of the world's first heart transplant. Surgeons managed to trepan his skull and save his life. Just. Again, the telling of this epic held the audience spellbound. Such stories are the talks the general public most enjoy.

In the 1960s some of the most talented photographers to have recorded the progress and actuality of our sport emerged: John Cleare, Leo Dickinson and Ken Wilson, the first two branching out into film and Ken into magazine and book publishing. Another type of lecture with wider appeal also emerged: the multimedia presentation. Originally developed in the USA, I remember the audience standing and cheering at the end of John Beatty's *Touch the Earth* performance at a Buxton conference in the 1970s. The use of dual projectors, sound and music was something few had then experienced.

John was not the first to produce such a presentation in the UK climbing world. As far as I know that accolade goes to Dennis Kemp, a professional photographer who worked for Kodak, and died tragically at Arapiles in Australia when a belay failed. He was a member of an expedition to Minapin in 1958, and once Carousel projectors had been developed in the 1960s put together a multimedia show about that expedition and some other subsequent climbs. There is a record of him giving such a performance at a Newcastle college around this date, in his role as a member of Kodak's educational unit.

The 1970s and 1980s saw big audiences for famous stars like Chris Bonington and Doug Scott. But the days of lecturing with transparencies and slide projectors have long been overtaken by the digital revolution. The box of slides is no more.

Traditional lecturers are still around: Stephen Venables, Doug Scott, Rebecca Stephens, Chris Bonington *et al*. But there is a new kid on the block, a new style of patter merchant, owing more to the digital revolution and stand-up comedy than stiff upper lip British understatement. The two best proponents I've seen in action are Niall Grimes, who is really a climber's lecturer, and Andy Kirkpatrick who has a wider appeal, especially to younger audiences. A reviewer of one of his lectures observed: 'He turned tales of near-death into philosophical and comic scenarios worthy of Samuel Beckett or Monty Python.' I can't imagine a reviewer writing that about any climbing lecturer of a previous generation.

Maybe climbing lecturing has always been a part of show business? You need to perform to do it well and to win the audience's approval. It's interesting that most of those who are good at climbing lecturing are not good at after-dinner speaking. That requires an entirely different skill, one that seems to be in short supply at present. Even so, lecturing about our sport appears as popular as ever. What began life as an eccentric theatre show by Albert Smith is now practised in every country where rock climbing and mountaineering are popular. However photography develops in the future, climbing lecturing will continue to be in demand for quite some time to come.

History

Matterhorn and Val Tournanche (early dawn). George Barnard. 1869.
Watercolour. 42 x 70cm. *(Alpine Club Collection HE117P)*

MICK CONEFREY

'Machiavellian Bastardy?'

The First Ascent of K2

K2 from Concordia. *(Conefrey collection)*

At about 6pm on 31 July 1954, Achille Compagnoni and Lino Lacedelli became the first men to stand on the summit of K2. That much is certain. Precisely how they got there is not. The 1954 Italian K2 expedition

Achille Compagnoni on the Summit of K2. *(From Mountain World 1955)*

was among the most rancorous in the history of mountaineering. Almost as soon as the team got home the lawsuits started. They argued about everything from expedition finances, to the rights to the film, to the leadership of Ardito Desio. The bitterest and longest running dispute, however, was of a much more fundamental nature.

Walter Bonatti, the youngest member of the team, claimed the two men who reached the summit had lied about key elements of their ascent. He fought a long, hard battle to get his version of events accepted in Italy and in the international climbing world. But did Bonatti get it right? And how much weight should now be given to the role of Robert Marshall, the self-acknowledged armchair mountaineer who played a decisive role in the controversy?

Today Bonatti is widely acclaimed as among the very best of his generation but in 1954 he was the youngest member of the K2 team. During the early stages he did not do any of the lead climbing but at the end he was entrusted with a vital task. In an epic of endurance, Bonatti and the Hunza porter Amir Mahdi carried two 18kg oxygen sets from their seventh camp at 7440m to around 8100m. They got within shouting distance of the summit pair but were unable to reach their tent and were forced to spend the night in the open. On the following day they descended, leaving Compagnoni and Lacedelli to retrieve the sets and head for the history books. Remarkably, Bonatti survived unscathed but Mahdi suffered severe frostbite.

This episode received very little coverage in Desio's official expedition book, *The Conquest of K2*, but in 1961 Bonatti published his first autobiography, *Le Mie Montagne*, and gave a detailed account of what happened. He was very critical of the summit pair, accusing them of placing their final camp so high that it was impossible to reach and then abandoning the support party to their fate. Bonatti portrayed Compagnoni as a man on the edge of exhaustion, so jealous of his position as climbing leader that he was prepared to endanger fellow team-members' lives.

Three years later, a report appeared in an Italian newspaper, based on an interview with Compagnoni. This told a very different story. It accused Bonatti of trying to make an unauthorized attempt on the summit, abandoning his partner Mahdi and most damagingly, of using some of Compagnoni and Lacedelli's oxygen during his high-altitude bivouac. Bonatti denied all the charges, sued for defamation and won the case. But the arguments didn't stop.

Over the next 40 years he waged a one-man guerilla campaign against the Italian climbing establishment, demanding that the official history of the expedition should be revised to recognize his vital supporting role and acknowledge the selfish behaviour of the summit pair and the lies that they had told. Bonatti argued that none of the altitudes or timings in *The Conquest of K2* could be trusted and, crucially, nor could Compagnoni and Lacedelli's claim that they reached the summit under their own steam.

According to interviews given by Compagnoni, the oxygen ran out between 100-200m from the top. He and Lacedelli kept on going though and even carried their heavy sets all the way to the top, because they were so awkward to remove and because they wanted to leave something as proof they had made it.

Bonatti poured scorn on this and denounced it as the 'base lie' of the whole story, which could easily be disproved using common sense and mathematics. In the first instance, it was simply absurd to maintain that anyone would carry an 18kg oxygen set to the top of the world's second highest mountain after the gas had ran out. Secondly, by looking at their climbing rates with and without oxygen, and comparing the capacity of their sets to the length of time it took to climb K2, he concluded that there must have been some gas left.

Bonatti published a book outlining his case, but no one paid that much attention. After years of arguments over K2, there was no appetite in Italy for yet more controversy. Then something unexpected happened: an Australian surgeon called Robert Marshall entered the fray.

Marshall was a keen trekker and an avid reader of climbing books. A long time fan of Bonatti, he became convinced that a grave injustice had been done. In 1993 he wrote an article in which he claimed to have found photographic evidence to prove that Compagnoni was lying.

The photos in question had appeared in the 1955 edition of a discontinued review, *The Mountain World*. One was the classic picture of Lacedelli standing next to his oxygen set, the other showed Compagnoni on the summit – wearing his oxygen mask. This, Marshall claimed, was absolute proof that the oxygen lasted all the way – why else would he have the mask on?

When the article was translated and published in Italy it garnered huge publicity and convinced many that Bonatti was right. Marshall spoke at conferences and translated the Penguin edition of Bonatti's bestselling book, *The Mountains of My Life;* it included his analysis of the summit photographs and a long piece in which he outlined the elaborate conspiracy theory, which he believed lay behind the story.

Today no one questions Robert Marshall's writings on K2 but if you look at them in detail, they are significantly flawed. In the first instance Marshall implied that there had been some sort of cover-up, with the photograph of Compagnoni on the summit missing from the 'official version', replaced with a blurred image where he has no mask on. There is no evidence for this and no sense that anyone had tried to suppress an incriminating image: the images in question were the very first two summit pictures to appear in the Italian press, published in *Il Corriere Della Sera* on 28 September 1954, long before any books appeared, under the headline 'The first photographic documentation of the events'. *The Mountain World* was not an obscure journal; it was a well-funded and well-known annual publication from the Swiss Foundation for Alpine Research and released in the same year as Desio's book.

Regarding the photograph of Compagnoni, Marshall assumed that the oxygen was connected and still flowing but this is impossible to determine from a still photograph and it is not even clear where the tube from Compagnoni's mask terminates. When Compagnoni was challenged, he explained that he was using the mask to warm the freezing air. Robert Marshall dismissed this out of hand but it was supported both by Lacedelli and Eric Abram, the Italian team's oxygen controller. The Italians were using open-circuit sets. Their supplementary oxygen was routed via a mixing box, or 'lung', where it was combined with ambient air. When the oxygen ran out it was still possible to breathe through the mask.

In a long interview from 2004, Abram confirmed that it was common-place on the Italian expedition for climbers to wear their masks and breathing tubes to warm the freezing air in 1954. A year earlier in 1953, two members of Charlie Houston's American K2 team wore 'Arctic breathers', a kind of sock on top of their mouths, for the same purpose. Then and now, in the Arctic and Antarctic masks are worn for this very reason.

Furthermore, Marshall focused almost exclusively on a single summit photograph, and ignored the four other summit images of Compagnoni in which he is not wearing a mask. The photographic and film evidence makes it absolutely clear that he spent at least some time on the summit without recourse to any supplementary oxygen.

As for Lacedelli, Marshall could not find an image with his mask on, so he came up with an elaborate theory that the ice visible on Lacedelli's beard was either caused by condensation of water vapour, indicating that he had just taken it off, or by a loose fitting mask that he had just removed. There are two obvious problems with this: first there are photographs of Lacedelli and other climbers with ice on their beards much lower down the mountain when they were not using oxygen or wearing masks. Second, if Marshall was right and ice formed when Lacedelli took his mask off, then why in all the photographs and footage of Compagnoni without a mask, is there no tell-tale ice on *his* beard?

Marshall claimed that these photographs were the key to the oxygen controversy, but he didn't notice something very telling: Compagnoni and Lacedelli had jettisoned one of their cylinders on the way up. Marshall always maintained that they carried three cylinders, a full 18kg, to the summit. But this is not the case. The middle cylinder is missing from each set. This is hard to see on the black and white pictures but is clear in the film footage and the colour summit photographs.

Like the equipment taken to Everest in 1953, the sets used by the Italian team were designed to allow for easy attachment and removal of cylinders. Every time a bottle ran out, it could be discarded; the more oxygen you used, the lighter your set became. So why did Compagnoni and Lacedelli only throw away one empty cylinder? Even if Bonatti was right and their final bottle contained some remaining oxygen, why did they carry the other bottle, which must have been used? If reducing weight was their priority, this does not make sense. There are two possible explanations: either they didn't have the time, energy or ability to remove them, or their sets had been assembled incorrectly. Either way, the fact that they must have carried at least one empty cylinder lends credence to their account.

The most important visual evidence however is found in the expedition film, *Italia K2*, which unlike most of the photographs was shot in colour. The Italian team were equipped with two types of oxygen cylinder: a large number of red bottles made by Dalmine, an Italian steel foundry with no track record in mountaineering, and a smaller number of blue bottles, made by Drager, one of Europe's leading oxygen companies. Drager had provided equipment for both the Swiss Everest expedition of 1952 and the

German Nanga Parbat expedition of 1953.

The Dalmine bottles had a maximum capacity of ten hours but when tested on the mountain many of them leaked. The Drager bottles were filled to higher pressure and, in theory, lasted for twelve hours. The plan was to use the Dalmine bottles for the low altitude work and then switch to the Drager cylinders for the final attempt. That's not what happened though. The expedition film shows that one of the oxygen sets on the summit was equipped with bright red Dalmine cylinders. It is not clear why this happened but somewhere in the confusion of the last days, the plan to use only Drager sets went awry.

The other striking fact, which neither Marshall nor Bonatti mentioned, was that the only time oxygen was used in 1954 was on the last day. Of the roughly 230 cylinders transported out to Pakistan, only six were used for climbing. Unlike Hillary and Tenzing, who used supplementary oxygen several times in the build-up to their summit bid on Everest, Compagnoni and Lacedelli had hardly any experience with it. And unlike Ed Hillary, who spent the night of 28 May 1953 checking and re-checking his and Tenzing's equipment, Compagnoni and Lacedelli did not get hold of their sets until the morning of their ascent and had no time to make sure they worked properly.

The oxygen sets of the early 1950s were crude and prone to failure. Though they had a good reputation, no Drager set had ever been used at really high altitude. The 1952 Swiss Everest expedition barely got above the South Col and members of the Austro-German Nanga Parbat expedition of 1953 hardly used their Drager sets either. Herman Buhl reached the summit of Nanga Parbat powered by his lungs, willpower and amphetamines – not bottled oxygen.

Supplementary oxygen was used in 1953 on the first ascent of Everest, but if you look in detail at the experience of that expedition, the British team frequently had problems. Cylinders leaked, valves froze up, tubes became choked with ice; oxygen seemed to run out at just the wrong moment. The first summit attempt by Bourdillon and Evans was undone by faulty oxygen equipment and Tenzing had problems with his set on the way to the summit.

In this context, the fact Compagnoni and Lacedelli had virtually no experience, were using a set never intended for the summit, and climbing in an era when oxygen equipment was prone to failure, makes it much more likely that they were telling the truth and that their oxygen did run out early. Both Bonatti and Marshall made the mistake of applying 1980s standards to a 1950s story. Modern oxygen sets might be relatively reliable, but those of the 1950s were not.

This wasn't the only example of Robert Marshall looking at the past with modern day eyes. According to Marshall's commentary on K2, as published in *The Mountains of My Life* and then elaborated on in his book *K2 Lies and Treachery*, the story of the oxygen running out early was the lynchpin of an elaborate conspiracy theory, what he called a typical piece

Lino Lacedelli on the summit of K2 in 1954, first
published in *Mountain World* in 1955.

of 'Machiavellian bastardy', designed to make Bonatti the scapegoat for his
partner Mahdi's frostbite.

Bonatti had emerged from his bivouac physically unscathed, but Mahdi
later had all his toes amputated. According to Marshall, Desio was very
worried that this incident would sully the reputation of his historic victory.
Marshall envisaged a series of meetings between Compagnoni, Desio and
an irate Mohammed Ata-Ullah, the Pakistani liaison officer assigned to the
Italian team, out of which emerged a plan to blame Bonatti, the youngest
and most expendable member of the team, and thus avoid any criticism of
the triumphant summit pair for placing their final camp so high. Marshall
backed up his theory by referring to angry reports in the Pakistani press
and an affidavit made in response to the Italian ambassador in Karachi in
September 1954, to clarify events on the mountain.

There are no letters, diary entries, memos or any archival evidence to support this. The idea of Ata-Ullah storming into Desio's tent to demand an explanation for Mahdi's frostbite makes no historical sense. The Italian expedition had the personal approval of the Pakistani prime minister, the Pakistani army had built the bridges that enabled the Italians to reach K2 more quickly than any previous expedition and Compagnoni and Lacedelli had planted the national flag on the summit of Pakistan's highest mountain. Would Ata-Ullah really have had the temerity, or the desire, to create a public scandal when he and everyone else was so thrilled at the first ascent of K2?

In the 1950s mountaineering was seen as an inherently dangerous sport and frostbite as one of its occupational hazards – for both Western climbers and their Eastern assistants. Only a few years earlier Maurice Herzog had famously lost all his toes and most of his fingers on Annapurna and the last two K2 expeditions, in 1939 and 1953, had resulted in the deaths of two American climbers and three Sherpas. Robert Marshall ignored the fact that both Compagnoni and Lacedelli also came down from the mountain with severe frostbite, while their colleague, Mario Puchoz, lost his life right at the beginning of the expedition. There would have been sympathy for Mahdi's frostbite but Desio would not have feared a scandal.

As for the idea that he was frightened by the Pakistani press, Desio could not have read any angry press reports, because he did not leave K2 with the climbing team, instead staying in the Karakoram for a secondary scientific expedition. When critical press reports were published in Karachi at the beginning of September, he was many miles away on the Biafo Glacier and had no idea what was being written. Furthermore, the negative press coverage did not focus on Mahdi's frostbite, but rather on the mistaken idea that the Italians had prevented him from reaching the summit, because they wanted to keep that privilege for themselves. In the affidavit made to the Italian ambassador, signed by Bonatti and Compagnoni, there is no mention of Mahdi's frostbite.

Compagnoni rejected the accusations of Marshall and Bonatti but he did not take either of them to court. Instead he appealed to patriotic values and called for all the mud slinging to stop. To some this might seem suspicious but Compagnoni was 80 when Marshall's article was published and after spending years in court on a failed attempt to get a share of the K2 film's profits, would have had no appetite for another legal battle. He was a tough, sometimes abrasive character; he did not have Walter Bonatti's charisma or his climbing record. This does not make him a liar.

As for Lacedelli, both Bonatti and Marshall portrayed him as Compagnoni's toady, but the two men were neither friends before the expedition, nor afterwards. When in 1955 Compagnoni sued the producers of the expedition film, Lacedelli did not support him and even signed a team letter condemning his actions. In his book *K2, the Price of Conquest* Lacedelli was very critical of Compagnoni but he insisted that the story about the oxygen running out was true, whatever Bonatti or Marshall wrote 30 or 40 years later. He was certain that it had, because he experienced it.

Bonatti's 'mathematical proofs' are rarely questioned but they too have problems. His timetable for the summit day was inconsistent; he conflated Compagnoni's book, *Men on K2*, and Desio's 1955 book, *The Conquest of K2*, into one mythical 'official version' and refused to accept the evidence of Pino Gallotti, another Italian climber who witnessed the events and kept a detailed diary. Robert Marshall put his faith in Bonatti because he was an honourable man but this is not a story about personalities – it's about oxygen sets. All the historical evidence indicates that it was much more likely for something to have gone wrong with Compagnoni and Lacedelli's equipment than for it to have worked perfectly.

Bonatti won his libel case in 1966. He did not need to rewrite the whole story of the summit day to prove that he had been wronged; the judge accepted that he had neither abandoned Mahdi, tried to stage an 'unofficial' attempt nor used any of the summit team's oxygen. Robert Marshall did not need to concoct a complex conspiracy theory to explain the photographs taken on the summit. The simple version, that Compagnoni and Lacedelli were telling the truth, that the oxygen ran out as a result of 'cock-up rather than conspiracy' as Jim Curran might have put it, has holes and problems and contradictions, but on balance it is far more historically plausible than Bonatti's or Marshall's elaborate version of events.

Hillary and Tenzing left a small cross and some sweets on the summit of Everest. Herman Buhl left his ice axe on the summit of Nanga Parbat. Lacedelli and Compagnoni carried their empty oxygen sets to the summit of K2 and left them as a marker. It might sound strange, it might sound irrational, but in extraordinary situations people often behave in extraordinary ways. Elaborate conspiracy theories are just an attempt to bring order to the chaos of life – reality is frequently much stranger.

PETER FOSTER & GARETH JONES

Sacking the Editor

T Graham Brown (centre) with Basil Goodfellow (left)
and Peter Lloyd (right) at Courmayeur, 1952.
*(Used with permission of the trustees of the National
Library of Scotland.)*

'I have come to the conclusion that the time has arrived to make a change in the editorship of the Journal,' wrote Sir Edwin Herbert [a], president of the Alpine Club, to Prof T Graham Brown, the incumbent editor. He continued: 'What procedure would you like me to adopt?'[1]

If he was expecting Graham Brown to fall on his sword and resign he did not know his man, despite 30 years of friendship. So, at a meeting of the Club's committee in January 1954, Herbert proposed that Graham Brown should be dismissed to which the Committee agreed with one dissenting voice. What lay behind this action, unique in the annals of the *Alpine Journal*? The charge sheet included the seemingly trivial, such as imposing a house-style that eschewed the use of Christian names and, more irritatingly, that the *Journal* never appeared on time; but the hanging offence was that Graham Brown had upset Geoffrey Winthrop Young.

Graham Brown had been reluctant to accept the editorship. Responding

266

to a sounding letter from T S Blakeney [b], the Club's assistant secretary, he wrote in September 1948: 'Longstaff [President 1947-50] asked me a year ago if I would be willing to edit the *Journal*, and quite a lot of other people have asked me the same thing... In every case I have said "No" emphatically...'[2] He added: '... I do not feel well fitted for the work, which I also dislike.'[3]

He was aware of his dilatoriness as a correspondent and tendency to procrastinate over tasks that bored him; he was, for example, habitually late with his income tax returns. Furthermore, he was nursing a grievance. He believed that he had been offered the position of vice-president of the Club only for the committee to have second thoughts and propose Raymond Greene[c] instead. Slighted, Graham Brown was not inclined to help, but Longstaff continued to press him. At last, having received a formal request from the committee expressing its unanimity, Graham Brown relented: 'I feel that I can no longer allow my private feelings to sway me, and it is therefore with feelings of inadequacy that I accept.'[4]

Graham Brown seemed well suited to the role. He had wide mountaineering experience and an extensive network of contacts, including foreign mountaineers. He had retired from the chair of physiology at Cardiff and, as a scientist, prized accuracy and truth. But Longstaff, commenting on Graham Brown's 'absurd addiction to absolute accuracy', warned: 'Speaking – or writing – the exact truth just breeds SWARMS [*sic*] of enemies.'[5]

Graham Brown assumed the role of editor in 1949 and his appointment met with widespread approval. His first number led with an article entitled 'Alpine Uplift', written by G E Howard[d], the theme of which was that contemporary mountaineering literature was tending to become too concerned with 'mystical emotions and elevated thoughts' rather than climbing action. No names were mentioned but the purveyors of 'uplift' recognised themselves. Arnold Lunn[e] thought the article was 'a good-humoured but definite attack on the Schuster-Young-Lunn school of alpine writers, to say nothing of Smythe, and our bunch cannot let our case go by default.'[6] He riposted with a paper, 'Alpine Puritanism', which Graham Brown duly published.

If Graham Brown's first number ruffled a few feathers, his second contained the seeds of his downfall. Douglas Busk[f] had submitted an article in which he had employed the Christian names of his companions. Graham Brown indicated that he did not favour their use but allowed them to appear in the proofs, which were approved by Busk, and then deleted them. Busk was furious and wanted to escalate the matter to the committee. Tom Brocklebank[g] was also annoyed that changes had been made to a review he had written. This editorial high-handedness would be used against him in the future.

However, it was an article Graham Brown wrote on the history of climbing on the Innominata Face of Mont Blanc that raised a furore. To a dispassionate reader, this was a detailed and rather tedious account. Even

Geoffrey Winthrop Young, writer and outdoor educator (AC president 1941-1943). *(Alpine Club Photo Library).*

reading between the lines it is difficult to see what caused offence, but Young wrote to the president Claude Elliott[h] that: 'from the nature of its assertions and innuendo, [the article] was clearly intended to belittle my mountaineering reputation.' It constituted 'a breach with our Club tradition and a grave discourtesy to a Member of the Club.'[7]

Elliott, who would later recall that his presidency was blighted by having to deal with Graham Brown, whom he found 'abominable', replied to Young that: 'The sooner he [TGB] ceases to be Editor the better.'[8]

Graham Brown claimed not to understand what the fuss was about and replied disingenuously to Elliott: 'You write… as if there was some sort of feud between us [TGB and GWY],' adding 'I have already asked you for the specific points to which GWY objects, because my only aim is accuracy in all matters of history and I shall of course correct any mistakes which I have made inadvertently...'[9]

However there had been some foul play. A rumour was circulating that Young had removed a page from Sir Edward Davidson's diary because the entry depreciated his performance on the south face of the Täschhorn in 1906. This climb had become a legend of Alpine achievement, not least due to Young's account in his book *On High Hills*. Pasted into the back of Davidson's diary is a letter from Young to Elliott, written at the beginning of 1950, in which he denied having tampered with the notebook and attacked Graham Brown, who he suspected of spreading the rumour, calling him 'base-minded' and a 'liar'.[10]

The extent to which Graham Brown propagated the story is unclear but he did have form, exemplified by his long-standing feud with Frank Smythe. [Editor's note: See 'The Brenva Feud', Foster & Jones, Vol 118, pp223-230] From the chronology of the letters to Elliott, it seems it was the discovery of this rumour that enraged Young and subsequently he saw malice in anything Graham Brown wrote concerning him. But, however much he impugned Graham Brown, there remained the inconvenient fact that the page that had previously been present was now missing and that in the interval the notebooks had been in Young's possession for safekeeping during the Second World War.

In the meantime Graham Brown, in common with his predecessors, was faced with the challenges of delivering the *Alpine Journal* within budget and on time. Longstaff had promised assistance to Graham Brown, which was provided by Blakeney and Emlyn Jones, who was appointed as assistant editor. Blakeney soon grew weary of Graham Brown, who often disappeared on climbing and sailing trips in Scotland and was incommunicado while his correspondence accumulated at the Marine Hotel in Mallaig. Blakeney felt that he was being imposed upon. Later he would claim that the fact that the *Journal* appeared at all 'owed little to the Editor's efforts and much to those who assisted him.'[11]

In October 1950 he wrote to the honorary secretary Basil Goodfellow setting out Graham Brown's 'defects' as editor and suggested 'that it may be necessary to get rid of G-B [*sic*] as editor.' Although Blakeney endeavoured to maintain cordial working relations with Graham Brown, privately he took the opportunity to defame him. In response to a request for information from Lunn, who was preparing an obituary of Smythe, Blakeney wrote at length, disparaging Graham Brown's climbing ability and his contribution to the Brenva Face routes. To Smythe's widow, Nona, he wrote that Graham Brown 'is unreasonable and has a malicious mind' and advised her 'to slaughter him' in her planned biography of Frank.[12]

1951 saw the publication of Young's book, *Mountains with a Difference*. The possibility that Graham Brown would review it for the *Journal* caused panic in the Club. Elliott begged him not to do so. He denied that the request was special pleading for a friend but was rather an attempt to fend off another row; meanwhile he approached Lord Schuster, behind Graham Brown's back, to ask him to write a review. Even Graham Brown's friends, fearing a split in the Club, urged him not to do it. In the end, C F Meade wrote a generous review.

In February 1952 Graham Brown recorded that the meeting of the Alpine Club committee 'went well' and that the 'atmosphere was much improved,' such that afterwards he could enjoy a 'very pleasant' dinner with Elliott and vice-president Leslie Shadbolt. But on 23 September 1952 the editorship of the *Journal* was once again an item on the agenda for the committee. R W Lloyd wrote to warn Graham Brown that: '... a perfect storm blew up over the journal, your enemies had a first class innings... They want your resignation.' [13]

The first ascent of Everest in May 1953 generated a sense of urgency amongst the senior officers of the Club, who were anxious to capitalise on the success. Sir Edwin Herbert, who had succeeded Elliott as president, exhorted Graham Brown to ensure that the *Journal* reporting the climb appeared at the end of October or, at the latest, the beginning of November and importantly, before the *Geographical Journal* in order to scoop the rival Royal Geographical Society. R W Lloyd, treasurer of the Club, hoped large sales of the *Alpine Journal* would generate some badly needed income.

The required schedule was impractical from the outset. By the beginning of September, Sir John Hunt had just managed to submit an account, written jointly with Mike Westmacott, – 'a terribly rushed job' – with an abridged version of his diary, and added that he had also sent copies of the article to French and Swiss journals, Hunt's action being endorsed by the Alpine Club. Now Graham Brown found himself in an unwanted race with foreign journals to publish first. The October deadline had already been missed and there were more delays, some of which were outside Graham Brown's control. Nevertheless there had been a lack of editorial focus resulting in the late return of proofs and the *Journal* eventually appeared on 15 December, after his continental competitors but still just in advance of the *Geographical Journal*.

Smarting from the loss of priority and reacting to a number of complaints from members of the Club, Herbert wrote to Graham Brown informing him of his intention to remove him from the editorship. The dossier of 'serious complaints' comprised just ten letters, all written in December 1953. Young and his friends, Brocklebank, Busk and Lunn were responsible for eight of the letters; Greene and W H Murray[i] wrote one each. Blakeney, exasperated and disaffected, orchestrated the protest and connived with Busk. The late appearance of the *Journal* was a common theme of the complainants.

Young had found additional reason to take offence. He criticised Graham Brown for publishing a brief article, written by Blakeney, in which it was correctly pointed out that Young had erroneously claimed the first descent of the Schaligrat in his books. Young demanded to know from Herbert whether Graham Brown was to continue as editor and if he were, threatened to take further action.[14] Murray's letter was completely different in tone and content and raised important concerns: 'I am at last compelled to write you despite a very natural reluctance – for I count Graham Brown as a friend whom I deeply respect...

The Editorship of the Journal has been too long uncreative and has formed for itself a rut that grows annually deeper. I and several other members of the Club who joined the recently formed Alpine Climbing Group were impelled to do so because it had become no longer possible within the AC to keep ourselves adequately informed about Alpine climbing developments... The AJ has become the last place one looks to get news of routes and reconnaissances.' [15]

Here, at least, was some cogent criticism for the committee to consider.

The committee met on 12 January 1954. In anticipation of its decision regarding the editorship, Busk wrote to Herbert from Addis Ababa, where he was serving as ambassador to Ethiopia: 'I have arranged for prayers to be said in all Coptic churches.' [16]

Above: Sir Edwin Savory Herbert, later Baron Tangley (President 1953-1956). Below: Sir Claude Aurelius Elliott, headmaster and provost of Eton (President 1950-1953).
(Alpine Club Photo Library)

Graham Brown had been invited to attend the meeting but, unbeknown to the committee, was in hospital in Fort William recovering from injuries sustained in a fall whilst descending a hillside in Glencoe. At the meeting, the committee, with one dissenting voice, R W Lloyd's, agreed to dismiss Graham Brown and appointed F H Keenlyside as editor in his place. Herbert and the Committee maintained the fiction that the reason for Graham Brown's sacking was the 'impracticability of carrying on the Journal with the editor so far away [ie Cardiff] from London.' [17] In fact, he was ousted as a result of an old-fashioned Alpine Club row.

Graham Brown suspected intrigue but recognised that there was no going

back. True to form, he examined forensically the evidence against him. He maintained that his published statements concerning Young's climbs were historically accurate and thought it 'absurd' that he should have apologised for them. At the beginning of March 1954, he made a statement defending himself to a General Meeting of the Club. His friend, R W Lloyd, described the mood of the evening: '…although nothing was said when he sat down, (everybody was too surprised to say anything) when he got up to make a short speech about the paper he was very strongly applauded. It seemed to me that he had the sympathy of the room.'[18]

Herbert gained a different impression and wrote to Graham Brown: '…the general feeling after your statement was that it was a pity… that it should have been made.' [19] Later, he recalled that Graham Brown took his dismissal 'very badly' and 'for some years refused to speak to me or even to acknowledge my presence… [but] …suddenly one day out of the blue I had a little note from him saying that we were far too old friends to quarrel, and what about having lunch together? We lunched at the Athenaeum as though nothing had happened and our friendship was thus resumed.' [20]

Acknowledgement

We thank the Alpine Club and National Library of Scotland for permission to reproduce quotations from material in their possession.

Notes

a E S Herbert (1899-1973) fatefully introduced Graham Brown to F S Smythe at Montenvers in 1927.
b T S Blakeney (1903-1976) Salaried assistant secretary of the Club. In 1928, at Smythe's invitation, he had joined him and Graham Brown for an attempt on the Route Major.
c C R Greene (1901-1982) A lifelong friend of Smythe.
d G E Howard (1877-1956) Known for his wit and vice-president 1952-3.
e A H Lunn (1888-1974) 'had an almost mystical apprehension of eternal beauty as he contemplated his beloved mountains.' [21]
f D L Busk (1906-1990) Old Etonian and diplomat. Together with Smythe, he had formed the 'Young Shavers', a ginger group which sought to challenge the 'Old Stagers' and reform the Alpine Club.
g T A Brocklebank (1908-1984) Eton schoolmaster. A celebrated oarsman and a member of the 1933 expedition to Everest.
h C A Elliott (1888-1973) Headmaster and Provost of Eton – nicknamed 'The Emperor'. During the First World War he served in the Friends' Ambulance Unit with Young, who was best man at his wedding.
i W H Murray (1913-1996) was a passionate believer in 'Uplift'. His friend, Bill Mackenzie, thought that Murray 'saw an angel in every pitch'. [22]

References

1. E S Herbert to Graham Brown (GB) 16 Dec 53; National Library of Scotland (NLS) Acc 4338/12
2. GB to T Blakeney 30 Sep 1948; NLS Acc 4338/12
3. GB to F^C Oughton 7 Oct 1948; NLS Acc 4338/12
4. GB to A Malcolm 11 Oct 1948; NLS Acc 4338/8
5. T Longstaff to GB 11 Feb 1950; NLS Acc 4338/9
6. A Lunn to GB 15 Aug 1949; NLS Acc 4338/9
7. G Winthrop Young to C Elliott 17 Feb 1950; NLS Acc 4338/9
8. Hankinson A, *Geoffrey Winthrop Young*, Hodder & Stoughton (1995) p326
9. T Graham Brown GB to C Elliott 1 Mar 1950; NLS Acc 4338/9
10. Davidson Sir E, Notebook Vol 8; AC Archives C35
11. T Blakeney, 'The Alpine Journal and its editors III', AJ 1976; **81:** p160
12. T Blakeney to N Smythe 6 Dec 1951; Blakeney papers: British Library Add MS 63125
13. R W Lloyd to GB 24 Sep 1952; NLS Acc 4338/11
14. G W Young to E Herbert 22 Dec 1953; AC Archives B59 (1)
15. W H Murray to E Herbert 1 Dec 1953; AC Archives B59 (1)
16. D Busk to E Herbert 2 Jan 1954; A.C. Archives B59 (1)
17. E S Herbert to GB 28 Jan 1954; NLS Acc 4338/13
18. R W Lloyd to E Herbert 10 Mar 1954; AC Archives B59 (1)
19. E S Herbert to GB 8 Mar 1954; NLS. Acc 4338/13
20. E S Herbert, *T Graham Brown – a footnote to history*; AJ 1966 **71:** pp51-7
21. Dictionary of National Biography 1971-1980; OUP 1986
22. Lloyd-Jones, R *The Sunlit Summit: the life of WH Murray;* Sandstone Press 2013 p xviii

KOEN VAN LOOCKE

The Shaping of Nineteenth Century Guiding

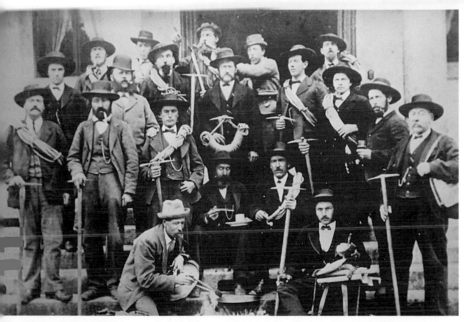

The guides at Meiringen. Developing guiding standards was harder in less famous Alpine resorts. *(Meiringen Museum)*

Nowadays mountain tourism is immensely popular. Between 120 to 170 million people visit mountain regions around the world annually, taking up 15 to 20 percent of the global tourism market, and their number continues to grow.[1] Around the world, more than 6000 official mountain guides lead a fraction of these people in the mountains,[2] allowing people to climb objectives or explore regions they otherwise would not. In a mountain guide they find someone who is capable of leading them safely, hopefully in good company. This article examines how this profession began and developed throughout the nineteenth century, and looks at the influence of mountaineers, and Alpine associations, in particular the Alpine Club and Swiss Alpine Club (SAC). My focus will be on Chamonix in France (before 1792, and between 1815 and 1860 it was part of the kingdom Piedmont-Sardinia), and to a lesser degree Valais (Wallis) and the Bernese Oberland in Switzerland. The most important period is between the 1850s and the

Melchior Anderegg, among the greatest of Victorian guides. *(Meiringen Museum)*

1870s.

We are familiar with the idea that from early times until the nineteenth century, most people tried to avoid the Alps, believing them inhabited by dragons and demons. People only crossed the Alps when it was really necessary for trade or pilgrimage and they remained largely unexplored. Local peasants explored their surroundings, and occasionally climbed mountains, but they wrote almost nothing about their exploits and the Alps remained truly a terra incognita to foreigners.[3]

At the end of the eighteenth century, thanks to the Enlightenment and then the fashion for the sublime, more people started to find their way to the Alps, in this period mostly to Chamonix. Thanks to the era's scientists, poets, artists and philosophers, people changed their view of mountains. They began to appreciate mountains as places of beauty. Because of this new fascination for the mountains by wealthy and mostly upper middle class people, the Alps became a more dynamic region.

Most people who came to Chamonix wanted to take a look at the mighty glaciers and the stupendous scenery surrounding the village and, because tourists were not at all familiar with mountain hiking, they hired local peasants to guide them and it is here that the origins of the profession of mountain guiding is found. Local people now had an extra source of income and improved their precarious economic situation. During the first half of the nineteenth century, mountain tourism was concentrated in Chamonix. Other important places, mainly in the Bernese Oberland and Valais, would not catch up with Chamonix until the 1850s and 1860s.

Chamonix was visited by between two and three thousand tourists annually at the beginning of the nineteenth century, and so more and more local people could earn extra wages as mountain guides.[4] The more challenging tours provided were those towards or on glaciers. The hardest excursion was the ascent of Mont Blanc, first summited in 1786.[5] This ascent gave a boost to tourism in Chamonix and would lead to the creation of the first professional organization for mountain guides: La Compagnie des Guides de Chamonix (CGC), in 1821.[6]

The main reason for establishing the first mountain guides association in the world was the success of mountain tourism but was triggered by an accident in 1820, known as the Hamel accident, on the slopes of Mont Blanc when three local guides perished. The accident made it clear that there was an urgent need for clear rules about who was able to act as a mountain guide, a mule driver or a porter, and who was not qualified for any of those tasks. Elsewhere it would take at least until the 1850s and 1860s before similar rules were introduced.

Besides its qualifications, the CGC also had some important rules. Best known was the *tour de role*, a rotation system in which all guides had the same opportunity to guide on different excursions. Furthermore, the CGC decided the number of guides a tourist was obliged to hire, and the rates of all excursions they offered were fixed. Thanks to this rotation system, each guide had the same opportunities to guide on financially more attractive trips. When tourists came to Chamonix, they could not choose a guide or decide how many guides they wanted. It was the CGC who assigned him or her one or more guides, depending on the complexity of their trip.[7] Finally, the CGC had a monopoly in the Chamonix-Mont Blanc region on mountain guiding. Foreign guides were not allowed to guide people within this region.

Although in this period the first steps were taken towards a more professional approach to mountain guiding, until the middle of the nineteenth century it was still not possible to speak of a true professionalism. Mountain guides remained farmers or herdsmen who occasionally guided tourists on smaller mountains, glaciers or on hiking trips. Even the guides who served in the CGC were not full-time guides. They spent only a small, albeit financially important amount of time in the mountains guiding tourists. And because they did not spend much time climbing, they did not feel the need to improve themselves much, and therefore their climbing abilities remained mediocre. It would take until the 1860s for this situation to change.

From the 1850s onwards more mountaineers came to the Alps to climb successfully almost all the still unclimbed peaks. For several reasons, between 1855 and 1865, British mountaineers took a dominant position in the Western Alps (Table 1 and 2).[8] This inflow of mountaineers would have some major consequences on mountaineering in general, but more specifically, they had a large influence on the profession of mountain guides.

First of all, mountaineers wanting to climb new peaks persuaded some mountain guides to improve themselves and to develop their climbing capacities. In order to keep guiding these mountaineers, many guides had to start climbing on a level much higher than before. If they did not, they risked losing their clients. The establishment of the AC in 1857 also influenced the professionalisation of mountain guiding, albeit rather indirectly.

The AC was the first mountaineering association, and though the Club was not directly linked to guiding, it was the example for other Alpine associations founded in the decades after 1857.[9] Unlike the AC, these new clubs actually were linked to mountain guiding.[10]

Gradually they started to organize and professionalise mountain guiding, by organizing courses to test the qualities of guides and establishing official mountain guide qualifications and certificates, by handing over *Führerbücher* to licensed guides as a way to check on their progress, drafting rules of conduct and offering insurance to guides.[11] Insurance was first implemented by the CGC to support injured guides or the families of dead guides. Later, Alpine associations would offer this kind of insurance to mountain guides. The idea, however, was not an immediate success, as many guides remained uninsured. In Switzerland only around one hundred guides were insured in the 1870s, and not more than four hundred towards the end of the century. Furthermore, the compensation insured guides received was often not sufficient, and most guides, in case of an accident, depended on charity from mountaineers and Alpine associations.[12] This would only change rapidly after the establishment of mountain guides associations at the end of the century.

In Switzerland, cantonal authorities were to a large extent responsible for the organization and control of mountain guides.[13] Regulations were first implemented in Bern in 1856, in Valais in 1857 and these were followed by other cantons.[14] SAC, after its establishment in 1863, took some responsibilities towards mountain guides, offering mountain guide courses, through its sections, and trying to get as many guides as possible insured.[15]

Only from the 1870s onwards were local mountain guides associations established in the Alps. It would take until the beginning of the twentieth century before regional or cantonal mountain guides associations were established.[16] One of their main purposes, besides improving and promoting mountain guiding, was – and is – to look after the interests of the affiliated guides. The interests of Alpine associations and those of mountain guides did not always correspond with each other. By organising themselves, mountain guides were better able to look after their own interests.[17]

The AC was not located within the Alps, and therefore had no official connection with guiding, which meant the Club could only influence it indirectly, by collaborating with other Alpine associations, not least the SAC, and regional authorities. The AC had another impact on the professionalisation of mountain guiding; it was thanks to such associations that mountaineering became better known and more widely accepted. Although the AC was only a small association (Table 3), it had a major impact on the number of British people travelling to the Alps. Many members of the AC were enthusiastic writers producing books and journals about the Alps, which gave many people across Europe the stimulus to go there.[18] Simultaneously, these writings contributed to the image of mountaineering as something dominated by the British, even though there were many tourists of other nationalities as well. In Chamonix the number of tourists rose from c1500 in 1800 to 3000 in 1830, and 12,000 in 1865.[19] A look at numbers of members of different Alpine associations confirms the increasing flow of tourists and mountaineers to the Alps (table 3). This increase gave mountain guiding a boost.[20] However, at first this development did not have a positive effect on the quality of mountain guiding.[21]

In the 1850s and 1860s, there was a considerable gap between the level of guiding in well-known districts like Zermatt, Grindelwald, or Chamonix and lesser-known districts like the Dauphiné, the Val d'Hérens or the Val d'Aosta. The reason for the early success of the former villages can to a large extent be traced back to their surroundings. The presence of Mont Blanc, the Matterhorn or the massif of the Wetterhorn, Eiger and Jungfrau gave these villages a huge advantage over others. These mountains, because of their height, distinct shape and majesty attracted more tourists than other villages in the Alps could hope for. As more tourists went to these districts, they needed to develop at a faster rate than other districts, no matter how beautiful or pristine these were and so guiding developed more slowly in less visited regions.

Criticism of guides from less developed districts in the Alps was not exceptional. Mid nineteenth century travel stories, guidebooks or diaries of mountaineers often refer to the low quality of tourism and mountain guiding.[22] In time, due to the efforts of the alpine associations and the influx of tourists this would change gradually. There was also frequent complaining about the CGC. The reasons can be found in their rules, with which many mountaineers and Alpine associations did not agree.[23] First, there was the rotation system. One great advantage was that it created equality among mountain guides. It had, however, several disadvantages. When mountaineers wanted to make more difficult excursions, they wanted someone they knew and trusted, or at least someone they had heard of. In Chamonix this was not possible; the CGC would assign one or more guides to the mountaineer.[24] The system often created incompetent guides, or guides were assigned to excursions they were not suited for. Not many guides were completely inept, but they often lacked the required skills on certain types of terrain. Some guides preferred climbing on ice or snow, while others preferred rocks. Due to the rotation system, guides could not choose their clients or their excursions. If everyone had the same opportunities to guide on tougher or easier jobs, why would one invest in trying to improve? Moreover, less competent guides were sometimes assigned to difficult climbs, endangering themselves, their clients and the image of mountain guiding in general. [25]

These shortcomings became increasingly noticeable.[26] In the 1870s, under pressure from both the AC and SAC, which even took this issue – among others – to the regional government in Annecy and the French ministry of the interior, the CGC would eventually, albeit reluctantly, abolish this rotation system, at least partially, in 1879: 'travellers are free in the choice of their guides; when they don't have a preference, guides will offer their services based on the rotation system.'[27] In the 1860s, there were already some exceptions to this rule. Experienced mountaineers and members of the AC could choose their guides and the number they considered necessary.[28]

Another source of frustration for many mountaineers, guides and Alpine associations was the monopoly on mountain guiding of the CGC around Chamonix. Before the 1860s, guides who were not affiliated with the CGC were not allowed to guide anyone in the region. Mountaineers who wanted to scale mountains in this region with foreign guides were not allowed and they were obliged to hire local guides. Only later was this rule made less strict; after around 1860 foreign guides were allowed, although often reluctantly.[29]

An extra reason for contesting this monopoly was that the CGC offered only a small, not very challenging number of excursions and climbs. From the 1850s onwards, more mountaineers were climbing harder mountains; this rule made it impossible to climb such mountains around Chamonix. The growing influx of tourists in Chamonix and elsewhere from the 1850s onwards also had an effect.[30] An increased demand for mountain guides combined with lax admission requirements only intensified existing problems concerning the quality of mountain guiding in Chamonix. In the 1870s, the AC claimed several Chamonix guides did not meet the requirements to become a mountain guide, but still became one, even showing tourists false certificates of ascents they had supposedly made. After these allegations, CGC regulations were tightened.[31] An important consequence of all this was that the lead in guiding the CGC had established in earlier years was now diminishing. Thanks to the efforts of the SAC and the AC, alterations were made to the, often outdated, regulations of the CGC.[32] From then on relations between the CGC, and the AC and SAC improved considerably.

The danger of hiring incompetent guides did not only exist in Chamonix. Most districts in the Alps had bad or incompetent guides, or even impostors. To avert the danger of hiring incompetent guides, measures were taken by Alpine associations and local authorities. Guide courses and certificates and also *Führerbücher* were meant to fight these problems. The latter were booklets, kept by mountain guides, in which clients had to write down their experiences with their guides. When a client wanted to hire a guide, he could consult these booklets before he decided whether this particular guide had the right capabilities for his ambitions. Guides were obliged to have them always to hand.[33] These booklets made it increasingly difficult for incompetent guides or impostors to keep guiding tourists which, in time, led to a general improvement of guiding standards.

In Britain, the AC tried to do the same by making lists of guides, in which members could write down their experiences with a particular mountain guide.[34] Even though most of these descriptions were very stereotypical, often praising the courage or strength of mountain guides, comments from fellow mountaineers could prevent climbers or tourists from hiring incompetent guides as well as help guides to make a career.

The Alpine Club's telegram to Anderegg's son following Melchior's death in 1914. In 2014 the Club was present at the unveiling of a new statue of Anderegg and his client Leslie Stephen. *(Meiringen Museum)*

Despite the flaws and criticism of the CGC one should not forget its importance and influence on mountain guiding. It was the first of its kind and had a major impact on the development of the profession. In addition, problems with incompetent guides were not restricted to Chamonix. On the contrary, compared to many other districts in the Alps, the average mountain guide at Chamonix was better skilled.

Furthermore, most tourists who came to Chamonix did not encounter any problems with their guides, or with the rules of the CGC.[35] Criticism came more often from experienced mountaineers, in whose opinion guides needed to excel in their profession. Many guides did not meet the high requirements these experienced mountaineers set, even though they were perfectly capable of leading tourists on less challenging tours. Elite mountaineers were, however, most often heard, and their criticism often overshadowed the positive remarks given by clients who were less demanding. This has led to an overly negative view of the CGC.

There was an enormous gap between the guides hired by tourists at the end of the eighteenth century and the mountain guides who were active between the 1860s and 1880s. These first guides were more peasants than guides, with only limited mountaineering skills. Only around the middle of the nineteenth century did things started to change as more and more tourists started visiting the Alps. The subsequent demand for mountain guides made it clear there was a need to find a way to guarantee that mountain guides had the appropriate skills and capacities to guide tourists and mountaineers in the mountains.

With the establishment of Alpine associations in the 1860s, after the example of the AC, guiding professionalism received a boost, with courses, certificates and *Führerbücher*. They set rates for excursions as well as rules of conduct for guides. They reported mischief and fraud and criticised the policy of certain mountain guides associations to improve their services. The AC, which is often neglected in regard to mountain guiding, influenced mountain guiding in an indirect way. They often urged or assisted other Alpine associations in dealing with issues they thought needed improvement.

The AC's pressure in reshaping the CGC in the 1860s and 1870s is a perfect example of how the Club altered the outlook of mountain guiding. Not only the Alpine associations and local or regional governments influenced this development, but mountaineers themselves, by their numbers or by their skills and urge to explore the Alps. This process continued until the end of the nineteenth century, when a number of important changes impacted on guiding: the growing number of guideless climbers, which was 'not done' beforehand;[36] the decline of long engagements, when before engagements of several weeks were not exceptional; and the beginning of skiing, which made it possible for the first time to be a mountain guide all year round. These and other changes altered the outlook of mountain guiding profoundly.

Table 1. Ascents on Mont Blanc between 1786 and 1878 by nationality

Nationality	Number of mountaineers	Percentage
British (& Irish)	448	57.4
French	132	16.9
German	36	4.6
American	76	9.7
Swiss	39	5
Italian	19	2.4
Others*	31	4
Total	781**	100

* Spain, Belgium, Poland, Sweden, Russia, Austria, Netherlands and Norway.
** Mont Blanc was climbed 629 times by 781 mountaineers in this period. These numbers do not bring into account the number of guides who climbed Mont Blanc with their clients.
Source: La Compagnie des Guides de Chamonix.

Table 2. Number of tourists in Chamonix by nationality in 1865

Nationality	Number of tourists	Percentage
British (and Irish)	3669	31.1
American	3004	25.5
French	2747	23.3
German	1097	9.3
Italian	214	1.8
Belgian	227	1.9
Others*	831	7.1
Total	11789	100

* Russia (173), Switzerland (119), Netherlands (108), Spain (43), Turkey (4), India (2), Not Classified (382). Source: Paul Guichonnet, 'La Saison Touristique de 1865 à Chamonix', *Revue de géographie alpine* 32, no. 4 (1944): 604-605.

Table 3. Members of different European alpine associations

Year	SAC	CAF	DAV*	ÖAV*	CAI	AC
1863	257			643	200 (1864)	158 (1861)
1870	1191		1070	1400	400	298 (1871)
1874	1988	607	3682		2011	361 (1875)
1878	2106	2535	7600		3459	
1883	2560	4688	11086		3683	
1888	2831	5497	21661		4409	509 (1891)
1896	4992	5868	38442		4213	611 (1901)
2013	142787	88000	1037922	470000	311641	1529

* The *Deutscher Alpenverein* and *Österreichischer Alpenverein* merged in 1874 to form the *Deutscher und Österreichischer Alpenverein* (DuÖAV). After the Second World War DuÖAV split up again in to the Austrian Alpine Club (ÖAV) and German Alpine Club (DAV). Sources: Jahrbuch der Schweizer Alpenclub, Annuaire du Club Alpin Français, The Alpine Journal, Zeitschrift des Deutschen und des Osterreichischen Alpenvereins, William AB Coolidge, *The Alps in Nature and History*, London (1908), p440.

Notes
1. Data according to UNEP (United Nations Environment Programme) and ICIMOD (International Centre for Integrated Mountain Development). Ester Kruk, *Two Decades of Mountain Tourism in ICIMOD*, 1989-2009 (2010)
2. In 2012 there were 5986 official IFMGA (International Federation of Mountain Guides Associations) guides. IFMGA 'is the only organisation that represents the profession of the mountain guides worldwide.' There are, however, several national mountain guides associations around the world, which are not affiliated with the IFMGA. Worldwide, consequently, there are more mountain guides than those 5986, most of which are active in Europe and North America. International Federation of Mountain Guides (2012), 2.2
3. Reto Furter, Urbanisierung – Transitverkehr – Bädetourismus – Alpinismus. Indikatoren zum Hintergrund des Alpendiskurses 15. Bis 19. Jahrhundert, Chur (2005), pp147-148.

4. Fabrizio Bartaletti, 'What Role Do the Alps Play Within World Tourism?' (2008). http://
alpsknowhow.cipra.org/background_topics/alps_and_tourism/alps_and_tourism_chapter_
introduction.html (accessed 15 February 2014)

5. First summited by Dr Michel-Gabriel Paccard and Jacques Balmat, two local people from
Chamonix (the latter hired by Horace Bénédict de Saussure from Geneva). The following
year, de Saussure himself ascended Mont Blanc. Horace-Bénédict De Saussure, *Voyages Dans
les Alpes: Précédes d'un Essai Sur l'Histoire Naturelle des Environs de Genève* vol 4 (Neuchâtel,
1803), p474.

6. Created in 1821 and ratified by the Sardinian Government in 1823.

7. 'Règlement des guides de Chamonix,' Bulletin du C.A.F. 2 (1879): pp59-62; John Ball, *A
guide to the Western Alps* (London, 1866), p194.

8. Between 1851 and 1900 around 1000 mountains were first ascended in the Alps. Approximately 350 of those were completed by British climbers, 100 between 1861 and 1867.
Between 1854 and 1865, the Golden Age of mountaineering, British mountaineers climbed 31
4000m peaks, compared to only four by other nationalities. Furter, Urbanisierung – Transitverkehr – Bädetourismus – Alpinismus , pp109-148; Daniel Anker, Come nacque l'alpinismo.
Dall'esplorazione delle Alpi alla fondazione dei Club Alpini (1786–1874): Erstbesteigungen
in den Schweizer Alpen 1740-1850 (Varallo, 2014), pp1-3; Peter H. Hansen, 'Albert Smith,
the AC, and the Invention of Mountaineering in Mid-Victorian Britain,' *The Journal of British
Studies* 34, no. 3 (July, 1995): pp300-324.

9. Letters relating to formation of AC: 1857-1858, AC Archives, 1922/B65. In 1862 the
Österreichischer Alpenverein, in 1863 the Schweizer Alpen-club /Club Alpin Suisse (SAC/
CAS) , also in 1863 the Club Alpino Italiano (CAI), the Deutscher Alpenverein (DAV) in
1869 and the Club Alpin Français (CAF) in 1874.

10. Direction Centrale, 'Rapport Annuel de la Direction Centrale,' Annuaire du Club Alpin
Français 1 (1875): pp483-485; M Ulrich, 'Statuten des Schweizer Alpenclub,' *Jahrbuch des
Schweizer Alpenclub* 6 (1870): p565.

11. Rules of conduct were drafted for guides as well as tourists in order to protect both against
misbehaviour. These rules are a clear indicator of the social differences that often existed
between mostly upper middle-class mountaineers and lower class guides: Peter H Hansen,
'Albert Smith, the AC, and the Invention of Mountaineering in Mid-Victorian Britain,' *The
Journal of British Studies* 34, no 3 (July, 1995): p310; C S Bennet, *The Golden Age of Moun-
taineering*: 1850-1870, 1950, 1922/C146, AC Archives; Rousseau, Règlement et Tarif de la
Compagnie des Guides de Chamonix , pp5-26; Abel Lemercier, 'Le Règlement des Guides de
Chamonix,' *Bulletin du CAF* 8 (1885): pp291-293; *Gesetz, Reglement & Tarif für den Fürherdienst
im Canton Valais* , pp3-22; Andrea Hungerbühler, 'Vom 'Ignoranten' zum Idealschweizer,' in
Helvetia Club: 150 Jahre Schweizer Alpen-Club SAC, ed Daniel Anker (Bern, 2013): pp82-85.

12. Gidl, Die Städter Entdecken die Alpen, 166; H, 'Personation of a Guide,' *Alpine Journal* 1
(1864): pp44-45; Douglas W Freshfield, 'Alpine Notes: Insurance for guides,'; *Alpine Journal*
9 (1880): p49; William A B Coolidge, 'Alpine Notes,' *Alpine Journal* 10 (1882): pp278-279;
Jahrbuch des Schweizer Alpenclub, vol. 11-7 p33, 1875-1897; J E Grob, 'Chronik,' *Jahrbuch des
Schweizer Alpenclub* 22 (1887): p495; Douglas W. Freshfield (ed), 'Alpine Notes: Insurance for
guides,' p49.

13. Gesetz, Reglement & Tarif für den Führerdienst im Canton Valais, Article 1; Rousseau,
Règlement et Tarif de la Compagnie des Guides de Chamonix, p24 ; Rousseau, Règlement
et Tarif de la Compagnie des Guides de Chamonix , pp13-14; Gesetz, Reglement & Tarif für
den Führerdienst im Canton Valais, Article 17; p22.

14. Andrea Hungerbühler, *Könige der Alpen: Zur Kultur des Bergführerberufs* (Bielefield, 2013),
p76.

15. M Ulrich, 'Chronik,' *Jahrbuch des Schweizer Alpenclub* 6 (1870): p547; M Ulrich, 'Statuten
des Schweizer Alpenclub,' p565; J E Grob, 'Chronik,' *Jahrbuch des Schweizer Alpenclub* 20
(1884): pp549-550; J E Grob, 'Chronik,' *Jahrbuch des Schweizer Alpenclub* 23 (1888): p646.

16. F.A. Monnier, 'Rapport du Comité Central,' *Jahrbuch des Schweizer Alpenclub* 32 (1897)
: 402.; Hungerbühler, *Könige der Alpen*, pp84-89: In Switzerland, cantonal associations were
only established at the beginning of the twentieth century in Valais, Bern, Graubunden, and
Uri (founded between 1904 and 1909). A national mountain guides association Schweizer
Bergführer Verband (SBV) was established in 1942, followed by the Syndicat National des
Guides de Montagne (SNGM) in France in 1946. Similar associations were founded in

1966 in Austria Verband der Österreichischen Berg- und Schiführer (VÖBS), and in 1968 in Germany Verband Deutscher Berg- und Skifuührer (VDBS).
17. Hungerbühler, *Könige der Alpen*, p442.
18. Douglas W Freshfield (ed), 'Alpine Notes,' *Alpine Journal* 6 (1874): p312.
19. Of which one in three was British or Irish. Guichonnet, 'La Saison Touristique de 1865 à Chamonix,' pp603-604.
20. In Chamonix, the number of guides rose from 46 in 1821 to 156 in 1845, to 298 in 1898. In Switzerland we can assume a similar increase in the number of mountain guides. This can be deduced from the growing number of tourists in the Alps and members of the different Alpine associations during the second half of the nineteenth century, as well as the increasing number of insured mountain guides in Switzerland. Due to the lack of guides associations in the Alps during the nineteenth century, hardly any official numbers were registered before the turn of the century, which makes it very difficult to give an exact number.
21. Karl Baedeker, *Switzerland with the Neighbouring Lakes of Northern Italy, Savoy and the Adjacent Districts of Piedmont, Lombardy and the Tyrol.* Handbook for Travellers, London, (1863), XXIX.
22. Thomas G Bonney, *The Alpine Regions of Switzerland*, Cambridge (1868), p177; Leslie Stephen, *The Playground of Europe* (1871); Alfred Wills, *Wandering Among the High Alps* London, (1858), p85.
23. Freshfield (ed.), 'Alpine Notes' (1874), p312.
24. Ronald W Clark, *The Early Alpine Guides*, London (1949), p74.
25. Clark, *The Early Alpine Guides*, p79; Freshfield, 'Alpine Notes,' (1874): p312.
26. Chaubet, *Histoire de la Compagnie des Guides de Chamonix* , pp76-79; Centralcomité des Schweizer Alpenclub, 'Elfter Geschäftsbericht des Centralcomité des Schweizer Alpenclub,' pp664-665; Freshfield (ed), 'Alpine Notes' (1874), p314.
27. M Ulrich, 'Die Sektionen', *Jahrbuch des Schweizer Alpenclub* 6 (1870): pp553-554; Centralcomité des Schweizer Alpenclub, 'Elfter Geschäftsbericht des Centralcomité des Schweizer Alpenclub', *Jahrbuch des Schweizer Alpenclub* 10 (1875): pp664-665, Freshfield (ed), 'Alpine Notes' (1874), p311; Douglas W Freshfield (ed), 'Alpine Notes,' *Alpine Journal* 7 (1876): pp42-43; 'Règlement des Guides de Chamonix,' pp59-62; Douglas W Freshfield (ed), 'Alpine Notes,' *Alpine Journal* 9 (1880): p308; Freshfield (ed), 'Alpine Notes' (1876), p42.
28. During the 1870s, the AC and SAC suggested an division of mountain guides in different classes to tackle this issue. This categorisation would never be implemented. The abolition of the rotation system, as well as better and stricter courses to become a guide made this categorisation redundant. Ball, *A Guide to the Western Alps*, p194; Freshfield (ed), 'Alpine Notes' (1874), pp306-315.
29. Trevor Braham, *When the Alps Cast Their Spell: Mountaineers of the Alpine Golden Age* (Glasgow, 2004), p150.
30. Guichonnet, *La Saison Touristique de 1865 à Chamonix*, pp603-608; Baedeker, Switzerland with the Neighbouring Lakes of Northern Italy, Savoy and the Adjacent Districts of Piedmont, Lombardy and the Tyrol, XXIX.
31. Chaubet, *Histoire de la Compagnie des Guides de Chamonix* , pp77-78; Freshfield, 'Alpine Notes' (1874), p311.
32. Douglas W Freshfield (ed), 'Alpine Notes' (1880), p308; 'Règlement des guides de Chamonix', pp59-62.
33. *Gesetz, Reglement & Tarif für den Fürherdienst im Canton Valais*, p1
34. List of Guides, c1866, AC Archives, 1922/C88; A Roth, 'Gletscherfuührer'; *Jahrbuch des Schweizer Alpenclub* 1 (1864): pp572-581; SAC likewise published in its annual journal a non-exhaustive list of guides, classified by district, with the ascents accomplished during the last year. SAC, 'Gletscherführer'; *Jahrbuch des Schweizer Alpenclub* 2 (1865): pp529-542.
35. Ball, *A Guide to the Western Alps*, pp193-194.
36. Tyndall, *New Fragments*, London, (1892), p457; William A B Coolidge, *The Alps in Nature and History*, London, (1908), p327; Braham, *When the Alps Cast their Spell*, p168.

C A RUSSELL

One Hundred Years Ago

*Zermatt in 1915 was a desert. Its busy street was empty. Its shops were
shut. Half of its hotels were closed, and the other half more than half empty.
The Zermatt-Visp and Gornergrat railways ran very few trains, and carried a
very unremunerative number of passengers. Hardly anyone could be seen on
mountain paths, no one on the peaks.*

The circumstances described by Edward Broome, who travelled to
neutral Switzerland with members of his family, were experienced in
many Alpine resorts following the outbreak of the First World War. As the
only English mountaineer in the district Broome did all he could to assist
the local guides, who had fallen on hard times. He engaged his friends
Aloys and Josef Pollinger for ascents of the Alphubel and Monte Rosa and
recommended other guides to interested visitors.

In July a disappointing consequence of the conflict was the disrup-
tion of proposed arrangements to mark the jubilee of the first ascent of
the Matterhorn. The international committee appointed to supervise the
arrangements had been unable to meet and the planned celebrations were
cancelled.

During the summer progress was made in connection with an important
project on the north-east, Hörnli ridge of the Matterhorn. After protracted
negotiations between the Swiss Alpine Club and the commune of Zermatt
and in the face of much unsettled weather, a small emergency hut funded
by a donation from the Belgian industrialist Ernest Solvay was constructed
at a height of some 4000m by the end of the season.

The bitter fighting in the Dolomites following Italy's entry to the war
in May led to the death of one of the great guides in the region. Sepp
Innerkofler, who had previously distinguished himself by laying a tele-
phone line up the north face of the Kleine Zinne – the Cima Piccola di
Lavaredo – volunteered to attack a number of Italian troops who had occupied the summit of the neighbouring Paternkofel – the Paterno. Early in
July Innerkofler succeeded in climbing the peak with other guides but the
plan ended in tragedy when he was killed on the summit plateau.

In May a major engineering project was completed more than a year
behind schedule.

*A new railway link between France, Switzerland and Italy – the Frasne-
Vallorbe Railway, including the Mont d'Or Tunnel through the Jura – was
opened for traffic last Sunday without any ceremony.*

Mount Edith Cavell, Canadian Rockies. *(Travel Alberta)*

Serious difficulties were encountered during construction of the line including frequent inflows of water in the tunnel, which is 6km in length.

In July celebrations were held to mark the completion of a new Swiss mountain railway. The line, nearly 11km long, connects Leuk in the Rhône valley with Leukerbad, the resort below the Gemmi Pass in the western Bernese Alps.

In the Caucasus, where foreign mountaineers were unable to continue their exploration, S Golubev and other Russian climbers completed a number of successful expeditions in the central region. After making the first ascents of several peaks in the Adyrsu district including Sarikol (4160m) and Kichkidar (4370m) they reached the summit of the unclimbed Pik Shchurovsky (4259m) above the Ushba plateau by way of the south-east ridge.

During the year some climbing was possible in other mountain regions not directly affected by the conflict. In South Africa W T Cobern and other members of the Mountain Club continued their exploration of Table Mountain (1087m). Several notable new ascents were completed including *Africa Corner*, *Spring Needle* and *Zig-Zag Route*, all outstanding climbs for the period.

In South America in September the Norwegian climber Eilert Sundt and a companion almost made the first winter ascent of Aconcagua (6959m). After reaching the summit ridge from the Horcones valley they were prevented by dangerous snow conditions from completing the short distance to the summit.

In New Zealand Conrad Kain commenced his second season in the Southern Alps after being invited by the government tourist department to join the guiding staff at the Hermitage Hotel. Employed as assistant to Peter Graham the chief guide, Kain completed many fine climbs including the first ascent of Mount Meeson (2699m), one of the peaks on the Main Divide above the Tasman glacier. After returning to Canada he joined Albert and Elizabeth MacCarthy's party to lead a number of successful climbs including the first ascent of Jumbo Mountain (3399m), one of the high peaks in the Purcell range.

Further north in the Rockies A J Gilmour and E W D Holway made the first ascent of the peak later named Mount Edith Cavell (3363m) in honour of the British nurse executed in October for assisting Allied soldiers to escape from German-occupied Belgium.

In January the death occurred of a famous guide from the Dauphiné. Pierre Gaspard *père* is remembered for his outstanding climbs in the region including the first ascents of the western peak or Grand Pic of the Meije and the south face of the Barre des Écrins.

An event which aroused considerable interest was the publication of *The Conquest of Mount Cook and other Climbs* by the Australian climber Freda Du Faur. The work was reviewed in the *Alpine Journal* where it was described as 'one of the best and most comprehensive books dealing with the New Zealand Alps that have yet been published.'

At the annual general meeting of the Alpine Club in December the President, Lord Justice Pickford, referred to the high cost of the war to the Club. During the year five members had lost their lives on active service including Bernard Head, killed at Gallipoli in August, whose party had made the first ascent of Mount Aspiring (3036m) in the Southern Alps. With no end to the conflict in sight Broome spoke for all members when he hoped that it would not be long before 'we shall again be free to flock back to the High Alps, free to scramble up our favourite peaks at our own sweet will, and free to meet our brethren on common ground.'

Area Notes

The Matterhorn. The Matterhorn and Gorner Glacier. John Singer Sargent.
1870. Watercolour and graphite. 38.8 x 27cm. Harvard Art Museums/Fogg
Museum, Gift of Mrs. Francis Ormond, 1937.2.
(Imaging Department © President and Fellows of Harvard College)

LINDSAY GRIFFIN

Alps & Dolomites 2014

The north face of the Grandes Jorasses: 1. *Rolling Stones*, 2. *Directe de l'Amitié*, 3. Polish Combination, 4. *Couzy-Desmaison Route* on Pointe Marguerite. *(Lindsay Griffin)*

2014 was a poor year for significant new routes or notable ascents, not only in the Alps but in most of the Greater Ranges. This was largely down to weather. The 2013-14 winter in the Alps was generally poor, and although the spring had a few 'moments', July and August were dire, and will be remembered as such by all those who sat in rain-sodden campsites throughout the Alps. One campsite manager, north of Chamonix, reported 26 consecutive days of rain. Sadly, there were many accidents, one of the most serious taking place on the Aiguille d'Argentière, when a guide and his five clients were killed in a single incident.

However, come September come the sun – a situation that lasted more or less the entire month. Plenty of snow on the mountains, combined with the drop in temperature that September brings, produced fantastic conditions, particularly on the major north faces. However, while it was the autumn that saw the most productive activity, there were several significant events in the early part of the year.

On the north face of the Grandes Jorasses young Slovenians Luka Kranjc

The west face of the Plan showing the line of *Pilier Septientrionale*. *(Lindsay Griffin)*

and Luka Lindic made the first free ascent of *Rolling Stones* (1200m, ED3) on the Walker Spur. First climbed in 1979 by Czechs Kutil, Prochaska, Slechta and Svejda at VI A3 M, the route has seen few repeats. The two Lukas climbed free at M8, spending four days on the face in March, and finding the crux a delicate and dangerous pitch originally graded A2/A3, on which they passed an ancient rusty bolt.

In the Aiguilles, Chamonix-based activists Jeff Mercier and Korra Pesce made the first free and possibly only the second overall ascent of a little-known Chris Bonington route on the west face of the Aiguille du Plan. In 1965 Bonington climbed three major new routes in the Mont Blanc Massif, culminating, after several attempts, in the *Right-hand Pillar of Brouillard*. The second of these, on which he was accompanied by the American Lito Tejada-Flores, took the obvious left-hand pillar of the Plan's west face via 'delightful climbing of IV and V, with a short section of V+ and one of A1', as far as the headwall. The latter was split by a continuous deep diedre, c200m high and formed of excellent granite. However, facing almost north and therefore getting very little sun, it proved to be heavily iced. The crux was A3, though the pair used no more than 20 aid points on the entire 700m TD+ route, known as the *Pilier Septientrionale*. The pair felt that in good conditions the route would give 'enjoyable climbing of a high order of difficulty', but unfortunately it seems that this idea never took off.

Over the years the lower spur has been subjected to much rockfall, leaving it unpleasantly broken, so Mercier and Pesce climbed the couloir alongside to the headwall, which they began at 11:30am, and were on the summit at 6pm, having enjoyed well protected climbing up deep chimneys, and cracks of all sizes up to M7 in standard. That night they had their feet safely under the table in the Requin Hut, well impressed that the crux section, which they had climbed fast and free in 6½ hours, had taken Bonington and Tejada-Flores only 4½ hours more, almost 50 years ago and with gear that bears no comparison with that used today.

Czechs Jan Straka and Pavel Vritik dispelled any suggestion that worthy independent lines – or gaps – on the big faces of the Mont Blanc Massif are non-existent, by climbing *Le Vol du Dragon* on Les Droites. The pair climbed for a total of 37 hours and made three bivouacs in early March before completing their new line on the 1200m north-east face between the Bergland Pillar and the North-east Spur. They began with the line of weakness between the normal start to the North-east Spur (*Authenac-Tournier*, 1937) and the 1983 *König-Suhubiette Couloir*. Much higher up they crossed the latter to finish via the top section of the Bergland Pillar, probably following ground first climbed in 1991 by Chris Dale and Jim Kerr, when the latter pair made the first direct ascent of the pillar at ED2 (the original Lackner-Messner route climbs mostly in a depression on the left side). Difficulties found on *Vol du Dragon* were M7+ with one pitch of A2.

Sadly, Marco Anghileri, an accomplished Dolomite climber, guide, and son of a famous Italian climber, was killed while attempting a winter solo of the Central Pillar of Frêney. Anghileri was last seen three pitches from the top of the *Chandelle*, having completed more or less all the independent climbing on the 1983 Jori Bardill Route. His body was recovered from below the Hidden Pillar. Judging by the extremely mangled state of the rope and ripped protection, and the fact that at this point the climber is very close to the couloir between the Hidden and Central pillars, the rescue team recorded a distinct possibility that he was swept from the wall by a large ice avalanche.

In the Valais the current trend towards, and increased media coverage of, speed ascents saw Italian guide Hervé Barmasse complete an impressive one-day, solo, link-up on the Matterhorn. Barmasse linked all four ridges of this iconic Swiss-Italian peak on a day of excellent weather towards the end of the winter season. In 1965 René Arnold and Joseph Graven started from the 3300m Bossi Bivouac hut a little above the Breuiljoch, followed the standard line up the Furggen Ridge (1150m, D-/D), descended the Hörnli Ridge (1220m, AD), crossed the Matterhorn Glacier to the Zmutt Ridge, climbed it (c 1200m, D), and descended the Italian (Lion) Ridge (c 1400m, AD/AD+), carrying on down to the village of Breuil in the Valtournenche, which they reached after a total of 19½ hours. In September 1985 Hervé's father, Marco, decided to repeat this, solo, but elected to start with the more difficult *Furggen Direct*, first climbed in 1941 by Carrel, Chiara and Perino. This gives 150m of sustained rock climbing

Coeurs de Géants on the north-west face of the Dent du Géant. *(Lindsay Griffin)*

from IV-V+ in the section above the shoulder. Marco Barmasse started at the Bossi Bivouac hut, made most likely the first solo ascent of the *Furggen Direct*, and continued to repeat the Arnold-Graven link-up, reaching the Abruzzi Hut (2802m), below the Italian Ridge, in a total of 15 hours.

Hervé decided to repeat his father's 1985 enchainment, only this time in the cold and snowy conditions of winter. He left the Bossi Bivouac at 5:45am and his time of 17 hours took him to the Carrel Hut on the Italian Ridge, where his father was waiting in support. Barmasse's ascent of the *Furggen Direct* is perhaps the first winter solo.

Less significant, but interesting because of their esoteric nature, were routes put up by local climbers who were able to utilise rare spells of good weather and conditions to climb new ground in less well-known corners of the Alps, where there is still much potential. The Grandes Murailles are a collection of summits on the west side of the upper Valtournenche, with the most shapely peaks being Punta Sella (3878m) and Punta Giordano (3872m), together known as Les Jumeaux. The coombe below these summits provides the most important venue in the region for serious icefall enthusiasts. One of the cardinal routes here is the *Cascatone Couloir*, a Gian Carlo Grassi ED1 from 1986. Italians François Cazzanelli and Roberto Ferraris added a new line to the wall between Punta Sella and Becca di Guin (3805m) to its south, climbing 850m to the ridge crest at V/4. They then finished (with a variant) up the 1877 original route to the top of Punta Sella.

In one of the less familiar sub ranges in the pre-Alps south of the Bregaglia, (Italian) AC member Tito Arosio and two companions put up the 650m *Mera Dimel* (AI4 M6) on the Anticime delle Quatro Matte, a little visited corner of the Presolana Range.

Further east in the Presanella Group Giovanni Ghezzi and Davide Lorenzi put up *Clean Climb* on the north face of Monte Nero (3344m), a 480m trad protected mixed route on granite at IV M4.

A little later in the year Christopher Baud, Brice Bouillanne and Jonathan Charlet added a new route to the very rarely climbed north-west face of the Dent du Géant. Relatively short (c380m), with a slightly convoluted approach, the face is predominately high altitude rock, and as such was considered 'out of condition' unless very dry, when other objective problems presented themselves. It was finally climbed in 1981 by Italians Benedetti and Luigi, who recorded it as an icy rock route, with a difficulty of TD. This route, and indeed the exact location of the line,

Alessandro Lolli on the fine hanging diedre (IV+) of *Canalone Grigio. (Marco Blatto)*

has somewhat fallen into obscurity. The new route is essentially mixed on surprisingly excellent rock, with much sustained dry tooling at around M5, a crux of M5+, and a fine little ice couloir on pitch three. *Coeurs de Géants* (ED) has 10 pitches/560m of climbing. A quick escape from the summit is made these days by three long rappels down the south-east face from bolted anchors. Using these, the trio reached the Torino Hut in 1½ hours from the summit.

AC members Tom Prentice and Simon Richardson completed a 20-year quest by climbing a new rock route on the remote east face of Mont Greuvettaz. The story behind *Il Solitario Pilastro* ('*Lonely Pillar'*, 500m, TD+ 6a+) appears elsewhere in this Journal.

Another Italian AC member Marco Blatto climbed two new alpine rock routes away from the high mountains, above the head of the Lanzo Valley on peaks close to the French border, just south of the Orco/Gran Paradiso. In August, with Alessandro Lolli, he put up *Canalone Grigio*, which is an integral ascent of the south-south-east ridge of Punta Clavarino (3260m), a long climb at D- (V-). The pair accessed the ridge from the Paolo Daviso Hut at 2280m. The following month Blatto also added *Tempo Scaduto* on the northeast buttress of the Poire du Mulinet (2850m), a short route (c

Above: The north-west face of the Aiguille de Talèfre and below: one of the linking mixed pitches on the ascent of the north-west face of the Aiguille de Talèfre. *(Tim Elson)*

210m) at VII and A1 climbed from the Bivacco Ferreri-Rivero (2207m) with Stefano Giaccone.

The high mountains would come alive again in September as hard mixed routes came into 'once in a lifetime' conditions. This was best exemplified with an unprecedented number of ascents of most of the big routes on the north face of the Grandes Jorasses. This face, now the crucible of modern mixed climbing on serious big walls, is no doubt even more fashionable since the publication of Julian Désécures, 212-page dedicated guidebook, which details all the climbs on the north face, all the mixed routes on the east face, and the descent routes on the south flank. Hundreds of alpinists are reported to have climbed the face during the autumn, with the most popular line, the Colton-MacIntyre, often sporting queues.

Martin Elias and Korra Pesce climbed the 1100m *Directe de l'Amitié* as a mixed route at M7 A3 over two days. This major line to Pointe Whymper, climbed in the winter of 1974 and with few repeats, has yet to see a free ascent: in 1994 a French team, making the third ascent in more dangerous, dry, summer conditions, eliminated much of the aid, recording difficulties of 6c/7a A1.

The 'Polish' route was apparently in excellent condition and received its first (Korra Pesce) and second (Philippe Angelo) solo ascents in the space of little over a week. Both climbers followed a combination of the 1970 (*Chrobak-Poreba-Wroz*) and 1975 (*Kurtyka-Kukuczka-Lukaszewski*) Polish routes to the summit of Pointe Hélène. Pesce climbed the route in just 2hr 10 minutes, quoting the technicalities as around WI5, and descending the south flank; Angelo finished by traversing the Rochefort, reaching the Torino Hut the same day.

On the Marguerite Spur Sébastien Bohin, Bertrand Delapierre, Julien Désécures, Jon Griffith and Korra Pesce climbed icy variants to the 850m *Couzy-Desmaison Route*, another rarely repeated line due to its reputation for very poor rock. First climbed in 1958 at a grade of TD V+ A1, the first winter and second ascent had to wait until February 1975, with the first summer repeat the same year (by the Burgess twins and Paul Moores). The five-man multi-national team didn't follow the original line but took advantage of the exceptional conditions to climb ephemeral ice smears a little left of the route to about half-height, from where they more or less followed the original line. The final chimney and exit onto the west ridge, which Couzy and Desmaison climbed at UIAA 'IV, V and A1', was a series of magnificent ice pitches. The team climbed the entire route to Pointe Marguerite (4065m) all free at around M5, and descended the west ridge to the Canzio Bivouac on the Col des Grandes Jorasses the same day. Whilst not exactly an independent new route, this represents a modern way to tackle a traditional, if rarely visited, rock line. It was also one of five routes climbed in 2014 by AC member Griffith on the north face of the Grandes Jorasses, bringing his overall total to 10.

Italian activist Enrico Bonino put up a couple of technical mixed climbs above Combe Maudit. With Luca Breveglieri and Oliver Colaye he first

Convenient climbing? Looking into the Cunningham Couloir on the Aiguille du Midi. From the left edge of the lower building (the viewing platform) mixed ground drops directly to a triangular ridged snowpatch, with a steep corner falling to its right. *Double Dave* takes this line. *(Lindsay Griffin)*

climbed the 500m *Saumons et Glaçons* (M5+ WI5 R) parallel to and left of the classic *Filo d'Arianna* (Faré-Grassi-Longhi, 1984) on the Third Pillar, East Face of Mont Maudit. He returned for *An...ice surprise* (M7 WI5 A1+), which climbs the steep front of the buttress left of the *Androsace Couloir* (Gabarrou-Muller, 1979). On the first attempt Bonino and the talented female alpinist Giulia Venturelli were stopped by the entry pitch, but the pair came back armed with copperheads and RURPs, and forced this section to steep, thin, mixed ground above. They terminated the route atop the buttress, where the angle eases.

On the 600m north-west face of the Aiguille de Talèfre AC members Tim Elson and Max Folkett made a minor variant – *The Clueless Variation* – climbing a section of new ground between *Nuit Caline* and the classic 1978 *Dufour Route*. In common with many new lines, this was climbed in error, the pair originally planning to follow the *Dufour*. However, they were only able to cross the bergschrund at its extreme left, where steep moves followed by an ice groove at Scottish V (the crux) led to the point where the *Dufour* moves left and the normally narrow gully of *Nuit Caline* continues direct, left of the *North-west Couloir* (the Gabarrou brothers, 1978). Elson and Folkett continued up *Nuit Caline*, then broke out left on a mixed pitch, continued up the gully above, and reached mixed ground on the right side of the central icefield. They were now just right of the Gabarrou-Ponti route (*Voie de Droite*) and realised that the *Dufour* lay far to the left again. They made a rising traverse into the *Dufour's* upper gully and followed it to the summit. The route was quite sustained at around Scottish IV, but featured much 'snice', which although good for the feet, meant axes kept ripping: hence the need to keep to more mixed terrain in the lower section. The north-west face lies in a quiet corner of the Mont Blanc Massif and is relatively overlooked compared to other faces, yet Elson and Folkett found the climbing excellent, with no fixed gear.

On the Aiguille du Midi Dave Almond and Dave Garry climbed two, possibly new, short mixed routes on the side wall of the Cunningham Couloir. The steep mixed flanks of the upper Cunningham Couloir have grown in popularity, given the relatively easy access and short but technical lines. Coming out of the top cable car station and crossing the bridge to the central summit, the climbs are clearly visible down to the right and are accessed by gaining the bed of the couloir via an airy free rappel from the bridge. François Burnei and the late Romain Vogler were more or less the first to investigate the potential, when they rappelled from the bridge in 1980, descended the couloir for 300m, then climbed a fine mixed line (M4) out to the Cosmiques Arête. Whilst most activity takes place on the true left (south) bank of the couloir, below the Cosmiques Arête, Almond and Garry tackled features on the more sunny north bank. The first route, *Club Tropicana* (120m, M6+), climbed with Tom Coney, starts about 60m below the end of the first rappel, and has a first pitch crux. The second, *Double Dave* (145m, M7 or Scottish VII, 8) follows a steep icy corner to an obvious triangular snow patch, then easier ground to below the viewing platform on the north summit. This is very much climbing in the public eye.

One day before the official 2014-15 season Chamonix based guides and AC members Jon Bracey and Matt Helliker climbed five possibly-new pitches on the north-west face of the Tour Ronde, to create the 250m *Chancer*. This short but intense line climbs steep ground between the 1977 *Cordier Route*, and the 1967 *Mazars-Rébuffat Couloir*. In a biting cold wind, the pair climbed three pitches of relatively amenable mixed ground to reach a steep rock buttress split by a corner system containing a very narrow seam of ice. Helliker despatched the crux 55m pitch, using delicate ice and hooks, at M6 to gain a good stance. A further steady pitch brought the two to a small notch on the crest of the ridge overlooking the *Mazars-Rébuffat*, into which they rappelled and then descended.

Two highly notable ascents took place in the Écrins. In the spring and on the north-west face of Ailefroide Occidentale (3954m), following the huge gully left of *Voie des Plaques*, Antoine Avenas, Jonathan Isoard and Hélias Millerioux put up *Le Reactor*, a 1000m line at 6b M7 WI5+, R. Snatching a brief weather window in August, Max Bonniot and Mathieu Maynadier established *Été Blizzard* (M6+, 4, 70°), first on the left side of the north face of the Meije (3983m), and then along the north spur right of the *Gravelotte Couloir*. The ice was thin and protection sparse. They then continued across the range to attempt a repeat of *Le Reactor*. They climbed the first part to where it touches the *Voie des Plaques*, but then decided to escape right up the latter.

There is little of an outstanding nature to report from the Dolomites, though each year many new routes are added to the wealth of rock, much of it less than perfect, that exists throughout this vast expanse of limestone.

On the famous Tofana di Rozes, Simon Gietl and Daniel Tavanini put up the 10-pitch (320m) *No Credit* on the south face at X-, the route breaching

Matt Helliker tracing the crux M6 pitch of *Chancer* on the north-west face of the Tour Ronde. *(Jon Bracey)*

huge red overhangs (with some dubious rock) with no use of a drill (trad gear and pegs for belays and protection throughout). Tom Ballard climbed more than 60 routes in the Dolomites during the summer, with several first solo ascents. Perhaps the most notable from this talented alpinist and son of the late Alison Hargreaves was the *Toni Egger Memorial Route* on the Rotwand, a 400m VIII+ climbed all free and solo.

Scotland's Dave MacLeod put up an important variation on the north face of the Cime Ovest when he climbed 130m of new ground, which starts up the 1968 *Bauer-Rudolph* aid climb, then continues direct to reach the 8c crux of Alex Huber's *Pan Aroma*, up which it finishes. The new ground features a long endurance pitch of 8a+. MacLeod climbed this with Alan Cassidy, who shortly before had climbed *Bellavista* (8c) on the same face with Rob Sutton.

SIMON RICHARDSON

Scottish Winter 2014-15

The 2015 winter was a remarkable one, and full of contrasts. Although
the season was short, starting in December and finishing for many
in March, it was an action-packed four months. The weather was often
stormy, but the wet autumn meant that as the mountains cooled down in
January, the mid-level gullies and smears began to weep copious amounts
of ice providing many opportunities for those poised to take advantage.
Despite the presence of the ice, the technical highlights were mixed routes:
Guy Robertson and Greg Boswell's three new Grade Xs and Boswell's new
Grade XII in the Northern Corries. Two of these Grade Xs were climbed
on sight and are the start of a new chapter in the history of Scottish winter
climbing.

Despite these outstanding successes, opinions are sharply divided as to
whether or not it was a good winter. Ice conditions may have been excellent, but with few periods of settled weather, there were limited opportunities to climb. To the frustration of many climbers, many of the best
days occurred mid-week. The statistics bear this out with almost 70% of
new routes climbed Monday to Friday – a surprising statistic considering
that most climbers operate at weekends. As always, flexibility was key
and Andy Nisbet, the grand master of Scottish winter climbing, showed
the way by being perfectly in tune with weather patterns and making first
ascents of many mid-level ice routes.

Grade X Hat Trick

Greg Boswell and Guy Robertson started their remarkable run of
cutting-edge routes on 19 January when they made the first ascent of *The
Greatest Show on Earth* (X,10) on the north face of Cul Mor in Coigach.
This awe-inspiring route takes the blank wall on the right side of Coire
Gorm. It is defended by a large overhang and is plum vertical above, and
was considered by the last generation to be a problem for the next generation. And so it was – Robertson led the first pitch, a steep icefall leading to
a small terrace below the overhang, before handing over to Boswell who
then made one of his finest leads by pulling through the roof and climbing
the poorly protected wall above. This was the first time a new Grade X
had been climbed on sight, although Nick Bullock's lead of the crux pitch
of *Nevermore* on Lochnagar last season hinted that this breakthrough was
not far away.

Four days later, Roberson and Boswell turned their attention to the
100m-high Broad Terrace Wall on Creag an Dubh Loch. The angle tips

Guy Robertson leading the first pitch of *The Greatest Show on Earth* (X,10) on Cul Mor during the first ascent. The route continues up the wall above starting from the small ice smear up and left of Guy's head. The ascent enters Scottish winter climbing history as the first on-sight of a new Grade X. *(Greg Boswell)*

considerably the wrong side of vertical between the lines of *Sword of Damocles* and *Culloden*, and in summer this section is breached by two mythical climbs – *Flodden* (E6) and *Range War* (E4). *Range War* is the steeper line, but the first pitch is very vegetated and the route has only been climbed a handful of times since its first ascent by Kenny Spence and Duncan McCallum in July 1983.

Boswell had walked into Dubh Loch seven times to attempt the route, and finally on 22 January the stars aligned; Boswell and Robertson found the cliff white with hoar frost and dripping with icicles and frozen turf. They climbed an alternative first pitch left of the original summer line to the Grass Balcony, a welcome ledge in a sea of overhanging rock. Boswell then led the daunting 35m-long overhanging crux pitch (graded British 6a in summer), pulling on huge reserves of physical and mental strength, leaving Robertson the top pitch of thick bulging ice. The pair gave *Range War (Winter Variation)* the same grade as *The Greatest Show in Earth* at X,10.

Ten days later, Robertson and Boswell teamed up with Uisdean Hawthorn and succeeded on the long sought-after first winter ascent of *The Messiah* on Beinn Bhan. The route was possibly first climbed by Creag Dhu climbers George Shields and Bob Jarvie in summer 1972, but their ascent was not recorded, and the route passed into climbing folklore. The eight-pitch winter route was graded X,10 and completed a remarkable hat trick of three new Grade Xs. 'We didn't intend to go out and climb three new Grade Xs in succession,' Greg explained. 'We've been waiting for these

Greg Boswell just after his spectacular 10 metre fall from *Banana
Wall* (XII,12) in Coire an Lochain
in the Northern Corries. After
lowering down for a rest, Boswell
then led the route on his second
attempt that day. *(Masa Sakano)*

routes for the past few seasons,
and with the stormy weather
this winter, they all came into
perfect condition... all the
training and route planning
paid off... and to have them be
three hard routes is the perfect
scenario. Scottish winter at its
best!'

Banana Wall

Greg Boswell's final groundbreaking ascent of the season
took place on 25 February
when he succeeded on the awe-
inspiring *Banana Wall* (XII,12) in Coire an Lochain on Cairn Gorm, with
Masa Sakano. This continuously sustained route, which takes the overhanging wall between *Fallout Corner* and *Bavarinthia*, is only the second
route in Scotland ever to be given a Grade XII rating.

Boswell first tried the route in 2011, but after two failed attempts, he
abseiled the line to see if it could be protected. The wall is so undercut
that he hung too far out to gain any useful information. With four more
years of winter experience under his belt and fresh from his superb trio of
new Grade Xs, Boswell felt ready for a return visit. On his first attempt he
took a 10m fall when a placement ripped. After a break he tried again and
successfully led the pitch. Sakano followed and they completed the route
in the dark whilst battling a rising storm. 'The route is crazy steep but the
protection is there if you can hang on long enough to place it,' Boswell
explained. 'It is by far the most sustained thing I've done in Scotland.'
Boswell considers *Banana Wall* to be M11, which makes it one of the most
difficult technical mixed routes ever climbed by placing the gear on the
lead.

Early Season

After a very warm November, the winter season finally got underway in
the first week of December, as westerly winds brought snow to the higher
tops. As usual, The Northern Corries were the most popular venue and there
were ascents of *The Message*, *Pot of Gold*, *Hidden Chimney* and *Invernookie*

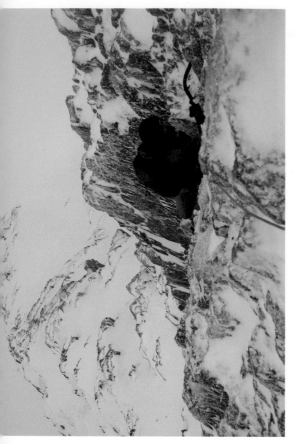

Roger Webb nearing the top of the crux pitch of *Tenterhooks* (VII,8) on Ben Nevis during the first ascent.
(Simon Richardson)

in Coire an t-Sneachda, and over in Coire an Lochain, *Savage Slit* and *Ewen Buttress* were also climbed.

The first new route of the season fell to Ally and Gav Swinton on Creagan Cha-no on Cairn Gorm, where they made the first ascent of *Punching Numbers* (VI,7), the steep crack-line right of *Mac's Crack*. A couple of days later on Ben Nevis, Will Sim and Andy Inglis set the pace with the second ascent of *Toma-hawk Crack* (VIII,9). This excellent route to the right of Sioux Wall on Number Three Gully Buttress was first climbed by Greg Boswell and Adam Russell in November 2012.

Ferocious storms the following week relented in mid-December providing a welcome weather window. Martin Moran and Robin Thomas visited Beinn Eighe and made the first winter ascent of *Boggle* (VIII,8) on the Eastern Ramparts. 'It was worth the wait and a special thrill to climb a Robin Smith route in winter,' Moran said afterwards. The same day, Guy Robertson and Greg Boswell pulled off the second ascent of *Culloden* (IX,9) on Creag an Dubh Loch's formidable Broad Terrace Wall. This exceptionally steep summer E2 was first climbed in winter by Iain Small, Gordon Lennox and Tony Stone in December 2010. *Culloden* was an inspired route choice as Creag an Dubh Loch is not normally considered an early season venue.

The weather on the run-up to Christmas continued stormy and unsettled but as ever, Andy Nisbet was on hand to visit the right place at the right time. On Stob Ban he made the first ascent of *Flying Saucer* (VI,7) with Steve Perry and on Aonach Mor he added *Gonzo* (IV,4) to the Ribbed Walls with Jonathan Preston.

The weather finally settled down between Christmas and New Year and Uisdean Hawthorn and Murdoch Jamieson nipped in for the second ascent of *Boggle* on Beinn Eighe – an unusually quick repeat of a major route. Three days later, Hawthorn teamed up with Callum Johnson on Ben Nevis to climb *Super G* (VI,6) on the Little Brenva Face This ephemeral ice route had probably not had a second ascent since it was first climbed by Hannah Burrows-Smith and Dave McGimpsey in March 2002. Also on the Ben, Iain Small and Tony Stone had a productive couple of days making third ascents of *The Brass Monkey* (VII,8) and *The Great Corner* (VIII,8).

Across in Glen Coe, Andy Nelson, Kenny Grant and Keith Ball added an excellent mixed route to Stob Coire nan Lochan. The sustained three-pitch *Tried and Tested* (VII,7) climbs the chimney-corner formed by the spur of Central Buttress and the wall of *Satyr* and was described as being 'at the sporty end of its grade.' Roger Webb and Simon Richardson took advantage of a short sudden freeze after the New Year thaw to make the first ascent of *Tenterhooks* (VII,8) on Ben Nevis. This steep, icy mixed climb on Creag Coire na Ciste between *Central Rib* and *Tinkerbell* brought the first part of the season to a close as more storms rushed in from the Atlantic.

Cold and Snowy

The stormy weather finally settled down in mid-January and a cold and snowy spell set in. The snow line was low, which made route choice difficult, but winter climbers are becoming increasingly adept at hunting out the most appropriate venues for the prevailing conditions, and soon a host of excellent routes were being climbed.

Many of the most notable ascents were early repeats, and Erik Baillot and Rob Bryniarski set the ball rolling with the second ascent of *The Sea, The Sea* on Slioch. This legendary Grade VII was first climbed by Roger Webb and Neil Wilson 20 years ago and is the second winter route on Slioch's huge Atlantic Wall to see a repeat. Clearly on a roll, Baillot made the third winter ascent of *Enigma* (VII,7) on Mainreachan Buttress the following weekend, and nearby, Andy Inglis and Will Sim made the second winter ascent of the technical *Pale Rider* (VIII,9) on Beinn Eighe. Further north, Helen Rennard and Simon Yearsley made the third winter ascent of *Castro* (VII,7) on Sgurr an Fhidhleir and two days later Rennard joined the small group of climbers who have climbed this magnificent feature more than once in winter, by making an ascent of the *Nose Direct* (VII,7) with Simon Davidson and Neil Silver.

The relatively low-lying Giant's Wall on Beinn Bhan saw the most activity however, with an early repeat of *The Godfather* (VIII,8) by Neil Adams and Graham McGrath and the second ascent of *Godzilla* (IX,9) by Iain Small, Murdoch Jamieson and Andy Inglis. Small and Jamieson returned a few days later to make the second ascent of *The God Delusion* (IX,9). This Robertson-Benson creation from 2008 is considered one of the most demanding winter routes in the Northern Highlands and was described by Small as 'a masterpiece in route finding.'

Elsewhere in the north-west, Andy Nisbet, Jonathan Preston and Dave McGimpsey added *Jinky* (V,5) to the Western Cliffs of Quinag which

Murdoch Jamieson leading pitch 6 of *The God Delusion* (IX,9) on The Giant's Wall on Beinn Bhan. *(Iain Small)*

are always a good choice when snow levels are low, and James Edwards and Neil Wilson found *Sideshow* (IV,6), a good looking chimney-line in Coire Gorm on Cul Mor. Over on Mainreachan Buttress, Iain Small and Murdoch Jamieson climbed a spectacular series of bulging ice pitches approximating to the summer route *Private Eye* (VIII,8), and further east, Andy Nisbet and Jonathan Preston added *Twerk* (V,5) to the rarely visited Coire nan Eun in the Fannaichs.

Classic Conditions

In early February the temperature rose, but cold clear nights transformed the snow into névé and the drainage lines filled with ice. On the west face of Aonach Beag, Andy Nisbet and Steve Perry had a great day climbing *Axiom* (III), the central gully on the lower face (a line so obvious that everyone thought it had been done before), *Santa* (V,5), the icy corner left of Prominent Chimney, and the steep *Right-Hand Branch to Bottleneck Gully* (VII,7).

But Ben Nevis was where the finest conditions were to be found, especially on the mid-height ice routes. The snow was frozen hard and the bright sunny weather made it feel more like spring than early February. For the first time in many years *Gemini* and *The Shield Direct* on Carn Dearg Buttress came into excellent condition and both routes saw dozens of ascents. Nearby, *The Bewildabeast* (VI,6), a Mark Garthwaite–Adam Wainwright route from 1995 saw its first ever repeats with all the parties raving about the quality of the climbing and the sensational positions.

On the new route front, Malcolm Bass, Simon Yearsley and Neil Silver succeeded on a long-standing objective with the first ascent of *Cousinade* (VII,8). This route climbs the front face of Cousin's Buttress using a steep groove spotted by Bass on the second of his previous attempts with Yearsley in 2013. Pride of place went to Andy Inglis and Iain Small for their first winter ascent of *Teufel Grooves* (IX,9) on Raeburn's Buttress. This steep route takes the hanging corner on the right flank, but rather than start up the summer HVS which uses the first section *The Crack*, Small found an independent direct entry. Inglis then made a superb lead of the crux pitch. 'It looked very intimidating from below,' Small explained. 'It was an overhanging corner-crack that had no hooks, just torques, and at the belay Andy's ropes were hanging free in space. Yeah, it was steep!'

As February progressed, the focus increasingly turned to ice and Uisdean Hawthorn climbed an impressive triptych of routes. He started off with the first ascent of *Han Solo* (VIII,7) on Ben Nevis, a thin ice drool hanging above the first pitch of *Storm Trooper* on the left side of Creag Coire na Ciste. 'Uisdean's lead of the smear was impressive,' Guy Robertson commented later. 'The ice was maybe only about three inches thick at best, and a lot thinner in places. All in all it was a pretty cool cerebral experience and I'd have thought one of the harder bits of ice the Ben has to offer.' The next day Hawthorn linked up with Iain Small and Murdoch Jamieson to make an ascent of *The Fly Direct*, the highly prized thin ice gully on Creag Meagaidh's Pinnacle Buttress. Seeing that the neighbouring *Extasy* (a Grade VIII that you really shouldn't fall off) was in condition, the trio returned the following day to make the fourth ascent. 'I would have been delighted to climb just one of these routes in a season but to climb them both in two days, after doing a new route on Ben Nevis the day before, left me on a high,' Uisdean said afterwards.

Ice conditions improved further on Ben Nevis and many teams took their fill on rarely formed modern classics such as such as *The Shroud*, *Mega*

Steve Perry below the Tower during the first winter ascent of the 470m-long *Tower Ridge* (V,6) on the north-west face of Ben Hope. *(Andy Nisbet)*

Route X and *Boomer's Requiem*. Michael Barnard and John MacLeod took advantage of the rarely formed ice to make the first ascent of *Shear Fear* (VI,5), the direct continuation to *Vanishing Gully* and the steep *Superdirect Finish* (VI,5) to *Nordwand Direct*.

More mixed in nature was *Inception* (V,7) a line of grooves and chimneys in the Fawlty Towers area of Secondary Tower Ridge by Steve Holmes and Duncan Curry, and the technical *Red Dragon* (VIII,9) by Dave MacLeod and Helen Rennard that takes the steep crack and wall just left of *The Urchin* on the east side of Tower Ridge. Also on the Ben, seasoned regulars Dave Rudkin and Keith Ball notched up an important repeat with the second winter ascent of *The Crack* (VIII,8) on the front face of Raeburn's Buttress. Further east, Andy Nisbet, Steve Perry and Dan Bailey added the excellent-looking line of *Navigator* (VI,6) to Stob a'Choire Mheadhoin, a secluded cliff that can only be seen from the West Highland Railway.

Nisbet and Perry had an impressive run in the North West notching up *Barbie* (V,6) on Beinn Liath Mhor (with Sandy Allan), *Batman* (VI,7) on the Northern Pinnacles face of Mullach nan Rathain on Liathach and the first winter ascent of *Tower Ridge* (V,6) on Ben Hope. The last route was something of a coup being 470m long and snatched in fairytale conditions of deep rime in advance of a warm front rushing up from the south. Guy Robertson and Uisdean Hawthorn made a successful raid on An Teallach and came away with the first ascent of *Low Riders* (VII,8), a prominent line of corners on the steep lower section of Minor Rib.

In the Cairngorms, Nisbet and Perry continued their good run with first ascents of the icy *Blood Hound* (VI,6) on Lurcher's Crag (again with Sandy Allan) and the steep *Waive Wall* (V,7) in the rarely visited Coire Garbhlach. The most impressive achievement in the Cairngorms however was visiting German climber Ines Papert's ascent of *The Hurting* (XI,11) in Coire an t-Sneachda. This was the fifth overall and first female ascent, but these statistics only tell half the story. The route was climbed on the last day of her visit (after an attempt two days before) during terrible weather with winds gusting over 100mph on the tops. Papert's fall-free ascent of *The Hurting* is almost certainly the finest yet, but remarkably this 10-year-old test-piece still awaits an onsight ascent.

Late Season Blues

The weather finally settled down in the middle of March allowing Iain Small to make two excellent additions to Ben Nevis. Starting off with Blair Fyffe, he climbed the *Piece Maker* (VIII,9), a steep mixed line between *Clefthanger* and *The Angry Chair*, on the east flank of Tower Ridge. This high and sheltered part of the mountain retains mixed climbing conditions longer than other venues. Two days later Small teamed up with Uisdean Hawthorn to make the first ascent of *Call Me Ishmael* (VIII,9) on Indicator Wall, an ephemeral and challenging route to the left of *Stormy Petrel*.

Perhaps the most noteworthy late season event however was the development of An Riabhachan by Andy Nisbet who climbed a remarkable 17 new routes in three days. This remote corrie had only been visited a couple of times before by winter climbers and illustrates the remaining potential for exploratory mountaineering potential in the Scottish Highlands. And needless to say Nisbet's visits were perfectly timed, as by the end of March the spring thaw had well and truly set in.

BRUCE NORMAND

China & Tibet 2014

Burnag Kangri from the north-west. *(Bruce Normand)*

Access to all areas of Tibet continues to be highly restricted, with a turf war between the Tibetan Tourist Board and the Public Security Bureau over responsibility for foreigners exacerbating tight 'national security' controls. All counties in eastern Tibet continued to be completely closed to foreigners, other than Tamotsu Nakamura and his team (see his article in this volume), as were all border areas east of Shishapangma, with the exception of the 8000m summits. Beyond these peaks and some regular, guided 6000m hikes, only one new route appears to have been climbed in 2014.

Access to Xinjiang remains possible despite a very major security clampdown, both due to and contributing to a general escalation of dissatisfaction and unrest among the Uighur population. One up-side of Beijing's heavy-handed policies for third parties is the official intent, at all costs, to maintain an appearance of normalcy and 'business as usual'. For the China Xinjiang Mountaineering Association, however, normal business means driving the costs ever higher, and spiralling logistical, permit and Liaison Officer prices combined with an extremely unhelpful attitude to anyone not applying for a tourist-brochure activity (in essence, a Muztagh Ata trek) are keeping activity levels very low. Despite this situation, 2014 did see six different teams visit all four of Xinjiang's major mountain ranges.

Access to Sichuan appears to have become significantly easier, with rather little in the way of official opposition to climbing around Siguniang Shan, where the vast majority of activity continues to be concentrated. One reason for an overall easing of regulations may be the completion of a project to build PAP (People's Armed Police) Headquarters in every village in the western part of the province, and certainly self-immolations are no longer making the news. However, teams with permits obtained at the national or provincial level may still face local opposition, although this has not been tested due to recent activities concentrating on 'known' regions. Climbers did not help their own cause in the Siguniang area in 2014, with two fatalities very early in the year causing an official curfew to be imposed on ice-climbers, and two more fatal accidents in summer and early winter leading to more aggravation of the authorities. The reaction of said authorities to the final accident, which left two bodies lying in the open for more than six weeks while the issuing of death certificates to the grieving parents was blocked, suggests that they would prefer to wash their hands of anything climbing-related; the situation concerning the bodies and the parents was resolved only by the persistence and decisive action of two visiting foreigners, Marcos Costa and Enzo Oddo.

Glacier approach below P6184. *(Bruce Normand)*

This report will also contain climbs from 2013 which, due to often slow confession rates on the part of activists in the region, went unreported in the previous edition of the area notes.

Tibet, Lapche Kang Range

Gyao Kang (6735m) is one of a number of rounded peaks in this border range between Cho Oyu and Menlungtse, and enjoys easy access from the village of Tingri on the Friendship Highway. In spring 2012, Paulo Grobel (France) made the first known ascent by the west ridge, and in autumn 2014 he returned with a group of fellow countrymen to climb the east ridge. Both all-snow routes are graded PD+ and were completed in a day from a high camp.

Tibet, West Nyanchentanglha and Chomolhari Ranges

Chinese couple Zhou Peng and Li Shuang own a vehicle and enjoy access to Tibet of which non-Chinese can only dream. As part of a long road trip in 2013, in September they climbed two summits in the West Nyanchentanglha Range, directly north of Lhasa. P5955 and P6192 are located on the south side of the road and railway, and both were climbed by their north-western aspects. Later in the month, and climbing with colleagues Yang Bo and Zhang Hao, Zhou and Li made a one-day ski ascent, from a drive-in high camp at 5800m, of Chomolhari Kang (7034m).

Tibet, Shishapangma Range

The Shishapangma Range remains accessible to climbers and offers some unclimbed and highly technical targets. Two teams in the area in autumn 2013 were foiled on their primary objectives by persistently poor weather but made notable climbs on acclimatisation peaks. Max Bonniot and Sébastien Moatti (France) made the first known ascent of Sursun Ri (6535m), finding short sections of mixed climbing to M4 and ice to 70° on the north-east ridge. Luka Lindic, Nejc Marcic, Marko Prezelj, Luka Strazar and Martin Zumer (Slovenia) climbed a new route on Ice Tooth (6200m), finding hard rock followed by easy mixed and snow climbing on the east ridge and upper east face.

Xinjiang, Tien Shan

The Kokshaal Too range of the western Tien Shan is famous for tall granite walls, particularly around Kyzyl Asker (5842m) and Pik Byeliy ('Grand Poobah', 5697m). Teams choosing to avoid the costs and officialdom of Xinjiang can approach from Kyrgyzstan but cross into Chinese territory by the Window Col to reach the bases of their routes. The Russian team of Dmitri Golovchenko, Dmitri Grigoriev and Sergei Nilov returned this way to a line on the south-south-east face of Kyzyl Asker which they started in 2009, completing *War and Peace* (1350m, ED, 6b, A2, M6) over 12 days on the wall. The Ecuadorean team of Rafael Caceres, Estoban Mena, Nicolas Navarette and Carla Perez did approach from Xinjiang, albeit with only hiking permits, and despite poor weather were able to climb a 1100m line further to the right on the same face (*Sal con Cebolla*, 5.12a, C1, WI5+, M6+).

The same region also saw significant action in 2013 climbs, with Nicolas Favresse, Stephane Hanssens, Sean Villaneuva and Evrard Wendenbaum establishing the *Belgian Route* (1400m, 7b+, M6/7) on the prow of the South Pillar of Kyzyl Asker, to the left of the Russian (2007) and *War and Peace* lines. Bas Vischer led a Dutch team to the Great Walls of China (5186m), abutting the same glacier, and after some abortive rock-climbing efforts by all six team members, he, Vincent Perrin and Bas van der Smeede were successful on an alpine ice line to the northern top. Nearby, Mike Libecki, Ethan Pringle (both USA) and Liv Sansoz (France) established a new alpine rock line (5.12 R) in the valley of Peak Byeliy.

Elsewhere in the Tien Shan in 2014, the British team of Boris Korzh and Sam Thompson was able to reach the Xuelian Range without undue bureaucratic problems but was shut down by weather. Elsewhere in northern Xinjiang, in 2013 a large team of foreign rock climbers based in eastern China was able to renegotiate access to the Koktokay valley, a region of granite walls close to the Mongolian border, and to establish a number of new rock-climbing routes, primarily in cracks of all sizes.

Xinjiang, Pamir

One of the guided groups in the region around Kongur and Muztagh Ata was on the lookout for something new and different. Led by Luis Stitzinger and assisted by Singi Lama and Chongba Sherpa, a team of 14 Austrian and German climbers reached the unclimbed summit of Kokodag Dome (7137m).

Jesse Mease during an acclimatisation climb on P6184. *(Bruce Normand)*

Xinjiang, Kun Lun

A British team led by John Town made an attempt on Liushen Tag (6535m) in the central part of the range, finding extremely dry conditions in September and extremely expensive permit arrangements. Although unsuccessful on their primary objective, Zaheer Durrani, Gus Morton, Stefan Jachmich and Susan Jensen all climbed a local snow peak, P6004.

Xinjiang, Karakoram

A large international group led by Bruce Normand was able to gain access to the upper Shaksgam Valley. Across from the Gasherbrums, the Kulchintubulak valley leads to the Kizil Davan (5700m), first crossed in 2010 by Andrei Lebedev's extreme-trekking team, and thence to the Zug-Shaksgam, a region never visited by climbers (Eric Shipton was in exploration mode when he passed through in 1930). From a base camp at 4100m on the Kulchintubulak River, the group split up into its separate teams, consisting of Rob Duncan, Jesse Mease (both USA) and Normand (UK),

Kaimuk Kangri from the west. *(Bruce Normand)*

P6490 and its neighbours. *(Bruce Normand)*

Lukas Brexler, Harald Kirschenhofer, and Christof Nettekoven (Germany) and Ales Holc and Peter Meznar (Slovenia), while Dymtro Shapovalov (Ukraine) joined both the Anglophone and German teams for different climbs. In contrast to the Pakistan side of the range, the Xinjiang side is dry and very warm in summer, meaning that all but the largest glaciers stop above 4500m. A lack of summer pastures ensures no human traffic and thus no trails. River crossings are a primary danger and the existence of horizontal limestone bands at several places throughout the otherwise execrable shale makes for some very serious slot canyons on all the approaches. The Anglophones and Shapovalov acclimatised by exploring the region around the Kizil Davan, reaching the snowy summits of P6184 and P5858 on either side of the col, but found an ice route on the north face of Durbin Kangri I to be impossible (baked ice and friable rock). The

Durban Kangri I: Jesse Mease searching in vain for climbable ice low on the route. *(Bruce Normand)*

Germans were active in the same area, climbing P6102 to the west of the Kizil Davan with Shapovalov. The Slovenians explored the valley to the north and west of Durbin Kangri II, climbing a 6200m snow peak.

The Germans and Shapovalov then left for home, after Brexler and Shapovalov had made an ascent of Kulchintubulak Tower (5290m), directly above base camp. Duncan, Mease and Normand spent six days trekking to the Zug-Shaksgam and back, but an attempt on Burnag Kangri was foiled by a slot canyon on the approach. Holc and Meznar returned to their valley for an attempt on Durbin Kangri II, but disappeared and were not heard from again. The other three climbers tried various search options, again frustrated by high water in all the rivers and canyons, and finally were able to get several helicopter overflights by the Chinese military, but were unable to find any sign of the missing duo.

Qinghai, Tanggula Shan

A remote region on the Qinghai side of the range was visited in 2013 by Singaporeans David Lim and Mohd Rozani bin Maarof, resulting in the ascents of two snow peaks, Sangay Ri (6000m) and Longyala West (6000m).

Above: The North Face of Kawarani I. *(Bruce Normand)*

Left: Climbing the North Face of Kawarani I. *(Bruce Normand)*

Sichuan, Gongkala Shan
Kawarani I (5992m) was climbed from the north side in winter by Marcos Costa (Brazil) and Bruce Normand. After a two-day approach from the road end, they found the north face to be 40-50° snow or snow gullies from bottom to top and climbed it from their forward camp in a day.

Sichuan, Shaluli Shan
In the central part of the range and close to Xiashe is the Jarjinjabo massif, which offers a wide selection of alpine rock possibilities on reasonable granite. Teams active in the region in summer 2014 included Garrett Bradley, Mike Dobie and Christopher Miller (USA), who completed a 10-pitch route on the south face of Jabo Tower, and Marcos Costa, Liu Yunqing and Zhou Lei, who completed seven new routes of varying lengths, up to a difficulty of 5.12b. Dobie and Zhou also visited in October 2013 with Andrew Hedesh

Top right: Approaching the North Face of Kawarani I. *(Marcos Costa)*
Below right:View from the south of (from left to right) P6684 (Long Shan), P6468 (two summits) and P6388. *(Chu Shan)*

to establish one rock route to the summit of one of the many local peaks and one snow route to the summit of P5550.

Sichuan, Daxue Shan

To the north of the Minya Konka Range lies the isolated summit of Yala (5820m), the object of many expeditions before its first ascent in 2006 by Malcolm Bass and Pat Deavoll. An unknown route is believed to have been climbed by Christine Boskoff and Charlie Fowler, also in 2006 and directly before their deaths on Genyen. Whether or not it was by this route, Marcos Costa and Bruce Normand made the probable third ascent in winter 2014 by the central couloir on the west face, climbing from a base camp at the hot springs (4100m) to the summit via snow and three mixed pitches. They bivouacked on the summit ridge before descending the following day.

Costa and Normand were then joined by Garrett Bradley for a visit to the chain of unclimbed 6000m peaks forming the southern and eastern extension of Minya Konka. From the obvious approach valley to the south of P6468 and west of

View from the summit ridge of Kawarani I. *(Bruce Normand)*

P6410 (Tai Shan, climbed from the eastern side in 1981), they ascended grass, mobile talus and dry glacial ice for two days to reach a camp at 5200m on P6468. A summit attempt the following day was abandoned at 6000m in high winds, but after moving to a higher camp on a 'rest' day the team was awarded a break in the winds, accompanied by significant clouds and light snow. They climbed the south-south-west ridge on low-angle ice and high-angle snow to the nearest summit, but found themselves

on a western peak, with the eastern one (presumably P6468) slightly higher and distant by 700m of steep, crevassed terrain. This was then the first ascent of P6460.

Also in the Minya Konka Range, but at its northern end, is

Marcos Costa on the summit ridge of Kawarani I. *(Bruce Normand)*

Bruce Normand with Minya Konka (left) and Long Shan (right) behind. *(Marcos Costa)*

the shapely triangle of Little Konka (5928m). Simon Gietl, Vittorio Messini and Daniel Tavernini (Italy) climbed it in October 2014 by the north-west ridge, finding difficulties up to 60° snow and M5, as well as signs of a previous attempt. They then made the first ascent, on snow and rock up to UIAA VI-, of a 5860m summit they named Tyrol Shan.

Sichuan, Qionglai Shan

Mountaineering in the Qionglai Range is concentrated in the three adjacent valleys of Bipenggou, Changpinggou and Shuangqiaogou. On the Bipeng (northern) side, Marcos Costa, Huang Siyuan (Azuo), Liu Yunqin (Simone) and Jon Otto made the first ascent of Crown Peak (Huangguan Feng, 5515m) in October 2014 by a nine-pitch route of mixed ice and granite. They named their line *Coronation* (550m, TD, AI4, M4/5), climbed in two days with one bivouac.

The Changping valley affords access to Siguniang and to the pyramidal Pomiu, of which more below, but new-route activity was limited to a 2013 ascent by Erik Hartz, Neil Kauffman and Felix Parham (USA) of a 5178m peak at the northern end of valley, which they named Joey Shan after a late friend. Their route involved nine pitches of technical climbing up to 5.9.

On the Shuangqiaogou side, 2014 started with a first known ascent of Lierenfeng (5362m) by Marcos Costa, Yann Delavoux (France) and Liu Zhixiong, who soloed different lines on the east face. The striking triangular peak of Abi was given a partial new route, in the form of a mixed variant to the left of the south face/south-east ridge line, by Liu Zhixiong. Given the prevalence of routes climbed or led by foreigners, it is heartening to report that Goromiti (also Ruyuebaojing, 5609m), on the ridge

East ridge and eastern peak of Yala from the summit. *(Bruce Normand)*

separating the Shuangqiao and Changping valleys and formerly the highest unclimbed peak in the region, was climbed by a small Chinese team in winter 2013. Veteran Li Zhongli and newcomers Li Di and Liu Zhixiong encountered very low-snow conditions on the south-east ridge, which they graded 5.7, M2.

It is disheartening to report that mountaineering in the region in 2014 ended on a very low note, with the deaths of Hu Jiaping and Liu Zhixiong in an apparent abseiling accident while descending from a climb of Siguniang (6250m). Reports differ as to whether they had climbed by the direct south-face route *Free Spirits* (Yan/Zhou 2009) or a variation. Both were accomplished sport climbers rather early in their alpine careers. The fiasco over their body non-recovery (they had to be placed in a crevasse) was noted above.

Shuangqiaogou is also the undisputed capital of alpine rock climbing in China and 2014 saw a plethora of new routes added to the many spires and summits. Unfortunately, the post-monsoon season started badly in August when veteran climber Wu Peng died in a possibly hypothermia-induced fall during a descent from Pomiu (Celestial Peak, 5413m; this climb was the probable third ascent of the south-east ridge). In September, Marcos Costa and Pat Goodman climbed a 1000m 5.10+ route on the south ridge of P5467, directly to the south of Seerdengpu, the dominant peak at the north end of the valley. Turning their attention to the many walls of the Daogou side-valley, they climbed a 300m 5.11 route on the south-west face of P5184 and

Yala from the north. *(Bruce Normand)*

a long route with a 5.11 finish on the south pillar of Daogou East (5462m). Also in September and in Daogou, Gu Qizhi and Wu Donghua climbed a new 700m route on the Shark's Fin (5086m) over two days, encountering difficulties up to 5.11a and A2 and making a high bivouac. Another group exploring the potential of the Daogou valley was Aurélie Didillon, Simon Duverney, Elodie Lecomte and Sébastien Ratel (France), who climbed P5120, which they named 'Four Pigs Peak,' by a 600m east face/north ridge route graded 7b, A2. Meanwhile, Jim Donini and Cameron Kern (USA) climbed a line on the south face of P5182 in the Changping valley with difficulties up to 5.10. When winter forces him to wear gloves, adoptive local activist Marcos Costa has been working on

Climbers low on the SSW ridge of P6460 with P6468 behind. *(Garrett Bradley)*

West face of Yala. *(Bruce Normand)*

establishing a hard mixed and dry-tooling scene in China, which by the end of winter 2014 had resulted in 14 new lines up to M11.

Several routes were also established in 2013 which went unreported in the previous edition. Next to the monolith of Potala Shan, the south-west face of Eagle Rock saw new routes from a team of Dong Jinyun, Wang Zhiming and Zhao Heng (650m, 5.11a), by Marcos Costa climbing solo (650m, 5.10+) and by Keita Kanehara and Kenji Onodera (Japan, 650m, 5.11). Elsewhere, Dave Anderson (USA) and Yi Szu-Ting (Taiwan), climbing with Li Yunching, established a 450m, 5.10- route on the southern ridge of Seerdengpu and, with Zheng Chaohui, made the first ascent of Dayantianwu (5240m) by a 600m route on the south face which they graded 5.10 R/X.

Shaanxi, Qin Mountains

China's sages, hermits and holy men have long understood the value of steep mountains, although their wisdom does not seem to have been passed on to modern local governments and tourism authorities. However, the many granite peaks of Hua Shan, the western peak of the 'Five Great Mountains' which stand as major landmarks in Chinese history as much as geography, have recently been open to low-profile climbing activities. In July, China's most experienced hard new route artist, He Chuan, took up the challenge of the 600m south face of the South Peak (at 2154m also the highest), producing a hard-fought 20-pitch testpiece of wide cracks and chimneys (5.10+ R C2+) which he climbed with Zhu Xiaofei. Elsewhere in the range, Yang Fan and Ye Yun climbed an 18-pitch route on another granitic feature, Qiezi Feng (Aubergine Peak), finding long and varied cracks up to 5.12b.

Indian Himalaya 2013

Border pillars at Chaukan pass. *(Harish Kapadia)*

In 2013 there were 31 expeditions from foreign countries and 67 Indian expeditions to the Indian Himalaya. Though the majority of them aimed for the routinely climbed peaks, a few attempted new peaks or routes. Unfortunately, many pre-monsoon expeditions to Garhwal and Kumaun suffered due to catastrophic heavy rains and their after-effects. Floods in the upper reaches of the Kedarnath valley trapped more than 50,000 pilgrims, and it is reported that at least 15,000 pilgrims died. The area has not yet returned to normal.

A selection of expeditions to new areas, new peaks and routes are below.

ARUNACHAL PRADESH

Chaukan Pass (2419m)

The Chaukan pass on the India-Burma border was reached by a team from Mumbai, led by Harish Kapadia. Trekking 157km along the muddy Miao-Vijaynagar road, they reached the Noa Dihing river. For several of the river crossings they had to construct small bridges and cut across thick forest. Finally a steep climb led them to the pass, which had not been

North face of Kuchela Dhura (6250m). *(Dhruv Joshi)*

visited by a civilian party for decades. During World War II a British party crossing this pass from Putao to Miao was trapped due to monsoon floods, and barely survived. The team also crossed into Burma from Pangsu pass and viewed the historic 'Lake of No Return'. (Article *HJ* 69)

SIKKIM

Tingchenkhang (6010m)

In May 2013, Manash Brooah led 15 members of the Assam Mountaineering Association of Guwahati on an attempt on Tingchenkhang. After establishing base camp near Lamuney, the team established one high camp on the western slopes of the mountain. On 14 May, the team made a summit attempt but had to stop at about 5580m as the ropes fixed had either been damaged or carried away by an avalanche. One more attempt was made on 15 May but again the summit proved elusive.

UTTARAKHAND

Trisul (7120 m)

An Indian army team approached this high mountain from the Raunthi glacier, under the leadership of Brigadier Ashok Abbey (president of the Himalayan Club). They climbed the west ridge and established three high camps. On 30 May 2013, the team of Naib Subedar Madan Singh, Hav

Matwar Singh, Lance Naik Min Bahadur Tamang, Rifleman Yashpal and Paratrooper Ashok Kumar left Camp 3 at 02.30. After crossing the col between Trisul I and II, they reached the summit at 09.20. The team also had planned to traverse all three summits of the Trisul massif but, due to unstable snow conditions, the traverse was called off. On 31 May, Nk Bishnu Bahadur developed major symptoms of high altitude sickness at Camp 3. Excellent team work resulted in a successful evacuation to base camp. On 3 June, another team comprised of Subedar Kunwar Singh, Capt Brijesh Kumar, Rifleman Pratap Singh and Rifleman Sunil Rai also reached the summit of Trisul I. (Article *HJ* 69)

Kuchela Dhura (6250m)

In the post-monsoon season of 2013, an expedition to this unclimbed peak was sponsored by the Indian Mountaineering Foundation and led by Dhruv Joshi. After crossing Martoli village, base camp was established at 4173m on the right bank of Lwan gad. They placed two higher camps and the summit camp was at 6064m. On 6 September 2013, the leader, Vijay, Chitramohan and Wallambok reached the summit and achieved the first ascent of Kuchela Dhura. (Note *HJ* 69)

Nanda Devi East (7434m)

In early May 2013, a team under the leadership of Anindya Mukherjee established base camp at Bidalgwar (4300m) and fixed ropes to Longstaff col. After establishing Camp 2 on the narrow south ridge at 6200m, the team attempted to reach the summit in semi-alpine style but had to abort the climb due to high winds and technical difficulties. (Note *HJ* 69)

Manda II (6568m)

Shekhar Ghosh and 10 expedition members of Nilkantha Abhijatri Sangh, WB, attempted Manda II in May-June 2013. The team established base camp on 30 May on the right bank of Kedar Ganga river, opposite Kedar Kharak, at 4400m. They established three higher camps on the western side of the mountain. Their fixed ropes were exhausted after reaching 6120m and, deciding that to climb further without fixed ropes was risky, they called off the attempt on 9 June 2013. On 11 June one of the members, Biswajit Bose, suffered respiratory problems at base camp. The team evacuated him and took him to Gangotri on 13 June but at the local health centre he was declared dead.

Mana (7274m)

In May 2013, Cyrus Shroff led an Indian expedition of four. The team established base camp (4120m) on the right bank of the confluence of Uttar and Dakkhni Nakthani gad on 18 May. The team entered the Uttar Nakthani glacier and established three high camps, fixing a few ropes on difficult portions. They first tried to reach Gupta khal but then shifted to a gully leading to the upper icefields. They established their highest camp

Chaukhamba col from Badrinath side. *(Debabrata Mukherjee)*

(Camp 2) at 5600m on 26 May. Unfortunately, the weather turned and gale force winds made movement dangerous and tricky. They abandoned the climb at 5900m.

Chaukhamba IV (6854m)

An American expedition led by James Ryrie Norton attempted Chaukhamba IV in September 2013. On 15 September, the team established base camp at Sundervan in the Gangotri glacier area, and attempted the mountain from the western/ south-western side. After ABC, they established Camp 1 at 5180m but had to call off the attempt because of heavy snowfall in the area.

First Crossing of Chaukhamba col (6053m)

In July 1912, CF Meade reached the col between Chaukhamba I and Januhut, hiking from a high camp on Bhagirath Kharak glacier. He did not cross the col. He stood there for a while, got a glimpse of the Gangotri glacier on the other side, and then returned the way he came. In May 2013, Debabrata Mukherjee and his team of four climbers and two high altitude supporters climbed up the Bhagirath Kharak glacier to the Chaukhamba col and descended to the Gangotri glacier, thus linking Badrinath with Gangotri. The team was awarded the Second Jagdish C Nanavati Award for Excellence in Mountaineering. (Article *HJ* 69)

HIMACHAL PRADESH

Khhang Shiling (6360m)

Cosmin Andron and some friends from Romania joined 'Climba-thon 2013', organised by the Indian Mountaineering Foundation, in the Bara Shigri glacier in July-August 2013. During the event Cosmin and eight others, including friends and a few trainees, climbed Khhang Shil-ling (6360m) by a new route on the north-west face, from the Bara Shigri glacier. They also attempted Kullu Makalu (6349m) but had to turn back due to rockfall. (Note *HJ* 69)

KR V (6258m)

On 12 June, a team of Coalfield Nature Lovers, WB, established base camp (4700m) near Baralacha la. After establishing two more camps, on 19 June, leader Paresh Chandra Nath, Subrata Roy and two Sherpas reached the summit of KR V.

The Bhadrakali Pathfinders Adventurers, WB, led by Debabrata Mukherjee, began their approach march on 30 August from Baralacha la towards Chandratal. They reached Transit Camp (4718m) that night, and on 31 August their base camp (4955m) beyond Tokpo Gongma. After continuing on the Koa Rong glacier, skirting below the hanging glaciers of KR VII they established Camp 1 (5304 m) on 3 November. The summit camp was established on 5 November at 5705m, below the east face of KR V. On 6 September, by 15.15 they had climbed up to 6089m by a new route on the east face but had to turn back because of lack of time and protection. They feel that most of the earlier teams have not identified KR V properly and thus have made wrong claims. (The HC mountain climbing authen-tication team led by Divyesh Muni *prima facie* agrees with this statement; their detailed analysis will be published in *HJ* 70.)

KR II (6187m)

After establishing base camp at 4650m, Spandan Kumar Malik and the Kolkata Trekkers Youth, WB, established three high camps and climbed the east ridge of the mountain. From the summit camp at 5630m, on 30 August, Mohene, Indranil and three high altitude supporters reached the summit at 07.50 in whiteout conditions. Though they did not have any clear views, they could locate and photograph the snow picket left at the summit in 2011 by a team from West Bengal (Sonarpur Arohi Club).

P6080m, Miyar valley

In 2012 the Scottish Zanskar Expedition attempted a couple of unclimbed 6000m peaks in the Namkha Tokpo. They had climbed one peak and attempted another. However, a potential route up the south face was spotted, and in June 2013 Rob Adams, Bob Hamilton, Steve Kennedy, Andy Nisbet (leader) and Susan Jensen returned to attempt an ascent from the Himachal Pradesh (as opposed to Zanskar) side of the range. After

Pensilungpa glacier. *(Derek Buckle)*

establishing base camp (4500m) in a subsidiary valley to the Miyar valley, heavy snowfall over several days limited the time for approach to that objective so they made a first ascent of P6080m after establishing ABC at 5400m. All the team members climbed the southwest face of the mountain to reach the summit on 20 June. Many smaller summits were also climbed by the team.

JAMMU & KASHMIR

ZANSKAR AND KISHTWAR

Hagshu (6515m)

In July 2013, a team consisting of Bryan Hylenski, Jake Preston, Jonn Jeannerret, Gabe Thomas and Dan Kopperud aimed for Hagshu, P6055m and P6035m located in the Hagshu glacier. They approached the area starting from Akshow village near Ringdom and placed three high camps above ABC. They could reach 6440m on Hagshu before turning back due to bad weather conditions. They achieved two first ascents during the expedition: P6035m was climbed on 19 July and P6055m (their altimeter registered 6191m at the summit) was climbed on 28 July. (Article *HJ* 69).

P5700m (Kange glacier)

A French team of three, led by Chance Emmanuel, began their trek from Akshow village and on 8 September established base camp at 3800m near the snout of the Kange glacier. They established one more camp at 4500m. From this camp the leader and Donadey Nicolas climbed the north face in alpine style, to reach the summit on 25 September in one push.

P5802m and P5825m (Pensilungpa glacier)

In September-October 2013 a British team from the Alpine Club, consisting of Derek Buckle (leader), Mike Pinney, Chris Storie and Tony Westcott, visited the Pensilungpa glacier in the Zanskar region. In addition to general exploration of the area, they made the first ascents of two summits on the Pensilungpa-Durung Drung divide: P5802m (proposed name Hidden Peak) and P5825m (proposed name Twin Peak). (Note *HJ* 69)

Kishtwar Kailash (6451m)

Brits Mick Fowler and Paul Ramsden completed the first ascent of Kishtwar Kailash in alpine style from 4 to 10 October 2013, climbing 1500m on the south-west face. They were supported by Mike Morrison and Rob Smith. The team approached the mountain from Machail village and entered Dharlang nala. Base camp was established at 4000m; after acclimatisation and reconnaissance, the peak was climbed in a week, in alpine style. (Article *HJ* 69)

LADAKH

Jungdung Kangri (6060m)

James Monypenny (UK) and Cory Hall (Canada) made the first ascent of Jungdung Kangri, which lies hidden in the Palzampiu valley of Ladakh. The team first tried to gain access from the south through Likir, however the pass could not be crossed by mules. They then headed north by road to the Nubra valley. After a two day walk with a couple of mules, the team reached base camp at 5090m in a pristine alpine meadow. A high camp was established at 5522m, below the west side of Jungdung Kangri. From there they reached the summit by a route which they named *The Monypenny Hall of Fame* (650 m, ED1 90° A2++) in an alpine style ascent.

P6046m, Kang Yabat range

A small British team under the leadership of Douglas Briton climbed P 6046m in the Kang Yabat range, in the Gya area of Ladakh. From Salsal on the Manali-Leh highway, the team followed the Yabat river to approach the mountain. After establishing three camps and a bivouac above base camp, Caroline McCann and Matt Jones reached the summit via the south face of the mountain. They proposed the name Cha Ri, meaning a mountain looking like a large bird. (Note *HJ* 69)

EAST KARAKORAM

Chamshen (7017m), North Shukpa Kunchang glacier

A joint Indian-British team led by Divyesh Muni and Victor Saunders entered Sakang Lungpa and made the first crossing of the Sakang col (6150m) to reach North Shukpa Kunchang glacier. On the night of 14 August, a wind blast from an avalanche down the north face of Saser Kangri II struck the camp on the glacier, and Andy Parkin suffered major injuries as he and his tent were thrown into a crevasse. After being pulled out of the crevasse by Susan Jensen and Victor Saunders, he was rescued

Summit camp on Lung Khor glacier. Left – right: South-east Shupka Kunchang glacier, Pyramidal peak, Sagtogpa glacier and Ngapo Kangri. *(IAF 2013 Expedition)*

by Indian Air Force helicopters in very unfavourable weather conditions. On 21 August, all four remaining members of the expedition and six supporting Sherpas reached the summit of Chamshen by the west ridge. (Article *HJ* 69)

Plateau Peak (7300m)

The Himalayan Club Kolkata section team, under the leadership of Debraj Dutta and consisting of eight members and 10 high altitude supporters, achieved the first ascent of this giant of the East Karakoram. This peak was attempted many times during last few years by various Indian and joint expeditions without success. The Himalayan Club team approached the mountain from the west via the Phukpoche glacier. After establishing three high camps, four members and five high altitude supporters reached the summit on 31 July 2013. (Article *HJ* 69)

Rongdo valley explorations and climbs

An Indian Air Force team of 12 members under the leadership of Gp Capt VK Sashindran explored the Rongdo valley and climbed seven peaks during a 35-day expedition in May-June 2013. This was only the third expedition in the valley. After establishing base camp at 4790m, from a few high camps they climbed Sa'i Lhamo (6030m), Khyung Kangri (6183m), Chu Skeyes Kangri (6053m), Langpoche (5968m), Odgsal I (6234m), Odgsal II (6028m) and Charok (6123m). They also attempted Lung Khor (6160m), previously climbed and identified as Gazgazri by a Canadian team in 2012. (Article *HJ* 69)

Other News

Dr MS Gill, past president of the Himalayan Club has had a long, abiding and continued interest in the Himalaya on a personal as well as professional level. As a fitting tribute, the Himalayan Club has conferred upon him the title of President Emeritus.

For the last 35 years at least, Harish Kapadia has been a personality very closely associated with the *Himalayan Journal*. He has been editor of the *Journal* for over three decades, is the Human Wikipedia of the Indian Himalaya and has authored several books on areas and aspects of the Himalaya. In recognition of his tireless contribution, the Himalayan Club has conferred upon Harish Kapadia the title of Editor Emeritus.

The Second Jagdish C Nanavati Award for Excellence in Mountaineering was awarded to Debabrata Mukherjee for exploration over the Chaukhamba col, a high-risk but wonderful maiden exploration of a very difficult route. This exploration linked the Bhagirath Kharak glacier with the Gangotri glacier, a most direct route.

The Second Jagdish Nanavati Garud Medal for outstanding support staff was awarded to a Darjeeling Sherpa, an unassuming man of few words but immense strength and pride in his work: Pemba Norbu, affectionately known as King Kong.

Jim Perrin received the Seventh Kekoo Naoroji Book Award for Himalayan Literature for his book *Shipton and Tilman*, which is a rare and wry insight into the lives of these iterant adventurers.

I am thankful to Harish Kapadia, Nandini Purandare, Lindsay Griffin and the staff of Indian Mountaineering Foundation for their valuable inputs.

IAN WALL

Nepal

Spring 2014

The avalanche in the Everest Ice Fall at 06.45 on 18 April 2014 was, tragically, the main news coming out of Nepal during the spring season. As a result of poor risk assessment, commercialism and financial incentives, the lives of 16 locals were lost, 13 of whom were Sherpas: Aash Bahadur Gurung, Dorje Khatri, Ang Kazi (Ankaji) Sherpa, Ang Tshiri Sherpa, Chhewang Sherpa, Chhiring Ongchu Sherpa, Dorje Sherpa, Lhakpa Tenjing Sherpa, Mingma Nuru Sherpa, Nima Sherpa, Pasang Karma Sherpa, Pem Tenji Sherpa, Phur Temba Sherpa, Phurba Ongyal Sherpa, Tenzing Chhotar Sherpa, Thendorje (Thendu Dorje) Sherpa. Another Sherpa died from AMS and two others died in other accidents on the mountain.

Although this event brought the Everest season to an abrupt end, the intrigue and drama were not over. Immediately after the incident Everest was reported as being 'closed' and all expeditions agreed to leave, either as a mark of respect for those who had died, or for other reasons. However, Chinese climber Jing Wang, with the help of Phurba Gyaltsen Sherpa (Managing Director of Himalayan Sherpa Adventure), secured a second 2014 season permit and the service of a helicopter to fly Wang directly to Camp 2, from where she made her ascent of Everest; she summitted on 23 May together with Lhakpa Gyalzen Sherpa, Pasang Dawa Sherpa and Riten Jangbu (Tashi) Sherpa. Jing Wang wanted to complete the Seven Summits and reach the two Poles within the shortest time span on record. On the descent she was airlifted out by helicopter from the Western Cwm. Wang was received in Kathmandu by a deputation from the Nepal Government who, in June 2014, awarded her not only the Everest Summit Certificate but also the International Mountaineer of the Year Award, an honour also bestowed on Sir Edmund Hillary. In effect, the Government were supporting the fact that Everest had not in fact been 'closed'. It has been suggested that the Sherpas on Wang's expedition received US$10,000 per head in salary plus a bonus of US$2,000; she is also reported as having donated US$30,000 to the Namche Bazaar community hospital, plus, of course, paying for her second permit.

Despite the Everest drama the season continued on other summits and with other expeditions. **Ama Dablam** (6812m) received eight ascents between 2 April and 13 May, by two Austrians, one Nepali, one German and four Ukrainians.

Arniko Chuli (6039m), situated in the Mustang region at the northern edge of the range between Lo and Dolpo, received five ascents, by three

Dragmorpa Ri (6185m), with line taken by Korean-Nepali team on second official ascent. First ascent was in 2013 by Russian Roman Gretzky, starting further left but following largely the same line. *(Korean Dragmorpa Expedition Collection)*

Swiss and two Nepali climbers on 18 May. **Cho Oyu** (8201m) had 31 ascents between 17 and 24 May with climbers from Switzerland, Austria, Nepal, the USA, Russian, the Ukraine and Sweden reaching the summit. **Dhaulagiri** (8167m) had 13 ascents with climbers from Nepal, China, Peru and South Korea summiting on 18 May.

Dragmorpa Ri (6185m) (Langtang) received its second ascent on 21 April by two Korean and three Nepali climbers, following a line further to the west of the Russian line taken on the first ascent.

On **Everest** (8848m), the north side received great attention with 94 ascents being made between 23 and 25 May by climbers from China, Nepal, Bulgaria, Russia, the UK, Ireland, France, Poland, the Ukraine, India, Switzerland, France, Germany, Finland, Austria, Denmark, Canada and Malta; all reached the summit.

Kangchenjunga (8586m) had 33 successful ascents between 17 and 20 May with climbers from Italy, Japan, Nepal, Finland, Spain, India, Russia and Bulgaria all reaching the summit.

Lobuche East (6119m) was ascended on 27 April by a three-man Ukrainian expedition.

Makalu (8462m) had 48 ascents with climbers from Switzerland, Germany, France, Nepal, Canada, Greece, Singapore, Japan, Russia, the

The west ridge of Lugula (6899m) seen from the south. (G) Korean Gate. (M) Minerva snowfield rises gently on the far side of the skyline ridge. (T) Tiger Ridge. (H) Hong's Step. *(Peter Jensen-Choi)*

USA, the Netherlands and Australia; all attempts were completed between 17 and 25 May.

Putha Hiunchuli (7246m) was ascended on 18 May by four Austrian climbers.

Thameserku (6623m) was climbed on 3 May by two Russians.

Lugula (6899m) in the Damodar Himal was ascended (the first official ascent by the south couloir and west ridge) on 23 April by two Koreans (Hong Seung-gi and Bum Won-taek) and two Nepali climbers (Lakpa Sherpa and Feme Sherpa). On 10 April the expedition arrived in Phu. Base camp was established at 5050m on the Bharchapk Glacier; advanced base camp was established a further three kilometres up the valley at 5450m. The team established two more camps before reaching the summit, the first on a small ridge leading to the couloir that drops down from the col between Bhrikuti Sail and Lugula. The second camp was on the crest of Lugula's west ridge (the border between Tibet and Nepal). Fixed ropes were used to safeguard the initial friable rocky ridge. On 18 April the team was forced back to base camp to collect more technical gear that they felt was needed to surmount the 80°, 60m of steep ice leading to the col. By 22 April, Hong Seung-gi had completed the route to the west ridge. On 23 April five members set out for the summit but due to the exposed nature of the ridge and the increasing wind strength two expedition members decided to retreat from 6550m. The remaining team reached the summit at 09.10 on 23 April and then returned to base camp by 24 April, after spending the night at camp 2. A French expedition made an unauthorised ascent of Lugula in 2010 via the south face and upper south-west ridge.

This season sadly saw other fatal incidents, including two Russians on Ama Dablam, a Nepali climber who was not involved with the Everest avalanche disaster but died as a member of an Everest Expedition, a Nepali climber and a French climber in separate expeditions on Makalu, and two Nepalese climbers and an Indian climber died on Yalung Kang.

In total for the spring season in Nepal records show that 12 expedition

Everest. *(Ian Wall)*

peaks were climbed by 161 foreign mountaineers and 116 Nepali climbers. Four foreign mountaineers and 20 Nepalese climbers were killed in the process.

Everest 2015 (as at 17 April 2015)

Changes to Everest Policy

Some changes have been implemented as a result of the Everest avalanche and ensuing discussions.

The Everest permit fee has been increased to US$11,000. There have been changes and increased benefits made available in the insurance arrangements and medical care allowances for the Nepalese high-altitude mountain workers; special provision has also been made concerning the future education of the children of the deceased guides. Insurance cover for the Nepalese climbers has now been increased: Sirdar 15 lakh, High Altitude Worker 15 lakh, Liaison Officer 12 lakh, cook 10 lakh, kitchen helper 8 lakh, porters 6 lakh, medical coverage 3 lakh, rescue coverage (per team) 10 lakh. A lakh is approximately US$1,000.

All expedition members must attend a briefing on 'Climbing Everest' given by a member of the Ministry. The Nepal Government has announced that the permits issued in 2014 would be valid up to 2019. Helicopters, apart from on rescue missions, have been banned above Base Camp. David

Change to Ice Fall route on Everest: dashed line – previous, solid – current.
(Ian Wall)

Breashears was acting in a supporting role to the Sagarmatha Pollution Control Committee (SPCC) by providing his aerial Ice Fall images to help identify the best route this season. There was also an Integrated Service Information Centre at Base Camp where service personnel will be based, to which expeditions should report as the season progresses. The route through the Ice Fall has been changed to avoid the danger spots. The route now starts from the bottom right of the Ice Fall but it keeps in the centre avoiding the area of last year's avalanche and dangers from Lhotse, finally exiting slightly right of a mid-point at the top.

Nepali operators have increased their hold in the expedition market, reducing the sector previously held by international operators. They are offering Everest expedition support for lower prices than the foreign operators, in the US$25-35,000 range compared to foreign operators from within the US$40-65,000 range. However, there is a huge difference in what you get for your money. When most of the costs related to permits, insurance and staff wages are controlled by the Ministry, effectively setting a baseline tariff, it is difficult to see how the Nepali operators can make such enormous savings. Rumours are now circulating stemming from the guides associations concerning the 'Everest Industry' and relating to the fact that soon activities will be governed by industrial regulations policies.

There was a big media presence at Base Camp this year, including the BBC who sent regular updates back to their BBC news desk.

This information has only been reported in various media platforms and is not substantiated. We'll know what the story is after it happens.

Autumn 2014

On 6 October a low-pressure system formed under the influence of a cyclonic, high altitude circulatory system of air above the Andaman Sea; this developed into a Severe Cyclonic Storm on 9 October. On 12 October 'Cyclone Hudhud', as it became known, having rapidly intensified, moved across Nepal. In the Annapurna region nearly 2m of snow fell within 12 hours, and on 14 October an avalanche on the Thorong La trapped 21 guides and trekkers who were subsequently rescued on 15 October. The search and rescue operation continued for the next four days by which time 400 people had been rescued, with many more extricating themselves from the dangers. As a result of this incident in the upper Manang district of the Annapurna Circuit, 43 people were reported as having died from exhaustion, hypothermia and carbon monoxide poisoning while many more were treated for frostbite. This incident is registered as Nepal's worst trekking disaster.

The meteorological situation developed at the very beginning of the season; consequently nearly all itineraries and expeditions were either rapidly changed or cancelled.

MARCELO SCANU

Argentina

Argentina saw a lot of exploration and many first ascents in 2014, but the area around Mendoza is the place to be these days, rather than the usual northern or central Andes. The steep granite towers and spires of Mendoza are being visited by a new generation of climbers.

Salta

Pirámide Alejandro Lewis. This fine, 4800m rocky pyramid is part of the Nevado de Cachi and is named for a late Argentine climber. It lies in the Quebrada de la Hoyada, on the way from Las Pailas. In November, Matias Cruz and Facundo Juárez Zapiola opened a new route, *Trankahuasi* (200m, F5+/F6b+). The routes is four pitches via a crack that takes a diagonal line on the left of the south wall, finishing to the summit by the west face. This was Juárez Zapiola's second route here: in 2011 he climbed a line with Patricio Payrola on the south face (200m, F6a).

Catamarca

Sierra Nevada. On 5 November, after a difficult approach, an Argentine team ascended the highest unclimbed peak in the Argentine Sierra Nevada (6160m). The whole area is a desert, nothing but arid, rocky and barren territory; it is one of the most savage in all of Argentina and South America. The team was composed of Guillermo Almaraz, Eduardo Namur, Henri Barret, Walter Sinay and Claudio Recchia. Their line of ascent took the border of the East Glacier (Glaciar Este), with camps at 5180m and 5520m.

La Rioja

Caldera del Inca. Caldera del Inca is a giant crater encircled by several 6000m peaks. Basques Jabi Txibon, Joseba Txibon, Arkatu Etxeberria and Arkaitz Ibarra (the last being resident in Argentina) prepared for the traverse of the caldera peaks by acclimatising in Laguna Brava for several days as they waited for the strong winds to subside. On 25 February they began the traverse with the mighty Volcán Bonete Chico (6759m), climbing the main and north Summits. On the Cordón de los Pioneros, a ridge north of Bonete, they climbed the Pico Cichitti (6164m) and the Pico Bravo (6193m) (called Pico C and Pico B, respectively, by John Biggar's book); both of these were on 27 February. On 2 March they established a base camp at 5300m to ascend Pissis (c6800m), and the next day attempted the southeast gully on one of the lower summits of Pissis (UPAME, 6790m) but only reached 6200m because of high winds. On 4 March, Jabi and Arkaitz reach the east summit, Ejército Argentino (6738m), at 5pm. The next day they camped at the base of the Gemelos after a difficult traverse in volcanic terrain with dry creeks and covered in loose volcanic ash. On 6 March they climbed Gemelos Norte (6110m) and Gemelos Sur; the latter peak is only two metres lower than the former but had remained unclimbed until that day. They took two more days to reach the base of Baboso (6078m), the volcano that finished the traverse to the huge crater. They climbed Baboso by the south ridge in very fierce winds.

Cerro Comecaballos. On 4 April, the virgin summit of Cerro Comecaballos (5199m), which is on the border with Chile, was ascended via its east face by Guillermo Almaraz, Eduardo Namur, Oscar Balmaceda and Gerardo Cano.

San Juan

Cordillera de Ansilta. In October, the well-known Argentine climbers Gabriel Fava and Wenny Sánchez ascended a route on an impressive needle in the Cordillera de Ansilta (San Juan Province). This ridge has seven principal peaks ranging between 5116m and 5996m.

The needle is found on the eastern side of the Pico 7 de Ansilta (5780m). Pico 7 is the southernmost peak of the range and is surrounded by glaciers. The brown granite spire, named Nico Made (c 4600m) is one of many that have recently been discovered. The route was christened *Alegría* ('joy' in Spanish, possibly a reference to the beautifully clean cracks) (230m, F6c). The pair descended the steep wall with eight rappels. It has been said that there are higher walls in the area, even as tall as 400 metres. To reach the needle from the town of Barreal, they rode 30 kilometres to the Estancia del Río Blanco, then walked two days and 18 kilometres to the base of the walls.

Mendoza

Cerro Piramidal del Potrero Escondido. Argentines Lucas Amuchástegui, Juan Bautista Alonso and Pablo Laumann departed on 16 September from Punta de Vacas, reaching the Río Chorrillos (some 18 kilometres from the start) at 12pm. The next day they continued trekking the Quebrada de Chorrillos, on the third day reaching the first step that had very different conditions from what they had seen in photos from preceding years. This year they had deep snow, followed by mixed terrain and snow gullies. On the third rope length they arrived at a rock band but left it to the next day because of lack of time, leaving fixed ropes. On day four they climbed through the rock band and set up camp at 3800m at 3am. On the fifth day they camped at 4200m, and on the sixth Pablo and Lucas departed at 6.20am to traverse a 30°-60° glacier and a bergschrund. The wall they found had more deep snow and steepened up to 75°. The final rope length on the wall was also at 75° but in deep snow with little protection. They finally reached the summit (5386m) at 6.30pm but left after a few minutes because they could see a big storm approaching. They arrived safely at camp at 4.30am after getting lost in the complex route. In a two-day, 40

Cerro Piramidal del Potrero Escondido (5386m). *(Glauco Muratti)*

kilometre hike, doused by storm, they reached Punta de Vacas.

The 500m route has been named *Alto Guiso* (something like Good Stew in Argentine slang – the all day meal), rated D, 75°, AI3, M3/4. The mountain has had two other ascents, the first one in 1965 from the west and another in 2005 from the Quebrada del Potrero Escondido.

Cerro Albardón del Potrero Escondido. This summit is part of the Cordón del Potrero Escondido – Los Clonquis, a nearly virgin zone. Argentines Adrián Petrocelli and Glauco Muratti departed from Punta de Vacas. Their approach involved 8-10 hours walking per day, every day interrupted

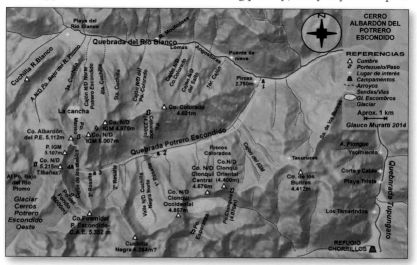

Cerro Albardón del Potrero Escondido (5112m). *(Glauco Muratti)*

by snowfall. They erected four camps and approached by the Quebrada Potrero Escondido.

The lack of winter snowfall, combined with hot conditions that season, made the terrain more difficult. The natural lines between the second, third and fourth camps (3300m, 3950m and 4500m) are normally couloirs with avalanche cones. This time, the lack of snow meant that there was only black ice or rotten ice waterfalls with objective danger – especially if one fell into the natural caves carved by the flowing water. Climbing protection was sparse. The last section was easy 40° snow. The pair reached the summit on 20 November as a storm approached the mountain. Nothing was found on the summit (5112m), verifying that the Spanish 1965 expedition hadn't climbed the peak. They returned to Punta de Vacas in two days with the always-present afternoon snowfall.

Cajón de Arenales. In late October, Gabriel Fava and Wenny Sánchez ascended a new route on the c3300m Aguja El Marinero located in the Cajón de Arenales near Tunuyán (Mendoza). The route (200m, F7a) was called *Libérate y Baila* and takes a direct line in the centre of the spire's south face through corners and splitter cracks.

Torres del Campanario. This 5090m tower has granite that is very similar to Patagonia, and some fine new lines were opened in March. An Argentine expedition approached the tower in the Cordillera Frontal, erecting a camp at 4300m after dealing with a difficult scree zone that extends between 4100m and 4600m; they then crossed the Paso Tucson to establish base camp. Diego Nakamura and Lucas Alzamora opened *Días de Insomnio* (305m, F6c+/A0). Carloncho Guerra and Macarena Zanotti opened a route nearby calling it *Che gil otario* (350m, F7a). The two groups met

Torres del Campanario - Torre del Este
Días de insomnio 6c+/A0 - 305m
Diego Nakamura - Lucas Alzamora
Marzo 2014

Torres del Campanario (5090m). *(Diego Nakamura)*

Torre Blanca de Ectelion
Vía "Chaparral"
10 largos 475m / 6b
Sosneado - Mendoza
Marzo 2014

on the summit of one of the three satellite peaks but did not continue to the highest peak, descending by another way where they found remains of previous attempts.

Also in March, Luciano Fiorenza and Pablo Pontoriero were active in the same zone. They opened a line on Aguja El Topo that they called *Gato con guantes... escala mejor* (180m, F6c). After ascending a tricky glacier well-endowed with snow-covered penitentes they reached Cerro Krakus (c4900m) to study the mountain. On 17 March they climbed *No hay pìcaro sin suerte* (300m, F6b) on

Torre Blanca de Ectelion. Unfinished lines are previous attempts.
(Diego Nakamura)

Negro Pabellón (6086m). *(Mauro Schmiedt)*

excellent granite, to the highest summit of Torres del Campanario.

Torre Blanca de Ectelion. Diego Nakamura and partners have climbed many spires in the Sosneado group in these last years, finishing the last virgin spire in March. On Torre Blanca de Ectelion, which is on the east flank of Cerro de los Pantanos. Diego Nakamura and Lucas Alzamora ascended a route that they christened *Chaparral* (F5+/6a with a few moves of F6b). The 475m ascent took 10 pitches and they descended by a scree slope. This was their fourth attempt to climb this spire; the three previous were on the green line as shown on the photo but the last section had proved too insecure.

Cerro Negro Pabellón. Cerro Negro Pabellón (6086m, S 33° 26' 59.9" W 69° 42' 09.7") is a rarely visited peak in the Cordón de las Delicias being the highest in the Cordillera Frontal of Mendoza province. Prior to 2014, it had three ascents: the first in 1953 by climbers from Mendoza (although it is not clear if they climbed the highest summit or the summit slightly east); Japanese in 1969 and Mendozans again in 1984.

Camp at 3300m. *(Mauro Schmiedt)*

A expedition took place from 15 to 23 November. Argentines Lucas Gómez, Guillermo Ferri, Mauro Schmiedt and Diego Cavassa opened a new access from Portillo Argentino: 96.5 kilometres long with a total of 8081 metres of height gain. The other groups approached from the Río Tunuyán; this one came from

On route with the false summit. Tupungato to the left. *(Mauro Schmiedt)*

the Arroyo la Olla followed by the Arroyo Negro. They descended the Río Tunuyán on the return. Camp 2 was erected at 3920m and the group split in two. Gómez and Ferri ascended a virgin 5039m peak, calling it Cerro Bautismo. Schmiedt and Cavassa erected two more camps, the final one being camp 4 (S33° 29' 19.52" W 69° 42' 06.11"). On 20 November they departed at 6:30am, reaching the summit at 1:55pm by a variant of the Japanese route (north-west ridge) and on the summit found a cairn with an ice axe left by the 1984 expedition. On descent they reached their camp at 7:30pm.

Correction: In last year's *Notes* I wrote about a first ascent of the Argentine face of Olivares del Límite (6220m), an enormous glaciated massif lying along the Argentine province of San Juan and the border with Chile. While there had been no record of ascents from Argentina, we now know that there had been some previous ascents because Glauco Muratti had left a record in the summit book. In some areas of Argentina, and in the Andes in general, there is still relatively little information regarding climbing activity.

New Zealand

New Zealanders were productive in the mountains again in 2014. Fiordland proved a popular venue, with much of the new route activity taking place in the Darran Mountains. A few notable ascents have also been recorded in the Mt Aspiring and Aoraki Mt Cook national parks.

Fiordland

The south face of Mt Suter, at the head of Falls Creek, fell at the hands of Ben Dare and Stephen Skelton. The pair climbed a grand couloir of ice that cleaves the imposing face from base to summit before enduring a cold bivouac and long descent.

The NZAC Southland Section Darrans Winter Climbing Meet happened again, and was a success again. Jaz Morris, Allan Uren and Al Walker sent the *Tunnel of Love* on the Tunnel Bluffs. Reg Measures and Kieran Parsons got sucked into *The Vortex* (5, 10p), also on the Tunnel Bluffs. Karl Greasley, Olivia Barron and Niall McLean did a new line left of *Double Vision* called *Ptero-vision*. Mike Buchanan and Jaz Morris wrapped up proceedings with a nifty little two-pitch line in the same vicinity as the aforementioned routes.

In February, Ben Dare and Daniel Joll did their second new route on the south face of Marian Peak; *Mater Dei* is grade 20 and 1000m long. Ben and Daniel also completed a variation to the original line on the south face of East Twin in March. Danilo Hegg, Max Olsen, Peter Wilson and James Thornton completed the first crossing from Mackay Creek into the Transit via a steep climb on the eastern side of the cirque at the head of the valley. In March, Stephen Skelton and Allan Uren ventured onto the south face of Barrier Peak and completed a new rock route. Sticking to the traditional naming convention for the face, they titled their climb the *Uren/Skelton* (19, 5–6p).

On 27–30 March, Guy McKinnon completed the first solo of the Kaipo Wall via the *Range Rover Route,* finding some real adventure along the way.

On 22–24 November 2013 Stanley Mulvany, Paula Macfarlane and Reece Mackenzie made the first ascent of the South Ridge of Mills Peak. Stanley, Paula and Reece also ventured onto Mitre Peak in winter to make the possible first winter ascent; it may be that Mike Berry previously climbed Mitre in winter.

In February, Kester Brown and Stephen Skelton got up *The Little Hard Climb* (I, 22, 4p) on the west side of the Petit Dur, and *Russian Gas Pedal Direct* (III, 20, 8p) on the west face of Taiaroa. Greg Jack, Troy Mattingley and Jean Tompkins got *Chumped* (I, 21, 3p), which is also on the west side

Ben Dare approaching another sustained vertical section of ice on the first
ascent of the south face of Mount Suter, Earl Mountains, Fiordland.
(Stephen Skelton)

of the Petit Dur, before they went *Up the Guts* (I, 22, 5p), on the north face
of the Rothorn. Greg, Troy and Kester also claimed they were *Over the Rain
Bro* (II, 19, 6p), on the first pillar of the south-east ridge of Tuhawaiki.

In February and March 2014, Georg Pollinger and Anton (Toni) Baumgartner, both from Germany, made first ascents of the following routes in
Fiordland: *Headbanger* (18, 6p), on the first pillar of the south-east ridge of
Mt Tuhawaiki; *Golden Octopus* (Ungraded, 9+p), on the second pillar of the
south-east ridge of Mt Tuhawaiki; *Rising High* (20/21, 8p), on the east face
of Karetai Peak; *Reise durch den Wahnsinn* (Ungraded, 10p), on the south
face of Mt Makere; *The Blast* (21, 4p), on the Diamond Face of Moir's
Mate; *Marder der Lüfte* (16, 5p), on the west face of Adelaide Peak; and
Infinite Sky (Ungraded, 9p), on Gento Peak (Pk1705), in the Bowen valley.

Late additions to the Central Darrans include first ascents of *Kilroy Wuz
Ere* (II, 21, by Richard Thomson, Dave Vass and Rich Turner) and *Brothers
in Arms* (II, 22, by James Spiers and Rich Turner) on the north-west face
of Nga Mokopuna (a pinnacled peak between Te Wera and Karetai). Zac
Orme and Troy Mattingley put up *Yeah, Nah, Dur* (I, 24) on the east face
of the Mighty Dur, and *Mr Mercedes* (I, 19) on the north-west side of the
Rothorn, both in Te Puoho Basin. Finally, on the first buttress of the south-
east ridge of Tuhawaiki, above Rainbow Lake, Kieran Parsons and Mike
Buchanan managed to *Weigh a Pie* (II, 19).

Mt Aspiring National Park

Guy McKinnon pulled off the climb of the millennium when he
completed the long-awaited second winter ascent of the east face of Popes
Nose, in impeccable style. Notably, Guy walked in and out via the West
Matukituki, climbed solo *and* attempted to link the east face into the north-
east face of Mt Aspiring. Guy was also active in the park in the preceding
autumn. On 9 March he achieved the first solo (and third overall) ascent
of the east face of Fastness Peak, following approximately the line of the
Dickson/Sveticic Route. Erik Bradshaw had also been occupied with Fastness, making the first ascent of the south face of the peak in early February.

In September 2013, Alexis Belton and Jaz Morris climbed six pitches
of compact, snow-covered schist on the first ascent of a new route on the
south face of Glengyle Peak, taking the central gully. In early September
2014, Ben Dare and Daniel Joll found a new line on the right-hand side
of the south face of Mt Aspiring; they climbed 12 pitches, the hardest of
which was grade M4, to produce *Shooting Star*. Ben was in the same area
back in June, climbing some good ice-cragging-style routes on the south-
west side of Mt French with Stephen Skelton.

Southern Lakes

On the Remarkables, new ice and mixed routes were made aplenty.
On the south face of Single Cone Ben Dare and Danny Murphy climbed
Eclipse (M6+, WI2, 125m)—a large corner of ice and then rock. Ben Dare,
Stephen Skelton and Adam Carlson climbed *The Principal's Daughter* (M5+,

The south face of Mt Aspiring (top) and the east face of Popes Nose (right) from the ridge between the Avalanche and Hood glaciers, Mt Aspiring National Park. This photo was taken by Guy McKinnon the day before he climbed the east face of Popes Nose. *(Guy McKInnon)*

4p) on the Telecom Tower in thin early season conditions. Stephen joined forces later in the season with Graham Johnson to claim *Naturalisation* (20, M6, 7p) on the west face of Double Cone.

A slew of new routes were completed during the frenzy of the annual Remarkables Ice and Mixed Festival. Those who did the hardest climbs were rewarded with swag and glory, the honours went to Jono Clarke and Diane Drayton this year for *Boys Don't Cry* (M6+) and *Bad Corner* (M4) respectively. Freddy Varengo won the Osprey Packs Double to Single Cone Traverse Race.

On 11 January, Ben Dare ascended the previously unclimbed North-east Buttress (15/16, 700m) of Somnus. On 25 January, Adam Carlson and Ben Dare made the first ascent of the East Face (MC3,14/15) of F-Knob, opposite Emily Peak from Emily Pass, near the Routeburn valley. In early March, Martin Hawes and Derek Chinn climbed a new grade 16-ish route on the west face of Emily Peak, in the Humboldt Mountains.

Aoraki Mount Cook area

In early December 2013, Ben Dare soloed the first ascent of a line left of *Runts in Paradise* on the south face of Nazomi. Also in December 2013 Kieran Parsons and Rob Frost approached the upper Landsborough via the Karangarua valley and proceeded to do the first ascent of the massive North-west Ridge of Mt Burns. The pair descended the Mueller to Mount Cook village. Not long after, on 11 January, Guy McKinnon soloed a new link-up on the south face of Mt Hicks. *Dance Commander* (MC4+) is an accessible but engaging route and is not as relentlessly steep as the other climbs on the face.

In August, Chris Elliot and Lee Mackintosh climbed a new ice line on the 19th called *Natural Selection* (IV); the route climbs on the south side of the buttress that forms the toe of the west ridge of Mt Darwin. On the 28th, Steve Eastwood and Taichiro Naka made the first winter ascent of the north-west face of Douglas Peak.

Other areas

During the NZAC Arthur's Pass Winter Climbing Meet, Sarwan Chand and Jack Grinsted climbed a new route up a 150m couloir on Mt Speight's north-east ridge; their route is called *Camp Mum* and is grade MC3/4. Ben Dare made the first winter ascent of the south-east face (MC5, 450m, WI4-, M4) of Ferintosh Peak in the Ben Ohau Range on 8 July. Steve Harris and Pete Harris ticked off the first ascent of the west face of Lyttle Peak on the Navigator Range; their route is called *The Architect* (MC4-, 16, 500m).

Mount Everest Foundation
Expedition Reports

SUMMARISED BY GLYN HUGHES

The Mount Everest Foundation [**www.mef.org.uk**] was set up as a Registered Charity following the first successful ascent of Everest in 1953, and was initially financed from the surplus funds and subsequent royalties of that expedition. It is a continuing initiative between the Alpine Club and the Royal Geographical Society (with the Institute of British Geographers).

Surprisingly, the word 'mountaineering' does not appear anywhere in its Memorandum and Articles, the prime object being the promotion of 'exploration' in mountain areas: this is mainly geographic, but also includes the application of other exploratory disciplines in these areas, such as geology, botany and zoology

It has now distributed well over £1,000,000 to more than 1600 British and New Zealand expeditions planning such exploration. Most of the grants have been awarded to ambitious young climbers who help to maintain Britain's reputation as one of the world's leading exploratory nations. In return for supporting an expedition, all that the MEF asks is a comprehensive report. Once received, copies are lodged in the Alpine Club Library, the Royal Geographical Society, the British Mountaineering Council and the Alan Rouse Memorial Collection in Sheffield Central Library.

Donations to assist the work of the MEF are more welcome than ever, so if you have previously benefited from MEF grants, why not include a bequest to the Foundation in your will?

The following notes summarise reports from the expeditions supported during 2014, and are divided into geographical areas.

AMERICA – NORTH & CENTRAL

Revelations, Alaska Expedition 2014 - Graham Zimmerman and Clint Helander (April 2014).

The objectives of this team were the first ascents of the west face of the Titanic and the north face of Jezebel in the Revelations Range, which is at the south-western edge of the Alaska Range. They flew into the north-east fork of the Big River glacier by ski plane, and established a base camp. The north face of Jezebel looked unsafe due to snow conditions. On 21 April they set out for the west face of the Titanic, and climbed unroped for 1700ft to the headwall where they roped up. There followed 2200ft of technical climbing of up to M6 and 5.8, and they reached the summit 16.5 hours after leaving base camp. They descended by traversing the summit ridge to the north, and then descending the east face. After a two day rest they set out to explore another cirque to the south of their base camp, but while skiing back Graham took a 40ft crevasse fall. He managed to extract himself, but had damaged his knee, which ended their climbing, and they were flown back out to Seattle. Graham had ruptured a ligament, but after surgery and physiotherapy expects to be back in 2015.   MEF ref 14-17

Brady Icefield Expedition 2014 – Paul Knott and Kieren Parsons (April/May 2014).
The primary objective was the first ascent of the east ridge of Mt Crillon in the Glacier Bay National Park, with first ascents in the Mt Abbe area as secondary objectives. They flew into a base camp at 3922ft in a bay south-east of Pk 7950ft. Heavy snowfall and unseasonably warm weather made the approach to the ridge too avalanche threatened, so they made a 20 kilometre traverse on the Brady Icefield to the area north of Mt Bertha, where they reached a high bowl overlooking the Johns Hopkins Glacier. From here on 6 May they made the first ascents of two peaks, 7507ft and 7274ft, and were able to identify the south-east ridge of Pk 8290ft as a viable objective. The following day they climbed this ridge, which involved a series of knife-edged corniced mushrooms and towers leading to the final rock pyramid. This was of superb granite and gave secure climbing on three pitches of up to 5.7. Conditions on the descent by the same route were made more difficult by the warm weather, but fortunately the ski plane was able to pick them up from the foot of the mountain, saving them from a repeat of the 20 kilometre traverse. The team identified significant further climbing opportunities in the area.   MEF ref 14-20

AMERICA – SOUTH & ANTARCTICA

Graham Silvestre Patagonia Expedition – Peter Graham and Ben Silvestre (January/February 2014).
An expedition with the objective of new routes on rock in the FitzRoy and Cerro Torre massifs. The prevailing cold and snowy conditions meant a change of objectives to mixed and ice routes. An attempt on *Exocet* on Cerro Stanhardt was aborted because of falling ice due to the warm conditions. While passing the time bouldering during bad weather Peter Graham injured his knee which put him out of action for a few days. Their first success was a repeat of *Super Domo*, a new route on Dome Blanco, which gave 10 pitches of excellent mixed climbing. An attempt on *Supercanaletta* on FitzRoy failed in violent winds, but was followed by a successful ascent of *Exocet* in difficult conditions. A final weather window just gave them time for another attempt on FitzRoy by *Mate, Porro y Todo lo Demas*, which yielded to a three-day assault. The team had summited three peaks by good routes, but not the hoped-for first ascents.   MEF ref 14-04

APEX 4 Bolivia 2014 – Ailsa Angharad-Campbell, Alex Christides, Alice Ojeda, Alistair Rocke, Arabella Kennard, Calum Stannett, Cameron

Richardson, Charlotte Bentley, Chris Graham, Eilidh Potter, Eleanor Dow, Eleanor Lee, Ellie Dickson, Ellie Heath, Gordon Paterson, Guido Peles, Harry Newmark, Mhairi Leeson, Millie Wood, Nandesh Patel, Rob Gilhespy, Sandy Jackson, Shona Main (leader), Stewart Rodney, Tom Beddis, Wayne Pringle, and Xu Teo (June/July 2014).

The objectives were to collect physiological and genetic data from young healthy volunteers at low, moderate, and high altitude in order to gain insight into the process of acclimatisation. The expedition was based in an abandoned ski lodge on the Chalkaltya Mountain near La Paz.

Tests carried out on expedition members included chest ultrasonography to assess for the presence of subclinical pulmonary oedema and changes in heart function, ultrasound scans of the eye to detect swelling of the optic nerve as an indicator of cerebral oedema, blood samples to identify changes in gene expression, as well as blood coagulation and clotting function. The evaluation of this data will take several months, but will provide information directly applicable to those spending time at high altitude, and to help develop patient-specific approaches to care and treatment. MEF ref 14-16

San Lorenzo East Face Expedition – Matt Helliker and Jon Bracey (September/October 2014).

The objective was the unclimbed east face of San Lorenzo, a 3706m peak on the Chile/Argentina border just north of the Perito Moreno National Park. They arranged to ship their gear in advance by courier, rather than paying excess baggage rates on the flight. This proved not to have been a good decision as the courier lost the baggage. While waiting for their gear in El Calafate they purchased food and arranged onward transport to the road head. As time went by they realised there was no way that they could recover the gear with enough time to continue the expedition. They gave all the food and other provisions bought locally to a charity for the homeless in El Calafate and flew home. The lesson learnt was not to ship equipment in advance to South America.   MEF ref 14-19

GREENLAND & ARCTIC

Wall to Wall 2014 – Cath Alldred, Sion Brocklehurst, Robert Durran, Pat Ingram, and Simon Smith (July/August 2014).

The objective was the establishment of new routes in the Fox Jaw Cirque, Trillingerne, East Greenland. The team were flown to the island of Kulusuk from Reykyavik, and continued by boat to the head of Tasilq Fjord. A base camp was established close to the Cirque. The team successfully completed a total of four new routes of up to 400m, three on Baby Molar and one on Left Rabbit Ear, and made attempts on a further three routes. These were aborted when the apparently safe lines ran out. Repeats of longer routes of 600m on Incisor were also attempted, but not completed. The climbing was generally bold, high quality slab climbing with long run-outs on gneiss of variable quality. There is still a great deal of climbing potential with hard lines on the most accessible formations, and much more in the more remote locations. MEF ref 14-27.

Monitoring of ice-marginal dynamics in West Greenland – Joseph Mallalieu, Duncan Quincey, and Jonathan Carrivick (July/August 2014). This was a scientific expedition to monitor changes in the ice margins of the Russel glacier, and quantify ice-marginal lake formation and drainage. This will benefit the community of Kangerlussuaq who have experienced destruction of infrastructure and evacuation as a result of outburst floods. The expedition was successful in installing a total of 15 cameras, and the site will be revisited in the summer of 2015 to download the information recorded. A previous visit had identified an accessible ice ramp leading to an area of less fractured ice behind the ice margin, and it was intended to install GPS transmitters here to record ice margin movement. Unfortunately the ice ramp was found to be have become heavily fractured, and installation of the transmitters was no longer possible. A final report will be produced after collection and examination of the camera data this summer. MEF ref 14-28

HIMALAYA – INDIA

British Expedition to Janahut – Malcolm Bass and Simon Yearsley (May/June 2014).
The original plan was to attempt the south-west face of Rimo III in the East Karakoram, but permission was denied. Plan B was an attempt on the north-east face of Chaukhamba IV in the Garhwal Himalaya. They established an advanced base near the head of the Gangotri Glacier, and reconnoitred Chaukhamba. Strong westerly winds had deposited massive volumes of snow on the east faces, which made the proposed ascent too dangerous, so they came up with plan C, an attempt on the unclimbed Janahut (6805m). Janahut had been attempted a number of times before, but the highest point so far achieved was about 6500m. They decided to attempt the South-west Buttress, which had been tried previously by Andy Brown and Paul Figg. After two days of climbing, mainly at night when the face was safely frozen, they reached the top of the buttress itself, and made a bivouac at about 6300m, a few rope lengths along a steep ridge of hard ice. The third day gave superb and exciting climbing further up the ice ridge and to a long horizontal section of ridge. Two hard pitches led to the top of a feature called the Castle at about 6660m. It was late, the summit was 140m above, and their tent and food were 360m below, so they decided to descend. After a day resting and eating at the bivouac site, two further days were spent descending by the east side of the mountain to the advanced base camp. MEF ref 14-07.

British Hagshu Expedition 2014 – Mick Fowler, Paul Ramsden, Steve Burns, and Ian Cartwright (September/October 2014).

The team was given permission well in advance for an attempt on the north face of Hagshu, a 6657m peak in Jammu and Kashmir. Shortly before leaving they discovered that the IMF had issued another permit for the face to a Slovenian team, and on arrival that yet another had been issued to an American team. A base camp was established on the true left bank of the Hagshu Glacier, and from here the entire team climbed a peak of 5680m just north-west of Hagshu for acclimatisation. When they returned to the base camp they found that the Slovenians were already established on the north face, and so decided to try a prominent slanting line on the north-east face. Three days of mixed climbing, including hard ice, led to the foot of the summit buttress. The following day they traversed to the right edge of the summit buttress to join the Slovenian route, and then enjoyed some steep and sunny rock climbing to just below the unclimbed north summit. The following day they continued over the north summit, and then a beautiful ridge to the main summit, and descent via the south-east ridge taken by the first ascensionists. While Fowler and Ramsden were on Hagshu, Burns and Cartwright had climbed an attractive, unnamed peak of about 6000m west of the base camp, and a Himalayan brown bear had made regular visits to the camp.   MEF ref 14-10

2014 British Spiti Expedition – Derek Buckle, Dave Broadhead, Mike Cocker, Geoff Cohen and Hamish Irvine (August/October 2014).
Exploration of unclimbed peaks and sub-valleys in the eastern Lingti nala region of the Indian Himalaya, with Kamen Gyalmo (6470m) as the main objective. This peak had been suggested by Harish Kapadia as a worthwhile objective, although actually getting to the mountain might be a problem. The team penetrated deep into the relatively unexplored region east of the Lingti nala, and after a multi-day trek over difficult terrain established a base camp at 5130m. Two advanced base camps and a further two high camps were subsequently established, from which it was possible to explore, and map by GPS, the high plateau region including and surrounding Lagma (5796m). This exploration took in three additional tops and two significant previously unclimbed outlier peaks of 5924m and 5927m. Pk 5924, tentatively called Chota Sgurr, lies at the start of a broad, intricate cirque enclosing the upper Talung nala and Kamen Gyalmo (6470m), one of the team's primary objectives. Complex terrain and deep, impassible canyons prevented easy access to Kamen Gyalmo via the Lingti nala and ultimately meant that they had insufficient time to mount a meaningful attempt.
                                                        MEF ref 14-11

HIMALAYA – NEPAL

Anidesha Chuli 2014 Expedition – Paul Hersey, Shelley Hersey, and John Price (April/May 2014).
Anidesha Chuli (6900m), aka White Wave, is located in north-eastern Nepal, and had been attempted by another New Zealand party a year

earlier. The approach was from Kathmandu to Taplejung by bus, and then a 10-day trek to base camp at 4800m on the Ramdang glacier. John became ill on the walk in, but responded to a change of antibiotic. Camp 1 was set up at 5200m, where Paul showed signs first of acute mountain sickness, and then of high altitude cerebral oedema, so he was evacuated to base camp where his condition slowly improved. John and Shelley continued with acclimatisation to camp 2 at 5400m, and then to 5600m, struggling through waist deep snow. After a thunderstorm and heavy snow they retreated to base camp, and a week of poor weather followed. It was decided that Paul would stay at base camp during the next attempt, so John and Shelley returned to camp 1 in the first break in the weather. They pushed on to 5700m, but found snow conditions worse, sometimes chest deep, and when another storm hit they decided to abandon the climb.

MEF ref 14-03

Lumba Sumba Peak 2014 – Paul Vardy, Helen Caunce, Dave Barker, Rory Sellar, Ken Hopper, and Phil Booth (April/May 2014).
Lumba Sumba (5672m) is located in eastern Nepal, and forms the watershed of the Arun and Tamor river systems. The approach was by air and jeep to Taplejung, and 11 days in the approach and setting up base camp. The team found a hidden couloir which gave them access around the right hand side of a glacier to a steep snow slope leading to the north ridge. This was followed to the summit in mixed conditions up to grade III. Only two days were needed on the mountain, and five of the six climbing members of the expedition summited. There was a daily pattern of thunderstorms or snow showers in the afternoons. There were four days when this did not occur, two of which were the days on the mountain.   MEF ref 14-15

PAKISTAN

New Zealand Hindu Kush 2014 – Pat Deavoll and Chris Todd (June/July 2014).
Objectives were first ascents of Langua-tai-Barfi (7011m) and the SE face of Shakawr (7076m) in the Hindu Kush of north-west Pakistan. The approach was by a two-day walk-in from the road head at Zondangram to the Roshgol Glacier. After acclimatising up to 5200m on the slopes surrounding base camp they established an advance base camp at the head of the glacier, 15km from base. They set up a further three camps to a high point of about 6200m on the north ridge of Langua-tai-Barfi, which forms the border between Afghanistan and Pakistan. The climbing had involved stretches of deep snow, and mixed rock and ice, although it did not require pitching. They left for the summit the next day at 1am, and climbed for 14 hours through deep unconsolidated snow in very low temperatures. At 5pm they estimated a further 4/5 hours to the summit, and in deteriorating weather and whiteout conditions they turned back to their high camp.

They retreated to base camp the following day. Shortage of time prevented any attempt on Shakawr.   MEF ref 14-08.

Muchu Chhish Expedition 2014 – Pete Thompson, Tim Oates, and Phil De-Beger (August/September 2014).
Muchu Chhish is one of a number of 7000m peaks on a high ridge known as the Batura Wall in the Batura Mustagh, the westernmost part of the Karakoram. The intention was to follow the Polish route up the south ridge of Batura VI, climbed during the first ascent of Batura V. They planned to leave the Polish route at 7260m, and traverse east below Batura VI to the ridge between Batura VI and Muchu Chhish, following this to the summit. They set off on an alpine-style attempt, but found that a long traverse which they had hoped to climb unroped was hard ice. Realising that climbing in pitches would be too slow for them to climb the mountain they decided to retreat at about 6000m. After resting at their advanced base they inspected their secondary objective, the south-east couloir of Gutum Talji, but decided not to attempt this because of the lack of ice in the couloir. They then decided on a change of scenery and drove to Sust in upper Hunza, and then to Morkhoon village, and the Morkhoon Valley. They set up a base camp at 4300m, and identified Pregar as an objective. Oates and De-Beger bivouacked at 4900m and made an attempt on the south face, but retreated from 5600m due to unconsolidated snow.
                                                                    MEF ref 14-21

Link Sar Expedition 2014 – Jonathan Griffith and Kevin Mahoney (July/August 2014).
The objective was the first ascent of Link Sar (7041m) in the Charakusa Valley, a peak attempted in two previous expeditions by Griffith. The approach was by air to Skardu, road to Hushe, and a two-day walk-in to base camp at 4300m. For acclimatisation they climbed Sulu Peak (6000m) and bivouacked on the summit, where Griffith suffered from altitude sickness. They decided to continue acclimatisation at an advanced base below the north face of Link Sar at 5400m, and after two nights here went back to base to wait for a weather window. The chosen route was to climb the north face, traverse the 1km ridge from the west summit to the main summit, and descend the south face. In spite of conditions on the face being by far the worse they had seen, and deteriorating weather, they managed to top out of the north face after three tough days, but the conditions were too dangerous for them to continue to the west summit. They believed that in good conditions they would have had a good chance of completing the route.   MEF ref 14-29

CHINA AND TIBET

Shaksgam Expedition 2014 – Bruce Normand and Jesse Mease (June/ July 2014).

Normand and Mease shared logistics with German and Slovenian expeditions, but climbed independently. Their goal was the exploration of mountains north of the Upper Shaksgam River in the Karakoram of Chinese Xinjiang, and in particular attempts on the unclimbed Durbin Kangri I (6952m), Kaimuk Kangri (6952m), and Burnag Kangri (6821m). The approach was by Landcruiser from Kashgar to Ilik, and then on foot with camels for the gear, to a base camp at 4100m up the Kulchintubulak River 3km off the Shaksgam. An advance base was set up further up the valley at 4800m, and they continued up the Kizil Davan Pass to acclimatise at 5600m. The daytime weather was extremely warm. They set off from ABC for a four-day push up the north face of Durbin Kangri I, but their attempt was short lived when the ice on the face was found to be hollow with running water behind, covering extremely poor rock. They then considered an attempt on the north-east flank of the mountain, but decided against this after seeing a huge avalanche sweep down this face. Instead they crossed the Kizil Davan to try their luck in the Zug-Shaksgam, and explore approaches to Burnag Gangri. Failing to find a feasible route, and with deteriorating weather, they retreated to ABC. At base camp they learned that the Slovenians were missing and overdue, and so started a search which turned out to be fruitless. The search continued with the assistance of a military helicopter, but no trace was found. MEF ref 14-12

British Liushen Tag Expedition 2014 – John Town, Zaheer Durrani, Stefan Jachmich, Susan Jensen, Gus Morton, and Alison Stockwell (September 2014).

An attempt on the unclimbed Liushen Tag (6595m) in the Kun Lun mountains of Xinjiang province, by its southern flank. The approach was by air via Urumchi to Hotan, and thence by road to Keria, Pulu, and Subashi. Base camp was established at 4959m, and they began to explore possible approaches to the upper part of the south spur of the mountain. The first 5km of the route proved good going, and a camp was placed below a prominent feature named the Tower, at the highest source of running water at 5400m. Meanwhile the first ascent of a peak of 6004m south of base camp was made to gain a view of the ridge beyond the Tower. This revealed a feature called the Castle, a 150m fin of rock which might be climbed direct on rock, or passed to the west on snow. A high point of 5900m on the left flank of the Tower was reached by Jensen and Jachmich, but they were forced to retire because of illness. By this time the unavailability of water had become a problem, time was running out, so they retreated. Another 400m of the south spur remained to be climbed, and from there a corniced ridge led to a subsidiary peak, and then on to the south summit (c6500m), which blocked the view of the main summit. MEF ref 14-22

British Chinese Tien Shan Expedition 2014 – Sam Thompson and Boris Korzh (July/August 2014).
The main objective was the first ascent of the north face of Khanjaylak I (5424m), with a secondary the north-west spur of Xuelian East, in the Xuelian Massif in the Chinese Tien Shan.
The expedition got off to a slow start after Thompson's kitbag was lost by the airline, and delays at a police checkpoint. Because of the delay they decided to abandon the attempt on Khanjaylak, and concentrate on Xuelian East. They began acclimatising on a peak near base camp, and then established an advanced base about 18km east of base at about 4100m on the Muzart Glacier. After closer inspection of the route, they changed their plan to climbing the east ridge of Xulian East, and continuing with a traverse of Xulian Feng, which had not been climbed from the east. They continued with their acclimatisation during a week of good weather, and set up an advanced base camp. Unfortunately the weather then deteriorated, with frequent snowstorms, mild temperatures, and poor visibility. Taking advantage of a weather window they did manage to climb up to the east ridge of Xuelian East, reaching 5200m. They were then caught in a snowstorm which lasted two days, and with no sign of improvement and depleted supplies they returned to base camp.   MEF ref 14-25

CENTRAL ASIA

Reaching the Roof – Ski Tajikistan 2014 – Susanna Walker, Phillip Mark Thomas, Richard Jones, and Tom Coney (April/May 2014).
Objectives were to climb and ski unexplored peaks of 5000-6000m in the Vanj Range in Pamirs. From Dushanbe travel to Poi Mazor was by 4x4, and from there to the RGS Glacier by Russian military lorry. Base camp was established at the base of RGS Glacier, and advanced base camp at the foot of Bear Glacier and Abdulkahor Glacier. During the exploration of Bear Glacier, Walker fell and suffered a suspected broken leg, and descended to ABC. Three of the party set a further two camps on Abdulkahor Glacier, from which they hoped to climb a 6000m peak at its head. With the onset of bad weather they changed objective and climbed a peak of 5313m via the west ridge, descending on skis. Returning to the RGS Glacier, they next headed up the Nedhuk Glacier to a camp at 3700m, from which they climbed the north face of Nedhuk 1 (5100m), again descending by ski. Having completed two first ascents, and concerned for Walker's leg, they called the expedition short and returned home.   MEF ref 14-02

Little Poobah 2014 – Adrian Dye, Scott Gillespie, Ian Peachey, Robert Middleton, Hannah Moulton and Huw Goodall (August 2014).
Objectives were to explore the Fersmana Valley area on the east side of the Western Kokshaal Too in Kyrgyzstan, focusing on new alpine rock routes on the faces either side of the Fersmana Valley, and the first ascents of a

number of peaks of up to 5481m.

The approach was by air to Bishkek, then by a UAZ 6-wheel-drive truck provided by logistics company ITMC. They were dropped off some distance from the desired base camp at c3400m on the west side of the Fersmana Valley, but as this was downhill the carries were not too difficult. During a two-week period the party made a total of six first ascents of peaks in the range 4500-4900m with grades up to D, and also a number of multi-pitch rock routes on lower crags of VS and HVS grades. The attempt on Little Poobah itself (5481m) failed due to poor snow conditions. MEF ref 14-13

Demar Djangart Expedition 2014 – Jamie Goodhart, Stuart Worsfold, Stuart Lade, Jill Plummer, Paul Padman, Liz Holley, Zoe Strong, Max Streeton and Alex Reed (August 2014).

Objectives were the ascent of unclimbed peaks in a remote area of the Djangart mountains, and an attempt on the north ridge of Khan Tengri. Because of the remoteness of the area the team were flown in by helicopter from Maida Adyr, a base 12 hours by 4x4 from Bishkek. The team split into two groups, and between them explored three glacier systems, one group on the most easterly glacier in the region, the other a small glacier to the west of this, and then a hanging glacier further to the west. Between them they made 11 first ascents of peaks between 4500m and 5100m, and put up one new alpine length rock route. Afterwards one group was flown by helicopter to Khan Tengri North base camp, and spent a week getting to camp 2. Fresh snow made conditions very difficult, and eventually deterioration in the weather led them to descend and fly out. MEF ref 14-14

Muzkol Expedition 2014 – Rebecca Coles, Simon Verspeak, Rhys Huws, and John Vincent – (July/August 2014).

An attempt on an unnamed and unclimbed peak of c6123m in the Muzkol Valley in the Tajikistan Pamirs. The peak had been attempted previously by Rebecca Coles in 2011, but they failed because of difficulties too great for the skills and equipment then available to the team. As the Muzkol valley is in the north-east of Tajikistan, they approached through Kyrgyzstan, flying into Osh. From there they travelled by jeep via Murghab to the Muzkol. Donkeys were used to carry further into Muzkol, and finally they ferried gear to a base camp at 4300m. They put in a high camp at 4900m, and from here climbed to a col at 5500m, where they stashed their gear. On the summit day they returned to the col, and traversed to the base of the west ridge. Coles and Verspeak climbed 50° snow slopes diagonally to the ridge, and followed this to a high point of 5900m. The ridge was a mixture of rock scrambling, snow patches, and low-angled ice pitches up to AD+. They stopped due to loose rock and a lack of snow. Huws and Vincent had climbed a more direct line reaching the ridge just below the high point. This was sustained D+/TD- with poor snow at the top. Both teams retreated by abseil. Coles and Verspeak explored another line further up the valley, but found that glacial retreat had left rock slabs and serac walls barring progress. Meanwhile Huws and Vincent were tempted to try a peak on the opposite side of the river above base camp, on which they eventually succeeded on with a 14-hour day. The ascent involved several hours of scree trudging, then a 50° snow slope, ending up on the summit ridge. The grade was judged to be approximately D.   MEF ref 14-18

Jiptik 2014 – Edward Lemon, John Proctor, and Martin Jones (July/ August 2014).
The original objective had been the north face of Muz Tok, an unclimbed 5000m peak in the Jiptik valley, Batken, Kyrgyzstan. This had to be changed as it involved an approach through the Tajikistani enclave of Vorukh, and one member was denied a Tajikistan visa, and also because of troubles in the Tajikistan/Kyrgyzstan border area. They decided instead to explore the valleys south of Zardaly, with an approach which avoids Vorukh. The Yashil-Kel valley gave three objectives, all peaks of 5000m plus, and the Tutek-Su valley a number of 4000m peaks. The approach was by saloon car from Osh to Batken, 4WD onward to Zardaly, and then on foot with donkeys to the base camp at the junction of the Yashil-Kul valley and the Ak-Terek river.
They first explored the Yashil-Kul valley, where the valley floor was at 2200m to 3000m, and the adjacent mountains up to 5300m, and with no access to the upper slopes from most of the valley. They investigated possibilities at the top of the valley, but found that the receding glacier had made progress impossible. An attempt on a snow peak of 5285m was blocked by a large and impassable icefall. They then explored Tutek-Su, where landslides and avalanches led to slow progress up the valley. By the time they reached the foot of the target peaks, they realised they no longer had time to tackle them, as they were predominantly steep rock spires. They concluded that the Yashil-Kul valley offers no climbing possibilities, but the unclimbed peaks above the western fork of the Tutek-Su are probably accessible.   MEF ref 14-23

Navlikin 2014 Expedition – Emily Ward, Dave Searle, Libby Southgate, Emma Crome, Cora Moffat, Sam Simpson, James Matthews, Joel Evans, and Simon Tracey (September/October 2014).
The main objective was an unclimbed peak of 5611m to the north of Pik Byeliy in the Western Kokshaal Too in Kyrgyzstan, along with a number of peaks, believed unclimbed, along the southern boundary of the Navlikin glacier. The party flew to Bishkek, and enjoyed an acclimatisation visit to the Ala-Archa national park, with an overnight stop at the Racek hut. They then drove into the mountains via Naryn in a URAL truck. The plan was to access the head of the Navlikin basin by crossing a col at the top of the Kotur glacier, and attempt one or more unclimbed 5000m peaks. Unfortunately only four of the party made it over the col, and they were pinned down by a storm and failed to summit anything. However the members did manage to climb all the peaks around the lower part of the Kotur glacier,

including two peaks which do not appear on the map. All climbing was in alpine style, and a total of 13 routes were completed. Subsequent research showed that all the peaks had been climbed previously, though many of the routes were new ones. MEF ref 14-24

MYANMAR

Shan Plateau Expedition 2013-4 – Peter Talling, Lui Hong, Fleur Loveridge, Paul Mackrill and Ben Wright (December 2013-January 2014). This was the fifth in a series of British Shan Plateau caving expeditions in the Southern Shan State in Myanmar (Burma), focussing on the area around Ywangan. A new feature of this expedition was that the members were allowed to stay in local villages outside Ywangan, closer to the caves to be explored, and also giving closer contact with the community. The first part of the expedition was based in Linwe village, from which they explored caves around a large closed depression in the area known as Dragon Lake. Here they mapped five new cave systems, and established connections with other neighbouring systems. The second part was based at Kyauk Ngauk village, hoping to extend the previously explored Kyauk Khaung system into a neighbouring cave, but the technical nature of the caving did not allow this. However, a new final pitch did make this the deepest mapped cave in Myanmar. In total the expedition mapped 5km of caves at eight sites, recorded a further 16 sites of speleological interest, and increased the understanding of the hydrogeology of the area.

MEF ref 14-05

Reviews

The Matterhorn from Riffelalp. Gabriel Loppé. 1879. Oil. 96 x 73cm.
(Alpine Club Collection HE019P)

Reviews

One Day as a Tiger
Alex MacIntyre and the birth of light and fast alpinism
John Porter
Vertebrate Publishing, 2014, pp244, £20

The 1979 *American Alpine Journal* was an outstanding volume for mountaineering achievement: the previous year, Americans led by Jim Whittaker had completed a 40-year quest by reaching the summit of K2 and the American Women's Himalayan Expedition, led by Arlene Blum, had confirmed, in the words of the T-shirt, that 'a woman's place is on top' with an ascent of Annapurna I.

Another big name in the contents list was that of Chris Bonington with an account of the ambitious British attempt on K2's unclimbed west ridge. Like the women's expedition, which saw the deaths of Alison Chadwick-Onyszkiewicz and Vera Watson, the Brits also suffered tragedy, Nick Estcourt being swept away in an avalanche. Bonington notes that the west ridge climbers 'numbered only eight.' He added: 'we had all had enough of big expeditions.'

Only eight? What then of two other expeditions recorded in the 1979 *AAJ* with just four Americans on the north ridge of Latok I, and four climbers (two Poles, one Brit and one American) on the south buttress of Changabang? Admittedly both peaks fall short of the debilitating 8000m contour, but the style in which these super-hard routes were tackled, indeed the whole aura around the expeditions, speaks of a different age of alpinism – different from heavy-duty *bundobusts* of the past, yet also qualitatively different from the age that would soon follow it, with top-flight alpinists incorporated into the entertainment industry, however pure in spirit the participants.

The Brit on Changabang in 1978 was Alex MacIntyre, the primary subject of this long-anticipated book; the American is its author John Porter, though after decades living in Cumbria, Porter is surely now best described as an Anglo-American and is, after all, a recent vice-president of the Alpine Club.

First, a couple of quotes from that 1979 *AAJ* which in the restrained language of the time give a flavour of what the young Turks of alpinism were up to. Michael Kennedy on Latok I: 'We had been on the climb so long that it seemed as if this was the only thing we had ever known. Memories faded into the distant past. Each day was routine: get up, put on a brew, eat, boots on, dress against cold, pack the gear, climb, haul loads, hack out a platform, eat, sleep – the details were all the same, the days alike, blurred into a simple ritual of the climb.'[1]

John Porter recalled day seven on Changabang, heading to the upper icefield they'd dubbed the 'Cyclops' Eye': The last pitch gave Alex an exercise in one-arm ice-axe pull-ups after the lower half of the icicle he was climbing collapsed under him.

'We traversed to the left side of the Cyclops' Eye and fixed a rope in an icy gully before returning to join the others at the spectacular bivouac nicked in a small ridge in the icefield. I was suffering on alternate nights from stomach pain and this was one of them. Sleep came only as a series of quick nightmares. Krzysztof's groans continually brought me back to the reality of our position. He had not eaten for four days and was losing coherence. I prayed for the summit next day and entertained myself with the glittering stars and the gradual dawn that gathered around the distant peaks of Nepal.'[2]

And the world knew nothing of any of this at the time. Kennedy's 'simple ritual of the climb' went on for 26 days uninterrupted by satellite phone-calls and Porter could count the glittering stars without thoughts of updating his blog or obligations to sponsors. While the Changabang and Latok I climbs – and that of the NE face of Koh-i-Bandaka, Afghanistan, in 1977 by MacIntyre, Porter and Voytek Kurtyka – seem modern in concept and character, they took place, as Porter points out, at a time closer to the Second World War than to today.

The marketing men had yet to discover the selling power of mountaineering; expeditions of the sort that launched MacIntyre's star may have had a cobbled together feel – 'privateering' is how Porter describes it – but there was a freewheeling *joie de vivre* about them that seems absent from today's professional scene.

Yet the fun was fading from MacIntyre's climbing too. Porter contrasts the Alex with whom he sang 'Be kind to your web-footed friends!' – on a freezing Andean bivouac during the first ascent of Nevado III, in Peru's Cordillera Blanca – to the goal-focused professional and BMC national officer he became only a couple of years later, spurred on by an ascent of Dhaulagiri's east face. Four years and two weeks after standing on the summit of Changabang, Alex MacIntyre was dead. On 15 October 1982, a single hurtling stone struck his helmet, smashing it apart and extinguishing one of the leading lights in a generation of outstanding alpinists. He was just 28 years old.

Porter's penetrating biography of his friend and climbing partner suggests inevitability in MacIntyre's fate. A life once so seemingly carefree took on a more ominous trajectory. Maybe it wouldn't have necessarily ended there, that day on the south face of Annapurna, but ambition was driving him

1. *American Alpine Journal*, vol 22 (1979), 24-28. (The north ridge route remains uncompleted.)
2. Ibid 29-35

Alex MacIntyre at base camp, Koh-i-Bandaka, Wakhan Corridor, 1977.
(John Porter)

ever closer to the edge. And MacIntyre knew it. He had dark premonitions about Annapurna, confiding to Porter on the eve of the fateful attempt that he had been having 'scary dreams'.

MacIntyre's partner that day was René Ghilini, a French-Italian alpinist at least as aggressively ambitious as MacIntyre himself. Porter, suffering from diarrhoea and out-performed by his younger companions, had opted out of the summit bid and witnessed the accident through his camera lens from just above base camp.

Porter's candid admissions about his own doubts and fears, along with his charting of MacIntyre's change in character from climbing vagabond to professional alpinist with a tick list are two of the engrossing aspects of this book. For many readers, I suspect, it will also be a nostalgia trip, through the glory days of the Leeds University Union Climbing Club, the era of John Syrett, Alan Manson, Roger Baxter-Jones, Brian Hall and

Descending the original route on Changabang after the first ascent of the south face. From *One Day as a Tiger*. *(John Porter)*

'habitual student' Bernard Newman (how could I leave out of this abbreviated list of luminaries my erstwhile successor in the editor's chair?).

These were years when climbing was laced with sex, drugs and loud music. I hesitate over the usual third element of that trio; this was the 1970s, rock and roll was being overtaken by punk and 1960s radicalism by a sort of cheery nihilism. The hard edge of Thatcherism lurked around the corner. Porter is a natural social commentator; he captures the zeitgeist perfectly and doesn't, unlike others, make the mistake of attributing anarchic behaviour exclusively to climbers. He has a broader vision.

One Day is in several respects a unique eyewitness account of a scene hitherto only sketchily recorded between the exhaustively chronicled exploits of climbing's elder statesmen (Bonington, Scott, Messner and their contemporaries) and the British rock climbing renaissance more recently detailed by, among others, Ron Fawcett, Ben Moon and Johnny Dawes. And only Porter could write with such first-hand authority on expeditioning with Polish teams, notably Andrzej Zawada and Voytek Kurtyka. Black-marketeering, being smuggled across the USSR by train and into Afghanistan en route for Koh-i-Bandaka: the tales coalesce into a unique portrait of Cold War climbing.

The idea of writing a biography formed in Porter's mind only a couple of years after the Annapurna accident. Much of the detail about MacIntyre's early years came from conversations with Alex's mother, Jean MacIntyre. Yet the book went on hold after Mrs MacIntyre was diagnosed with terminal cancer. 'If you have to finish the book do so when I'm gone,' she had asked. And Porter complied. (The weakest parts of the book are to my mind two magazine articles by MacIntyre himself, inclusions useful as first-hand narrative perhaps, but rambling and juvenile in style.)

I hope John feels he has another book in him and that it won't be quite so long in gestation. He writes with an easy fluency and an insider's knowledge of the mountaineering scene stretching back five decades. Over that time he's watched climbing evolve into 'an established part of the entertainment industry', on which he offers thoughtful opinion. And then there's the matter of risk. As John notes, MacIntyre was one of a generation that 'all but climbed itself into extinction'. Was that down to bad luck? No one could have predicted the trajectory of that single stone. Was it poor judgement or obsessive ambition? He reflects on this briefly, concluding: 'Alex was unlucky, but his ambition pushed him to extremes.'

One Day deservedly scooped the Grand Prize at the 2014 Banff Mountain Book Festival and I would confidently expect that by the time this *AJ* appears Porter will be on the shortlist for the 2015 Boardman Tasker Prize, and a likely winner. And then? There is so much more I'd like to read from John Porter.

Stephen Goodwin

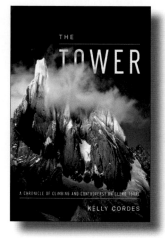

The Tower
A chronicle of climbing and controversy on Cerro Torre
Kelly Cordes
Patagonia, 2014, pp400, US$27.95

'Calm around Cerro Torre never lasts,' Kelly Cordes writes early in his comprehensive and compelling history of this exceptional mountain. He's talking about the weather of course, but right from the start the controversy Cerro Torre engendered matched its reputation for sticking its elegant snout into some of the world's worst weather. 'A shriek turned to stone,' Reinhold Messner called it, but only when the wind blows. Under blue skies and high pressure it's the closest you can imagine to mountaineering perfection, a kind of Platonic ideal of what a climbing challenge should be. It provokes something akin to lust. Lionel Terray put it neatly, looking over at Cerro Torre from the summit of FitzRoy in 1952: 'Now there's a mountain worth risking one's skin for!'

Seven years and a day after Terray's judgement, an Italian émigré called Cesarino Fava left a snow cave on the Torre Glacier for one final attempt to see something of his two companions. They had been gone for six days, the last three of them in a horrendous storm, the wind overhead howling like a jet engine. He was preparing himself to descend and tell the world that Cesare Maestri and Toni Egger were dead. Then he saw something in the snow, and rushed uphill towards it. The shape turned out to be the half-dead form of Maestri who looked up at Fava and said: 'Toni, Toni, Toni.'

The story Maestri told the world of a brilliant, nervy dash up the frozen cliff of Cerro Torre to the summit, and the harrowing descent, ending with Egger being swept to his death in an avalanche, has been revealed to all but a cadre of committed believers in Italy to be a fraud. Anyone who had any lingering doubts about this would have had them sorely tested by Rolando Garibotti's 2004 seminal article in the *American Alpine Journal*, titled 'A Mountain Unveiled: A Revealing Analysis of Cerro Torre's Tallest Tale.' Despite the fact this important article was translated into Italian, it has never been challenged.

Why do we need anything more than Garibotti's exemplary essay? Much has happened in the intervening years. Patagonian climbing has, thanks to the arrival of excellent and timely weather forecasts, changed the game forever. Garibotti himself, together with Ermanno Salvaterra and Alessandro Beltrami, climbed, more or less, the route Maestri claimed and found no trace of the 1959 attempt above the already discovered fixed ropes that end a thousand feet from the ground and three thousand short of the summit. This despite Maestri claiming to have placed '60 or 70' bolts on his desperate retreat from the top.

But Cordes does much more than simply bring the story up to date. He does several other important things, beyond telling a fascinating and important story with verve and energy. There is, for instance, a useful chapter where he considers the likelihood that it was technically possible for Egger to have climbed the freakish sheet of ice that Maestri said covered the mountain and allowed them to succeed. Given the ice tools available, and what the very best ice climbers were doing elsewhere, including Egger himself on Jirishanca, it's inconceivable.

Cordes successfully brings together the past and the present, particularly the free ascent of Maestri's 1970 abomination dubbed the Compressor Route and the removal of its bolts. In doing so he touches on quite profound ideas to do with sovereignty and how the mythology of the past becomes some kind of intellectual property, to be fought over and owned. (These issues are very current, and extend to how commercial climbing is practised now in the Himalaya, with fixed ropes expanding a lucrative market.)

Maestri's second route on Cerro Torre took a line up the south-east ridge, a route tried in 1968 by a British team that included Dougal Haston, Martin Boysen, Mick Burke and Pete Crew. The British came close to success. Had Haston not dropped their bolt kit, a few studs would have seen them past the crux and perhaps to the summit. When they came home, they expressed doubts about Maestri's 1959 claim to a route that looked even harder than the one they'd tried. Maestri was enraged and set out for Patagonia with a petrol-driven drill and hundreds of bolts: 'I return and attack their routes, the routes they were not able to climb. I will humiliate them, and they will feel ashamed of having doubted me.' Despite creating something akin to a *via ferrata*, he still didn't quite reach the summit.

When Hayden Kennedy from the US and Jason Kruk from Canada did the first 'fair means' ascent of the south-east ridge in 2013, after scores of repeats of the Compressor Route, they decided, standing on the summit, to remove Maestri's bolts, particularly from the headwall, chopping around 120 as they descended. Their actions were bitterly resented in the town of Chaltén – a place that simply didn't exist in 1968 and has been built literally on the back of mountain tourism – where locals attempted to threaten and intimidate Kruk and Kennedy, seemingly for the crime of destroying their livelihood.

As it happens, interest in the Compressor Route was already waning before the bolts were chopped and many climbers around the world, certainly those with a clear view of what alpinism should be, hailed their actions as a bold step in the right direction. This was a restatement of what Mummery had argued back in the nineteenth century – that you can climb anything given enough technology, but that doesn't mean you should.

Cordes skilfully weaves together the long decades of the Maestri controversy with these modern developments, and in doing so reveals how the legend of Maestri and Egger – and also of the third team member from 1959, Cesarino Fava – has become a legend that draws people in, along with the beauty of Patagonia and the quality of the climbing. Undermine the legend, and people feel threatened, as though it were some religious myth that deserves defending.

He opens and closes the book with Fava, interviewing his son about the 'ascent' in 1959, and then revealing at the end that Fava lied, not just about Cerro Torre, but about other events in his life, in particular the circumstances of a rescue attempt on Aconcagua. Rolo Garibotti and Reinhold Messner both seem to agree that Fava wasn't just an accomplice but more of a driving force in the concoction of Maestri's claim, making critical interventions in support of Maestri, even when the Spider of the Dolomites seemed close to revealing the truth. Cordes reveals how this charming man kept secrets.

There are one or two small omissions. I would, for example, like to know much more about the early history of both Cesare Maestri and Toni Egger; these men were born in the same country, but the vagaries of history drove Egger to a new home in Austria. What was Maestri's early life really like? I would have liked also a little more on the significant contribution of Eastern European climbers like Silvo Karo. But these are minor points.

For those who argue that this story must be left in the past, this strong and highly readable contribution to climbing history should make them think again. Not only does it show how the past impinges on the present, it makes an urgent case for those most affected – Toni Egger's family – to be told what really happened. It asks searching questions about what kind of world we want mountaineering to be – one where honesty and compassion are paramount, or one where the comforting lies of the past are allowed to infect the future.

Ed Douglas

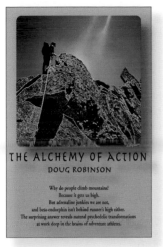

The Alchemy of Action
Doug Robinson
Moving Over Stone, 2013, pp210, US$24

There's a passage you may know from Yvon Chouinard. He's on the seventh and penultimate day on El Cap's Muir Wall, forging a new route with T M Herbert. The unremitting effort has left them pretty spaced out.

'With the more receptive senses we now appreciated everything around us,' Chouinard wrote. 'Each individual crystal in the granite stood out in bold relief. The varied shapes of the clouds never ceased to attract our attention. For the first time we noticed tiny bugs that were all over the walls, so tiny they were barely noticeable... This unity with our joyous surroundings, this ultra penetrating perception gave us a feeling of contentment that we had not had for years.'[3]

I hope you've experienced such moments of clarity and calm in the mountains yourself. It's a big part of why we go there; well, it is for me, even if I push myself nowhere near so hard as Chouinard and Herbert.

But what's going on here? What brings about this enhanced state of awareness, of being, even? Doug Robinson has been turning over this question for most of a long and active mountain life. He had a strong hunch back in the 1960s when the sub-cultures of Haight-Ashbury and climbing coalesced in Yosemite. LSD was the catalyst as climbers at Camp 4 enacted Timothy Leary's memorable dictum: 'Turn on, tune in, drop out.'

Robinson soon realized that the chemically induced state of mind he derived from LSD and marijuana was eerily like the one that arose spontaneously out of the intensity of his life on the Valley's granite walls. As he put in a seminal essay, 'The Climber as Visionary', published in 1969 in *Ascent*, climbing and its attendant fear 'produces a chemical climate in the body that is conducive to visionary experience'.

The idea sounded plausible – not dissimilar to the visionary states induced by mystics through fasting or other extreme austerities – but at the time might best have been described as well-founded speculation. With *The Alchemy of Action*, Robinson brings us up to date. Neuroscience has moved on dramatically in recent years and the old 'metabolic voyager' thinks his case is now all but proved. So do I.

Actually Robinson is only just ahead of the curve with *Alchemy*. After suffering under decades of repressive legislation, research into psychedelic drugs is enjoying a productive renaissance. You can hardly open a weekend supplement these days without reading of the wonders of ayahuasca or the potential of LSD to treat obsessive-compulsive disorder or alleviate the

3. 'Muir Wall – El Capitan', Yvon Chouinard, *American Alpine Journal* 1966, pp46-51

anxiety of the dying. Professor David Nutt, the government's former drugs tsar, told *The Independent*[4] that people on a psychedelic trip often experience being at one with the world, or even with the universe. The fear of dying subsides as the sense of self breaks down. They exist beyond their body. That experience can give them a sense of perpetuity, of being permanent, of being part of the cycle of life, which of course we all are.

How can such a sane and humane person have been selected by ministers as their chief policy advisor of drugs? Unsurprisingly, Prof Nutt was sacked in 2009 after saying ecstasy, cannabis and LSD were less dangerous than alcohol and tobacco.

What has all this science got to do with climbing? Well, Robinson sees it as an answer to the 'why?' question. Why climb mountains? Simple! Because it gets us high.

Answering the 'how?' question is more complicated. In fact it becomes so complicated that well into *Alchemy* Robinson suggests that less engaged readers skip the 'dense' chapters on brain chemistry and jump straight to his wrap-up. But I advise you to stick with it. It's your brain after all. And if as you gulp at the sketchy nature of that barely-in-reach hold your life is going to depend upon, it's fascinating to know that your brain is at that moment releasing a mix of chemicals, including a tiny shot of DMT (dimethyltryptamine), one of the most fiercely potent psychedelics known to man. Thus fortified, you will cruise the move. And you will feel great! (Let's hope so anyway.) Another good reason to stick with it through every page of *Alchemy* is that however many authoritative tracts you might read on this subject, nobody will tell it in such a zany, folksy way as Doug Robinson.

Alchemy is a joyous trip, guided by a knowing roshi who blends the insight of Aldous Huxley (much referenced) and the romance of John Muir with the vernacular of The Dude in *The Big Lebowski*. Take the following breakdown of the brain juices that flow when we're out on the edge. (Climbing, ski-mountaineering, running: Robinson loves them all.)

'Start with noradrenaline. Alert, alive. It's what your Starbucks or your Red Bull turns into inside your head...

Now add dopamine, pleasure itself. Mr Feelgood. And of course sultry Ms Feelgood too. The dopamine molecule is a close relative of noradrenaline. They are essentially sisters, trading outfit and maybe flirting with the same boys...

Another relative, serotonin, joins the mix. This cousin is pretty familiar too, and runs with a lot of the same brain enzymes...'

And so it jives on. The three hormones above are well studied and acknowledged. But then Robinson adds two more ingredients to the cocktail... 'the fizzy stuff that goes in with a flourish at the end, just before the wedge of lime and, of course, a tiny umbrella.'

The first is anandamide, the human hormone that mimics marijuana, but stronger. Anandamide is now the researchers' hormone of choice for

4. 'Why I think the terminally ill should take LSD', *The Independent*, 7 March 2015

explaining 'runner's high', superceding beta-endorphin which in retrospect seems to have been way over-hyped as a candidate. Anandamide by itself could easily account for climber's euphoria, indeed for the remarkable enriching of consciousness attending all our edgier games. (Before you slip into your trainers and dash round the block to generate a shot of this stuff, bear in mind that to achieve an anandamide high you'll have to run hard for at least 50 minutes.)

Finally comes DMT, made not in the lab or ingested as ayahuasca, cooked up from the caapi vine and other plants, but generated naturally in the brain. Robinson is running a bit ahead of scientific agreement here, but that's part of the book's excitement. He contends that in the right circumstances – 'heady times where a dash of fear blends into high human function – a drop of this wickedly strong, but entirely organic, substance gets released into the brain, 'adding a jolt of Technicolor to the rewards of playing on the edge'.

So that's the hormone cocktail that Robinson believes hooks us in. There is plenty about LSD and other mind-bending chemicals in *Alchemy*; indeed the book might as well be Paisley-patterned so rich is its portrait of the 1960s – cue walk-on parts for *The Grateful Dead*, Gary Snyder, Joni Mitchell and more, and of course a bigger part for the Haight alchemist himself, Owsley Stanley. When customers complained to Owsley that his acid had dished them a nightmare, his standard reply was: 'Aww, man, you shoulda taken half!'

Robinson, however, is not advocating we trip out on LSD all over again. He's mellowed and gone organic. Far better the naturally occurring psychedelics like DMT cooked up in our brains on steep rock or as skis turn towards the fall line. No more overdose, instead a more subtle, threshold dose.

Climbing is a physical meditation, Robinson believes. If your brain delivers an organic high with freshly altered perceptions, then revel in them. 'What could be better than to be awash in the beauty of life rather than tripping out beyond it?'

Owsley Stanley is history. With this stimulating and original book it is now Doug Robinson who is the alchemist, turning wit, words and dedicated personal research to wisdom. And as he says of the hormonal cocktail served up on the edge: How could you resist?

Stephen Goodwin

• *The Alchemy of Action can be bought via the website movingoverstone.com*

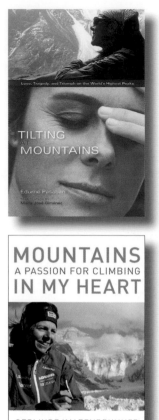

Tilting at Mountains
Edurne Pasaban
Mountaineers Books, 2014, pp218, £14.95

Mountains in my Heart
Gerlinde Kaltenbrunner
Mountaineers Books, 2014, pp304, £14.25

These two books relive the journeys of the only women in the world, so far, to have undisputedly climbed all fourteen 8000-metre summits. Clearly, with such a unified goal, the books share many similar experiences, but Pasaban and Kaltenbrunner have sufficiently different life stories to tell that the books complement rather than compete with each other.

Neither woman claims to have had all fourteen peaks as an initial goal. By 2007, however, when Pasaban had successfully climbed nine and Kaltenbrunner ten summits, the possibility of achieving a 'full house' became an incentive but never, each claims, a competition between them. The alleged rivalry was left for the media to enjoy. The two women were, and remain, firm friends; they stood on the summits of Broad Peak and Dhaulagiri together in 2007 and 2008.

Both books, although translated, are easy and engaging reads and follow a chronological order from the first to the last 8000-metre peak. *Tilting at Mountains* would have benefited from a timeline of Pasaban's expeditions and a few photographs would have lightened the text, but these are minor criticisms. The book charts how, as a misfit at school, discovering her ability as a rock climber and, in particular, as a mountaineer unlocked a new identity for Pasaban. It provided 'a sort of escape, a lifeline, a way of living that was in line with my way of being in the world.'

For Pasaban, arguably more than for Kaltenbrunner, determining who she was, particularly after a suicide attempt in 2006, was critical to her unprecedented success as a mountaineer. In a curious paradox, high-altitude climbing both questioned and created her identity. For someone who became the first woman to climb all fourteen 8000-metre summits – with the dedication, pain, concentration, suffering and composure that entails – it is enlightening to observe how fragile that same person's self-confidence could be.

Such self-doubt emanated, to some extent, from an overprotective family, but undoubtedly was also a symptom of being a successful woman in the predominantly male world of Himalayan climbing. Pasaban wrestled in 2006 with whether she should give up mountaineering and become a 'normal' woman with husband, home and children – an issue many women, in different walks of life, often experience but, unlike Pasaban, often do not discuss so frankly. As she perceptively notes, 'the awareness of who you are isn't always easy to elucidate.' Kaltenbrunner was more assured of her place in the world and promptly ditched a boyfriend who clearly expected her to stop climbing once they married.

Kaltenbrunner, however, had the luxury of being 'protected by my family so I can be myself.' As a result she had fewer personal demons to vanquish than Pasaban. She also had more natural self-confidence and the advantage of meeting her future husband, the mountaineer Ralf Dujmovits, in 2003, who provided Kaltenbrunner with stability and constant support during much of her climbing career. Unlike accounts of most male climbers, personal relationships form an important part of both women's narratives, which, rather than being a distraction, provides a more holistic vision of how the mountains fit into their lives.

Because of their inevitable feminine perspective both books have an important message to convey, not only about women mountaineers but also by highlighting the oppressed position of women in Pakistan compared to those in Nepal, and of course to those in western societies. Both climbers encountered gender prejudice or worse. While Kaltenbrunner relates faintly amusing tales of Kazakh men having difficulty confronting her greater strength and all-round ability, (to say nothing of them being unwittingly subjected to expeditious use of tampons – a great story!), Pasaban recounts a more serious attempted rape. These two women's outstanding mountaineering achievements, often enacted in a society hostile to female freedom, makes the contrast to the lives of the indigenous women all the greater.

From 2003 Kaltenbrunner elected to climb in alpine style whenever possible rather than in a larger expedition group. This reflected growing self-confidence in her mountaineering ability and overall fitness. The developing relationship with Dujmovits also encouraged such an approach. Her extraordinary mental and physical condition meant Kaltenbrunner was often found continuing a climb when others, including her husband, chose to retreat. Something of the loner and the individualist emanates from her accounts. She frequently reached summits alone but this proved a source of enjoyment rather than one of fear or concern.

For both women, of course, an accurate knowledge of how far they could push themselves, both mentally and physically, was crucial. Luck and weather conditions, inevitably, also played major roles in determining the success or failure of a climb. As for most Himalayan mountaineers, there were many aborted attempts before all fourteen summits succumbed and each woman had one mountain that constantly defied them; for Pasaban it was Shisha Pangma and for Kaltenbrunner, K2. Although Pasaban may have been more cautious in her approach, she climbed all fourteen summits in just nine years while Kaltenbrunner took thirteen.

Both women's accounts, unsurprisingly, are characterised by physical and mental strength. Kaltenbrunner became the first woman to climb all 8000-metre summits without oxygen or high-altitude porters, something only fifteen people have achieved to date. Pasaban's recovery from the depths of depression to deal with the psychological rigours of Himalayan mountaineering is staggering. When she attempted K2 in 2004 there were no women still alive who had climbed it. Her mental resolve and recovery is an example for all who ponder the apparently insurmountable – mountains or otherwise. Kaltenbrunner's relationship with the mountains is informed and strengthened, to some degree, by a religious faith that she embraced at an early age. This merges into a mysticism embracing nature, mother earth and creativity that forms a crucial part of her connection with the mountains.

For such unprecedented success in the mountains both women paid a hefty price. Numerous climbing friends and colleagues died, often literally in front of their eyes; the women themselves frequently came close to experiencing similar fates. As Pasaban writes, mountaineering was 'a passion bordering on irrationality.'

These two books provide unique windows onto a world that is commonly satiated by visions of heroic masculinity. In demonstrating varying amounts of weakness, vulnerability and doubt counterpoised with iron determination, focus and athletic ability, the books are a welcome relief from such a commonly held trope. They provide, in their differing ways, what for some might present a new dimension to femininity. While Pasaban and Kaltenbrunner's Himalayan climbs cannot be anything other than inspiring, the overwhelming impression is that the mountains enabled a true sense of freedom, purpose and identity to occur to two different women from dissimilar backgrounds. Like women alpinists in the nineteenth century, who expressed similar feelings of liberty, I would suggest that women – in a world where their role in life is still much debated – experience such sensations in the mountains more profoundly than men. As Kaltenbrunner writes:

Up here, I am free; I can leave all responsibilities behind. I don't have to please anyone else... I can be at one with myself... I feel content, even-keeled and filled with joy... In the mountains, I feel very differently than I do down in the valley.

Clare Roche

• *Neither of these books has a UK edition but both are available from amazon. co.uk.*

Nanga Parbat 1970
Richard Sale and Jochen Hemmleb
Carreg Limited, 2014, pp 206, £25

Few mountains have generated such triumph and tragedy as Nanga Parbat. Its history resonates in Germany as effectively as Everest resounds in Britain. The first ascent of the vast Rupal Face by the brothers Rein-

hold and Günther Messner in 1970 and their traversing descent by the Diamir flank, so thoroughly explored in this account, echoes the drama and unanswered questions that Mallory and Irvine left for Everest historians. But the similarities soon end. The Messners certainly reached the summit but during the descent Günther died in an avalanche and Reinhold was severely injured, narrowly escaping with his life.

The controversy that erupted through a series of misunderstandings, accusations and legal battles has no equivalent on Everest but this close examination of the tragedy and disputes following the 1970 expedition draws together the background and the repercussions that still reverberate. Messner has added to the literary history of Nanga Parbat with his own accounts of the expedition translated into English, but around ten books about the mountain and its turbulent history have not been translated from the German.

The account recalls earlier history when Nanga Parbat was strewn with tragedy. In 1934 three German climbers and six Sherpas died and three years later seven more Germans and nine Sherpas were lost in an avalanche. One victim was Willy Merkl, half-brother of Karl Herrligkoffer, who organised the 1970 expedition, insisting that significant points on the Rupal face were named after climbers who had died on the mountain. The 1970 expedition comprised German, Austrian and Italian mountaineers with Messner, chosen for his alpine record, the acknowledged star of the show with younger brother Günther a late addition to the team. For Herrligkoffer, who directed progress from base camp, it was his third expedition to the mountain since 1953 when Hermann Buhl reached the summit in a daring solo attempt, establishing himself as a hero in Messner's eyes. Seventeen years later Messner himself was poised in a high camp on the Rupal face awaiting a rocket signal from below that would indicate the latest weather forecast: blue for fair weather, allowing more time to secure the difficult final section, and red for approaching bad weather that could give Messner the chance for a swift solo bid. The forecast was fine but a red rocket was wrongly fired; Messner set off to be joined, much to his surprise, by his brother.

The two pressed on to the top and then returned after bivouacing above a steep section of the Rupal face where Felix Kuen and Peter Scholz were making their own attempt on the summit. When Messner was within shouting distance but separated by a wall of vertical rock, an exchange between Messner and Kuen left Kuen with an impression that all was well and Messner believing that help was on the way. Günther at this stage was suffering, possibly from altitude sickness, and the brothers urgently needed a rope to safeguard a descent 'where one wrong step and it would be all over'. When no help came the Messners opted to descend by the Diamir face, which promised to be a less steep alternative. Again the brothers had to bivouac on the face. Günther died in an avalanche after Reinhold went ahead to find the best route. He was rescued by locals, severely frostbitten.

The accusations and writs soon began to fly: had the Messner brothers deliberately intended to make a traverse of the mountain, had Reinhold deliberately sacrificed his brother to achieve an historic first and who said what to whom in the shouted conversation between Reinhold and Felix Kuen? Other questions emerged: why, for example, was there no immediate effort to send a search party to the Diamir side of the mountain? The tangle of accusations and conflicting stories kept the lawyers busy and the battle lasted for years with Herrligkoffer among the most vociferous accusers. Messner's return to Nanga Parbat in search of his brother's body yielded a human fibula, which proved on DNA analysis to be most probably belonging to Günther Messner, and so the saga once more reignited.

Nanga Parbat 1970 is a thorough analysis of all the evidence in a wealth of books, statements and film about a controversial expedition surrounding someone acknowledged to be a giant among mountaineers. Messner has always fought back, sensitive to criticism. But the authors declare: 'At first it is understandable that a young man feels a victim when losing a brother with whom he had just shared the greatest triumph, under traumatic and life-threatening circumstances – and subsequently becomes the subject of accusations from a doubtful expedition leader as well as of criticism from colleagues and the media. Survivor's guilt is also a known phenomenon. Four decades after the events, however, and with Reinhold Messner able to look back on a life of ideational and material success, and enjoying a widespread fan base among both the public and the media, the victim role appears to be an artificially maintained construct and is no longer as convincing.' In the end, they conclude, the truly tragic figure is Messner himself.

Ronald Faux

Messner: My life at the limit
Interviews with Thomas Hüetlin
Translated by Tim Carruthers
Mountaineers Books, 2014, pp256, £13.34

This is the essential Messner, his life at the limit as the world's most renowned mountaineer. Being a series of well judged questions put to him by Thomas Hüetlin, *Der Spiegel* journalist and specialist interviewer of sporting personalities, the conversations brook no interruption yet reveal much about Messner's attitudes and the controversies that have dogged his life. The book extends previous interviews between the two and brings the Messner story up to date.

Why he has become so unassailably famous is worth a brief reminder: from rebellious boyhood Messner quickly became a bold and pioneering

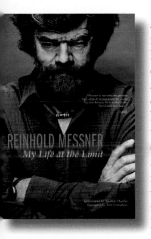

alpinist, climbing the Eigerwand in record time and moving to the Himalaya where the traverse of Nanga Parbat with his brother in 1970 ended in Günther's death and a lifetime of controversy. Messner's first ascent of Everest with Peter Habeler without bottled oxygen in 1978 was followed by solo ascents of Nanga Parbat and Everest. He was first to climb all the world's 8000m peaks and the highest summits on each of the world's seven continents. He brought alpine-style techniques to the highest mountains, reaching three 8000m summits in one season. His trek record includes 2800km across Antarctica via the South Pole, 2200km across Greenland, across Bhutan from east to west and solo across the Gobi desert. His attempt to traverse the North Pole failed when the ice he was on began to sink; he and his brother Hubert were rescued by Russian helicopter. His search for the elusive Yeti concluded by agreeing with the Dalai Lama that the creature was probably a Himalayan brown bear. As he assured Messner: 'We have got Yetis in the zoo in Lhasa.'

The 1970 expedition to Nanga Parbat was the first and most damaging clash with the mountaineering establishment and subject of a book reviewed elsewhere in this year's *Journal*. Because a wrong signal launched Messner on a solo attempt from high on the Rupal face, he was 'irritated' when his brother caught up with him. Together they reached the summit but they had no rope and without one Günther, already suffering from the altitude, refused to return down the Rupal face. Messner was asked whether he blamed himself for Günther's death: There is no one else to take the blame, only me. I bear full responsibility. That's why I don't understand why a few of the expedition members still keep trying to twist the story.'

After DNA analysis established that the bone found on Nanga Parbat originated from Günther, Reinhold was asked whether any of his former expedition members, who had accused him of sacrificing his brother to his own personal ambition, had apologised. 'No,' replies Messner. In the case of one stern critic whose wife moved in with Messner on a long-term relationship, this may have been easier to understand.

Hüetlin pulls no punches, suggesting that on Manaslu, his next eight-thousander, it all went wrong again. Why? 'It really did all go wrong again,' Messner acknowledges and vowed that from then on he would do it all on his own. 'Every time I went away with other people, something went wrong', he says. Messner reached the summit alone in terrible weather. Two other members of the expedition were lost. Once more the 'Herrligkoffer brigade' began recriminations, accusing Messner of being irresponsible, and in vigorously defending himself Messner created even more problems. A disagreement between Habeler and Messner following Habeler's account of their Everest climb was provoked by a ghost writer's version the publisher refused to correct, but the two are now friends once more.

In 1986 with all challenges completed and running out of high mountains to climb, and much to his publisher's regret after some best-selling books, Messner turned to exploring the world's wilderness areas. Antarctica demanded a different level of stoicism and Messner's sled-sail via the South Pole was with Arved Fuchs, the German explorer. Once again the expedition produced two contrasting versions of the outcome with Fuchs insisting he was the strong member of the partnership and had pulled Messner along; Messner pointed out that he was usually ahead, covering in six hours what took Fuchs seven and a half. Fuchs, according to Messner, had wanted to stop at the South Pole but was coaxed on by Messner to reach their destination 'in a strong silence and a partnership that had served its purpose.'

With his family settled in Juval castle above Naturno in the South Tyrol from whose walls Messner spectacularly fell, severely injuring a heel, he turned to politics and in 1999 won a seat on the Green list in the European parliament. For five years he served on the networks of the commission, the council and the parliament. His particular interest was the well-being of the hill farmers and village communities in the South Tyrol that desperately needed help. As for the European parliament, he had little time for the 'pompous blowhards who pretended to represent the interests of their voters, the lobbyists, or even Europe but are really just opportunists, trading political offices for favours and the mad, egotistical scramble for list places for the next elections – I loathed all that.'

With such thunder echoing around his reputation, Messner now approaches his seventies, establishing a legacy of six museums, the Messner Mountain Museums, reflecting many aspects of mountaineering and the mountain environment, all superbly located in the South Tyrol. He reflects on a very changed mountaineering world with some climbers achieving sensational performances but with regimented crowds queuing to climb Everest and treated by guides who behaved like kindergarten teachers.

Did he ever feel gratitude? 'Of course. I've had a fantastic time. The generation of climbers before me got to go on one or two expeditions in their whole life. We could do virtually anything we wanted to do. It was a crazy time. And I was lucky to survive it; lucky that I didn't make that one big mistake; lucky that, from 1972 onward, I was able to follow my dreams.'

This is a grand and thoughtful inquisition of mountaineering's most internationally famous personality.

Ronald Faux

• *Messner: My life at the limit is available through amazon.co.uk.*

Letters from Chamonix: stories and a novella
David Stevenson
Imaginary Mountain Surveyors, 2014, pp232, US$30/$4 e-book

The Mantis
Philip Temple
Vertebrate Digital, 2014, e-book only, £4.99

'The mountaineer has learnt a language which is but partly revealed to ordinary men.' This sentiment, expressed in the title story of David Stevenson's award-winning collection of seven short stories and a novella 'Letters From Chamonix' serves to explain a transformation in vision, a shift in focus from the everyday to the sublime or the unexpected, which can occur when climbers are severed from their tenuous links with familiar routines and wholly committed to the testing environments in which they choose to immerse themselves. Indeed, it is these moments of transcendence which illuminate the stories in this collection and bring a generous measure of understanding to what is, for non-climbers, often an incomprehensible pursuit.

'At The Eigergletscher' has gothic resonances; Broyles meets the mysterious Enga and they drift into an agreement to climb the north face of the Eiger. Her 'fangs', the bloody-tasting soup they consume and the faintly menacing castle-like hotel they stay in all subvert the traditional idea of preparations for a climbing trip. After a large meal, Broyles falls into a feverish, hallucinatory stupor from which he is awakened by a giant of a man who leads him unroped and at breakneck speed almost as far as Death Bivouac and then disappears. Broyles completes the route, never feeling in control, beset by terrors and, after awakening in his hotel room in the care of a doctor, is assured that his perception of events is false. This genre manipulation strays into magical realism and the unaccustomed insights and excessively heightened state this affords takes the reader into the realms of intense and often inexplicable transformational emotional experiences typical of those felt high in the mountains.

In 'After The Expedición' Richards is a disillusioned mountain guide – tired of inexperienced clients' unreasonable demands and expectations, worn out with the loss of friends, stripped of the joy and optimism he once had in climbing the mountains whose ascents have become routine, whose secrets have become too widely known. The truth of a porter's words ring hollowly: 'You go from peak to peak, from nothing to nothing to nothing.'

Richards' response is to strip himself, literally and metaphorically, of everything he possesses, leaving himself with no way back into the life he once knew. Only then and not in the euphoria he once felt in the high mountains does he really have the freedom to make the final choice as he shelters under a rock 'hoping dimly for one last night's sleep'. Those who climb would like to think of themselves as free, but the irony is that they are governed by an obsession so entrenched that it enslaves, leaving only the willingness to do its bidding.

The story 'The Orbit Of Celestial Bodies' is prefaced by a short extract from Wordsworth's 'Intimations of Immortality', in which he asserts that, pre-birth, we dwell in a purer realm, which children are able to remember and which suffuses their lives with magic until it withers with increasing age. Allan's extraordinary climbing ability – 'Allan acknowledged that he was well rehearsed for this, as if he had done it before, in a dream, perhaps?' – seems to emanate from such a source. It provides Ted, a climbing guide hired by Allan's father, with the opportunity to complete a route on the unclimbed Eleusinian Wall, a project first conceived of by Hans, his long-dead Austrian climbing partner and with which he is consumed.

Again, it is Stevenson's choice of form rather than descriptive detail, which best clarifies his purpose. He works with Ted's inexplicable, sudden and total disappearance from the climb – 'a sort of seam in the air that opened for a split second and inhaled him' – to explain those experiences which are beyond the reach of all but the few who inhabit the extremes.

Allan completes the climb after two days in 'a state of trance-like mystification, feeling privy to some large and unintelligible secret' knowing finally that it should have been he who disappeared, not Ted, but knowing also that his ability to climb like 'water in human form, flowing uphill' had deserted him and, far from regretting this loss, he knew with quiet certainty that he could at last return to himself.

In *Letters From Chamonix* it seems that Stevenson offers a seismic refocusing of vision, a series of sharply delineated encounters in which protagonists and readers are able to clarify their responses to extreme environments and situations, to motives and outcomes. His writing leaves space for readers to pursue their own lines of enquiry, his characters carry the emotional freight of each story but are never overwhelmed by it – and the need to read on is compelling.

The Mantis by Philip Temple is a fictional account of a first attempt on Puthemojar in the Karakoram – the mountain which eats its prey. The assertion in the blurb that the book is based on a 1980 publication, 'The Last Great Challenge', is a conceit – one which no doubt fulfils its purpose in intriguing readers in what is an overcrowded e-publishing market. However, it is redundant, as *The Mantis* stands firmly on its own two literary feet without need of extraneous support.

Temple sets himself the task of answering a number of questions about the pursuit of climbing – most notably on the spectrum of motivation. The dichotomy between teamwork and ambition is tackled particularly well, offering a consideration of how competitiveness and co-operation co-exist, albeit uneasily, on a climbing expedition.

Where *The Mantis* excels is in its detailed examination of group dynamics in the high mountains. Temple has created his characters with conflicting ambitions, which must be both harnessed and contained. The raw talent of the two newcomers, Chase and Wyllie, 'drunk with anticipation' and eager to make their mark, is balanced against the dogged, brilliant and unflinching Dodge and Strickland, the team's nominal leader, who must set his accomplished dealings with the media against his increasing awareness that his contact with high mountains had become a 'partial life he had constructed and conspired to propagate.'

One of the weaknesses of the book is that the narrative is not always consistent in the quality of its descriptions and comparisons; it veers from the evocative to the awkwardly expressed, too purple in tone, too unwieldy to convince: 'Strickland was forced to make the agonising reappraisal that is to the mind as the menopause is to the womb.'

Further, whilst precise detail is helpful in envisioning the technical details of a climb, there are occasions when these sections are simply too long and claw away the tension created by the ever present high-altitude risk. However, the squalor, colourful camaraderie and physical and mental strains of life in tents and snow holes are brilliantly captured, especially by means of the internal dialogues in which the climbers engage. These revealing interludes offer the reader a fascinating perspective into the dynamics of confinement and deprivation – slights acknowledged and resented, motivations re-examined, loyalties reconsidered and adjusted.

The book returns firmly to form in its closing chapters with Dodge's accident and subsequent abandonment, Chase's decision to go back and wait with him for the rescue which will never come and Strickland's decision to walk out of base camp, utterly spent and alone after his traumatic descent from the mountain – still determined to prove himself, still wanting to preserve the charade of the successful mountaineer. These episodes are handled with a careful balance of compassion and emotional exposure, giving them a pathos, which has its roots in old-fashioned morality on the one hand and, on the other, a deep-rooted instinct for survival in a cause that has long been lost. By forcing readers to make stark decisions about what they might have done in the same situations, Temple plunges us headfirst into an examination of our own moral codes and how they might have been found wanting.

Val Randall

• *Letters from Chamonix, which won the Banff Mountain Book Festival's Fiction Award, is available in print and e-book from www.imaginarymountains.com The Mantis is available for download from Amazon and Vertebrate Publishing.*

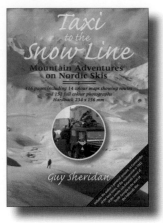

Taxi to the Snow Line
Guy Sheridan
White Peak Publishing, 2006, pp351, £20

Few, if any, contemporary British mountaineers can claim to have had a mountain named after them but Sheridan Peak in South Georgia recognises the author's achievement in commanding the small detachment of Marines and SAS that successfully recaptured South Georgia at the start of the Falklands War in 1982. Guy's harrowing account of his attempt to climb this elusive peak 16 years later with David Nicholls in an Antarctic blizzard is one of the many thrilling adventures described in this second volume of his life and times as a Nordic ski-mountaineer.

Sheridan is yet another Alpine Club member who has served with distinction in the Royal Marines, in his case for 31 years. Specialising in mountain and Arctic warfare, a natural progression through alpine and Himalayan mountaineering led him to the biathlon, that most demanding and exacting of winter sports which combines Nordic skiing and rifle shooting. After competing in the 1971 world championships, illness denied him a place in the 1972 Winter Olympic team. Eighteen winter seasons in Arctic Norway, his particular love, and various postings to Sarawak, Aden, Oman, the Balkans and East Africa gave Guy ample opportunity to mix his military duties with climbing and skiing. However, it was a chance meeting in 1974 with the Norwegian Everester Odd Eliassen that fired his passion for long distance, lightweight, self-sufficient Nordic ski expeditions to remote, untrammelled and, sometimes, hostile parts of the world.

While Guy's earlier book, *Tales of a Cross Country Skier,* describes prodigiously long traverses he and his companions made through Iran's Zagros Range, the Western Himalaya, the Yukon and Sierra Nevada, the present volume gives fuller accounts of those he did between 1989 and 2006 in the Drakensburg, Lapland, Iceland, Albania, California, Canadian Rockies and Zanskar. The final chapters recount sorties in his sixties to Kyrgyzstan, New Zealand and Iran. It is very well illustrated with many colour photographs and maps.

Such a remarkable catalogue of Nordic expeditions takes exceptional courage, stamina, resilience and technical competence and one can only envy Guy and his artist wife Mollie's inspired decision to have made their retirement home in the Pyrenees whose mountains he must know better than any other British mountaineer. These tales, by Britain's most outstanding Nordic ski mountaineer, read like some Norse saga and are told with humility, humour and self-deprecating modesty.

J G R Harding

• *Taxi to the Snow Line is available from the South Georgia Heritage Trust website.*

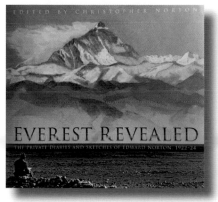

Everest Revealed
The private diaries and sketches of
Edward Norton, 1922-24
Edited by Christopher Norton
The History Press, 2014, pp158, £20

It must be a curious sensation to watch as your parent or grandparent is absorbed into myth, a process familiar either to the progeny of celebrities or, in the case of Edward Felix Norton, a collaborator in a famous enterprise – in his case, climbing Everest. Yet Norton's presence in the story is somewhat hazy. While the world apparently cannot have its fill of the enigmatic, romantic George Mallory or the youthful optimism of Andrew Irvine, or indeed the self-sacrifice and overall decency of Howard Somervell, Norton's name is less familiar. And yet he it was who set an altitude record of 28,128ft on 4 June, 1924, a record that would not be broken until the Swiss climbed high on the mountain in 1952.

Why the relative obscurity? One answer lies in the historian's selective gaze. Walt Unsworth, in his highly regarded account, introduces him thus: 'The sixth member of the climbing team was Major E F Norton, thirty-eight years old and a grandson of Sir Alfred Wills, the man whose ascent of the Wetterhorn in 1854 had begun the Golden Age of Alpine climbing. He was also distantly related to Mallory, but his experience of climbing appears to have been slight and the best that Younghusband could find to say of him in his Introduction to the 1922 expedition volume was that he was well known in India for his skill and interest in pig-sticking!'

You can see why many writers have fallen into the trap of gazing upon John Noel's brilliant portrait of Norton, in which he appears debonair, intelligent and reserved, with the tip of his right ear gone to frostbite adding a mark of glamorous experience, and think: conventional army officer of the Empire doing his duty. And yet here is the man who, for all his inexperience of hard climbing, despite our assumptions about his background, goes highest and comes back, and acts with compassion and sensitivity towards the survivors of this most famous climbing tragedy.

So this compendium of Norton's diaries, letters and watercolours is doubly welcome. First, it gives those of us with a passion for Everest history undiluted access to the thoughts and behaviour of one of the key men from those mesmerising early years. It also gives his grandson, who brought the material together so effectively, and his sons, who wrote the introduction, the chance to present their own ancestor in a congenial light.

Norton is not the greatest artist who ever lived, not even the best artist at Everest in 1924 given Somervell's presence, but his sketches and paintings not only have flair, not only exhibit a good eye, they have considerable wit as well. In fact, this is one of the great revelations of this delightful book: Norton was a good laugh. On reaching Langram bungalow in the second trekking party he writes: 'Geoff [Bruce] left us a half bottle of whisky – which turned out to be tea: we failed to connect this with April 1.' And then, later in April, after a wonderful morning indulging his great passion for bird-watching: 'Spent pm writing *Times* article – fearful tripe – I only hope the British public will like it.'

This sense of fun, something often missing from weighty accounts of imperial adventuring, is on show in a beautifully reproduced photograph of Norton, hand on hip, meeting the Dzongpen of Shekar a few days after his entry about meeting the British public's great appetite for tripe. Mallory stands alongside, his soft hat brought to a ludicrous point, the brim lifted slightly, to give himself the air of a simpleton. This is the quicksilver of the climbing life that falls into the cracks of history.

Japes aside, and with the leadership of the 1924 expedition in his hands following Bruce's withdrawal, it was left to Norton to offer consolation to those relatives waiting for news of how their loved ones met their end. His letter from base camp to Ruth Mallory is powerfully affecting and deeply compassionate:

'And then – on the mountain – I wish I could describe to you what he was like. Physically he was a wonder – the best of us without the least doubt from start to finish – but this hardly mattered for his great heart carried him on entirely independent of physical considerations. I really believe the struggle between him and the mountain had become a personal matter to him. He simply would not accept defeat and yet (from 1000 talks on the matter) I know how his determination was tempered with discretion; he fully realised his responsibility as leader of the climbing party – he and I saw eye to eye over the question of the absolute necessity of avoiding a single casualty even to conquer the mountain... He was a great mountaineer.'

It's the opinion of some that Mallory pushed on recklessly to reach the summit of Everest and took Irvine with him to his doom. You could argue that Norton is offering Ruth Mallory comfort in her darkest hours, and that he exaggerated Mallory's sense of caution; that he himself felt a level of responsibility for what had happened as the leader. The latter might be true, and I suppose the former might be too, but I think Norton believed what he said. 'I wish I could help you in your great grief,' he writes, repeating the sentiment at the end of the letter.

This beautifully produced and quietly moving book will do a great deal to advance our knowledge of Edward Norton beyond our expectations of his class and profession.

Ed Douglas

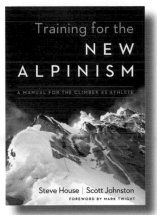

Training for the New Alpinism
A manual for the climber as athlete
Steve House and Scott Johnston
Patagonia, 2014, pp448, £24.95

A decade ago I bumped into Steve House at a presentation weekend for the *Piolet d'Or* mountaineering awards. I was nursing a hangover and making a beeline for the breakfast buffet while Steve was heading out for a two-hour run. The encounter reminded me how decathlete Daley Thompson made sure he did an extra-hard training session on Christmas Day because he knew his rivals would be taking things easy.

The reality of my own position compared to Steve's was even more obvious. I was a fully paid-up member of the traditional no-training culture, believing you should just climb as much as possible. The shortcomings of that ethos were patently obvious; Steve's dedicated preparation was one of the key reasons he was climbing several notches better than anyone in Britain at the time. That truth was underlined when Steve and fellow American Vince Anderson scooped the top prize that weekend for their extraordinary alpine-style new route on the Rupal Face of Nanga Parbat.

Nowadays the stigma of training for alpinism is lifting; the achievements of Ueli Steck are a shining example of what is possible if you systematically apply yourself. As a result Steve House and skiing and climbing coach Scott Johnston's new book have seized on the zeitgeist.

Training for the New Alpinism is an immediately impressive book. It is huge and lavishly illustrated with stunning shots of alpine training and practice from many of the current top players. The shots by Slovenian Marko Prezelj in particular get the pulse racing and clearly demonstrate the purpose of all the hard work listed in the book.

The first section of the book might seem a little daunting to the uninitiated, spending almost 150 pages detailing 'the methodology and physiology of endurance training'. The authors make no excuses for this. Steve has always had a reputation for taking his climbing seriously, and the book's recommendations are grounded in practice but also tested by sports science. Steve was well known in the past for the motto 'talk minus action equals zero;' this book is the embodiment of that ethos.

The science is nicely interspersed with stories illustrating practical lessons in the mountains written by a whole host of international stars from Voytek Kurtyka to Ines Papert and Ueli Steck to Peter Habeler. These words of wisdom aren't all from the sources you'd expect either; the book draws on the knowledge of endurance trail runners and rock climbers like Tony Yaniro. It was a nice surprise to see a valuable exposition of Soviet alpine training by Alexander Odintsov. The book often draws – bravely –

on Steve's own failures and mistakes, and is unafraid to debunk training myths where necessary, such as Mark Twight admitting the mistake of his exclusive obsession with fashionably short high-intensity training.

Chapters follow on such arcane subjects as periodisation, tapering, nutrition, altitude and mental fitness among several others. Steve and Scott cover every conceivable aspect of training for the mountains; there's even a section that would have hit a nerve with me a decade ago called 'Training by Climbing', explaining how this approach can be made effective by sound structure.

This manual will obviously appeal to top-end committed alpine climbers, but there is a lot here for mountaineers with more modest ambitions. The – comparatively slim – 60 or so pages of practical workouts are the best I've seen specifically for alpinists.

So far, the book is unique, offering the level of information and guidance taken for granted in more mainstream sports but until now unavailable to alpinists. It reminded me of Tim Noakes' legendary book *Lore of Running*, which is accepted as the bible of athletics. *Training for the New Alpinism* is a book of similar stature and is essential reading for anyone serious about preparing properly for the mountains.

Ian Parnell

Chamonix Mont-Blanc in 3D
A journey through the stereoscope from the 1850s to today
Peter Blair
Éditions Belvédère, 2014, pp128, €29 plus postage

I first came across 3D photography as an architecture student. It was 1972 and I had been offered an internship. (We didn't call it that then, we called it 'working for very little money while learning the job.') As the internship was to be in Japan, I couldn't bring the models I had made of my projects. Instead I made 3D slides of them from various angles, built a slide viewer, and thereby had a mobile portfolio of my work. I have been making 3D images ever since.

My method is based on taking stereo pairs with a single camera. I soon found that the best stereo modelling was done with a six-degree angle between the camera lines, which is also the angle between the eyes when looking at an object in your hands. I also found that dentists had been using the technique with x-ray images, by hanging up the plates and crossing their eyes to generate 3D images. The middle image, the overlapping one, was in stereo. It is all good harmless fun.

What I did not know was that stereo imagery is as old as photography itself. So I was delighted to be asked to review this book which under one set of covers combines images from the giants of Alpine photography – by Tairraz, Savioz, Couttet, Bisson, Braun and England – with some of my favourite subjects: a history of technology, 3D photography and the Chamonix valley.

This is a coffee table book, pleasant to hold and nicely printed. It also comes with a cunning little pop-up viewer. On each pair of pages is a paragraph or two of text and several stereo images.

Hold the viewer before you and suddenly, as if through a window in time, it comes to life.

We see the mountains and mountaineers of the Belle Époque. We see the nineteenth century Bossons Glacier bulging into the valley, the Argentière Glacier reaching almost down to the church and its cemetery, the Bois Glacier, now known as the Mer de Glace, overflowing moraines that are now cliffs of rubble more than a hundred metres high. Climbers scramble across fragile cornices, the void beneath their boots so much more abysmal in stereo. And among the peasants we witness the now archaic transhumance, the cows and sheep of pre-industrial Chamonix. With these views it is easy to add the sounds and smells of the age.

In an image from the next century, in 1924 in fact, there is an astounding shot of a ski jumper, flying through the air and captured in 3D forever. The final stereogram is of the author, also on skis, enjoying Grandes Montets in powder. It is all very good.

The texts accompanying the photographs are often not related but always fun to read. Some are quotes from Victorian visitors. Ruskin, Byron, Turner all make an appearance; there are also descriptions of everyday life, for instance how the Bossons Glacier was mined for ice to be transported as far afield as Geneva. There is also an explanation of the changing technology of photography during the period. There is a serendipitous quality to the texts; they are nuggets of pleasure. Chamonix in 3D is recommended

Victor Saunders

• *The English edition of Chamonix in 3D is currently available only from Peter Blair (peter3dblair@gmail.com).*

Higher Ground
A mountain guide's life
Martin Moran
Sandstone Press, 2014, pp278, £14.99

Martin Moran's qualification as an accountant in 1980 seems an improbable start to a successful career as an international mountain guide. But his passion for the mountains overtook his talent for figures and he sped through the guides' training scheme, qualifying in 1985. In addition to his work as a guide, he and Simon Jenkins completed one of the few non-stop

traverses of the Alpine 4000m peaks in 1993, using only foot and pedal power to get from the Bernina to the Dauphiné in just 52 days, including a 33-hour circumnavigation of the Mer de Glace skyline. It was testament to the scale of this achievement that a number of local guides questioned whether they had actually done it.

Guiding as a profession has sometimes had a mixed reputation. In the nineteenth and early twentieth centuries, it was largely regarded as a partnership of equals, one partner with local knowledge, the other with similar technical prowess but even greater ambition. In the latter part of the twentieth century, it became tainted with the notion of 'cheating', perhaps due to the number of clients pulled up peaks like Mont Blanc and the Matterhorn. While this remains true of the honeypot routes, British guiding came of age during the period covered in Martin's book. In a time-pressured world, it is also seen as a convenient way for competent mountaineers to achieve their objectives quickly, often when climbing partners are difficult to organise.

Moran's guiding career is different from the norm in two major respects. The first is that he used guiding to explore new places and paths less trodden; the other is the fact that Martin ran a guiding business, employing other guides to do some of the work, unlike the vast majority who are sole traders.

Anecdotes about the vast array of clients Martin has worked with form the backbone of the book. Any reader familiar with the places described will thrive on the local references: the Cuillin Ridge, the winter routes in Torridon or some of the Alpine peaks. He has picked out plenty of 'characters', some of them setting him personal rather than technical challenges. Martin is at all times honest about these encounters, the joys and frustrations they caused, but also his own shortcomings when his patience was tried.

But it is the sense of exploration and freshness that captures the difference in approach from average. Two areas in particular realise Martin's dream to explore new places with clients: Norway and northern India. Both have provided workplaces that would be beyond the comfort zone of the average guide from the Alps. And it is the descriptions of these expeditions that show off a fascinating career in its best light and take the reader to places of which they too can dream.

For the non-mountaineer, the book is an interesting travelogue with anecdotes of human relations. For the mountaineer, it is a compelling and fascinating account of a familiar world seen in a new light.

Chris Dodd

Ski Touring: a practical manual
Bruce Goodlad
Pesda Press, 2015, pp280, £16.99

Ski touring, ski mountaineering, call it what you will, mountain travel on skis is a craft, and like all crafts it takes time and attention to learn. Some might elevate it from a craft to an art; inscribing perfect turns from a tight gully out to a fan of glorious powder. But this is a short review – no time to get into semantics.

Time was when learning a craft – joinery, machinist, newspaper reporter and the like – meant serving a 'proper' apprenticeship, three and a half years in the latter case, as I remember well. The apprenticeships trumpeted by ministers today seem little more than a spell of work experience. In ski-touring terms this would be like following a guide either for a day off-piste or a few days' hut-to-hutting in the Silvretta. It's a useful taster but craftsmanship remains far distant.

The model of the old apprenticeship is a good one for ski touring. Traditionally it would have comprised three or more years of on the job training, working alongside a time-served craftsman that's your couple of weeks in the Alps each spring, in the company either of experienced amateur tourers or a guide (as Bruce Goodlad is an IFMGA guide I feel obliged to include this route, though guided skiers can get lazy about learning). An additional requirement for any apprenticeship would have been 'block release' at the local 'tech'; the ski equivalent is an avalanche awareness or crevasse rescue course. Finally there would the manual: a hefty tome backing up your course work or skills you'd half-learned on the job with much needed explanation and refinement.

Bruce Goodlad's *Ski Touring* is that hefty tome. Subtitled *A Practical Manual: essential knowledge for off-piste, backcountry ski tourers and ski mountaineers*, it is the best exposition of the skills needed for safe (it can never be 100 percent safe) ski travel in the mountains that I have come across in 35 years addicted to this form of play. There's still new stuff for me to learn here – and plenty to revise. The meat of the book is the chapters on avalanches and rescue, glacier skiing and navigation – the 'solid tools' as Bruce calls them.

Decades ago the Swiss guide Martin Epp told me that if the choice was between clients who were good skiers but poor mountaineers or poor skiers but good mountaineers, he would prefer the former. The mountaineers may be competent and confident on the final summit climbs but hold the party up if they can't cope with tricky snow conditions on the descent – too much falling down and struggling back on their feet again. If any of this gives a twinge of recognition, you may benefit from the chapter on 'Downhill Skills' written by BASI instructor Alison Culshaw; really good advice on honing your technique.

The blurb on the cover says the book contains everything you need to make the transition from piste skiing to ski touring, and this is true in spades. Indeed it contains much for the experienced tourer to catch up on too. My worry would be that a would-be ski tourer might find some of the detail, say on creating a direct haul system for a crevasse rescue, so mind-boggling they'd dismiss touring and stick to the piste. But don't be deterred, the technical stuff can be learnt over time, using the manual as support.

Interspersed through the text are Bruce's 'Top Tips' – on anything from a Klemheist working best with the longer tail being in the direction of pull, to putting a slice of fresh ginger in your hot blackcurrant juice (of course you always carry root ginger on tour, don't you?). My own 'Top Tip', be you novice or veteran, is simple: buy this book.

Stephen Goodwin

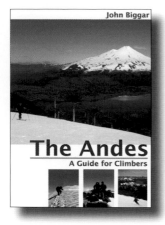

The Andes – A Guide for Climbers
John Biggar
Andes; 4th Edition, March 2015, pp352, £26.95

It is a gargantuan task to attempt to cover the whole of the Andean chain in one pocket-sized guidebook, but this is what John Biggar has accomplished in the fourth edition of his guide to Andean climbing. Following broadly the same format as earlier versions, the author first provides some extremely useful, indeed essential, introductory information that will be of particular value for those planning to visit South America for the first time. He then progresses southwards from Venezuela and Columbia through Ecuador, Peru and Bolivia to Argentina and Chile. The book describes routes on all of the major 6000m mountains, many of the more frequented 5000m mountains and the more popular peaks in Patagonia. In order to contain this vast wealth of information in such a compact volume the author has necessarily limited the detail provided, but this in no way detracts from its value to the experienced mountaineer. While most of the Andes are not noted for their ski touring, opportunities do exist, particularly at latitudes below 35°S and on individual mountains and glaciers further north. This volume has extended coverage for those that are keen to ski tour in South America.

In each section the author has provided colourful maps showing the general orientation and access to each peak alongside colour photographs indicating the major routes described. The inclusion of some key GPS waypoints is a bonus, but there is some way to go before this becomes a more comprehensive compilation.

John Biggar is a professional climber who has spent many seasons climbing in South America. He has first-hand experience of many of the mountains described in this book, but understandably he has been forced to rely on the accounts of others for those that he has not personally visited. References to other regional guidebooks are given, although no other English language guidebook offers the breadth of knowledge embraced by this book. It is a 'must have' for anyone planning to climb in South America.

Derek Buckle

The Calling: A Life Rocked by Mountains
Barry Blanchard
Patagonia, 2014, pp 429, US $27.95

Forgive me for starting the review of this great book with clichés. Perhaps it is more of a truism than a cliché, but it has to be said. Barry Blanchard and his tales of mountaineering are 'larger than life.' Mountains are of course very much larger than life. Despite their indifference and inanimate nature, they are as memorable as the many renowned mountaineers who populate the book, many of whom are equally and powerfully caught up by the call of the mountains.

Blanchard's many 'brothers in alpine style' are made to seem at once insignificant by the vast scale of the challenges they undertake yet god-like and almost unstoppable on the vast stage of one unclimbed face after another. The mountains are as much characters in the book as the climbers. Some chapters are dedicated to friends; e.g. Kevin and David to name but two chapter titles (for Kevin Doyle and Dave Cheeseman). Some chapters are the names of mountains; e.g. Mount Fay and Rakaposhi.

At one point the author describes the lines that alpinists make on the mountains like those of an artist's etching. And when the writing is this good, it is truly a form of art. At times there seem no boundaries, the mountains are canvases on which men and women pursue expression through mountaineering. The writing can one moment be quite delicate, capturing intimate details of a campsite or a bivouac conversation, and in the next paragraph down you are in the midst of an avalanche and a gripping struggle to survive.

Mountains are much larger than life, yet when climbing them, and describing those experiences as well as Blanchard does, you realise that he is very aware of the complexity of the sport that is his calling. For Blanchard, climbing is at once a very personal and an extreme form of engagement with life. But what sort of life engagement is it? This is a very old question that climbers ask themselves, and Blanchard tackles it without becoming analytical, philosophical or overly romantic. It is much simpler than that. It is as if someone like Blanchard who has truly known fear has no fear in truly telling it like it is.

The Calling is also a call into parallel life, and away from the life of his childhood. The mountains provide a life that is physically harder, more threatening, exhilarating, exhausting and overwhelming than the life Blanchard led as a child being brought up on the wrong side of the tracks in Calgary. Being in the mountains for Blanchard is solace, a place to forget bad things that happened to his family. Part of that forgetting is through the act of taking on the bad-ass things that mountains throw at you. The mountains erase his worldly concerns (most of the time). Being there on their unclimbed faces, the author finds a place in which he feels at home. But like the home of his childhood, the mountains are also broken; falling stones, collapsing seracs, endless avalanches, horrendous storms, injuries to friends and to himself. This is the parallel world of a true mountaineer.

There are some great one liners in the book that capture the climber's reality. During continuous nasty weather on a new route on the east face of Mt. Fay, Blanchard writes:

'… I turned out from the mountain and began screaming obscenities into the driving snow, challenging the storm. I wanted perfection in my alpinism and this is what you get. I spent what was left in my lungs and crumpled back into the slope. Carl caught up with me, waited ten heartbeats and then said; "hey, man, it don't gotta be fun to be fun."'

At first I could not quite explain to myself why the writing is so alive and vivid. In part it is because it is written fearlessly. In so doing, Blanchard finds many wonderful turns of phrase when describing his friends, the mountains, the 'real world' and the experiences shared by so few. For example, he goes to the north face of Mt. Alberta with Gregg Cronn:

'…a lean and tall American with elongated El Greco looks intensified by a black beard, and sad lack-bellied Benicio del Torro eyes. But his eyes were misleading because Gregg was easy to laugh . . . I'd get him guffawing with my ribald irreverent humour; "those lick-dick, conservative butt-knuckles wouldn't know leniency if it came up and bit his in the ass."'

Anyone who knows Barry Blanchard will know that's the way he is. He just comes out with things regardless of the audience and he is very entertaining and funny. It is part of his 'as I see it' nature. For British readers who remember Mo Antoine, they will find in Barry Blanchard a native American soul mate of Mo's.

Several days after introducing us to Gregg, they are approaching the top of Alberta's North Face:

'(Now) an ice filled groove and I hauled up my crampons once again. The rock and ice were so good and the angle was easing back. My climbing became a joy and I realized that I was the only expression of joy for many a mile and thousands of feet.'

This is compelling stuff, and compulsive reading, especially for mountaineers and anyone who loves the alpine world. It is compelling because his writing has a cinematic, IMAX, surround sound feel that envelopes the reader in the experience of dark, deep and dangerous mountains. The detail is almost tactile. You feel the cold, the pain, the altitude sickness. 'I hurt therefore I am' is one of the mottos of the book. The compulsive nature of the book comes from a deep love of the mountains and life, the wanting to just go climb as long as there is energy and daylight. And for the reader, you just want to be there, to grab the next pitch. Even though many of the climbers in the books are not well known in Britain and Europe, you get to know them through Blanchard's excellent characterisation. You want to know them better and share the experiences. The people in the book are as vivid and real as the contradictions and realities that the mountains can bring so unexpectedly, painfully and sometimes fatally.

The Calling is extremely well illustrated throughout with black and white photos relevant to the particular chapters and two sections of full colour plates. Oh, and I must not forget to mention the sex, drugs and rock and roll. The author provides us with suggested play lists for each chapter, indeed, as the subtitle suggests.

In his acknowledgements, Barry Blanchard pays tribute to the many great climbers who, through their writing, inspired him to climb. Among them are Walter Bonatti, Lionel Terray, Tom Patey, Gaston Rébuffat, Yvon Chouinard and many other familiar names. Barry Blanchard, for future generations of mountaineers, will be part of that 'play' list.

John Porter

Obituaries

Matterhorn. Edward Theodore Compton. 1880. Watercolour. 43 x 68cm.
(Alpine Club Collection HE118P)

In Memoriam

The Alpine Club Obituary	Year of Election (including to ACG)
Ralph Atkinson	1997
Una Bishop	1982
John Chadwick	1978
John Clegg	1955
Dennis Davis	1977
Gordon Gadsby	1985
Johannes Villiers de Graaff	1953
David Jamieson	1999
Emlyn Jones	1944
Brian 'Ned' Kelly	1968
Neil Mackenzie	Asp.2011, 2015
Richard Morgan	1960
John Peacock	1966
Bill Putnam	1972
Stephanie Roberts	2011
Les Swindin	1979
John Tyson	1952

As usual, the Editor will be pleased to receive obituaries for any of those above not included in the following pages.

Ralph Atkinson
1952 - 2014

Ralph Atkinson climbing on the slabs of Fournel, near Argentière, Ecrins. *(Andy Clarke)*

I met Ralph in 1989 when I moved to Wolverhampton, through our involvement with the Wolverhampton Mountaineering Club. Weekends in Wales and day trips to Matlock and the Roaches became the foundation for extended expeditions to the Alps including, in 1991, a fine six-day ski traverse of the *Haute Route*, Argentière to Zermatt, and ascents in 1993 of the Mönch and Jungfrau. Descending the Jungfrau in a storm, we could barely see each other. I slipped in the new snow and had to self-arrest, aided by the tension in the rope to Ralph. It worked, and I was soon back on the ridge, but when we dropped below the Rottalsattel and could speak to each other again, he had no idea that anything untoward had happened.

I recall long journeys by car enlivened by his wide-ranging taste in music. The keynote of many outings was his sense of fun. There were long stories, jokes or pithy one-liners. He had an appetite for the mountains that went back to his days training as a teacher in Wales, but he was never hungry. When anyone floated a particularly gnarly plan for the day, his response in his residual 'cockney twang' was often, ' 'Ang on a minute, I'm on me 'olidays!', a very understandable comment in that he had a demanding and responsible job in teaching.

In later years he experienced some back problems, possibly the legacy of too much squash-playing, which led to his retirement in 2004. That and my moves to Manchester, then Bristol, meant that we met less frequently. His focus also shifted after his marriage to Sue in 2008, in that they spent a lot of time travelling together. It is sad that, after finding such happiness, the time they shared should be cut short by his sudden illness.

I last met Ralph by chance when I was dropping friends off at the AC dinner in Buxton in 2013 and, as it turned out, we had time to catch up over a couple of drinks. I was hoping to get in touch in the autumn, so when I returned from six weeks abroad in mid-September I was shocked to hear that he was terminally ill with a brain tumour. He was always so full of life. His funeral took place on 6 October. He will be much missed by family and friends.
Dave Wynne-Jones

Andy Clarke writes: Ralph was a keen and skilful rock climber, mountaineer and skier throughout his adult life. He was a long-standing member of the Alpine Club (from 1997), the Eagle Ski Club and the Climbers' Club, besides playing an active role in his local Wolverhampton MC. He combined his passion for the mountains with a career as a popular and successful secondary school teacher of geography and as Pastoral Head.

Like many of his generation, Ralph's love of adventure was ignited by taking part in the Duke of Edinburgh's Award Scheme, which gave him his first taste of climbing. From his teenage years, it played a central role in his life: it was no accident that he chose Wrexham College to train as a teacher: it was the closest he could get to the mountains of North Wales.

Ralph rock climbed extensively in all the major regions of the UK. He made many summer and winter trips to the European Alps and over the years developed a particular love for the Écrins, so much so that he purchased an apartment in Puy St Vincent, down the Gyronde valley from Ailefroide. This provided an excellent base for climbing and skiing. Beyond Europe, he took part in a number of exploratory expeditions to Baffin Island, Greenland (with some eight first ascents in east Greenland) and the Karakoram, including two first ascents and a new route above the Barpu Glacier.

I first met Ralph around 15 years ago, through the local climbing club, and we became both climbing partners and close friends. Over the last few years in particular – ah, the joys of retirement and mid-week climbing! – we did hundreds of routes together, from 10m gritstone scarefests at his local crag, the Roaches, to long Alpine snow and rock routes near his home-from-home in the Gyronde valley.

Ralph remained a committed climber right until the point at which cancer robbed him of his mobility. I shall always treasure the memory of our last day out together, on the glorious gritstone of Stanage, warmed by the sun of early spring. He faced his illness with great fortitude and kept his sense of humour until the end. He died peacefully at home on 25 September 2014. He leaves a widow, Sue, stepdaughters Clare and Lisa and a sister, Pauline.

Lady Una Bishop 1918 - 2015

Una C C Padel was brought up in Carlisle, in Cumbria. Her earliest climbing memory was the ascent of Great Gable with her family at the age of 5.

Una married Sir George Bishop, who was later to be president of the Royal Geographical Society from 1983-87. In the 1960s, the couple spent time in British Guyana and Washington, because of the nature of Sir George's work with Booker McConnell. Their earliest climbs, however, were in the Alps, mainly of the classic kind: Mont Blanc, the Jungfrau, the Breithorn, the Tour Ronde, the Gran Paradiso and the Grande Casse, as well as many other lesser ascents.

Having discovered that India still lay within the sterling area, from 1967-80 Una and her husband undertook 18 expeditions to Kashmir. An early (1967) attempt on Kolahoi (5425m) was foiled just short of the summit because of a heavy fall of new snow. In 1970 they were in the Langtang, and the following year they accompanied W H Murray to Everest Base Camp (Nepal side). In 1974, they crossed the Mera La with their Sherpa, Pemba Norbu, and returned the following year to climb Gokyo Ri (5357m) in the Khumjung.

In 1976, their interest shifted to the Annapurna area, where they climbed Tharpu Chuli (Tent Peak) (5663m), returning to Pokhara via Jomsom and Muktinath. An attempt on Mera Peak (6476m) a year later ended in an epic three nights stranded on a ridge at about 4500m because of heavy new snow.

Una Bishop.

However, they returned to Mera Peak the following year for a successful ascent. Their climbing expeditions in this part of the world concluded in 1979 with an ascent of Chulu East (6200m) via the Marsyandi Valley and in 1980 the first ascent of Paldor West (5500m).

Lady Bishop joined the Alpine Club in 1982, at the same time as Sir George. During Sir George's tenure as president of the RGS, in the mid-80s, he and Una mounted a large scientific expedition to the unexplored Kimberley area of Western Australia. They made the first crossing of the King Leopold Range and visited various previously unknown sites and caves.

In later years, they were fond of returning to the Gran Paradiso area, and also particularly enjoyed walking in the Lozère part of the Cévennes, in Meyrueis.

Sir George died in 1999 and Lady Una in 2015; she died in High Wycombe, aged 96. She leaves an extensive family, but no children.

Catherine Moorehead

John Chadwick 1946 - 2015

The untimely death in February of John Chadwick, as the result of a fall above Red Tarn, Helvellyn, came as a great shock to all who knew him. It was no surprise that he was climbing alone in winter. John was at home in

John Chadwick. *(Chris Woodall)*

those hills; he was vastly experienced and spent as much time as possible wandering on them in all conditions. John was renowned for his immaculate, balletic climbing style; he was bold and adventurous but always careful in considering the next move. He was never hurried but always fast, a joy to watch and to be with, on rock or ice.

John was born in Ashton-under-Lyne. He became a keen student, with an appetite for learning that lasted all his life. I remember his holiday reading in later years to be huge volumes on psychology or astrophysics. While John was still at school, his father, an outdoor man, led him into the Peak District to experience its freedom, wind and heather: it was here that he was introduced to climbing on the Edges. Gritstone was an ideal medium for the enjoyment of precision and the search for perfection which became so much a part of John's character.

He graduated to Imperial College, London, to study chemistry and quickly joined fellow students from the Mountaineering Club. Bob Peckham fondly remembers those days when they would head off to North Wales or the Lake District in an ex-laundry van affectionately named the 'steam wagon'. John was soon climbing to a high standard and became a member of an ICMC Expedition to East Greenland in 1967. The expedition pioneered a new route into the Avantgarden area near Mount Forel by using local boats to travel up the Kangerlugssuaq Fjord, and then man-hauling sledges up the Glacier de France. The team then made several first and second ascents of peaks in this remote area.

In the early 1970s, John joined Bob Peckham in what was probably the first serious attempt to free climb out of the Gaping Ghyll main chamber. They reached a height level with the roof of the chamber before being stopped by excessive water flowing down the main V-groove. The feasibility of the route had, however, been demonstrated and it was completed by another team a year or so later.

Continuing his mountaineering, John visited the Alps and Dolomites each summer to build up his experience. He was a naturally reserved character who climbed because he enjoyed the challenge and saw no reason to shout about his exploits. Coupled with this was his meticulousness in planning and execution, so that he experienced very few epics or incidents.

He had an ability to read the conditions and was never afraid to turn back.

Many bold routes were done with his friend Graham Swainson. Perhaps those which made the greatest impression were the Nant-Blanc Face of the Aiguille Verte, the North Face of Les Drus and North-east Spur of the Droites. Graham remembers some cold bivouacs, but other than that no particular problems. About this time, John tested his toughness and resilience by soloing the West Ridge of the Aiguille Noire de Peuterey.

After working as a chemist from 1967 until 1971 at the Philips research labs in Redhill, he decided upon a career change and enrolled at Heriot Watt University, Edinburgh, to study town planning. Needless to say, John also made good use of his proximity to the Highlands. As a student he won a travel scholarship which enabled him to visit the Polish Tatra.

On graduating, he found a post working for Middlesbrough Council Planning Department and became associated with the Cleveland Mountaineering Club: he was happy to find that it was easy to visit the outcrops of North Yorkshire on his way home from work. He was soon pioneering new routes and solving many technical problems with his 'fancy footwork'. He met and married Marjorie, bought a house in Redcar and settled quickly into family life, although this change for Marjorie and her young daughter Joanne was a more radical alteration. Joanne remembers long car journeys each weekend, and even having their own flood-free hillock in the Ynys Ettws field.

With Pete Goodwin and other friends from Cleveland, John tackled high-quality rock climbs across Britain, from Cornwall to the Highlands, with routes such as *Torro, The Pinch, Carnivore, The Big Groove* and *Resolution* among the most memorable.

After his election as president of the Cleveland MC, John typically tackled the job in a professional manner, attending every meet, making a point of welcoming new members and sharing his knowledge and expertise with others. John was also a member of the Climbers' Club, becoming membership secretary.

In 2007, Marjorie and John moved to Gamblesby, near Penrith, where John took up fell-running. Simple jogging would never inspire John, so on his 63rd birthday he completed an unaccompanied Bob Graham round, the ever-attentive Marjorie refuelling him at every road-head. John's final achievement was a family affair: an ultimate triathlon from John O'Groats to Land's End involving cycling, running all the Scottish 4000ers and the English and Welsh 3000ers, as well as canoeing or swimming the longest lakes in each of these countries. Richard, Joanne's husband, did the cycling, Joanne and Marjorie the swimming and canoeing and, in very inclement conditions, John ran up all the hills. The whole venture took 10 days, an outstanding feat of organisation and stamina of which the whole family is justly very proud.

John was a rock climber, alpinist, skier and more recently a fell-runner of great ability, who died on the mountains he loved.

Chris Woodall

Dr E John Clegg
1925 - 2015

John Clegg on Kangchenjunga in 1955.
(Joe Brown coll.)

John Clegg was a graduate of Sheffield University Medical School where, as an undergraduate, he was a member of the Officer Training Corps and the Sheffield University Mountaineering Club (SUMC). In the late 1940s and early 1950s the SUMC was heavily involved in the exploration of local gritstone edges, leading to the publication of the *Sheffield Area* guidebook in 1953. John became a member of the Climbers' Club in 1946 and a member of the Alpine Club in 1955.

After his National Service in the Royal Army Medical Corps, John moved from Sheffield to a lectureship at Liverpool University, but maintained his service contacts through the Territorial Army, where he was attached to an airborne unit. While at Liverpool he became a member of the Wayfarers' Club and was invited to join the successful 1955 Kangchenjunga Expedition as its doctor. He returned to Sheffield shortly after this Himalayan trip before being appointed Regius Professor of Anatomy at Aberdeen University in 1977. From Aberdeen and up to the time of his retirement in 1992, he led a number of overseas expeditions to study the peoples of developing countries.

Although a mountaineer rather than a rock climber, in 1954 John organised and led the Climbers' Club Alpine meet at Blatten in the Lötschental, which was unfortunately blighted by poor conditions and frequent heavy rain. His rock climbing also had him involved in first ascents on Sheffield grit and helped open up the crags of the Grisedale Valley when the SUMC secured the lease to Ruthwaite Lodge in 1953.

Undoubtedly, the 1955 Kangchenjunga Expedition and its immediate aftermath were the highlight of John's mountaineering career. Charles Evans needed a doctor with mountain experience and John provided just that, along with being a singer with a stock of good songs, as the expedition discovered. The expedition book records the part he played in the ascent, in leading porters who were carrying loads to set up the early camps; improving the route with Streather, and his key role on the radio at base, transmitting weather reports and visual observations of summit attempts to those at high camps. The friendships formed during the expedition also led to a period of what was probably John's hardest climbing, when with Joe Brown he climbed a number of the classic routes in Wales.

He was a big, very strong man. At Liverpool, John played in the front row of the scrum for St Helens Rugby Union Football Club. His strength was also much in demand when the SUMC was rebuilding Ruthwaite Lodge in 1953, from its roofless shell; I was part of the group with John. The weather was idyllic: we all slept outside the building site, waking in still air and the sun's warmth to see it touching the summit of Place Fell beyond the bottom of the valley. Over the course of the work we became integrated with the local population, and a highlight for John was the Ullswater Foxhounds' New Year's Day Meet.

John and I shared the same sense of humour: he was a great raconteur. I look back to the many happy hours spent climbing, wandering, talking and singing in all weathers on Peak District crags, on Kinder Scout and while exploring the hills and crags of Eastern Lakeland. Memorable events range from a week of superb winter climbing based in Wasdale to a glorious late autumn day's climbing on Stanage Edge. Tired after our efforts, we sat in the late afternoon sun, idly reminiscing, waking suddenly to the realisation that the sun had set, that it was already quite dark and that we were enveloped in a thick, impenetrable mist. But we only had to get back to the road at Moscar Top and the Edge would guide us. We soon found that a compass would have been useful: when we reached the road, soaked from the knees down, we couldn't find the car! It was with much amusement that we debated how the *AJ* might have reported our predicament.

Frank Fitzgerald

Dennis Davis 1927 - 2015

Dennis Davis was a leading British mountaineer throughout the 1950s and 1960s. He achieved several outstanding winter ascents in the UK, dozens of *grandes courses* in the Alps, and highly significant climbs and expeditions in the Himalaya.

I first met Dennis in 1951 in Idwal. My older companion, Alf Beanland, and I (then aged 15) were rather in awe of him, for he was an alpinist. He had climbed in the Alps and even made some notable ascents such as the Brenva Spur, the Innominata and the Diable Ridge. Though of medium height, at that time he cut a rather dashing figure, spare, dark-haired and moustached.

Dennis was born in London. Contrary to a later image (due to a highly successful working career) he came from a working-class background. After a state-school education, he trained as a draughtsman. A crucial part of his development as a climber came when he was posted to work on Anglesey during this training, but he actually started his mountain activities on a visit to Skye in 1946.

In that year in Idwal, at the YHA, he met Ray Colledge; they agreed to climb together. Like Dennis, Ray was an ambitious mountaineer; in 1949 they set out on their first visit to the Alps. Today's climbers have little or no idea what that entailed, for it meant overcoming rationing, travelling by train, and being limited by money-exchange controls. From the outset, though, they headed for major objectives. Like Ray, Dennis had limited holidays, usually only two or three weeks, but over the next decade and a half they notched up a truly impressive list of ascents. There were only two or three a season but even today these climbs command great respect, such as the north face of the Triolet, the *Red Sentinel* on Mont Blanc, the *Cassin Route* on the Piz Badile, the north face of the Aiguille de Bionnassay, the north face of the Dent d'Hérens, the north face of the Grosshorn in the Bernese Oberland, the Macugnaga face of Monte Rosa, and many more.

In his early years as a climber Dennis had joined the Wayfarers' Club. Later, he also joined the Rucksack and the Karabiner MC, then the Alpine Club in 1977 (although before then he had been a member of the Alpine Climbing Group). Through his membership of the AC he met Charles Evans. Dennis tried to persuade Evans to include him in the party to attempt Kangchenjunga in 1955, but Evans advised him to build up his Himalayan experience by joining Alf Gregory's party travelling out to explore the Rolwaling Himalaya. This he did, and it proved to be good advice, for this was a highly successful expedition, making 19 first ascents of peaks in the 5500m-6000m category.

In 1957, Charles Evans approached Dennis to travel with him to Nepal to attempt Annapurna II (7937m). The party was to be just the two of them, accompanied by four Sherpas. Dennis had already agreed to go later that year with Alf Gregory to Distaghil Sar, but he was persuaded by Evans to take part in both outings. Conditions on Annapurna II turned out to be too unsettled, so they switched their attention to Annapurna IV (7525m) and summited successfully. Unfortunately, the attempt on Distaghil Sar was unsuccessful, owing to very poor weather conditions.

These expeditions were significant, for they supported the trend towards lightweight, alpine-style climbing in the Himalaya. Dennis's next expedition in 1961 was to be his greatest: the groundbreaking ascent of Nuptse (7861m) when he and Sherpa Tashi led the way to the summit, to be followed the next day by Chris Bonington, Les Brown and Jim Swallow. This expedition was compromised by some personality clashes, not helped by the party driving overland to and from Nepal in two Standard Vanguard cars, which needed continual mechanical attention. Dennis, as the only member of the party with real engineering knowledge, found himself often working into the night to keep the cars on the road, while his team-mates were of little help. At that time Dennis did not suffer fools gladly and he could be acerbic if rubbed the wrong way, but he had put so much into the Nuptse adventure: it cost him his job and his first marriage. On his return, he had to start his career again, for he was living out of a suitcase. Such trials naturally bred resentment.

I did get to know Dennis well at the end of 1959 when I moved to Derby. The city was a hotbed of climbing activity at that time; one of its presiding spirits was Nat Allen, with whom I reformed the Rock and Ice Club. Dennis attended some of our meets, and on occasion I climbed with him. In the big winter of 1962-3 we ascended *Pigott's Climb* on Clogwyn D'ur Arddu, in the coldest conditions I have ever known in the UK: the fourth member of our party, Eric Wallis, suffered frostbite to his fingers, the only case I have ever known in this country. We were staying in Idwal, but just getting to Llanberis was challenging on the icy roads. Dennis always drove as if he was in a rally, and in trying to keep up with him, Dez Hadlum crashed my vehicle into a wall. The climb was demanding: we climbed in two ropes until at the final cracks we were forced to join up in a foursome. I led the first crack, which was at my limit. Dennis joined me and as the final fissure looked desperately sheathed in ice, he climbed it in tricouni-studded boots. He traversed first out right, then attacked a thin crack in the wall above him, which he somehow managed to ascend. In following, Dez, Eric and I agreed none of us could have led this pitch in those conditions. Another memorable climb I made with Dennis at that time was the *Western Gully* of the Black Ladders. We were in the company of Ray Colledge, Derrick Burgess and Ray Handley. Dennis at that date preferred to climb such routes in his tricouni-studded boots, while the rest of us wore crampons.

Starting his working career again after Nuptse, Dennis trained as a chemical engineer, specialising in high-impact polystyrene. He became a project manager for Petro-Carbon, which was a part of the Costain group. This work took him to Romania, Finland, Poland and China. He was based in Poland in the mid-1960s and it was there that he met his second wife Renata. In every country he visited he made contact, wherever possible, with the climbing community, and in Poland he climbed nearly every weekend with climbers from Cracow. This led to one of his most outstanding climbs, the *Superdirettissima* in winter of the north face of Mieguszowicki, accompanied by the two then unknown but brilliant Polish alpinists, Voytek Kurtyka and Jacek Rusiecki. This first ascent in the Tatra mountains is still held in high regard by the local activists.

When a Polish party visited the UK in 1975, Dennis acted as one of the hosts. By then he was again well-established in his career, and in the Peak District he provided accommodation for the whole group at his house in Butterton. In Wales I have a vivid memory of this visit, particularly after climbing at Tremadog, when Zawada, the Polish leader, emerged ashen-faced out of Dennis's Lancia, to say that they had reached a speed of over 100mph on the return journey to our base at Plas y Brenin.

The Karabiner Club, based in the Manchester area, used to have a tradition of inviting non-members from the wider climbing world to be their president. The names of those who accepted this invitation are impressive: Eric Byrom, Fred Pigott, John Hunt, Nat Allen, myself and several others. Dennis accepted this invitation in 1964, and as I also found out when I took this on some years later, the KMC is one of the most active clubs in the country. One highlight of their meets list is a Fell Race. The Club has always boasted outstanding performers in this activity: members in the past have won the Karrimor Mountain Marathon. Dennis, when he became president, set about trying to win this event, for it is a handicap race. It really is a gruelling outing. But despite spending time researching and training over the course, Dennis never won the event. When I was the KMC president he confessed he would sooner have won the KMC fell race than climb the Eigerwand (I think this was meant as a joke!).

In later life, even after retiring, Dennis kept up with his rock climbing, regularly visiting north Pembroke over several years with Nat Allen or Claude Davies, producing several new routes. In almost his 70th year he visited the Rolwaling Himalaya again and teamed up with his old Sherpa friend from 1955, Rita. Despite the onset of arthritis he summited Lobutse East (6119m) after his British climbing partner had to cry off owing to altitude problems.

Because of difficulties with arthritis he then climbed less and less, though he kept up an interest in golf. Nat Allen ribbed him about this, dismissing him as never more than a 'hacker'. Then he developed osteoporosis and though he still appeared at climbing dinners (at the AC, Wayfarers', Rucksack and KMC) his active climbing days were over.

The last time I met him was at Ray Colledge's funeral in 2014. He still had an 'edge' about him and at this event delivered a fitting tribute about his old rope-mate. His last words to me were 'I will be next', said in a jocular manner. This, I believe, was typical of Dennis: he was harder on himself than he was on anyone else. Along with Ray Colledge, climbing together in a golden period for British alpinism, when many of today's techniques were adopted and breakthroughs made, he forged one of the strongest partnerships in the history of our sport.

Dennis Gray

Dr Johannes de Villiers Graaff 1928 - 2015

Dr Johannes de Villiers Graaff, universally known as Jannie, died in Cape Town on 6 January 2015 at the age of 86.

Jannie was an exceptionally talented man who used his talents to the full. Besides his remarkable record as a mountaineer, at the time of his death he was still regarded as a world authority on welfare economics. He combined his academic career with farming, banking and advising the South African government on tax policy.

Jannie was born in Muizenberg on 19 February 1928. He was the youngest of three brothers of whom the eldest was Sir de Villiers Graaff who inherited the baronetcy from his father and was leader of the opposition United Party during the 1960s and early 1970s. Jan Smuts was one of Jannie's godfathers.

He attended Western Province Preparatory School and Diocesan College (better known as Bishops) where he matriculated at the age of 15, obtaining the second-highest marks in the whole of South Africa. After graduating from the University of Cape Town, he lectured for a year at Wits

Jannie Graaff. *(Douglas Scott)*

University before going up to St John's College, Cambridge, where he completed his PhD in 1950, at the age of 22. His thesis was published as a book, *Theoretical Welfare Economics.* It was still prescribed reading for Cambridge students in the 1980s and remains a classic text in its field.

Jannie had started rock climbing on Table Mountain when he was at university in Cape Town. From then on, mountains and mountaineering became a passion which lasted for the rest of his life. He first visited the Alps while he was at Cambridge and it was on a skiing holiday that he met Clare Thomson, of whom her aunt, Janet Adam Smith, wrote, 'I had taken my niece Clare Thomson climbing in Arran, you might say up to O-level maybe, and with the Witch's Step, A-level. But I have seldom known anyone advance more rapidly to her PhD!'

Clare is a daughter of Sir George Thomson, at that time Master of Corpus Christi College, Cambridge. She was thus a granddaughter of the famous J J Thomson who discovered the electron. Both her father and grandfather were Nobel Laureates. Clare's family has had a long and very distinguished association with the Alpine Club, as chronicled in an article by Janet Adam Smith in the *Alpine Journal,* Volume 67. Jannie could not possibly have found a more suitable partner; they were married in 1951.

After returning to South Africa in 1953, Jannie bought a fruit farm in the Koue Bokkeveld mountains about 120 miles north of Cape Town. In due course, he became a world- renowned expert on agricultural economics, so much so that whenever he visited the USA he had an open invitation to lecture at Stanford. He was made a fellow of St John's College, Cambridge, in 1950, then Churchill College, Cambridge in 1965. He was later elected a fellow of All Souls, Oxford, which was an unusual honour for a Cambridge man. He and Clare spent several terms in Oxford during the 1980s.

Jannie was highly esteemed in the business world. He was a director of Nedbank for many years and among many other activities was the dominant intellectual figure on both the Margo Commission, which led to the introduction of VAT in South Africa, and the Katz Commission, which led to the restructuring of the Revenue Service as an independent body.

It is of course his record as a mountaineer which will be of most interest. Jannie and Clare spent their honeymoon climbing in the Dolomites, as

Janet Adam Smith puts it, '*sesto grado*'. They concentrated on the Sella Group and the Langkofel, where *inter alia* they climbed the Grohmannspitze and the difficult *Schmittkamin Route* on the Fünffingerspitze.

In January 1952 they participated in a large South African party which converged on Mount Kenya. The weather was excellent and a number of successful ascents were made.

Bob Davies, with Clare and Jannie, climbed Nelion by a route which avoided the so-called 'Rickety Cracks' section of Shipton's original route up the south-east ridge. This has become known as the *de Graaff Variation*, which is unfortunate because it should correctly be called either the *Graaff Variation* or the *de Villiers Graaff Variation*. Perhaps future compilers of guidebooks will note this.

Jannie and Clare then opened a new variation of *Mackinder's Route* up the Diamond Glacier. (It is often stated incorrectly that they merely repeated the original *Mackinder's Route* but Clare says that *Mackinder's Route* crosses the Diamond Glacier whereas their route took them directly up it to the Gate of the Mists.) It was a very fine effort in the days before modern ice-climbing equipment became available. They did not have ice-screws and of course were using long-shafted ice-axes. Typically, Jannie later told Janet Adam Smith that after cutting steps up the first rope-length on the diamond-hard glacier ice, a sudden thought came to him: 'I don't think Clare has been on ice before!'

They joined forces with Bob Davies and Pottie Thompson at the Nelion end of the Gate of the Mists. This latter pair had reached that point by the ordinary route. The two parties then combined for the ascent of Batian. After lunching on the summit they then returned to the Gate of the Mists and climbed Nelion with the aid of a fixed rope left by Davies and Thompson. They were off the rock by 18.40 and back at the Two Tarn Hut by 20.45 having left the hut at 03.30 that morning.

Jannie and Kenneth Snelson made a reconnaissance visit in 1950 to the Panch Chuli peaks without getting to the top of anything significant. In 1952, he and Clare were in Kullu and Spiti with Ken Berrill and Pasang Dawa Lama, a very highly esteemed member of the Buddhist hierarchy who greatly assisted them in their relationships with the local people. They crossed two new passes into Spiti and succeeded in finding the key to, and making the first ascent of, Deo Tibba (6001m). They also made the first ascent of Manirang (6593m), which was then the highest peak to have been climbed by a woman. They were narrowly foiled by bad weather from reaching the summit of Shilla (6132m).

A few years later they were in the Ruwenzori, and in unusually fine weather they climbed Mounts Baker, Margherita and Alexandra. Jannie and Bob Davies made a new route up the north-east face of Margherita.

Both Clare and Jannie were also very accomplished skiers. They bought an apartment in Zermatt conveniently close to the Sunnegga lift and from then on spent a month or so during the winter in Zermatt; they usually returned for a few weeks in the summer, using it as a base for downhill skiing, ski touring and mountaineering.

Between 1946 and 1962, Jannie participated in the opening of an extraordinary number of new routes in the mountains of South Africa including what were then some of the hardest routes on Table Mountain and the Cederberg. In 1946 he was in the party that made the first ascent of the Grosse Spitzkop in what is now Namibia, while in 1949 he opened nine new rock climbs on Table Mountain.

As he got older and rock climbing became too demanding, he took up kayaking at which he became very proficient. His other great interest was ornithology.

Jannie was always something of a recluse. It was difficult to get him to participate in social occasions although he was marvellous company when one had the opportunity to draw him out on subjects which interested him, like mountaineering and ornithology. He had a very dry and witty sense of humour and delighted in turning a subject round so as to reveal an unexpectedly amusing aspect.

In his old age he continued to spend most of his days at the offices of Graaff's Trust, of which he was chairman. It was from there that he had walked over to Long Street when he was unintentionally knocked over by a pedestrian and hit his head on the pavement, fracturing his skull. Typically he didn't mention this to anyone at the office but drove himself home. It soon, however, became apparent that he was not at all well and he was admitted to hospital where he later died of complications.

He was buried with his ice-axe and rope beside him at de Grendel, the family farm which his father had established and which is now a well-known wine estate.

He is sorely missed by Clare, his six children and 18 grandchildren.

Robin Richards

Gordon Joseph Gadsby 1932 - 2015

Gordon Gadsby was born in 1932 and died on 13 March 2015. His hometown was Nottingham, where he was educated; he graduated from Nottingham College of Art as a qualified lithographic printer. It was an inauspicious time for young graduates seeking employment in the immediate post-war period, since employers preferred demobilised, experienced practitioners. Consequently, Gordon joined Buxton and Atwell as a decorator where he served for 44 years until he retired at 58 on medical grounds. A practical advantage from this profession, to stand him in good stead as a rock climber and mountaineer, was that he became familiar with working at heights.

National Service in the Royal Air Force gave Gordon an opportunity to bring his artistic gifts to photography. He practised professionally, and on return to civilian life he successfully embraced photography to record his climbs, using first a Leica and then a succession of Nikons. He was a stal-

Gordon Gadsby. *(Bob Pettigrew coll.)*

wart supporter of Kodachrome, as the shelves in his study testify, and was never persuaded to convert to digital photography.

My own association with Gordon took place in two phases, separated by my ten years' service in India. The first phase occurred when a passion for mountains and mountaineering brought us together in 1952 on a basic mountaineering course.

J E B (Jerry) Wright of the Mountaineering Association and Kenneth Wall, inspector of schools for Nottingham Local Education Authority, established a Further Education course in mountaincraft, based at the Lenton Primary School on Gregory Boulevard, and appointed me to conduct it. The first mature student to enrol was Gordon, closely followed by the 14-year-old Doug Scott, later our illustrious president. Richly endowed with the British wilderness of Bleaklow and Kinder Scout, interspersed with upflung gritstone edges, the High Peak of Derbyshire was our doorstep outdoor laboratory and gymnasium, while the old-fashioned but stout wall bars of the school gym served as an infinite variety of belaying points for the teaching of rope techniques.

Gordon graduated naturally to membership of the Oread (Greek for 'mountain nymph') Mountaineering Club, described memorably by Sir Jack Longland as, 'that delightful, disreputable and defiant club, the Oread!'

That decade was marked by the flourishing social life of the Oread MC, at which Gordon excelled since he had a natural talent for friendship and community organization, and for communicating to others his love of mountains with all the fervour of an evangelist. Kipling's memorable couplet is applicable here:

So and no otherwise – so and no otherwise – hillmen desire their Hills!

The Oread attached great importance to its annual photographic competition and ensured high standards through a standing invitation to C Douglas Milner, doyen of the AC and the best mountain photographer in Britain, to judge the entries. Before Gordon's arrival in the Oread I had enjoyed some success in the competition using a Leica M2. Gordon, once a Leica man, had converted to a Nikon SLR and henceforth dominated the competition. In the belief that 'it was the ships not the men in them' which had dictated his success, I followed suit, but to no avail; Gordon's artistic skills coupled with 'through the lens composition' outclassed all the opposition and won the unstinting praise of Douglas Milner.

In my absence abroad, Gordon made a massive voluntary contribution to the mountaineering and social success of the Oread MC. Simultaneously, throughout Nottinghamshire and Derbyshire, he was in constant demand as a lecturer, recounting his mountaineering adventures illustrated by projected transparencies of the highest pictorial quality. Invariably he would be accompanied by his wife Margaret, who took the role of helpmeet, agent and secretary.

At this time he was also contributing extensively to mountaineering and outdoor journals. His majestic and evocative photograph of climbers on the summit of An Teallach in Wester Ross identified Eric Langmuir's *Mountaincraft and Leadership* through a record number of print runs. His personal unpublished journals number more than 50 and would be a rich source of material for the appropriate archive.

When I returned to Derbyshire in the 1980s, I persuaded Gordon to join the Club. In my letter of proposal I described him as a fine all-round mountaineer, an outstanding mountain photographer, and a staunch companion on the hill. His application was seconded by C Douglas Milner and supported by R F Gilbert and Robin Hodgkin. Gilbert wrote, 'I have known Gordon for years and have the utmost respect for him as a person, mountaineer, and brilliant mountain photographer. He would be a valuable addition to the Club.'

Beginning in the season 1960 when I introduced Gordon to the Alps with an ascent of the Weissmies, and traverses of the Mittaghorn and Fletschhorn with Doreen Gadsby and Wally Smith, every season up to 1984 (the year of his application to the Club) produced a rich cornucopia of Alpine expeditions of the higher grade, ranging across the European Alps from Norway down to Corsica, and to the High Tatra in the east. He will be remembered by his erstwhile companions on the hill as a classical alpinist and boon companion.

Robert Pettigrew

David Jamieson 1926 - 2014

Davie Jamieson, active to the end, had a stroke while out on his bicycle and died on 14 October 2014.

Apart from a short spell in the Royal Navy when he was very young, Davie's career led to a senior position in the then Ministry of Works (now Ministry of Public Buildings and Works). He always took a great interest in nature, wildlife and mountaineering and had an extensive knowledge of the environment. He climbed in Turkey, Cyprus and Kenya, and led one expedition, in 1965, to Arctic Norway. He also made an ascent of Jebel Shams (3009m) in Oman. Through his work, he met the Royal Air Force Mountain Rescue Team (RAFMRT) at RAF Nicosia in Cyprus and became a member.

He was very popular: the team even named a practice slab 'Jamieson's Rocks' after him. Later, he went to East Africa and climbed Kilimanjaro. While there, he and another MRT member saved two climbers suffering from hypoxia. Later still, he was posted to Kenya and climbed extensively, including an ascent of Nelion, with the Kenya Climbing Club. On his return to the UK he continued close contact with the RAFMR teams at Kinloss and Leuchars. He climbed frequently in Scotland and the Lakes.

Davie was a keen exponent of mountaineering in Turkey, his first expedition to the Aladaglar mountains taking place in 1963. He and I climbed Demirkazik ('Iron Pole', 3756m), the highest mountain in the western Taurus range, as well as Emler (3723m) and Kaldi Dag (3734m). He organised three more expeditions from the UK to that area; many more peaks were climbed. Davie had many good friends in Turkey, including Omer Tuzel, who had written the *Ala Dag* guidebook.

In addition to mountaineering, Davie was an avid sailor and member of his local Aberdour Sailing Club where he kept a boat. With two others from the sailing club, he sailed to Norway and back, an epic voyage! He was also an artist and had recently given four of his paintings to the Alpine Club.

Davie was a great companion on the hill with a fine sense of humour.

Pete Addis

J H Emlyn Jones MBE, CBE 1915 - 2014

John Hubert Emlyn Jones, known to all as Emlyn Jones, was a high-achiever in many fields. He served as president of the Climbers' Club from 1966 to 1969 and as president of the Alpine Club from 1980 to 1982; he earned an MBE for conspicuous gallantry during the Second World War; he served as High Sheriff of Buckinghamshire in 1967 and, in his post-war profession of Chartered Surveying, rose to high office in the Lands Tribunal, during which he was made a CBE. He remained active to the end of his life, climbing Snowdon in his 80s and, until he was 98, travelling from his home near Leighton Buzzard twice a week to play bridge at the Garrick Club in London.

He was born in Wales, on the Gower, where his parents took their holidays. He spent his early years in Llandudno where his father was a schoolmaster who worked and occasionally climbed with J M Archer Thompson, the school headmaster. One of Emlyn's proud possessions was a copy of the original Lliwedd guidebook, given to his father by Archer Thompson and inscribed with a poem by the same, describing the joys of climbing on Lliwedd in the rain. His father's love of the mountains was the inspiration for Emlyn's own interest in mountaineering. Emlyn left Wales for school in Dulwich when he was 14 and spent the rest of his life in England. However, he was always a fiercely patriotic Welshman and in his later years taught himself to speak Welsh. On leaving school, he qualified as a chartered surveyor with a firm in Liverpool, spending his weekends climbing in North Wales or the Lake District and his holidays in the Alps. He joined the Climbers' Club in 1939 and the Alpine Club in 1944.

His early career was interrupted by the war. He was commissioned into the Royal Engineers in 1940 and appointed to head one of the newly-formed bomb disposal units. His engineer's knowledge of explosives quickly developed into the skills required to defuse bombs, though not without some good fortune when he unknowingly tackled a new type of fuse designed to explode when withdrawn: luckily this was a faulty unit and provided essential training in methods of combatting this threat. Emlyn's work on this and other devices earned him the MBE (Military). By the age of 28 he was a major and in command of all the bomb-disposal companies in northwest London. Then, in 1944, the V1 rockets came into use by the Germans; as Emlyn said, 'They gave us no work – they all went off!' He was posted to France after D-Day and was involved in clearing mines, booby-traps and beach obstacles. A significant operation for Emlyn and his team was the destruction of the vast underground complex that was intended for the V3 Long Range 'super-guns' that would have bombarded central London.

Emlyn Jones

Emlyn Jones on the Welsh coast.

After being demobbed in 1946 he resumed his career, joining a chartered surveying practice in Birmingham, and also resumed his Alpine climbing. A notable season, described in the 1948 *CC Journal*, included the north ridge of the Dent Blanche and the long Moming ridge traversing over several summits from the Mountet to the Weisshorn. In 1950, he joined a surveying partnership in London, but had only been in the post for two days when H W Tilman invited him to join an exploration of the Annapurna region, a recently opened area that had been closed to Westerners since the seventeenth century. His partners agreed to him taking five months off, telling him that he would regret it forever if he didn't go. He went, enjoyed the exploration, but suffered all the depredations that legend associates with Tilman expeditions, his illness after eating a 'green' banana causing him never to eat the fruit again.

Back in the UK, his rock climbing was strong; he shared ropes with many of the leading climbers. In 1952 he went with Tony Moulam and John Churchill to climb a new route on Craig yr Ysfa. Moulam and Churchill took so long to work out the complicated line that it became too late for Emlyn to follow; instead, he went to the top of the crag in order to be able to lower a rope if required, although this proved unnecessary. The successful pair stood at the top of the climb with Emlyn, looking at the mist rolling in with the encroaching darkness, while wondering what to call their new line. Emlyn suggested a Welsh name, *Mur y Niwl* (Wall of the Mists), which the others happily accepted. He regretted not actually being on the first ascent, but was pleased to have found a classic name for a subsequently classic climb.

Around this time, John Hunt invited Emlyn to join the Everest squad for the 1953 expedition. As plans progressed, Emlyn missed the cut for the main party 'by a whisker', but he was invited to head a reserve team that would take up the challenge again in the autumn, should the spring attempt fail. Many years later at one of the Everest team reunions, he said that the Queen spoke to him about the joy of the nation at the announcement on Coronation Day of the expedition's success. He told her, 'Yes, Ma'am, but I'm afraid there were several of us whose joy was somewhat diminished!'

Emlyn Jones returned to the Himalaya in 1959, when he led his own expedition to the then unclimbed Ama Dablam, in Nepal. Emlyn had married Louise Hazell in 1954 and she was also planning to join the expedition, but became pregnant with their first child, daughter Eiluned, so stayed at home. Sadly, on what was to be the final push to the summit, George Fraser and Mike Harris (both Climbers' Club members) disappeared into clouds on the final, easier slopes. They were never seen again; their loss marked the end of Emlyn's Himalayan mountaineering.

In his later years, Emlyn developed his love of music, playing the cello, singing with the Madrigal Society and forming a 60-piece orchestra in Leighton Buzzard. In his career, through his work with the Land Tribunal, he became an authority on rating values and appeals, for which he was awarded the CBE.

I was privileged to interview Emlyn for the Climbers' Club Oral Archive in January 2011 and was impressed by his vitality, his humour and his memory. Several of his stories are touched upon in the tribute above which, though they cannot do justice to the man, hopefully give a flavour of his achievements in his long life.

He died, aged 98, in February 2014, and is survived by Louise and their three children.

David Medcalf

Brian 'Ned' Kelly
1934 - 2014

Ned was a Londoner, born and bred. As an evacuee from the Blitz, Slough was the first 'wild place' he encountered but, soon after returning to Islington, his home was demolished by a V2 rocket – luckily while Ned was at school and his parents at work. On leaving Holloway Grammar where he boxed, played cricket and the cornet, he joined a small engineering firm but soon escaped to a stockbroker's office. By the time his call-up came for National Service, he was playing in a local silver band, acting in amateur dramatics and enjoying long rides to youth hostels with a local cycling group.

Ned Kelly approaching Namche Bazaar during the 1971 International Everest South Face Expedition. *(John Cleare/Mountain Camera Picture Library)*

Recognising his talents, the Army posted Ned to the Intelligence Corps and sent him to Malaya where he learnt Malay before working as an intelligence analyst with Special Branch, tracking down communist terrorists in the jungle. After this a City office lost its appeal and in 1955 he managed to join the BBC as a Trainee Technical Operator in the then rapidly expanding Television Service, a job which involved rubbing shoulders with such celebrities as Gilbert Harding and Fanny Craddock, while working on such diverse programmes as Top of the Pops and Zoo Quest. Out of hours, he was cutting his teeth on Wealden sandstone with the North London MC.

In a calculated career move four years later, Ned joined TWW (Television Wales & West) in Bristol and, some way further north, the Mynydd CC as a climber. In due course, by now a producer, opportunities began to occur to merge profession and pleasure, and in the early spring of 1965 he 'set up' the first ascent, by Bonington, Cleare and Greenbank, of *Coronation Street*, that now-classic line up the impending 150m limestone wall of Cheddar Gorge. A month or two later he produced a spectacular and highly successful broadcast of the second ascent, tele-recorded the previous day (a production technique not to be confused with film or live television).

Doors opened, of course, and the following year Ned joined Dennis Gray's expedition to the unclimbed north ridge of Alpamayo, essentially as film-maker, although he himself nevertheless climbed to the north summit of the mountain in order to shoot the exposed and dangerous final arête to the main top, such professional dedication greatly impressing his more experienced companions. Networked on ITV and abroad, *The Magnificent Mountain* won the Italian Alpine Club's Mario Bello Prize at the Trento Film Festival. The judges remained unaware of the climb's sequel: winding down in the Andean foothills after the expedition, Ned and Dennis escaped a hijacking by drug dealers.

In 1967, Ned produced another climbing broadcast, this time for ITV's *World of Sport*, with Joe Brown leading a pretty, blonde physical education student up *Vector*, Joe's Tremadoc classic. Dennis, who as safety officer organised the rigging, recalls that the climbing was so exciting that the programme overran by almost an hour.

The following year, Ned joined the already world-famous BBC Natural History Unit, also based in Bristol.

In 1970, when the BBC 'bought' Norman Dyhrenfurth's International Expedition to attempt the still virgin south face of Everest (planned for the following year), Ned was named as film producer and enlisted as a full expedition member. His meticulous organisation of the film logistics and his tireless work as a regular support climber in the Western Cwm endeared him to the 21 other members from 10 nations. Despite the failure of the climb and the 'Rebellion of the Latins', the film, *Surrender to Everest*, (directed by Anthony Thomas) was shortlisted for a BAFTA award. On returning to Everest in 1975, Ned produced *Everest the Hard Way*, the film of the successful south-west face climb by Bonington's team.

The Natural History Unit gave free rein to Ned's delight in travel and exploration, and for over 20 years he worked in many of the world's wild places, frequently as producer with David Attenborough. When in 1974 Ian Howell and I explored the little known Paldor area in the Ganesh Himal, Ned had already made a helicopter reconnaissance and provided some useful photographs; we were able, officially, to name a prominent, shapely peaklet Neddy's Thumb.

Among Ned's favourite projects were *The Living Planet* (1984), *Life in the Freezer* (1993) and the *Voyages of Charles Darwin*. Indeed, it was during the filming of the latter series in 1977-78 that he met Suzanne, from Dublin, the ship's doctor and cook, whom he was later to marry. But she was not Ned's only prize, for in 1978 he won both a BAFTA, shared with Chris Ralling and director Martyn Friend, for the best factual series, and then in 1985 an Emmy for his work on *The Living Planet: A Portrait of the Earth*, a first-ever award to a nature programme.

After 21 years and many adventures at the BBC, Ned and Suzanne 'retired' to a remote rural farmhouse on the Isle of Wight and raised a family, a boy and a girl. Suzanne, meanwhile, worked as a senior medical consultant on the island while Ned continued to work as a freelance television producer and trek leader for Mountain Kingdoms, specialising in Nepal and Bhutan, between trips keeping fit on his mountain bike.

A man of many parts, Ned had been an actor in his youth: he played many roles as a member of the London Irish Theatre Group. He was a jazz enthusiast, a fine trumpet player and an entertaining speaker, frequently at club dinners. Indeed, with fellow member Brian Royle, he once wrote and produced an opera for the Mynydd Club's annual event. For the Everest 60th Anniversary celebrations, in aid of the MEF, Ned recorded one of his own compositions *Any Old Pitons* for Wanderlust, for the CD of climbing songs compiled by his old friend Dennis Gray and music producer Paul Cherry.

Ned, with his happy chuckle and ready wit, was great company, always enthusiastic and always ready with sound, practical advice. He kept up with the climbing world and was for some years a member of the BMC's Public Relations Committee. In retirement, Ned and Suzanne were generous hosts to climbers and old television colleagues who managed to brave the island ferry. He spent many hours carefully scanning back-numbers of the *Alpine Journal* into the digital archives, a task for which the Club is extremely grateful. His work in film and television is a worthy epitaph.

John Cleare

Dr Neil C W Mackenzie 1983 - 2015

With the untimely death of Neil Mackenzie in January 2015, British mountaineering has lost one of its most enthusiastic and adventurous characters. While Neil embodied the spirit of his beloved Scottish Highlands, his endless thirst for adventure extended far beyond. Naturally, he relished the summer and winter climbing that Scotland has to offer, with many trips to the north-west Highlands. He was also an enthusiastic fell-runner, musician, ski-mountaineer, snowboarder and surfer, while developing an accomplished academic career in biological research. His enthusiasm for life extended into any organisation that he was part of, including the Eagle Ski Club, Alpine Club and Varsity Outdoor Club (VOC), for whom he regularly led trips and training courses for younger and less experienced members.

The passion he shared for life also came through in his publications. These extended beyond his own academic research, with a scientific review published in the *Journal of the Association of Surgeons of GB and Ireland* entitled *The Molecular Mysteries of the High Mountains*. Neil also made contributions to several blogs, co-authored expedition reports for the Eagle Ski Club Alaska expedition (2013) and British Columbia expedition (2011), as well as publishing articles in the Eagle Ski Club yearbook, VOC journal and on UKClimbing.com.

Throughout his youth, Neil enjoyed many adventures in the Highlands, where he forged numerous close friendships. He made many ascents of rock climbs up to E1 5b, such as *The Big Top*, as well as winter climbs up to IV,5 around the UK. In 2008, Neil enjoyed his first Alpine summer season with close friends Andy Main and Andrew Warren, with ascents of the *Chèré Couloir, Midi-Plan traverse, Cosmiques Arête* and *Parat Seigneur* in the Aiguilles Rouges. His next adventures abroad were ski-mountaineering trips in 2010, with ascents of Mount Sir William (3200m) in the Adamant Range of British Columbia, with Ian Button, and an ascent of Piz Calderas (3397m) in Switzerland with close family friends Lewis Luyken, Reiner Luyken and Andy Main. Neil went on to make ascents of the *Hohlaubgrat* on the Allalinhorn and the *Dri Hornli Ridge* with Andy Main, Mark Jarvie and Andrew Warren.

I first met Neil in Glen Coe in June 2011. It was immediately apparent that his easy-going nature combined brilliantly with a strong drive for mountaineering, for example on the west face of Aonach Dubh. Throughout our expedition to the Northern Coast range of Alaska, Neil proved highly dependable and prepared to carry loads at any hour in any weather conditions, but he was also vital in maintaining team morale throughout some seriously soul-sapping conditions. It is a testament to his strength of character, indefatigable enthusiasm and sense of humour that we had a great time despite two weeks of gales and near constant rainfall. He also taught me the valuable lesson of how to enjoy wild environments to the full even when conditions prevent any mountaineering from taking place.

In April 2012 Neil made a ski-mountaineering ascent of the Ebnefluh (3962m) in the Bernese Oberland with Andy Main and Dave Macfie. This was to be his last ascent in the European Alps before he moved to British Columbia, where he found his ultimate land of adventures and made even more good friends. His notable ascents included the north buttress of Colchuck Peak (Cascades), east ridge of Alpha (BC), the north-east spur of Mount Matier, Stonecrop Face (BC) and the Fisher Chimneys on Mount Shuskan (Cascades). In 2012, Neil joined the Eagle Ski Club expedition to the Central Chugach range in Alaska. An aborted ski-mountaineering ascent of Mount Marcus Barker resulted in him making the likely first ascent of a peak above the Matanuska Glacier on the return journey. This expedition culminated in the first ascent of the *Wreckage of Petit Pimousse* (D, 5.10+, A0) in the Northern Cascades with Yan Pennec and Jens Von-Schmidt.

Neil's natural ability to unite and inspire people in a variety of adventures despite adverse circumstances was unique. His gift for making unlikely adventures happen despite daunting logistical challenges is a rare quality. His untimely death has curtailed years of adventures. His contributions to organisations and literature will be highly treasured for years to come. Above all, Neil was an excellent companion and his infectious smile combined with endless enthusiasm endeared him to many with whom he became close friends. They will all sorely miss him.

Adrian Dye

Elliott Skierszkan writes: I lived with Neil for the last year and a half of his life. We were fellow academics, members of the University of British Columbia's Varsity Outdoor Club, frequent trip partners and close friends. I shall miss poring over maps and guidebooks with Neil, to cook up some new adventure plans for the upcoming weekend.

The Coast Ranges of British Columbia are known for their heavily glaciated summits and deep valleys. It was in this magnificent place that Neil Mackenzie, Elena Cernicka and Stephanie Grothe lost their lives in a tragic climbing accident while attempting to summit Joffre Peak via its aesthetic Central Couloir, which splits this imposing mountain's north-east face. The three climbers were relatively recent immigrants to Vancouver: Elena, from Slovakia, Stephanie from Germany and nearing the completion of her PhD in Physics at the University of British Columbia (UBC), and Neil having arrived from Scotland for a post-doctoral fellowship in molecular biology at UBC.

Neil was raised, along with his older sister Caroline, in the village of Flichity, Inverness-shire, by their parents Angus and Margaret. Early on, he learned to love the outdoors, scrambling around the crag behind the family home. He attended primary school in Flichity and then secondary school in Fettes College, Edinburgh, where he became well-liked by his classmates for his jolly and sociable nature. He loved a drink and a laugh and was noticed for how he prioritised life above all else, although his teachers worried about his lack of interest in writing and literature. While he did not read his first book until he was 16, he soon became a very keen reader and by 19 had read *War and Peace*. An equal interest in history and sciences eventually led him to pursue the latter during his undergraduate years at Glasgow University, although he was also always fond of discussing history and politics.

His years in Glasgow were influential, as his social network expanded and diversified. He was described as having selflessly introduced an incredible number of people to each other, and having been the catalyst for many friendships and marriages. In Glasgow, Neil became enamoured with climbing after he and a few mates took up the sport. His scrawny body and hairless chin eventually morphed into a stacked climber's body with a massive beard.

Neil's natural curiosity eventually led him to complete a PhD in transgenic technologies at the University of Edinburgh. During this time, his passion for the outdoors also flourished. Within a week of having obtained his driver's licence in his late 20s, he had acquired a long-wheelbase high-top Transit van which would become an iconic fixture among Scotland's mountaineering community as it was spotted at various trailheads throughout the Highlands.

After completing his PhD, Neil struggled with the decision to pursue an academic career, or to devote himself in full to his mountaineering passion. Discussions eventually led to him accepting a post-doctoral position researching the pathways of bone and soft tissue mineralisation, on the condition that he would have time to do a month-long mountaineering and ski-touring trip to the Canadian Rockies before starting.

His post-doctoral study ended up being tremendously successful, although Neil would have never bragged about it himself. He managed to publish an impressive 11 papers and won a number of awards, including a travelling fellowship to work at a bone lab in San Diego, as well as an invitation to speak at Hokkaido University in Japan. In 2014, he was awarded the John Haddad Young Investigator Award by the American Society for Bone and Mineral Research for his work on mineralisation in tissues. Of course, Neil always did his best to ensure that his work travels would be combined with some form of mountaineering!

A successful grant application to the Canadian Institute of Health Research brought Neil to the UBC Faculty of Medicine's Centre for Blood Research for a second post-doctoral research period. Neil was thrilled about being granted the opportunity to come to Canada once again to pursue his work, while exploring this country's endless mountains.

At UBC, Neil naturally gravitated towards the university's very active Varsity Outdoor Club (VOC), where he made many friends, including Stephanie Grothe. A soft-hearted but chiselled mountaineer, he happily embarked on trips with people of all skill levels, making them feel comfortable and patiently teaching them the ways of the hills. He volunteered on numerous instructional VOC trips, passing on the hard-earned skills he himself had learned mostly without the safety of an instructor or guide. On more challenging climbs, Neil always kept his cool and would selflessly volunteer to take the sharp end of the rope and scout a passage to safety.

While his thoughts were often consumed by the mountains, deeper inside what really counted were his friends and family, in particular those back home. He would diligently Skype with his parents in Scotland, and always loved to see his little niece and nephew, whom he cared about deeply. As much as he was happy with his life in Vancouver, he missed his mates back home dearly.

A life-loving, adventurous, and modest man with an incredibly large heart, part of his legacy is demonstrated by looking at the connections and friendships which were created in his wake: in his departing, people from all walks of life whom Neil had introduced came together and joined in mourning and in celebrating the life of this tremendous character. The community mourns the loss of a truly great man whose life was cut short, but who in his 31 years has left a deep impression that will never be forgotten.

Editor's Note: While Neil was an Aspirant Member of the Club at the time of his death, his mountaineering CV was subsequently submitted to the Membership Committee, and Neil was posthumously designated a Full Member of the Club in March 2015.

Richard Morgan 1929 - 2015

Richard grew up in Hertfordshire and Surrey. Following boarding school, he gained a scholarship to King's College, Cambridge, where he read classics then history. At university, he discovered his love for climbing, often visiting North Wales and the Peak District on a Triumph motorbike. To celebrate the Queen's coronation in 1953, he climbed the spire of King's College Chapel, planting a home-made Union Jack on the spire. The authorities were outraged; scaffolding was used to remove it.

Richard's working career began in accountancy. He also completed a law degree and had a spell in management consultancy before progressing through various jobs as finance director in companies of increasing size. He retired aged 62 after a brain haemorrhage, from which he made a near-complete recovery. Until his mid-30s, every spare weekend and holiday was spent rock or Alpine climbing. He was leading E1 in the early 1960s and took great pleasure in transferring these rock skills to bigger challenges in the Alps.

His Alpine career was extensive; he climbed major peaks from 1952 until 2004. Until I was born in 1967 he did not miss a single year of Alpine climbing. Major mountain routes in the 1950s and 1960s included the Zmutt Ridge on the Matterhorn, *Guggi* on the Jungfrau, the Schreckhorn-Lauteraarhorn traverse and Triglav's north face.

Perhaps his favourite style of climbing was multi-pitch Alpine rock, and the climb he talked of most fondly was the *Comici* on the Cime Grande. It must have been very exciting in 1963, with only a bowline round his waist. He described a fall at one point, held by a body belay; the overhang was such that he could barely make contact with the rock with the tip of his toe. Later, he persuaded my mother that this peak would make an ideal honeymoon trophy.

Richard's life was transformed when he met my mother. He chose to press 'pause' in his climbing career; for many years he devoted himself to her and to the tough job of bringing up two very demanding boys. Alpine holidays turned to beach holidays until we boys were big enough to have family camping trips in the UK, then later in the Alps. Richard and I started climbing rocks together at Windgather; I was only one year old and have no recollection of it but the picture with me in a backpack is in the family's album. He fell off only once, apparently, fortunately with no consequences for either of us.

Climbing with Dad was an apprenticeship of movement skills, classical ropework, route-finding and self-confidence. This was an extension of the era of 'the leader never falls' as Dad was not a big fan of overcomplicating things with baggage such as helmets, harnesses, belay plates and rock-protection generally. I remember us being shown round Mark Vallance's Wild Country factory in Eyam when I was 10. Mark proudly showed us brand new, state-of-the-art camming devices, which he called 'Friends'. Clearly, they revolutionised climbing safety but we did not appear to need them. Even aged 15 on big routes in North Wales, I was still leading in classic 1960s style with only a bowline round my waist.

When I was 11, in 1978, we experienced possibly our most epic adventure together in Chamonix, doing the Charmoz-Grépon traverse. We did it all in big boots; I have strong memories of classic abseiling from the summits using only the rope. He had a thing about getting all the way down to the valley after a route; staying an extra night in the hut was never on the agenda. I was pretty exhausted walking all the way down from Plan de l'Aiguille to Chamonix in the dark. Even then, Richard was keen to drive on to Geneva. He had seemingly unstoppable energy.

I remember a conversation we had before dawn on another occasion as we set off from the Promontoire Hut to do the traverse of the Meije. 'Dad, you know we're climbing with these big, orange Eveready torches in between our teeth? You see those French guys? They've got torches on their heads. Can we get some?' So we modernised with headtorches, harnesses, rock gear and even got some 'Friends'. In my 20s and 30s, with Richard now in his 70s, we continued to enjoy Alpine adventures, now in modern style, doing numerous classic but challenging routes. Among others, we climbed the Matterhorn, the Dent Blanche, the Miroir d'Argentine and the *Triftigrat* on the Breithorn. He remained fitter than most people half his age and I remember the surprise when a rather tired-looking British mountain guide bumped into Richard and me on the summit of the Chardonnet. He was even more surprised to discover Richard had done it under guidebook time.

Richard spent many happy trips in the Alps, ski touring with his friends and contemporaries, doing numerous week-long hut-to-hut tours with other AC members. I had the pleasure of joining Mike Esten and Richard, aged 77, on his last multi-day ski tour, in central Switzerland. This was a challenging itinerary including staying in unguarded huts. On the final day we navigated to a snowy col in a whiteout, jumping off the cornice onto the glacier below before the final ski descent. His last climb, on the week he turned 80, was one of the most famous and classic UK rock routes, *Devil's Slide,* on Lundy, which we did together with my son, Sam, who was 10. We went over for the day, an uncertain procedure as on the crossing it was raining hard. But the weather was kind in the end and we managed to do perhaps the first ever three-generation ascent of that route.

Throughout his life, Richard always took great pleasure in introducing others to climbing and the great outdoors. For the last 25 years, with more time in retirement, he took on the key role of treasurer of the Mount Everest Foundation, a position which, despite lots of work, gave him great pleasure. It allowed him to keep in touch with the mountaineering community and in the process, with his financial expertise, enabled the fund to expand hugely in value to continue to support expeditions every year.

He became a member of the Climbers' Club in 1952 and was treasurer for six years. He became a member of the Alpine Club in 1960, and held over many years a number of positions such as vice-president and chairman of the finance sub-committee. He enjoyed many happy Alpine Club meets in the summer and skiing trips with AC members in the winter. He made many lifelong friends from the Club.

Richard battled bravely with failing kidneys and dialysis for the last few years. Despite not following his own advice he told me that although he had had a great working life, he had worked too hard. I won't make the same mistake, and I hope I can embrace life with as much passion, dedication and generosity as he did. He was a great Dad, a great role model and will be missed by a great many people.

Jon Morgan

John D C Peacock
1931 - 2014

John Peacock died on 20 August, 2014, aged 83. He will be remembered as a keen and able mountaineer, a congenial expedition member and brilliant leader, a planner who could think two jumps ahead and a man with a twinkle in his eye. Almost to the end of his life he seemed to be blessed with a lucky star.

John's first experience of the hills took place on Lakeland holidays starting in 1945. It was love at first sight; in 1947 he did his first rock climbs, tied to a

John Peacock in sledging harness as leader of the Combined Services Expedition to North Peary Land 1969. *(Bruce Reid/Chris Shorrocks coll.)*

hemp rope and in borrowed clinker-nailed boots, in Birkness Combe above Buttermere, most notably *Mitre Buttress* and the *Oxford and Cambridge Route*.

His early years were spent in a Gloucestershire village where, influenced by a family friend who was deeply engaged in the development of naval radar, he became fascinated with electronics. In the immediate aftermath of the war his rural grammar school had neither physics nor maths teachers: John was allowed to transfer to Cheltenham Grammar School for his sixth form. At Cheltenham, his world rapidly expanded and he not only won a place at Cambridge but also was one of twenty-five schoolboys from the UK (nearly all from public schools) to be chosen by the South African Aid to Britain Fund to fly out to Nairobi in a DC3 Dakota and then spend three months travelling to Cape Town by Landrover and bus. The group sailed home on the Union Castle line's *Warwick Castle*, a ship reputed to be the only vessel that rolled in dry dock.

At that point, National Service called. John received his officer training at Eaton Hall before being commissioned into the Royal Electrical and Mechanical Engineers. He was posted to a base in Kent. As luck would have it, the area fell under the command of the youngest brigadier in the Army. For some reason he took a shine to this young subaltern and encouraged him to stay in the service. John, however, elected to go to Cambridge, in 1952, on full army pay and allowances and then went on to spend at least two years on electronic research with the General Electric Company. He returned to the Army as a captain after five years, having never worn uniform.

At Cambridge the CUMC was at one of its high points, awash with luminaries such as George Band, Roger Chorley, Geoff Sutton, Eric Langmuir and Bob Downes. They became lifelong friends and although John was never a driving leader, he was a participant in many fine ascents. I recall he was very pleased with climbing the east face of the Grépon and the complete traverse of the Meije. He also took to the river with his normal enthusiasm. Hardly of the stature of an oarsman, he filled the back seat admirably and coxed the Lady Margaret Boat Club 1st Boat (LMBC is the boat club of St John's College) to Head of the River in both the Lent and May races, as well as coxing the crew in the Ladies' Plate at Henley. He was elected to the Leander Club. Almost incidentally he was awarded his degree in Mechanical Sciences.

John loved telling jokes and seemed to have an infinite reserve, from the crude to the cultivated. On a British Association of Ski Instructors course, he insisted on each member producing a fresh joke every morning at breakfast. He also had a few party tricks: one of those was playing the spoons (two spoons back to back in one hand while rattling them over the fingers of the other). Years ago, in Glen Brittle, I asked Mrs Macdonald if she could remember my brother. A moment's thought and then in that lovely West Highland brogue, she said, 'Oh now, that will be the boy who gets the music from the spoons.'

In 1964, John was selected as a member of a Combined Services Expedition to South Georgia. The main aim was to retrace Shackleton's 1916 route from King Haakon Bay to Stromness. This was the first crossing since the original one and had to rely on Shackleton's own description and sketches. The report describes John as 'conscientious and enthusiastic'. In the latter half of the 1960s, John led three expeditions to Greenland. The first was to introduce some officer cadets at Sandhurst (where by now he was an instructor) to the delights of expeditioning. The second was with the Army Mountaineering Association to peaks in West Greenland and the third, which he led with Bruce Reid as his deputy, was a four month Joint Services expedition to Peary Land, the most northerly region of Greenland. Every member of that expedition recalls it with great pleasure: among the comments, he is remembered for having played the spoons in the northernmost land on the globe, and everyone mentions his superb leadership.

His efforts were recognised by the Royal Geographical Society with the presentation in 1971 of the Ness Award.

John Peacock was promoted to lieutenant-colonel at about that time. There were wry comments about his absence from his desk at the Ministry of Defence when he joined the party, led by Alan Blackshaw, which made the first British ski traverse of the Alps, a route of more than 500 miles from Kaprun in Austria to Gap in France. Meanwhile, he was recruited to the planning team for the 1976 Army Everest Expedition. The preparation for Everest involved preliminary expeditions to Himachal Pradesh and to Nuptse. It became apparent that John had problems at altitude and for this reason he became base camp manager on the Everest expedition. Despite health difficulties, he was proud to have reached c6700m in the Western Cwm and thrilled that Brummie Stokes and Bronco Lane gained the summit. It should be added that when Harold Wilson announced the British withdrawal from East of Suez a committee was formed at the MOD to consider the personnel repercussions of that policy. John became a member and pushed strongly for the development of Adventurous Training in all branches of the forces, a policy which continues to this day.

Everest seemed a good point to have a change of course (he was 45 by then) and one fair wind blew him towards sailing. Another blew Sheila Ralph in his direction. Sheila had been John Hunt's PA at the Duke of Edinburgh's Award office. She says she and John had had each other in their sights for years. At the time they were married, Sheila was an editor at Heinemann and overnight became the 'Colonel's wife' at Rheindahlen, a remarkable feat in anyone's book. She tells the tale of a visit to the dentist in Germany and discovered that she was down as, 'Colonel Peacock – wife of '!

Sailing was his next interest; he went about it with his customary thoroughness, helped by Sheila's background. While in Germany he raced and cruised in the Baltic and when posted back to the UK he became commodore of the Royal Electrical and Mechanical Engineers (REME) Yacht Club; they sailed round Brittany, Ireland, Spain and the Mediterranean. In 1992 he was mate on REME's yacht *Master Craftsman* on a voyage across the Atlantic from Canada in which he qualified as an RYA Yachtmaster, Ocean.

By now a full colonel, John's penultimate posting with the army was as Commandant of the Princess Marina College for REME apprentices. He brought discipline and enthusiasm and self-confidence into the lives of many young men who had never experienced such things before. He told me it was the most satisfying job he had in his army career and he was delighted when Prince Philip accepted his invitation to take the salute at one of his passing-out parades.

John retired early from the army and, after a brief period as a bursar of a public school, became Director of the RYA Seamanship Foundation, a charity providing sailing opportunities for blind and handicapped sailors. Here, he was once again in his element, working actively with young people and, often with the skilled help of Sheila, taking blind crews across the Channel. On his final retirement from the Seamanship Foundation, the Peacocks moved to the village of Lustleigh in Devon. There, they threw themselves into village life with John becoming chairman of the Lustleigh Society, a role involving hosting many memorable parties.

John was elected to the Alpine Club in 1966 and served two terms on the committee, 1974-6 and 1984-6. He was also a member of Library Council from 1992 to 1999.

Ten months before his death, John went into hospital for a knee replacement. A day later he suffered a stroke from which he never recovered. He knew he was dying and had no fear of that. We talked of the old days, of the high hills and our shared love of Arthur Ransome's books. John's favourite was *We Didn't Mean To Go To Sea* and, struggling to speak, he quoted the words on the title page: 'Grab a chance and you won't be sorry for a might-have-been.'

Nigel Peacock

John Cleare writes: John Peacock in *Last Blue Mountain*.

I've often regretted that, apart from once in 1970, our paths crossed only socially, never long enough for further adventures – unless one considers working together, in which case running the Alpine Ski Club from 1993-6 was one such. John served as the power behind my presidential throne and was the most able and efficient hon secretary for which any organisation could have wished.

But few know that John was also a film star. Early in 1970 the BBC decided to re-tell the 1957 Haramosh epic, *Last Blue Mountain*, as a film 'reconstruction'. The crew was to be minimal: a courageous BBC Producer/ Fixer, myself as Cameraman/Director, Colonel Tony Streather in person to ensure accuracy and boost morale, and two climbing ski-bums from ISM as porters. The treatment was to be silent but with commentary and sound effects. Tony procured three experienced Army alpinists to act the parts of Emery, Culbert and Jillott, while Glenmore Lodge loaned us Bill March, their leading ice-climber, to take the heroic part of the young Streather. John Peacock was to be Emery, the survivor, with Jon Fleming and Brian Martindale the two tragic casualties.

On an aerial reconnaissance we selected the Zermatt Breithorn and its north-west coire as the main location. It possessed all the necessary Haramosh features: a 'Cardinal's Hat', a corniced ridge, a steep ice wall and a snow basin, albeit in miniature and mirror image. Meanwhile a nest of séracs on the Plateau Rosa would suffice for shooting falls and close-ups. We had the Theodule Hut opened up for us from where, for over two weeks in early March, we skied to work before dawn every day.

It snowed and blew hard when necessary, so conditions were almost authentic, apart from nights in the freezing hut. John and Bill built us an igloo on location to store equipment. John's part required some serious acting. Filming is a frustrating business, especially in such conditions, and he was tireless, always practical, always jolly, always patient, and always ready to climb up the slope again for yet another take. Off-set, John was ever ready to do more than his share of work and I couldn't help thinking what a brilliant chap he'd be to expedition with... and so it proved, but never with me.

Bill Putnam

William Lowell (Bill) Putnam III 1924 - 2014

In 2002, the Alpine Club of Canada (ΛCC) proposed that William L Putnam be elected an honorary member of the International Mountaineering and Climbing Federation (UIAA). This motion was seconded by the German, Japanese and South African Alpine Clubs. Bill's election added to the many other honours bestowed on him by the world's climbing community. These included: honorary memberships of the Appalachian Mountain Club (1976), the Alpine Club of Canada (1989), the Association of Canadian Mountain Guides (1990) and the American Alpine Club (1993).

Bill Putnam was born in New England in 1924. While studying geology at Harvard University during World War Two, he volunteered for service in the US Armed Forces. He saw combat in Italy as an officer with the 85th Mountain Infantry (part of the 10th Mountain Division). Wounded in combat, he was awarded the Purple Heart, the Silver Star and the Bronze Star medals. During his service, he made the ascent of various Apennine peaks, and in his own words, 'was shot at, too!'

In 1942 Bill, travelling by train to the old Glacier Station at Rogers Pass along with members of the Harvard Mountaineering Club, made his first visit to the Selkirk Mountains in western Canada. The result of this trip was, for Bill, the beginning of a love for the Canadian mountains that would last a lifetime.

This passion (he would make more than 62 first ascents in the Selkirks) made him, in 1957, the natural choice as editor of the American Alpine Club's Canadian guidebooks. His experience of the Selkirks, the American Rockies and the Canadian Rockies was extended in 1950 to an expedition to Alaska, making several first ascents in the Juneau Icefield group.

His mountaineering career had begun much earlier, however, with an ascent in 1934 of the Marmolata with his father. As he declared at the time, 'I have never climbed with a guide, unless I was one.' He occasionally returned to the Alps, perforce when on war service, but also in 1950 for an ascent of the Grossglockner by the *Hoffmannsweg*, laconically described as 'a drag'.

In 1946, as President of the Harvard Mountaineering Club, Bill led the first American ascent of Mount St Elias (5489m) in the Yukon Territory. Unfortunately, Bill's war injuries (shrapnel damage to his lungs) prevented him from going higher than about 5000m. Consequently, his formidable energies were turned towards revising and editing James Monroe Thorington's *Guide to the Interior Ranges of British Columbia*, a task which saw three updates and revisions, the last being in 1971. In addition to editing guidebooks for the AAC, Bill also authored over 20 books on a variety of historical and scientific subjects.

He was elected to the American Alpine Club's Board of Directors in 1969 and served in various capacities for 30 years, including president from 1974 to 1976 and honorary president from 2010-14. Bill represented both the Canadian and American Alpine Clubs on the Council of the UIAA from 1974 until he was elected vice-president of the UIAA, in which capacity he served from 1992 until 1996. During his period in office he was responsible, in 1982, for drafting one of the most visible acts of the UIAA, the Declaration of Kathmandu, calling for vigorous measures to protect the flora and fauna of the alpine environment worldwide, long one of his principal preoccupations.

In his business life, Bill was a successful TV broadcaster and the originator of the broadcast editorial (he was later elected to the Broadcasters' Hall of Fame). He also served as the sole trustee of the Lowell Observatory in Flagstaff, Arizona, the largest private astronomical observatory in the world. During his tenure as sole trustee (1987-2013) Bill was responsible for developing and funding the $4.3m Discovery Channel Telescope.

In 1965, Bill became responsible for constructing the first hut at the Fairy Meadows, a Panabode cabin, foreshadowed by his having worked on the Refugio Corsi in Italy during the war. In 1973, one year after becoming a member of the Alpine Club, he was instrumental in the building of the current structure. In the autumn of 2002, the Alpine Club of Canada approved that the Fairy Meadow Hut be renamed the Bill Putnam (Fairy Meadows) Hut in recognition of Bill's contribution to both the Alpine Club of Canada and Canadian mountaineering.

Bill's wife Kitty died in January 2014, followed by his own death in December of the same year. He is survived by his three children, Kathleen, Lowell and Erica.   *Mike Mortimer*

Dennis Gray writes: I first met Bill in the autumn of 1974 at a UIAA Executive meeting. He was representing the American Alpine Club and I had been similarly appointed to that role by the BMC. We immediately hit it off, as we had similar views about standing up for 'The Freedom of the Hills'.

Bill was a big man physically, and a typical Yankee, forthright and at times impatient at the slow and tortuous ways of the world body of mountaineering. In 1974, the UIAA was dominated by the representatives of the 'old established' European alpine clubs, the Swiss, the German, Austrian and French. Their very hierarchical way of working often had Bill chafing at the bit.

For the next 15 years until my retirement from the BMC in 1989, I met Bill in many locations at the UIAA Executive and General Assemblies. On several occasions we made common cause over such UIAA developments as the need to make the organisation truly international, to do which needed a future policy review (chaired by an Alpine Club member, Robert Leopold, from the Netherlands), leading to a new constitution, as well as such innovations as reciprocal rights in members' alpine huts. We also worked on the Kathmandu Declaration, with its great emphasis on conservation, as well as the beefing up of the work of the specialist committees, and many others.

Bill was a larger than life character. He had close contact with the Canadian Alpine Club, and often represented that body at the UIAA. Socially, Bill was good to be with: my keenest memory of him was of a night in Mexico City while we were both attending a UIAA meeting. The official of the Mexican mountaineering organisation who was supposed to be organising the event had run away with the funds; the country's government had needed to step in to take over the organisation at the last moment.

Bill and I were sharing a room. A government official arrived on our first evening to show us around the city. But instead of taking us downtown to see the tourist sites such as the Mariachi bands or a Hili game, he bundled us into a taxi and headed for a distant suburb. Our first port of call was a huge broken-down dance-hall, full of over-made-up portly middle-aged ladies slowly gyrating to beat music. Our next destination was a seedy bar full of ladies of the night; finally we reached another hostelry where a gaggle of transvestites were for some reason keen to make friends with my Yankee companion. We waited until the government man went to the toilet and made a run for it. We had no idea where we were, but Bill collared a local with a car, and after loading him with greenbacks, persuaded him to drive us back to our hotel. As we were staying in the only Hilton in Mexico City, we found our way back despite our halting Spanish. The government worker must have believed that Americans were more interested in the low-life of his city rather than high culture. But once back in our hotel room, Putnam made me swear to keep quiet about our adventures that night, for it would look bad for him in waspish Springfield, Massachusatts (Bill's home city), if stories surfaced!

Bill was a dynamic, progressive individual who gave so much of his time and own money to support the sport he loved. He made friends easily and everywhere, from Nepal to South Korea and beyond. I am sure he will be widely missed and I am happy and proud to have known him as a good friend.

Stephanie Roberts (previously Allan Yeend) 1952 - 2015

Stephanie, and those who knew her as Allan, remember her as full of the sense of adventure, instilling confidence wherever she went, always with humility and unpretentiousness. Though determined, she would always work at the pace of the weakest, and ensure everyone was looked after. Anyone who climbed with her knew they could trust her not only to be safe, but to have good judgment, and work in partnership.

Stephanie was born in 1952 in Christchurch, Dorset, as Allan Yeend, and grew up there in modest circumstances. Allan's father died when he was about nine, and this left a lasting impression on him. He was highly intelligent and entirely self-educated, having left school at 16, with a remarkable memory and interest in history, nature, philosophy and of course the mountains.

Moving out of home with characteristic determination, he quietly sorted everything out in advance, and simply announced it to an astonished and protesting mum as he packed his bag. This approach revealed his trademarks: a kind modesty and calm confidence.

He would often joke about his GCSE in gardening, his 'highest' educational qualification. In fact he was an extremely skilled boatbuilder, not just in his craftsmanship of cabinet-maker standard but also through a strong understanding of design and engineering. There is not a single Sadler sailing boat which does not bear some of his handiwork. When Sadler's closed, Allan carried on working in the industry at Sunseekers. On becoming Stephanie after her gender change in 2005, this work was continued after a brief period of trying out other occupations, including nursing the elderly.

Joining the Wessex Mountaineering Club in 1974, Allan quickly became respected as a very competent and safe climber and one of the club's best all-round mountaineers. By then he was already a regular at Swanage, making forays into the intimidating Boulder Ruckle. Nigel Coe found him playing frisbee at the castle with Richard Crewe and Dave Kyle; regular climbing partnerships were formed with Tim Dunsby, Steve and Pat Portnoi, Robin Wilson, John and Alan Walmsley and many others.

He would proudly show his new routes – in the sea! The fun of Swanage is a continuous supply of new routes, as the previous day's route would often have disintegrated. Always up to something, Allan recruited an unusual climbing partner – Sooty – in one of the Swanage quarries during filming of the TV series.

Not only into the hills, Allan was a top grade whitewater canoeist. He helped all his friends build canoes: these are still being used 35 years later.

On my only foray canoeing out to sea with Allan, we 'bumped' into a basking shark in Poole Bay. He remained totally calm, as if this was an everyday occurrence, but stayed between me and the big shark. He had a knack of finding the spectacular anywhere.

Every weekend saw Allan and the rest of us off to all parts of the UK to get to the crags. The driving took place at speed, with precision overtaking and micrometre clearance in the lanes of Cornwall. Superb at everything he did, his driving was exemplary even if at times on the far side of the law. Once, the police pulled him over, presumably expecting to fail his faded purple Cortina for some or other roadworthiness defect. After half an hour of inspection the police failed to find anything wrong, and with infallible aplomb Allan thanked them for this 'free MOT'. So the trusted Cortina with Allan at the wheel carried us all into the hills for many more years.

When the weather caved in, so did Allan. Many autumns were spent underground, crawling and grappling in South Wales, the Mendips, Peak and Yorkshire. Duck-diving through the sumps in Swildon's Hole tempted him fully into cave diving, and some pretty bold wreck diving as well. He cave dived with the likes of Rob Palmer. Perhaps the mountaineer in Allan kept him alive, unlike so many of his cave diver buddies. He did what every SCUBA diver dreams of, bringing up a ship's bell, this one from the *Waitara* off the south coast.

Allan Yeend on Fletschorn – Lagginhorn traverse, Saas Fee, 1988. *(John Walmsley)*

I met him in 1981, when I joined the Wessex MC. The Club had just bought a hut in Betws y Coed. Every fortnight we were up at the hut, rebuilding, carrying up materials. Allan built alpine-style bunk beds (which most of us had never even seen); we carried them up like meccano pieces, for assembly at the hut. They are still there 33 years later, yet another testament to Allan's skill and quality of workmanship. We would take a break from the hut and do a climb or go up a mountain. The sack was always ready to go on the hill, including the 'emergency rations' that had been in there since 1975, as old as the sack.

Rapidly, Allan became my partner and my climbing partner. When not in North Wales at the hut, we were climbing or caving in some other corner of Britain. We climbed the railway arches in Dorset before climbing walls were invented; we spent evenings after work at Swanage or on the Agglestone Rock. The Wessex was an active and vibrant club, and there was a core which built up into a happy climbing fraternity largely due to Allan's enthusiasm.

At times we practised sea-cliff rescue. Allan managed a rescue for real, when Paul Wallace, one of the Wessex elders, fell off, broke his hip and tumbled into a turbulent sea while soloing at Cattle Troughs. Allan thought things through, checked that a harness would not aggravate the injury, instructed us in how to make a rope stretcher, and supervised the haul to the top of the cliff as well as the subsequent smooth carry towards the ambulance. Paul recovered to carry on climbing.

Every summer meant a trip or two to the Alps. An embarrassing epic on what was to be a short training route, the Leiterspitzen, saw us benighted. A sudden thunderstorm swept over us. We were on a ridge near the summit, and with almost nowhere to hide. I kept the wet rope snaked and curled so it looked a bit less like a lightning conductor. Just by the summit Allan found a steep, seemingly bottomless gully off the ridge which looked far from ideal, but it did have a small ledge with an overhang above it, which kept some of the rain off. Allan had struck gold again: we sat on our ledge watching the pre-lightning strike up the gully before meeting the down stroke, mesmerized by this spectacular show within feet of us, while actually feeling quite safe. Having made the summit, the weather turned worse and, after descending for hours, snow and darkness forced us to bivvy. When the mist cleared next morning we were 50 metres above a road. Years later, I discovered books and files that Allan had studied, with comprehensive notes about the nature of thunderstorms in the mountains. This thoroughness in being prepared, learning and understanding everything in detail, was the case in whatever enterprise he took on, and kept him and the rest of us safe and alive on many occasions.

As Allan, his application for Full Member to the Alpine Club was accepted in 2000, and was active on UK and Alpine meets. She rejoined as Stephanie, her passion for the mountains still alive, becoming a Full Member in 2011. She had climbed most of the 4000m peaks in the Alps, but no-one would have known this, and wasn't anything she counted herself. Her achievements were about the adventures she shared with her friends.

As Stephanie she also realised another ambition, and developed her interest in Egyptology into a programme of study and research, for which she received a degree. She published two books, one revealing the real origins of Tahemaa, the mummy at the Bournemouth Natural Science Society. Her research took her and her partner Tony to Egypt many times. On one occasion they spied a forbidden entrance at a pyramid, and when the coast was clear Tony slid Indiana Jones style down the chute, with Stephanie close on his heels. They found rooms full of mummies standing around, looking surprised at these new visitors. Of course they were in big trouble, but got away with a fine and an incredible adventure.

The diagnosis of cancer was a hard one to accept. In the mountains she would figure out the geology to plan a safe escape route; when canoeing, she would know how the sea moved to avoid being crushed against rocks.

Though she said she did not want to go like this, the mountains and seas would never have claimed her. She was in harmony with the natural environment, her apparently uncanny judgment actually based on painstaking diligence and learning, and the ability to use a lifetime of experience. No wonder 'Allan was good to have in an emergency'.

Toto Gronlund

Les Swindin 1938 2015

Les Swindin. *(Barbara Swindin)*

Les Swindin was born in the London area, but at the outbreak of the Second World War went to West Yorkshire with his mother, whose family lived in Pudsey. His formative years were much influenced by his father, a professional footballer who had been goalkeeper for Arsenal Football Club in the 1930s and continued his career with Arsenal after spending the war years in the Army. When Les was 16, he and his parents moved to Peterborough, where he immediately started work in a chemical laboratory and studied part-time at the local technical college, graduating in 1963 with an external degree from the University of London.

During his time in Peterborough, Les played football and cricket as an amateur, and took an avid interest in jazz and folk music. Sport remained of great importance to Les throughout his life, although once he discovered mountaineering, around the time of his graduation, he became mainly a spectator. In 1965, having discovered it was not too late to train as a teacher, Les studied in Huddersfield for a PGCE in technical education. From 1966 until he retired 30 years later, he was a chemistry lecturer at Gloucester Technical College.

It was during his first year there that I met Les. We had separately joined the Gloucestershire Mountaineering Club within a month of each other. Our friendship and love of the mountains led us to marry in 1969, and over the next three decades we continued mountain climbing together on most weekends and for a large part of our lengthy college holidays. Les had a naturally athletic physique which was ideal for fast walking and fell-running. In his 40s, he took up orienteering, eventually winning national championships. With mountaineering friends, he ran in many fell races and mountain marathons, the Lowe Alpine Mountain Marathon probably being his favourite. At the age of 60, Les successfully completed the Joss Naylor Lakeland Challenge in 14 hours 30 minutes.

Les was introduced to climbing on the Isle of Skye in 1963 and returned there over and over again, traversing the Cuillin Ridge on several occasions, including the Greater Traverse and even the 'Greater Greater Traverse', encompassing not only Clach Glas and Blaven, but also the crossing of the Dubhs Ridge and back down to Glen Brittle in one continuous outing. Les also climbed all the Munros, saving the last few to do with me in 2000, thus ensuring that we 'compleated' together. Despite him being able to walk probably twice as fast as me, he patiently waited at intervals so that I could be with him on all the summits.

As a rock climber, Les was a traditionalist. He loved climbing on mountain crags all over the UK, especially in Snowdonia and the Lake District. It was always satisfying to climb with Les, as he instinctively knew how to climb swiftly and competently up the routes he chose. We never queued in those days, and I rarely spent too long at a belay point wondering when it would be my turn to follow. He encouraged me (and others) to climb up to (though within) our limits, while he himself often climbed more serious and more technical routes with other friends of similar ability to his own. The social life of the mountaineering world was always a joy to Les; he had a good sense of humour. Above all, he loved to chat about his climbing experiences, share his knowledge and encourage others.

These aspects of his personality were all the more apparent in his career as an alpinist. His first climbing holiday in the Alps was based at Zermatt, in 1965. There, as a complete novice, he climbed the Rimpfischhorn, Zinalrothorn and Matterhorn. In 1970, he introduced me to Alpine climbing, and from then on we climbed together in France, Italy and Switzerland for 25 years until I had to quit because of ill health. Climbing all the 4000m peaks was one achievement, but he rarely climbed to an Alpine summit simply in order to tick it off a list. Mostly, he chose particular routes for their apparent merits and sometimes climbed the same peak by two or more different ridges or, occasionally, faces. He was a natural leader and always climbed guideless. From 1980 onwards, he and I teamed up on many occasions with the late Pete Fleming. It was with Pete that Les climbed the Aiguille Blanche de Peuterey when, despite a sunny forecast, their outing turned into a three-day epic with 15cm of snowfall and many hours of constant thunder and lightning as they sat in an emergency bivouac on the south-east summit. It is testament to their skills that they escaped unharmed.

The number of Alpine routes that Les enjoyed is too large to count, but they all feature in the Alpine Club guidebooks that he edited. During his later visits to the Alps, active climbing was gradually replaced by many serious long walks and scrambles in order to take photographs to illustrate these guides. Les was determined to give other alpinists the best chance of finding the routes described.

In addition to summer climbing, Les also led approximately 20 ski tours in the Alps from the south-east of France to Austria. I accompanied him on half of these. Our friends and I all benefitted from his understanding of snow conditions and ability to find a safe way through complicated terrain, whatever the weather threw at us. Probably the greatest ski tour of all was for him, as well as for me, our traverse in 1981 through the Bernese Oberland from the Grimsel Pass to Stechelberg near Lauterbrunnen, accompanied by Alpine Club member Jay Turner and two other friends. In perfect weather, we stayed high for 10 days.

Sadly, Les's last decade was marred by the onset of Parkinson's Disease; his activities were prematurely curtailed despite his efforts to keep as fit as possible. Even at the end he could still walk faster than me, albeit only for a short distance. Les will be greatly missed by all his many friends, and especially by me. He was my loyal and loving husband as well as my climbing partner and 'unofficial mountain guide'.

Barbara Swindin

Lindsay Griffin writes: I'm not sure when I first met Les, though it would have been before the mid-1980s, when we first started working together on Alpine Club guidebooks. It may even have been in the early 1970s, when I first met Barbara, although I actually was not aware of that meeting until relatively recently, when I read her book. I was a young whippersnapper, camped in Chamonix, and like most other climbers there had no command of French at all, which meant that whatever information we could get on weather forecasts in those days – and it was little – we couldn't understand anyway. Similarly, the available guidebooks in English were often rudimentary in their descriptions. Then word began to spread through the encampment that Snell Sports, the main climbing shop in Chamonix, to where a lot of the British drifted on wet days, was employing an English girl who spoke fluent French. So Barbara became the centre of attention for a lot of British climbers, trying to find out what the weather really would be doing in three days' time.

In 1985, Les completed all the 4000m peaks on Robin Collomb's list, a lot of these with Barbara, who as we know eventually completed all but one. A year or so later, the Alpine Club decided to prepare a completely new series of guidebooks to the major European Alpine regions. These were to contain a wide selection of routes, across the grades, to cater for all abilities, the innovation being that they would be published by the Alpine Club itself. It was entirely appropriate that Les, who had been a member of the Club since 1979, spearheaded this initiative by taking on the important role of general editor: he continued in this office for the next 20 years. It was a time-consuming and often thankless job, yet one to which his determined approach and vast wealth of Alpine experience made him ideally suited. The first of these guides, in 1987, was John Brailsford's *Ecrins Massif*, closely followed by Ron James's single volume guide to the Dolomites. In the end, Les was responsible for the production of all Alpine Club guides from the mid-1980s onwards. He convinced a traditional club of the need for clear topo-diagrams, good photo-diagrams, moving to colour, and so on. And when he was unable to find or cajole authors into writing on a particular area, he simply wrote them himself. I know he really enjoyed producing two editions of the *Bernese Oberland and Valais Alps East*, the latter with his long-time climbing partner, Peter Fleming.

Most of these guides were written at a time where there was really no other viable English language alternative. That now has all changed, thanks to the vast increase in small European publishing firms which have realised that to be commercially successful with a diverse international mountaineering community, they had to include some sort of English version. In the middle of the last decade the AC realized it simply did not have the resources or drive to compete. Many of the guides, notably two that I wrote with considerable help from Les, *The Mont Blanc Massif* and the *The Bregaglia*, are seriously out of date, but in areas such as the Valais and Bernese Oberland where, despite climatic change, fashions have not much altered, those guides are still genuinely useful for the budding Alpinist.

This was an interesting era in the shaping of British Alpine climbing; these guidebooks determined the routes that were followed. Les made a significant contribution to this, and for that he gets my personal thanks, as well as a large thank you from the Alpine Club, in bringing its name to the fore not only in the UK but also throughout Europe.

I never got to climb with Les but I well remember walking as a foursome into a remote Welsh crag to tackle a couple of ice routes. We struggled to keep up on the approach and eventually gave up as he disappeared into the distance; we only met again back at the car, where he and his partner seemed to have been waiting for several hours. And that is how I'd like to remember him: super-fit, enthusiastic, and with that little smile at the end of the day suggesting that we relative youngsters still needed to put in a bit more work.

John Tyson. *(Tyson archive)*

John Tyson MC
1928 - 2014

John Baird Tyson was born in Partick, Scotland, and brought up in London, where his father was Surmaster (deputy head-master) of St Paul's School. He acquired a passion for climbing during family holidays in Scotland, France and Switzerland.

I first met John when, as a schoolboy, I spent a month at the Outward Bound Mountain School in Eskdale, where John was an instructor and Eric Shipton was Warden. It was evident even from this first contact that he was a very determined character who, once he had decided on a course of action, would see it through to the end in an almost obsessive way.

In his National Service during the Malayan Emergency, he won the Military Cross for leading his platoon with great determination against a group of guerillas, who were eliminated. While not unique, such medals were few and far between.

After demobilisation, John went to read Geography at Magdalen College, Oxford, and in 1952 led the first-ever Oxford University Scientific Expedition to the Himalaya. In addition to work on several high-altitude projects in the Tehri-Garhwal region, the team made first ascents of Gangotri I and Gangotri III, both above 6500m.

In the Alps, he had done such routes as the *Marinelli Couloir*, the Zmutt Ridge and the *Younggrat*. As a housemaster at Rugby School, over several seasons he introduced boys to guideless climbing in the Swiss and French Alps. His enthusiasm over the years led to many worthwhile routes being completed, many along the Haute Route.

In 1953, he and Bill Murray had made an exploratory journey to the Api and Nampa region in the far north-west of Nepal where they made the first ascent of several peaks in the 5500m-6000m range.

Around this time, he bought a house in Eskdale. There, he and his wife Phebe offered renowned hospitality to visiting mountaineers and other friends.

Then, in 1961, began John's obsession with Kanjiroba (6880m). This massif in west Nepal had become his blank on the map. Over the next nine years, he led expeditions through very rough country but, in spite of sustained efforts, he never reached the summit.

In 1964, I joined him in west Nepal. After a wonderful few weeks of surveying and climbing several peaks of around 5500m-6000m, we forced a route along the Langu Khola, the gorge of the Langu river, but turned off too early to get to the peak of Kanjiroba – no GPS at that time. The 1969 expedition learned from this and reached the mountain, but dangerous snow conditions precluded a successful attempt. John's final visit took place in 1998 when he had great pleasure in being reunited with Sherpas from the 1964 and 1969 expeditions. Kanjiroba had become 'John Tyson's mountain' to the extent that, when it was eventually climbed by a Japanese team, its leader sent a telegram to John to apologise; 'with your permission, we have climbed your mountain.' John was said to have been delighted.

Meanwhile, he was offered the headship of a school to be funded by the British government in Nepal, but political differences between the British and Indian governments prevented this coming to fruition immediately. Instead, he was appointed headmaster of another British-funded school in Bhutan, where he spent three years before being invited by the Nepalese government to run its school in Budhanilkantha, where he spent six happy years. Perhaps it was having done the Zmutt Ridge and *Younggrat* from a base in Zermatt but, in his later years, year after year, he returned to Zermatt to be among and to look at the mountains of his youth.

He is survived by his wife Phebe Pope, and their daughter and two sons.

John Cole

Alpine Club Notes

The Matterhorn from the slopes of the Unter Gabelhorn. Arthur Cust. 1881.
Watercolour. 34 x 53cm. *(Private Collection)*

Early Drawings of the Matterhorn

The early history of depicting the Matterhorn was described by Charles
Gos in 1923,[1] and more recently in a series of publications by Anton
Gattlen. The best known of these was his collaboration with Laura and
Giorgio Aliprandi[2] in 1978, followed by a comprehensive two-volume
survey of published prints in 1987,[3] and an abridged version from 1999[4]
concentrating on Zermatt. Readers whose interest is pricked by the Matterhorn pictures used at the front of each section in this year's AJ should find
more to stimulate them in these publications. They deal mostly with the
north side of the Alps. There was a comprehensive survey of early depic-

1. Gos, Charles, *Le cervin par l'image*. Editions Spes, Lausanne, 1923
2. Gattlen, Anton & Aliprandi, Laura e Giorgio. *Il Cervino e le sue stampe*. Collana, 1978. [German version: *Das Matterhorn im Bild*. Rotten-Verlag, Brig, 1979]
3. Gattlen, Anton, *Druckgrafische Ortsansichten des Wallis* 1548-1850. Rotten-Verlag, Brig, 1987 and *Druckgrafische Ortsansichten des Wallis* 1850-1899. Martigny, editions gravures, 1987. [French versions: *L'estampe topographique du Valais*, etc.]
4. Gattlen, Anton. *Zermatt – Druckgraphisches ansichten*. Rotten-Verlag, Visp, 1999

tions of the Aosta valley side of the Alps by Ada Peyrot, published in 1972,[5] but it contains few Matterhorn drawings.

Aside from some rather unconvincing drawings on old maps, no attempt to draw the Matterhorn was made until the visit of Marc-Theodore Bourrit in 1803. Bourrit is well known for illustrations of early books about Mont Blanc and Chamonix, particularly in collaboration with H B de Saussure. However, Gattlen dismissed Bourrit's effort: 'In his picture, the Matterhorn is seen as a not particularly distinct part of a mountain range, drawn from the Italian side of the Theodulpass.' [Gattlen, p16, author's translation] So the first clearly recognizable drawings of the Matterhorn are two rather impressive watercolours by Hans Conrad Escher von der Linth in 1806 – one of the Zermatt side on 14 August and – after a presumed crossing of the Theodul Pass – one of the Valtournanche side on 16 August. Escher had a most productive life as politician, engineer, scientist and artist.[6]

Escher's drawings might be thought remarkable for their faithful record of the mountain's topography: the east and north faces and enclosing ridges are very accurately drawn. However, in general, late eighteenth century drawing was faithful to topography; artists made their living by accurately rendering portraits of the faces and grand houses of the rich men that employed them, and these habits persisted when they turned to recording other subjects. It might also be thought remarkable that we had to wait until 1806 to see a decent drawing of the Matterhorn, but the Visp valley was inaccessible then, and Switzerland was enduring a period of exceptional political turmoil.

It wasn't until 1820 that the startling appearance of the Matterhorn became widely known. This was largely due to Johann-Jakob Meyer, who published an engraving of the northern side in the *Helvetischer Almanach* and various other publications. The Club has a faithful later copy of one of these by Johann-Jakob Sperli. Meyer's engraving and the badly faded watercolour on which it is based may be seen at www.jjmeyer.ch. Other engravings appeared in the 1820s and 1830s, notably a fine one by Johann Heinrich Meyer in 1829.[7]

The first artist from French Switzerland to draw the Matterhorn was perhaps the Genevan Alexandre Calame. His excellent drawing *Le Mont Servin*, appeared in a vanishingly rare book of lithographs in 1841.[8] I was unable to obtain a usable image of this. At this time James D Forbes also produced a drawing from the Riffelberg, 'Plate VII' in his *Travels through the Alps of Savoy* (1843). He described the Matterhorn as 'the most striking natural object I have seen, an inaccessible obelisk of rock.'

After the establishment of the Swiss Confederation in 1848, tourism flourished, and numerous attractive little books, illustrated with coloured lithographs, were published. Foreign artists took note, and came to

5. Peyrot, Ada, *La Valle d'Aosta nei Secoli*. Tipografia Torinese Editrice, 1972
6. Brandenberger, René, *Hans Conrad Escher von der Linth: die ersten panoramen der Alpen*. Baeschlin, 2002
7. Sauvan. Jean-Baptiste-Balthazar, Le Rhône. *Description historique et pittoresque de son cours depuis sa source jusqu'à la mer*. Various publishers, 1829
8. Calame, Alexandre, *Douze vues du Mont-Rose et la vallée de la Viège*. Lithographs printed by Schmid. Wessel, 1841

Zermatt, which grew rapidly from a mere scatter of houses to a village with hotels. John Ruskin came in August 1849, and made sketches of the north side on which the wonderful engravings in his *Modern Painters*[9] and some beautiful watercolours were based. Ruskin's diary recorded two days 'spent daguerrotyping'.[10] Charles Gos (p32) rather meanly suggested that these primitive photographs explained Ruskin's 'impeccable profiles', but one might consider Ruskin's superb draughtsmanship responsible. Another English artist who visited in the period before the first ascent was Edward William Cooke. Cooke's drawings were used to produce a splendid engraving for his friend John Tyndall.[11] The French artist Gabriel Loppé made several visits to Zermatt, producing some later pictures which rendered the mountain faithfully, but his early efforts drew it as a dagger of rock and ice piercing the skies[12] – certainly a valid and effective treatment.

Following the first ascent, the Matterhorn was drawn by too many artists to mention here, but splendid examples by Elijah Walton, George Barnard, John Singer Sargent, Edward Theodore Compton and Arthur Cust are presented at the start of later *Journal* sections.

Robin Campbell

9 . Ruskin, John, *Modern Painters: Volume 4, Part 5: Of Mountain Beauty*. Smith, Elder & Co. 1856
10. See Evans, Joan & Whitehouse, J II, *The diaries of John Ruskin 1848-1873*. Clarendon Press, Oxford, 1958
11. Tyndall, John, *Mountaineering in 1861: A vacation tour*. Longman Green, 1862
12. For example, a coloured lithograph published by Becherat of Geneva which was tipped into various tourist picture-books of the 1850s. I have seen it only in *Souvenirs de la Suisse et des Alpes* in the National Library of Scotland. This is given a guessed date of 1863, but 1850s seems more likely.

Robin Collomb: An Appreciation

Robin Collomb, who died in January at the age of 84, was an *eminence grise* in the mountain world, his West Col publishing imprint better known than his name. Although his lengthy alpine record more than qualified him for AC membership, he preferred to avoid any conflict of interest by remaining close to the Club, though never actually of it.

Son of a French engineer with Rolls Royce, in his teens Robin spent a year with an aunt in Nice, joined the Club Alpin Français and started to climb methodically throughout the Alps. After national service in the RAF – during which he claimed to have worn a uniform only rarely – he worked for the now long defunct Mountaineering Association, in summer as deputy chief instructor in the Alps (Hamish MacInnes and Ian Clough were among the temporary instructors) and in winter back in London producing *Mountain Craft*, the MA magazine. (This eventually metamorphosed into *Mountain* under the YHA.) Robin became a stalwart member of the London Mountaineering Club, itself originally an offshoot of the MA.

Jobs in printing and publishing allowed Robin to develop his expertise in the field and evening classes at St Martins (now Central St Martins) honed his artistic skills; throughout his life Robin produced bold paintings and delicate line drawings of mountains for both pleasure and business. Meanwhile, he was busy collecting and filing useful information from the journals of the continental Alpine clubs and other relevant sources, eventually enabling him to build a very successful business around this mine of information. His first book – *A Dictionary of Mountaineering* – was published in 1957 by Blackie.

One day in 1964 I received a letter from the editorial director at Secker & Warburg – one Robin Collomb – inviting me to lunch. His name rang a bell, wasn't he an alpine instructor with the Mountaineering Association? The upshot was the commission for my first book, *Rock Climbers in Action in Snowdonia*. My old school chum Tony Smythe added the text and the book was published in 1966, the first of an innovative series that Robin had planned covering British and Alpine climbing regions. While making the acquaintance, through the book, of several of the young, leading-edge climbers of the day, he noted the talents of the mercurial computer man Pete Crew.

In 1966 Robin joined Pergamon Press, recently acquired by Robert Maxwell MP, the later-notorious publishing tycoon, and moved to Maxwell's Oxford headquarters. Among the exciting new projects he initiated under Pergamon's auspices was a glossy, international mountain magazine. Remaining a well-kept secret, a team of high-powered regular contributors was recruited, Chris Brasher among them and, after an interesting lunch with Maxwell, Pete Crew was appointed as editor. My own task was to be art director and picture editor and an attractive advertiser's dummy was produced. Then, quite abruptly, Robin resigned his post. 'I want out before the CID move in,' he told me. 'The whole edifice is crooked.' Maxwell's subsequent career is well known, though it took many years for his fraud to be finally confirmed.

And so West Col was born. Initially a short-lived partnership with a Pergamon journalist named West, West Col handled all sorts of specialist and unusual publishing and printing assignments, but its forte was mountaineering guidebooks, for which there was an obvious gap in the market. Keeping overheads to a minimum, Robin worked from home in Goring-on-Thames where typesetting was done by a local girl using a then state of the art IBM golf-ball electric typewriter. Pete Crew was set up as guidebooks general editor, while specialists in each mountain area, in Britain, the Alps and elsewhere, were commissioned to assemble the contents. Meanwhile Robin personally wrote or compiled several useful reference volumes, an annotated list of all Alpine peaks for instance, besides many of his *Guide-Collomb* mountain-walking guides to extra-Alpine ranges. As catalyst-with-contacts, he was able to commission and place with mainstream publishers, books written by various mountain authors, including biographies of Joe Brown and Don Whillans. Meanwhile he ran the publishing programmes of the AC, the Scottish Mountaineering Trust and others, besides several important business clients in the City.

Another string to Robin's bow was maps. A subsidiary venture, Alpina Technica Services, specialised in graphic design and illustration and imported relevant Alpine maps via friends in Switzerland, undercutting

Robin Collomb in action on the pinnacle of *Pinnacle Ridge* (V.Diff.), Braich Ty Du, Carneddau, March 1965. *(John Cleare/Mountain Camera Picture Library)*

the over-priced official London importers. He continued with authorised reprints of rare or unobtainable maps of other mountain areas such as the Atlas and in due course commissioned definitive climbers' maps of Mount Kenya and Kilimanjaro.

Naturally Robin continued to climb himself, often visiting an area for which a guidebook was in preparation where he would check out the regular routes and the current valley facilities in person. Unfortunately in 1969 he was struck down by severe rheumatoid arthritis which blunted his climbing but never his ferocious appetite for work, and I recall him holding court, semi-crippled, in the Maloja campsite for the season, while pointing several powerful parties at the important routes and the obvious virgin lines in the Bernina and East Bergell massifs, with gratifying results. In later years, in remission of sorts but still in pain, Robin was active abroad, frequently with his wife Pam – an AC member in her own right – or various other companions, in the Picos, the Atlas, the Rockies, East Africa and elsewhere, inevitably resulting in yet more useful publications.

A family man with three daughters, Robin was highly regarded by both friends and business associates. He was a kindly, generous chap and good company, typically expounding his encyclopaedic knowledge of his subject while smoking a cigar or black cheroot before adding pointed comments laced with his usual dry humour. But despite his valuable input to the mountaineering world, some who knew Robin only by repute considered him controversial. Who was Collomb to pontificate about the Alps? A friend once jested that he'd climbed the *voie normale* on every significant alpine summit. While obviously an overstatement, when taken together with his comprehensive filing system, it qualified Robin to speak with considerable authority. How dare he make money from guidebooks! Surely the clubs should produce these at cost? But they didn't. And only recently have they got round to paying expenses and even small fees. The fact is that after West Col swung into action, guides to almost every Alpine area appeared, guides which would otherwise never have been published, and many delightful areas would have remained *terra incognita* to climbers from Britain and abroad. We owe Robin Collomb a considerable debt.

John Cleare

Kekoo Naoroji Award

The Kekoo Naoroji Book Award was founded by the Naoroji family in memory of Kekoo Naoroji, past president and great supporter of the Himalayan Club. Each year the award is given to an outstanding book on a Himalayan subject from entries received. In 2014, Tony Smythe won the prize for his outstanding memoir *My Father, Frank*. Tony Smythe writes: 'The Kekoo Naoroji Himalayan Literature Award ceremony followed Lindsay Griffin's lecture, *Escape from Mongolia*. I was called to the platform and Rishad Naoroji presented me with a certificate and a superb, lavishly produced volume of Himalayan photos taken by his illustrious climbing and environmentalist father Kekoo. This was accompanied by the presentation by the honorary treasurer, Divyesh Muni, of a freestanding metal shield inscribed with the HC logo.

'After my words of appreciation I then gave a talk with slides on *My Father, Frank*, the book and the man, rounding this off with a showing of the 1983 version of the BBC's TV production of the 1931 Kamet expedition film, with its professional commentary, perhaps more watchable than the somewhat hilarious BBC version of 1965. This is an opportunity for me to record my thanks to my hosts, and particularly organiser Rajesh Gadgil, for their great kindness, generosity and efficiency during my trip to India.'

Tony Smythe receives his Kekoo Naoroji Himalayan Literature Award from Rishad Naoroji and Divyesh Muni at the Himalayan Club.

Lines of Ascent: William Heaton Cooper

A certain generation of us grew up with William Heaton Cooper's guide-book crag drawings of the Lakes in the little brown Fell and Rock guidebook series originally edited by Harry Kelly. The latest exhibition in the archive gallery of William's Grasmere Studio, now the family business selling the work of four generations of artists, does much more than simply display his original crag drawings. It evokes a whole Lakeland climbing culture of the era before the Second World War when these guidebooks were initiated and reaches into the present with original drawings by the current Fell and Rock crag draftsman, Al Phizacklea, who opened the exhibition. Certainly William's large sketchbook drawings are at the centre of the show, with their amazing economy of line and simple repertoire of cross-hatching. But photographs, crag paintings, equipment, sketchbooks, letters and notes provide an insight into not only William's commitment to this guidebook job, but his unfailing passion for his life's work – catching the shifting spirit of specific mountains at specific moments in all the media and modes avail-able. So as well as his famous watercolours, there is a Cubist vision of Kirk-fell from 1930, an oil portrait of Gimmer, a 1938 linocut in three colours of 'Gimmer Crag and Bowfell' and, from an Alpine sketchbook of 1955, two drawings of people crammed into the interior of the old Couvercle Hut followed by a pencil sketch of the Grandes Jorasses.

William Heaton Cooper started illustrating Fell and Rock guidebooks in 1935 and continued for the next 50 years. The pages of Harry Kelly's diary for 3-6 June 1933 reveal that the first meeting of the guidebook committee included 'AT and AB Hargreaves, HC, self and Speaker, Pollitt and Doughty'. They were hands on. From Manchester Kelly drove for the meeting at Thornythwaite and on the Sunday they drove to Honister summit, walked to Pillar for *Hadrian's Wall* and *Nor' Nor' West Climb* before descending to Ennerdale for tea: 'Left 9.10pm. Honister 10.15pm'.

So William knew these crags intimately, upwards and downwards with his hands and his feet. In a 1938 note William wrote, 'Many a man grows old with a picture in his mind of summer evenings on the Pinnacle. Everyone has gone home for dinner, the crag that has been in shadow all day wakes up and comes to fresh life as the sun sets ablaze all the significant detail of the sound grey rock face that stretches in a clean sweep.' A 1936 pencil sketch of Pillar Rock's west face indicates volumes of mass for a later painting, rather than for guidebook purposes. It seems that his famous Esk Buttress watercolour with the golden shaft of light beside it – William did regard this as a religious painting – derived from a moment when he took his sketchbook and pencil out of his climbing sack 'to remind me of the design'.

Of course, William's son, AC member Julian Cooper, was inevitably tempted into the guidebook sketching business. His drawing of Beinn Eighe for the SMC Northern Highlands Area 1972 guidebook is on display, as is, by way of contrast, his 'Eiger Face' of 2005. This huge painting on two panels allows the sky only small triangles at the top corners as the full majesty of the crag, if one can call it that, literally falls in paint as the light catches odd bits of snow. The famous ice fields are ominously dark and integrated into the shadowed face. The presence of climbing history is part of the spirit of the crag that Julian has evoked here in an extension of his father's work.

Many people would want to pay tribute to the warm memory of using William's guidebook drawings to read Lakeland crags, but few could command so much authority as Gwen Moffat, now over 90 years old, who has contributed a personal statement to this exhibition: 'I still have those guides: over 60 years old, water-worn, mud-stained, dog-eared and annotated, and still consulted.' She says that William was 'a man who understood the soul of rock [...] something between a realist and an impressionist.' But almost hidden in the richness of documentation in this exhibition is a statement from John Hunt. Lining Crag, the evening sun-catcher above Eagle Crag, Borrowdale, was one of William's favourites, on which he made a new route, *Evening Wall*, with his loyal climbing partner, Jim Cameron. In August 1939 John Hunt climbed here with William before going off to war, taking with him in his kitbag William's book, *The Hills of Lakeland*. This is, perhaps, the most moving tribute of all.

Terry Gifford

Lines of Ascent, The Heaton Cooper Studio, Grasmere, November 2014 – Spring 2015

Monte Viso, also known as Monviso. *(Adele Long)*

The First Female Ascent of the Stone King

Dominating the Italian Cottian Alps, Monte Viso or Monviso (Occitan: *Vísol*; Piedmontese: *Brich Monviso* or *Viso*) stands higher than all its neighbouring peaks by about 500m. From its summit, on a fine day, a spectacular 360-degree panorama of the Alps unfolds, a view that inspired the title of Will McLewin's book *In Monte Viso's Horizon*; the mountain itself can be seen from many miles away. At 3841m Monviso is not the highest mountain in the Alps, neither is it the hardest, nor the most dramatic, but arguably it is one of the most majestic, fully deserving of its name *Il Re di Pietra* – the Stone King. Not many mountains can boast the same level of love and loyalty from the population over which it stands so regally. As Paulo Allemano, Mayor of Saluzzo, said of Monviso, it is 'a mountain that speaks to the soul and characterizes our lives.'

The first recorded ascent of Monviso was on 30 August 1861 by William Mathews, British mountaineer and a founding member of the Alpine Club accompanied by his friend Frederick Jacomb, a French lawyer, the Irish naturalist and politician John Ball, first president of the Club, and guides Jean-Baptiste and Michel Croz. The second ascent, done the following year between 3 and 4 July 1862, was by Francis Fox Tuckett, also a British mountaineer and former Alpine Club vice-president. The party on this occasion included the first Italian climber, Bartholomew Peyrotte, a mountain guide, and guides Peter and Michel Croz. This group were the first to camp for a night on the summit of Monviso.

L-r: Rya Tibawi, Caroline Phelan, Amanda Graham and Adele Long on the summit of Monviso. *(Adele Long)*

The first wholly Italian expedition to the summit was that of government minister Quintino Sella in 1863. The expedition was supposed to be guided by Bartholomew Peyrotte, already familiar with the route, but apparently he gave up. The climbers, who included the Piedmont noblemen Paolo e Giacinto Ballada of Saint-Robert and congressman Giovanni Barracco from Calabria, were accompanied by three local mountain guides: Raimondo Gertoux, Giuseppe Boudin and Giovan Battista Abbà. The event was a clever political propaganda drafted by Sella aimed at celebrating, through the 'heterogeneity' of the expedition, the recently achieved unification of Italy in 1861. In the wake of the enthusiasm that had accompanied the success of the climb, Sella went on to found the Italian Alpine Club in Turin.

Official records report the first female ascent of Monviso as that by Isabella Straton, born in 1838 in Sussex, southern England and Emmeline Lewis Lloyd of Wales. Emmeline is purported to have introduced Isabella to climbing, and in 1871 the pair climbed Monviso in the company of the guide Jean Charlet. Isabella had inherited all the family wealth at an early age and was thus able to pursue an independent life, which she chose to spend in the mountains. She married Jean Charlet, but was always known in the climbing circles as 'the Lady'. Both Emmeline and Isabella climbed for many years and made significant contributions to women's mountaineering. However, around 10 years ago, the diaries of a local woman, Alessandra Boarelli (née Re, 1838-1899) of Verzuolo, came to light. It emerged that Alessandra had had her eye on Monviso some six years prior to Emmeline and Isabella. Her quest for the summit commenced in 1863, when she made her first attempt, putting a camp in at passo Forcioline. Her guide was none other than Peyrotte, who decided, on that occasion, that the weather was too bad to continue. Fortunately her persistence paid off the following year, 1864, on 16 August; the 26-year-old Alessandra successfully summitted Monviso in the company of the 14-year-old daughter of the notary of Casteldelfino, Cecilia Fillia. The achievement was recorded in local newspapers. A plaque to commemorate these achievements has been erected in the open-air theatre in Casteldelfino. Alessandra was born in Turin and married the nobleman Emilio Boarelli in 1856; they had three children, daughters Isabella and Luisa and a son, Clemente. She is buried in the family chapel in the cemetery in Verzuolo. Little is known about Cecilia Fillia (1850-1937), who was unmarried.

In the words of Paula Bonavia, president of the CAI Saluzzo: 'Alessandra Boarelli was a 26-year- old... athletic and sporty, [and her achievements] should be remembered because she challenged the conventions of the time, going against the grain.' In the same spirit, on 1 September 2014, a group of four women from the Alpine Club and Climbers' Club set off, at the invitation of the CAI Saluzzo and the Piedmont tourist board, to celebrate the occasion of the 150th anniversary of Alessandra and Cecilia's ascent. After some acclimatisation, based at Rifugio Vallanta, taking in Punte Gastaldi (3210m) and Monte Losetta (3054m), the team crossed the passo Giacoletti (Grade II) to the Rifugio Quintino Sella. The following day they made the ascent of Monviso via the *voie normale*, in the company of Paolo Allemano, Dave Wynne-Jones and guide Sandro Paschetto; ice and snow conditions made it somewhat harder than the 'F' given in the guidebook.

*Ad Alessandra Boarelli
e Cecilia Fillia
nei 150 anni dalla prima
salita femminile al Monviso*

16 agosto 2014
Il Comune di Casteldelfino

At the summit they signed the special book to record the female ascents. Unfortunately the awful weather in the Alps that year had rendered Monviso unclimbable for many weeks and their summit successes were recorded as numbers 81 to 84, a long way short of the 1000 women the Italians hoped to get to the summit on that anniversary year. Nonetheless, the Italians appreciated the team's presence, exhibiting their famous hospitality and generosity.

Adele Long and Livio Perotti

Team: Adele Long, Amanda Graham, Caroline Phelan and Rya Tibawi. A film by Dave Wynne-Jones is available on vimeo.

ALPINE CLUB LIBRARY ANNUAL REPORT 2014

The year started with the accent on conservation work – particularly for books. Jerry Lovatt, our Hon Librarian, gained a grant from the British Mountaineering Council towards the re-binding of 20 of our historic mountain books from the nineteenth century; we augmented the fund with sales of surplus second-hand books. Work went ahead with expert help from Cyril Titus, a book restorer with many years of experience with the British

One of 20 hand-coloured aquatint plates in *Views in the Himala Mountains* by James Baillie Fraser, a large folio book published in 1820 and expertly rebound in 2014. *(Barbara Grigor-Taylor)*

Library. The elegant new bindings are a tribute to those members who helped build the book collection we have today. Other conservation work progressed with the high-resolution scanning of prints from the early photo albums in our collections, as part of our long-term digitisation project.

In the summer, the Library did some actual mountaineering. In 1864, AC members Frank Fox Tuckett and Reggie Macdonald attempted the first ascent of the Barre des Écrins (4102m) but time and weather caused the summit to elude them. Several days later, Edward Whymper, Horace Walker, Alphonse W Moore, and guides Michel Croz and Christian Almers Senior and Junior, succeeded. The commune of Valouise decided to hold a 150-year celebration climb and to open a small permanent alpinism exhibition in Ailefroide. The Library supplied two historic photos to the museum and we were invited to join some French climbers to repeat the climb. Sue Hare, who manages Library photo sales, myself, and three other AC members joined 70 climbers, including guides dressed as Whymper, Croz and the Almers, in the Refuge des Écrins. The weather began well and, after a pre-dawn start, the whole party gained the lower summit, that of the Dôme des

John Fairley and Sue Hare admiring newly re-bound book plates. *(Hywel Lloyd)*

The final ridge of the celebration climb of the Barre des Écrins, 150 years after the first ascent. *(Hywel Lloyd)*

Écrins (4015m). Then the weather closed in, but some climbers went on to the main summit. Celebrations continued that evening in Valouise and we presented the mayor with a photograph of Frank Tuckett, who has a local hut named after him.

The next invitation received by the library was to provide an exhibition, *The Treasures of the Alpine Club*, to run for around 10 months as part of the 2015 Chamonix celebrations of the Golden Age of Alpinism (broadly 1854 to 1865).

We negotiated a scheme to provide books, archives, artefacts, photos and paintings – around 200 items in all – for this, a process undertaken by Jerry, Glyn Hughes (Hon Archivist), Barbara Grigor-Taylor (Library Trustee), Peter Rowland (Hon Keeper of the Photographs) and John Fairley (Hon Keeper of the Pictures). Some items would be unique original artefacts, archives or paintings; other items would be images scanned from our collections of archival letters, photographic glass plates, and album photos. Fortunately, we now have a capable digitisation team in action in the photo library.

Clearly, everything would be insured, but we have to make extra provision for any possible loss of unique items. Our strategy is to scan or photograph every item with an image file size of at least 50 megapixels, thus

Messers Whymper and Croz seen
on the Barre des Écrins, July
2014. *(Hywel Lloyd)*

preserving a high-resolution image for posterity. Peter Rowland, Bernie Ingrams and Peter Payne have undertaken this task. John Fairley divided the paintings into two lots: one for summer exhibits and one for winter. This reduced the risk of total loss and reduced the exposure of watercolours to excessive light, which can fade these paintings.

At the time of writing, work is in progress to value every item and arrange high-security packing, transport and insurance for the moves to and from Chamonix. The exhibition was scheduled to run in the Musèe Alpin in the centre of Chamonix from late June 2015 through until after Easter 2016. When the collection returns to the AC, it will be exhibited in London and then in local shows in a number of places around the UK.

Finally, I know that all members will appreciate that these achievements have only been possible because of lots of difficult and time-consuming work by the experts on the library team. Our thanks are due to each one of them. The Chamonix Exhibition next year will be the library's tribute to the alpinists of the Golden Age.

Hywel Lloyd

Contributors

CHI-YOUNG AHN has had several attempts and successes on first ascents and new routes in the Himalaya. Ahn won the Asian Piolet d'Or for his pure alpine style ascent on Himjung in 2012, and again in 2014 for his Gasherbrum V first ascent. He guides, instructs and freelances on the side and has begun to get into backcountry skiing.

MALCOLM BASS has always been fascinated by exploration. At first he focused on caving and cave diving, but his head was turned by a winter trip to Ben Nevis and since then he has been absorbed by the process of trying to climb new routes in Scotland, Alaska, Pakistan, India and China. He and Paul Figg were nominated for a *Piolet d'Or* for their ascent of the west face of Vasuki Parbat in 2010.

PETER BLAIR was born in Scotland, is at home in Chamonix, and is an associate member of the Alpine Club, spending his free time enjoying the mountains on foot and on ski. A PhD graduate in chemical physics from Edinburgh University, he has always been fascinated by the science and magic of photography. He has written two books on stereoscopy – *Chamonix Mont Blanc in 3D* and *William England – a collector's catalogue*. For further information contact him at peter3dblair@gmail.com

ROGER BIRNSTINGL took his first Alpine holiday in 1946 with his family, staying at the Hotel Weisshorn in the val d'Annivier. There has been virtually no year since when he has not been somewhere in mountains of five continents. Likely the only AC member who earned his living as a bassoonist, he has played in orchestras ranging from the Chicago Symphony to the London Symphony. He left the latter to go to l'Orchestre de la Suisse Romande in Geneva, ideally placed to improve his rock climbing on the home crags of the Salève and climb the most famous 4000m peaks.

KESTER BROWN is the managing editor/designer of publications for the New Zealand Alpine Club. He produces the club's quarterly magazine *The Climber* and the annual *NZ Alpine Journal*. He is a rock climber and mountaineer of many years' standing and lives at Taylors Mistake Beach, NZ.

DEREK BUCKLE is a retired medicinal chemist now acting part-time as a consultant to the pharmaceutical industry. With plenty of free time he spends much of this rock climbing, ski touring and mountaineering in various parts of the world. Despite climbing, his greatest challenges are finding time to accompany his wife on more traditional holidays and the filling of his passport with exotic and expensive visas.

ROBIN CAMPBELL has held every office in the Scottish Mountaineering Club for which administrative competence is not required, including a long stint as editor in the 1960s and 1970s, and as archivist since 1997. Retired from a desultory career as an academic child psychologist, he now wastes his time and money collecting and studying old drawings and watercolours, particularly those depicting mountains before they were trampled into familiarity by the boots of mountaineers.

GEORGE CAVE works for much of the year as a design engineer in Warwick. In search of more adventurous peaks he developed in interest in planning expeditions abroad, particularly to central Asia. In recent years he has climbed or skied in Kyrgyzstan, Iran, Morocco and Russia, using his background in engineering and technology to take advantage of the latest digital mapping tools when planning ascents of unclimbed peaks.

JOHN CLEARE has been a freelance professional photographer for over 50 years but a climber for rather longer. Business and many expeditions have taken him all over the world, while he has several dozen books, several films and live TV broadcasts, more than a few new routes and several virgin summits to his credit. An ex-vice president of the AC and an ex-president of the Alpine Ski Club, he lives in remote Wiltshire.

MICK CONEFREY is a film-maker and writer, specialising in exploration and mountaineering. He is the author of *The Adventurer's Handbook*, *Everest 1953* and a forthcoming history of K2. His documentary, *The Ghosts of K2*, won several international awards.

ADRIAN DYE has recently retired from secondary school geography teaching after five years and is currently studying for an MSc in Polar and Alpine Change between mountaineering adventures. The adventures include mountaineering, and rock and winter climbing in the Alps and UK, Lofoten Islands and the Picos de Europa. He previously led an expedition to the coastal range of Alaska and took part in an expedition to the Cordillera Apolobamba of Bolivia.

EVELIO ECHEVARRIÁ is a professor of international literature, now retired, and has been an AC member since 1959. His mountaineering record includes many obscure peaks in South and North America. He specialises in the history and chronicling of Andean mountain ascents.

PETER FOSTER retired three years ago as a hospital physician and is researching the life of T Graham Brown. He has been a member of the Alpine Club since 1975.

MICK FOWLER works for Her Majesty's Revenue and Customs and, by way of contrast, likes to inject as much memorable adventure and excitement into his climbing ventures. He has climbed extensively in the UK and has regularly led expeditions to the greater ranges for more than 27 years. He has written two books, *Vertical Pleasure* (1995) and *On Thin Ice* (2005). Mick served as president of the Alpine Club from 2010-13.

RAJESH GADGIL is honorary editor of the *Himalayan Journal*. An avid explorer, he enjoys the barren landscapes of East Karakoram, Ladakh and Spiti. For more than three decades, he has been wandering the Himalaya and has many first ascents to his credit. Climbing new routes on the rock spires of the Western Ghats in his native land is his first love, though it has taken a back seat to his increased involvement with the Journal and family business.

DENNIS DILLON GRAY started climbing on Yorkshire gritstone in 1947. Secretary of the ACG, first national officer, then general secretary of the BMC, Dennis has visited over 60 countries and, following early retirement, enjoyed several trips to the Himalaya. More recently Dennis has travelled widely in China and undertaken three research projects, two involving spells in Xinjiang. He has written two autobiographies, two books of stories, a novel and a volume of poems, plays the banjolele and sings on three CDs of climbing themed songs.

LINDSAY GRIFFIN lives in North Wales, from where he continues to report on the developments in world mountaineering. An enthusiastic mind still tries to coax a less than enthusiastic body up pleasant bits of rock and ice, both at home and abroad. He is currently serving as AC President.

MARTIN HOOD After studying Japanese in Japan twice during the 1980s, Martin was sent to Tokyo in 1989 by a British bank. On the strength of one Alpine season, he quickly became involved in alpine climbing, *sawa-nobori* (river-gorge climbing) and ski mountaineering. Although he climbed a few of the *Hyakumeizan* – Makihata-yama in Niigata Prefecture was a favourite – his great interest in the book followed his return to Switzerland in 1995. Since then, he's returned to Japan to meet the author's son and climb a few more of those one hundred.

GLYN HUGHES is a some-time Hon Secretary of the Alpine Club, but now carries out the equally important roles of Hon Archivist and barman (or as the AC quaintly puts it, 'Chairman of the Wine Committee'). In 2014 he took on the near-impossible task of following Bill Ruthven as Hon Secretary of the Mount Everest Foundation.

SUSAN JENSEN grew up in Anchorage, Alaska, and started climbing some time shortly after the millennium while living in Surrey. Now in Scotland, she has a day job doing statistics for NHS Scotland and also works with the Scottish Mountaineering Trust Publications on the climbers' guides. These and the *Alpine Journal* are fitted in around summer and winter climbing, expeditions, sleep and cakes.

PETER JENSEN-CHOI is an American-Korean living in South Korea with his family. Peter is an associate editor for the *Korean Alpine Newsletter*, a Korean Alpine Club Technical Committee member and on their International Overseas Committee. He has a rock and ice guiding and instruction service and has climbed with Chi-young Ahn on a few Himalayan ascents.

CARADOC 'CRAG' JONES has recently returned from another of Julian Atwood's failed Marxist re-education programmes in the wilds of western Nepal, resuming manoeuvres as an adventurous house-husband. In between polishing surfaces he tries to: climb, convince his kids there's more to life than the climbing wall, convince his wife with ever more implausible reasons not to work, and chair the South Georgia Expeditions Advisory Panel on behalf of its government.

GARETH JONES was Professor, Cambridge Clinical School, UK. He has published *The Hypoxia Hilton*, which describes attempting to induce pulmonary oedema by acute exposure to altitude. Also *Aviat Space Environ Med* 2008; **79**:81 – 6; and *T Graham Brown, Behind the Scenes at the Cardiff Physiology Institute and The Brenva Feud.*

PAUL KNOTT started climbing in the UK, where he developed a passion for remote exploratory expeditions. Since 1990, he has climbed new routes in the St Elias and Fairweather ranges, in the Tien Shan and other mountains of Central Asia and Russia, and on desert alpine rock in Oman and Morocco. He now lives in Christchurch, New Zealand, where he has a busy life as a school academic, but still makes ample use of the nearby climbing, hill running, and skiing.

CATHERINE MOOREHEAD recently retired from being Mistress of Scholars at the Royal Grammar School, Guildford. She became a 'Compleat Munroist' in 1996, and has led expeditions to the Mongolian Altai, Kazakhstan, Zanskar, Xinjiang, Tibet and Bhutan. In 2013, she published *The K2 Man*, the biography of Godwin-Austen.

ANINDYA 'RAJA' MUKHERJEE works as a mountaineering expedition guide and trek leader in the Indian Himalaya. In the past decade or so he has participated in or led more than 35 expeditions, including climbing Nanda Devi East. He has also climbed and trekked in Tanzania, Greenland, Iceland, the Caucasus and the European Alps, and bicycled from the equator to tropic of Capricorn in Africa. Above all, his passion lies in exploring the lesser known valleys, glaciers and mountains of the Indian Himalaya.

TAMOTSU NAKAMURA has been climbing new routes in the greater ranges since his first successes in the Cordillera Blanca of Peru in 1961. He has lived in Pakistan, Mexico, New Zealand and Hong Kong and has made more than 30 trips exploring the 'Alps of Tibet'. In 2010 he retired as editor of the *Japanese Alpine News* but continues as contributing editor. He received the RGS Busk Medal in 2008 and more recently the Japan Sports Prize.

BERNARD NEWMAN started climbing the day England won the World Cup, so you'd think he'd be better at it by now. He joined the Leeds University Union Climbing Club in 1968 when Mike Mortimer was president, and was closely associated with that exceptional group of rock climbers and super-alpinists which included Syrett, MacIntyre, Baxter-Jones, Porter and Hall, without any of their talent rubbing off. One-time geologist, editor of *Mountain*, *Climber*, and Hon Editor of the *Alpine Journal*, Bernard is still a 'freelance' writer, editor and photographer.

BRUCE NORMAND is a professor of theoretical physics at Renmin University of China in Beijing, where his day job is research on electronic and magnetic materials. In the alpine world, he can normally be found putting up technical new routes on the world's least-known high mountains, his tally now extending to over 40 first ascents and new routes on 6000m peaks in Nepal, Pakistan, India and China. In 2007 he also climbed K2, making him the only Scotsman to have done so. Some of his ascents in China have gained recognition for their technical difficulty as well as their boldness and exploratory nature, leading to a *Piolet d'Or* in 2010 and a second nomination in 2011.

ALLAN PENTECOST is an honorary research fellow at the Freshwater Biological Association at Windermere. He has a particular interest in the plants that grow upon mountain rocks.

SIMON PIERSE is an artist and art historian with a special interest in Himalayan mountain art and its history. He is author of *Kangchenjunga: Imaging a Himalayan mountain* and in 2005 curated an exhibition of paintings and photographs of Kangchenjunga to mark the fiftieth anniversary of the first ascents. Simon is senior lecturer at Aberystwyth University, an artist associate of the Alpine Club and a member of the Royal Watercolour Society.

SIMON RICHARDSON is a petroleum engineer based in Aberdeen. Experience gained in the Alps, Andes, Patagonia, Canada, the Himalaya, Caucasus, Alaska and the Yukon is put to good use most winter weekends whilst exploring and climbing in the Scottish Highlands.

BJØRN RIIS-JOHANNESSEN is retired and lives in Geneva. He is a keen ski touring enthusiast and alpinist, pursuits he partakes in with the Alpine Club and as tour leader in the Swiss Alpine Club. He has participated in three expeditions to the Antarctic, lately to South Georgia and the Antarctic Peninsula as organiser and assistant expedition leader.

C A RUSSELL, who formerly worked with a City bank, devotes much of his time to mountaineering and related activities. He has climbed in many regions of the Alps, in the Pyrenees, East Africa, North America and the Himalaya.

VICTOR SAUNDERS was born in Lossiemouth and grew up in Peninsular Malaysia. He began climbing in the Alps in 1978 and has since climbed in the Andes, Antarctica, Papua, Rockies, Caucasus and across the Himalaya and Karakoram. Formerly a London-based architect, he is now an IFMGA guide based in Chamonix. His first book, *Elusive Summits*, won the Boardman Tasker Prize. In 2007 he received an honorary MA from the University of Stirling for services to Scottish mountaineering.

MARCELO SCANU is an Argentine climber who lives in Buenos Aires. He specialises in ascending virgin mountains and volcanoes in the Central Andes. His articles and photographs about alpinism, trekking, and mountain history, archaeology and ecology appear in prominent magazines in Europe and America. When not climbing, he works for a workers' union.

BOB SHEPTON was fortunate enough to find the cliffs of Lulworth and Portland unclimbed in the 1960s and '70s and set about steadily developing them. In latter years he has led Tilman-type expeditions to the west coast of Greenland and arctic Canada, sailing and climbing new routes from his boat, culminating in the 'Big Walls' expedition awarded a *Piolet d'Or* in 2011.

IAN SMITH is a librarian, now employed at Birkbeck College, University of London. He has written articles on Whymper, and was responsible for an edition of Whymper's first diary, *The Apprenticeship of a Mountaineer* (London Record Society, 2008). He is the author of a biography of Whymper, *Shadow of the Matterhorn* (Carreg, 2011) and has been climbing in the Alps for 35 years, repeating many of Whymper's first ascents, including the Matterhorn. He has also climbed in South America, Canada, Jordan, Ladakh and Kyrgyzstan. He is a member of the Alpine Club.

KAREN STOCKHAM cut her outdoor teeth in the Yorkshire Dales and Lake District in the 1980s and liked nothing better than getting wet and dirty in the caves and potholes of the limestone dales. As an adventurous walker she walks and scrambles in the French Alps, Scotland and the north of England and is currently combining her research interests in English Literature and mountaineering by reading the diaries of Dorothy Pilley.

JOHN TOWN is a retired university registrar and, until recently, AC Honorary Secretary. He has climbed in the Alps, Caucasus, Altai, Andes, Turkey and Kamchatka and explored little-known mountain areas of Mongolia, Yunnan, Xinjiang and Tibet. He is old enough to remember the days before satellite phones and GPS.

KOEN VAN LOOCKE After finishing his studies in history at the University of Ghent in 2012, he worked as a ski instructor in Switzerland before returning to Belgium after six months to work as a history teacher. While at university he wrote two masters dissertations on the history of mountaineering and is currently waiting to start a PhD at the University of Leuven about participation in mountaineering in Europe. In his spare time he tries to be outdoors as much as possible, cycling or climbing, or mountaineering and skiing in the holidays.

IAN WALL worked at Plas-y-Brenin in the 1960s. Since then Ian has climbed extensively throughout the UK, the Alps and in Norway. He was involved with the first round of the Kendal Mountain Film Festival in 1980. He has led treks in Africa, Ladakh, Tibet and Nepal, where he now lives and acts as an advisor to the Kathmandu International Mountain Film Festival, Kathmandu Environmental Education Project and in developing and training the Nepal Mountain Leader programme working closely with the Nepal Mountaineering Association.

ALEKSEY ZHOLOBENKO is an Anglo-Russian biochemist working in the sleepy Czech town of Olomouc. When he is not engrossed in tormenting microscopic life-forms and students, he enjoys steep, snowy places of all shapes and sizes.

Index 2015

A

Abbey, Ashok 324
Abraham, George 162
Aconcagua (6959m) 286
Adams, Neil 305
Adams, Rob 327
Addis, Pete 416
Adelaide Peak 347
Aguja El Marinero 341
Aguja El Topo 342
Ahn, Chi-Young 3
Aiguille d'Argentière 168, 291
Aiguille de Talèfre 296, 298
Aiguille du Midi 298, 299
Aiguilles Rouges 153, 155, 422
Aiguille Verte 161, 163, 405
Ailefroide Occidentale (3954m) 299
Akoguz 48
Alaska 91, 95, 100, 350, 421, 422, 432
Alchemy of Action (The), review 373
Alex MacIntyre and the birth of light and fast alpinism, review 365
Allardyce Range 135, 140
Alldred, Cath 352
Almaraz, Guillermo 338, 339
Almond, Dave 299
Alonso, Juan Bautista 339
Alphubel 284
Alpine Climbing Group 271
Alpine Club Library Annual Report 454
Alzamora, Lucas 343
Ama Dablam (6812m) 332, 334
Amuchástegui, Lucas 339
Andes (The) – A Guide for Climbers, review 394
Anderegg, Melchior 194, 274
Anderson, Dave 322
Anderson, Vince 389
Andron, Cosmin 327
Angelo, Philippe 297
Angharad-Campbell, Ailsa 351
Anghileri, Marco 293
Anidesha Chuli (6900m) 354
Annapurna 264, 337, 365, 366, 368, 369, 403, 408, 417
An Riabhachan 309

An Teallach 309
Anticime delle Quatro Matte 295
Aonach Beag 307
Aonach Mor 304
Aoraki Mount Cook 345, 349
Argentière Glacier 152, 391
Argentina (area notes) 338; 352
Armytage, J C 159
Arniko Chuli (6039m) 332
Arnold, René 293
Arosio, Tito 295
Arunachal Pradesh (area notes) 323
Astill, Tony 187
Ata-Ullah, Mohammed 263
Atkinson, Ralph 401
Avenas, Antoine 299

B

Baboso (6078m) 339
Baffin 113, 115, 116, 123, 124, 402
Bailey, Dan 309
Baillie, Rusty 177, 179
Baillot, Erik 305
Ballard, Tom 300
Ball, John 451
Ball, Keith 309
Banff Mountain Book Festival 370
Barnard, George 255
Barnard, Michael 308
Barre des Écrins (4102m) 162, 168, 286, 454, 455, 456
Barrier Peak 345
Barron, Olivia 345
Bass, Malcolm 10, 307, 317, 353, 457
Batura Mustagh 356
Batura VI 356
Baud, Christopher 295
Bauer, Paul 77, 79
Baumgartner, Anton (Toni) 347
Baxter-Jones, Roger 368
Beanland, Alf 407
Beard, Eric 182
Becca di Guin 294
Beinn Bhan 305
Beinn Eighe 304, 305, 450
Beinn Liath Mhor 309

Bell, Tom 55, 56
Belton, Alexis 347
Beltrami, Alessandro 371
Ben Hope 308, 309
Ben Nevis 304, 305, 307, 309, 457
Ben Ohau Range 349
Bergin, Jack 90
Berg, Peter 245
Bernese Oberland 273, 274, 408, 422, 439, 440
Bernina 448
Berry, Mike 345
Besso, Vittorio 173
Bhutan 74, 76, 90, 381, 421, 441
Biafo glacier 264
Biener, Franz 167
Biggar, John 338, 394
Birnstingl, Roger 168, 457
Bishkek 47, 55, 56, 57, 359, 360
Bishop, Lady Una 402
Bishop, Sir George 402
Bisson, Auguste-Rosalie 231
Blair, Peter 227, 390, 457
Blakeney, TS 267, 272
Blanchard, Barry 395
Blatto, Marco 295
Blondin, Charles 229
Blum, Arlene 365
Boarelli, Alessandra 452
Bobonng (6152m) 74
Bohin, Sébastien 297
Bonatti, Walter 250, 258, 397
Bonavia, Paula 453
Boner, Martin 90
Bonington, Chris 247, 250, 252, 292, 365, 408
Bonino, Enrico 297
Bonniot, Max 299, 312
Boskoff, Christine 317
Bossons Glacier 391
Boswell, Greg 301, 302, 303, 304
Bouillanne, Brice 295
Boysen, Martin 371
Bracey, Jon 299, 352
Bradley, Garrett 317, 321
Bradshaw, Erik 347
Brady glacier 98

Brasher, Chris 181, 184, 446
Braun, Adolph 231
Bray, Lillian 198
Breashears, David 335
Bregaglia 295, 440
Brett, John 239
Breveglieri, Luca 297
Brewster, David 228
British Mountaineering Council 250, 350
British Women's Patriotic League 193
Briton, Douglas 329
Broadhead, Dave 38, 354
Broad Peak 376
Brocklebank, Tom 267, 272
Broome, Edward 284
Brown, Andy 353
Brown, Joe 446
Brown, Kester 345, 457
Brown, T Graham 248, 266
Bryniarski, Rob 305
Buchanan, Mike 345, 347
Buckle, Derek 32, 35, 37, 38, 328, 354, 395, 457
Buhl, Herman 265
Bullock, Nick 301
Burke, Mick 371
Burma 323, 361
Burnag Kangri (6821m) 310, 315, 357
Burner, François 299
Burns, Steve 19
Burro (5269m) 103
Buscaini, Gino 147
Busk, Douglas 267

C
Cairn Gorm 303, 304
Cairngorms 309
Cajón de Arenales 341
Caldera del Inca 338
Calling (The) – A Life Rocked by Mountains, review 395
Campbell, Robin 445, 458
Carlson, Adam 347, 348
Carn Dearg Buttress 307
Carrel, Jean-Antoine 165-176, 293, 294
Carr, Herbert 194

Carrivick, Jonathan 353
Carr, Pauline and Tim 125
Carruthers, Tim 380
Cartwright, Chris 148
Cartwright, Ian 19
Cashin, Constant 184
Cassidy, Alan 300
Catamarca 338
Cavassa, Diego 343
Cave, George 209, 458
Cavour, Camillo 168
Cazzanelli, François 294
Celestial Peak 320
Central Darrans 347
Cerro Albardón del Potrero Escondido (5112m) 340, 341
Cerro Bautismo 344
Cerro Comecaballos 339
Cerro de los Pantanos 343
Cerro Krakus (c4900m) 342
Cerro Negro Pabellón (6086m) 343
Cerro Piramidal del Potrero Escondido (5386m) 339, 340
Cerro Torre 351, 370, 371, 372
Cervin/Cervino 111, 159, 168, 171, 172, 175, 176, 187
Cesen, Ales 20
Chadwick, John 403
Chadwick-Onyszkiewicz, Alison 365
Chamonix in articles: 148, 163, 168, 174, 229-233, 245, 273-283; in reviews: 383-385, 390, 391
Chamshen (7017m) 329
Chand, Sarwan 349
Changabang (6864m) 365, 366, 369
Chaohui, Zheng 322
Chardonnet 153, 154, 157, 426
Charlet, Jean 452
Charlet, Jonathan 295
Charok (6123m) 331
Chaukan Pass (2419m) 323
Chaukhamba col (6053m) 326
Chaukhamba IV (6854m) 326, 353
Chaupijanca 101-108
Cheeseman, Dave 395
Chimborazo 165

China (area notes) 310
Chinn, Derek 348
Chivers, Alan 178, 180
Chomolhari (7326m) 312
Cho Oyu 311, 333
Chota Sgurr 35, 38, 354
Chouinard, Yvon 373, 397
Chronicle of climbing and controversy on Cerro Torre (A), review 370
Chuan, He 322
Chulaktor 48
Chulu East (6200m) 403
Chu Skeyes Kangri (6053m) 331
Chyangdayng Khola 40
Cime Ovest 300
Clarke, Jono 348
Clark Glacier 100
Clark, Hugh 105
Clark's Nevado (5190m) 107
Cleare, John 177, 179, 181, 183, 184, 251, 419, 421, 430, 448, 458
Clegg, Dr E John 406
Climbing Days 189-198
Clough, Ian 250
Clyde River (Baffin) 115, 116
Cobern, W T 285
Coccomyxa dispar 219
Cocker, Mike 38, 354
Cohen, Geoff 38, 354
Coire an Lochain 303, 304
Coire an t-Sneachda 309
Coire Gorm on Cul Mor 306
Coire nan Eun 306
Colaye, Oliver 297
Cole, John 441
Coles, Rebecca 359
Colledge, Ray 407
Collomb, Robin 445
Combe Maudit 297
Comino, Gianni 148
Compagnie des Guides de Chamonix 275
Compagnoni, Achille 257
Compton, Edward Theodore 399
Condoraju (5115m) 107
Conefrey, Mick 257, 458
Coney, Tom 299

Contamine, André 148
Cooke, Edward William 207
Cook, Thomas 231
Cooper, Julian 450
Cooper, William Heaton 448
Cordes, Kelly 370
Cordillera Blanca 101, 102, 107, 366
Cordillera Chaupijanca 101-107
Cordillera de Ansilta 339
Cordillera Frontal 341
Cordillera Huallanca 101, 108
Cordillera Huayhuash 101, 102
Cordón de las Delicias 343
Costa, Marcos 311, 316, 317, 321
Crabbe, Davy 177
Cramer, John Antony 145
Creag an Dubh Loch 301, 304
Creag Coire na Ciste 305, 307
Creag Meagaidh 307
Crew, Pete 371, 446
Cronn, Gregg 396
Crown Peak (Huangguan Feng) 319
Croz, Michel 163, 166, 168, 169, 175, 451
Cruz, Matias 338
Cul Mor in Coigach 301
Culshaw, Alison 393
Cumberland Bay East 127, 128, 135
Cumbre de los Burros (5268m) 103
Curran, Jim 265
Cust, Arthur 443

D
Daguerre, Louis 246
Damodar Himal 334
Daogou East (5462m) 321
Dare, Ben 345
Darjeeling 241, 242, 331
Darran Mountains 345
Dauphiné 162, 277, 286, 392
Davidson, Simon 305
Davidson, Sir Edward 269
Davis, Dennis 407
Dayantianwu (5240m) 322
Deavoll, Pat 11, 317, 355
Delapierre, Bertrand 297
Delavoux, Yann 319

Dent Blanche 163, 191, 417, 426
Dent du Géant 294, 295
Désécures, Julian 297
Desio, Ardito 258
Destivelle, Catherine 251
Dhaulagiri (8167m) 333, 366, 376
Diamond Face of Moir's Mate 347
Dickinson, Leo 251
Didillon, Aurélie 321
Diemberger, Kurt 250
Di, Li 320
Ditto, Ben 113
Djangart range 212
Djanghorn 47, 48, 49, 50, 51, 52, 56
Dobie, Mike 316
Dodd, Chris 392
Dodo's Delight 113, 114
Dolomites 284, 404, 411, 439; area notes: 299
Donghua, Wu 321
Donini, Jim 321
Double Cone 348
Douglas, Ed 165, 166, 372, 388, 442
Douglas Peak 349
Doyle, Kevin 395
Dragmorpa Ri (6185m) 333
Drayton, Diane 348
Drygalskis Halvo 114, 123
Duda, Sylwia 137, 143
Duncan, Rob 313
Duplay, Benoit 137, 143
Durbin Kangri I, II 315
Durrani, Zaheer 313
Dutta, Debraj 330
Duverney, Simon 321
Dye, Adrian 57, 58, 63, 64, 358, 422
Dyhrenfurth, Norman 41, 420

E
Eagle Rock 322
Earl Mountains 346
East Bergell 448
Eastman, George 247
East Twin 345
Eastwood, Steve 349
Echevarría, Evelio 101, 108, 458
Ecuador 161, 165, 167, 394

Edwards, James 306
Egger, Toni 370, 372
Eiger 250, 277, 381
Ejército Argentino (6738m) 338
Elephant Island 136, 141
Elias, Martin 297
Eliassen, Odd 386
Elliot, Chris 349
Elliott, Sir Claude Aurelius 268, 271
Elson, Timothy 47, 298
Emily Peak 348
Emmanuel, Chance 328
Empson, William 190
Endurance 136, 141
England, William   227, 228, 229, 230, 231, 232, 233
Epp, Martin 393
Escher, Hans Conrad 444
Estcourt, Nick 365
Everest in articles: 247, 249, 261, 262, 265, 270; in area notes: 332-337; in reviews: 381, 382, 387; in obits: 403, 418, 419, 420, 421, 429
Everest Revealed, review 387

F
Fairley, John 455
Fairweather range 91, 100
Falkland Islands 127, 137, 143, 386
Fan, Yang 322
Fastness Peak 347
Faur, Freda Du 286
Faux, Ronald 380, 382
Fava, Cesarino 370, 372
Fava, Gabriel 339, 341
Favresse, Nico 117, 120, 124, 312
Favresse, Oli 113, 124
Ferintosh Peak 349
Ferraris, Roberto 294
Ferri, Guillermo 343
Fersmana 59, 62, 64, 358, 359
Figg, Paul 353, 457
Fillia, Cecilia 453
Fiordland 345, 346
Fiorenza, Luciano 342
Fitz Roy 351, 370

Folkett, Max 55, 56, 298
Forbes, James D 145
Fortuna Bay 140, 141
Foster, Peter 266, 458
Fowler, Charlie 317
Fowler, Mick 18, 19, 22, 30, 31, 329, 353, 458
Fox Jaw Cirque 352
Fox, Julian 127
Fraser, James Baillie 454
Frasne-Vallorbe Railway 284
Freeman-Attwood, Julian 126
Freshfield, Douglas 78
Frost, Rob 349
Frost, Tom 251
Fuchs, Arved 382
Fyffe, Blair 309

G
Gadgil, Rajesh 323, 459
Gadsby, Gordon Joseph 413
Gallotti, Pino 265
Gangkar Puensum (7570m) 74
Gangotri 11, 16, 17, 325, 326, 441, 353, 440, 441
Gangtok 78, 83
Garhwal 12, 249, 323, 353, 441
Garibotti, Rolando 371
Garry, Dave 299
Garthwaite, Mark 307
Garwood, Prof EJ 76, 78
Gasherbrum V 3-9
Gasherbrum VI 6
Gaspard, Pierre 286
Gattlen, Anton 443
Gauri Sankar 250
Gazgazri (also Lung Khor) (6160m) 331
Geiger, William A 197
Gemelos Norte (6110m) 339
Ghezzi, Giovanni 295
Ghilini, René 368
Ghosh, Shekhar 325
Giaccone, Stefano 297
Gibbs Fjörd 119, 120, 124
Gietl, Simon 299, 319
Gilbert, RF 415
Gill, Dr MS 331

Gillespie, Scott 64
Gill, John 251
Gilmour, AJ 286
Giobbi, D 105, 108
Giordano, Felice 169-176, 294
Givler, Alan 97
Glen Coe 305, 422
Glengyle Peak 347
Goikarla Rigyu 69, 71, 72
Golden Dragon (6614m) 73
Golovchenko, Dmitri 312
Golubev, S 285
Gómez, Lucas 343
Gongkala Shan 316
Goodall, Huw 64
Goodfellow, Basil 269
Goodhart, Jamie 359
Goodlad, Bruce 393
Goodman, Pat 320
Goodwin, Stephen 370, 375, 394
Google Earth 138, 209-214
Google Maps 210
Gornergrat 177, 284
Goromiti (also Ruyuebaojing) 319
Gove, Walter 97
Graaff, Dr Johannes de Villiers 410
Graham, Amanda 452
Graham, Peter 286, 351
Grand Cornier 163
Grandes Jorasses 147, 148, 157, 163, 168,
244, 291, 297, 449
Grandes Montets 391
Grandes Murailles 294
Grand Pic of the Meije 286
Grassi, Gian Carlo 148, 294
Graven, Joseph 293
Gray, Dennis 410, 432, 459
Great Walls of China (5186m) 312
Green, Dore 150
Greene, C R 272
Greene, Raymond 267
Greenland 20, 113, 162, 165, 166, 199,
352, 353, 381, 402, 404, 428, 462
Gregory, Alf 249
Griffin, Lindsay 439, 459
Griffith, Jonathan 297, 356

Grigoriev, Dmitri 312
Grigor-Taylor, Barbara 455
Grimes, Niall 252
Grinsted, Jack 349
Grobel, Paulo 311
Gronlund, Toto 437
Grytviken 141, 143
Gyao Kang (6735m) 311

H
Habeler, Peter 381, 389
Hadow, Douglas 169, 183
Hagshu 18-31, 328, 353, 354
Hall, Brian 368
Hall, Cory 329
Hamilton, Bob 327
Hanssens, Stéphane 312
Harding, Warren 250
Hardy, Thomas 162
Hargreaves, Alison 300
Harris, Pete 349
Harris, Steve 349
Hartz, Erik 319
Harwood, Dan 137, 143
Haston, Dougal 371
Haute Route 154, 401, 441
Hawes, Martin 348
Hawthorn, Uisdean 302, 307, 309
Head, Bernard 286
Heckmair, Anderl 250
Hedesh, Andrew 316
Hegg, Danilo 345
Helander, Clint 350
Helliker, Matt 299, 300, 352
Heng, Zhao 322
Herbert, E S 272
Herbert, Sir Edwin Savory 266, 270, 271
Herbert, T M 373
Herford, Siegfried 196
Herrligkoffer, Karl 379
Hersey, Paul 354
Herzog, Maurice 264
Hew, Cath 137
Hex River Mountains 251
Hey, Dr Richard 34
Higgins, Kevin 90

Higher Ground – A mountain guide's life, review 391
Hillary, Ed 262
Himachal Pradesh 32, 38, 327, 429
Hindu Kush 355
Hodgkin, Robin 415
Holland, C F 196
Holmes, Peter 34
Holway, E W D 286
Hood, Martin 199, 204, 459
Hooker, Sir Joseph 78
Hörnli Hut 177, 181
Hörnli Ridge 161, 167, 178, 284, 293
House, Steve 389
Houston, Charlie 261
Howard, G E 267, 272
Huamánhuequi (5338m) 107
Hua Shan 322
Huber, Alexander 300
Hüetlin, Thomas 380
Hughes, Glyn 350, 455, 459
Huinchuli 41, 42, 46
Humble, Ben 249
Humboldt Mountains 348
Hunt, Sir John 270, 409, 418, 429, 450
Hylenski, Bryan 328

I
Icebird 137, 140, 142
Ice Tooth (6200m) 312
Ikerasak Peak 122
Inchbold, John William 239
India (area notes) 323
Inglis, Andy 305, 307
Instituto Geográfico Nacional (formerly Instituto Geográfico Militar) of Peru 101,108
Irvine, Andrew 387
Irvine, Hamish 38, 354
Isoard, Jonathan 299
Italian Alpine Club 170, 420

J
Jabo Tower 316
Jachmich, Stefan 313
Jack, Greg 345

Jagdish Nanavati Garud Medal 331
Jagersky, Dusan 97
James Caird 136, 141
Jamieson, David 415
Jamieson, Murdoch 305, 306, 307
Jammu & Kashmir (area notes) 328
Janahut 10, 16, 17, 353
Jannu 241
Japanese Alpine Club 200, 203
Jarjinjabo massif 316
Jarvie, Bob 302
Jensen-Choi, Peter 3, 460
Jensen, Susan 313, 327, 329, 459
Jiaping, Hu 320
Jinyun, Dong 322
Johns Hopkins glacier 91, 96, 100
Johnson, Graham 348
Johnston, Scott 389
Joll, Daniel 345, 347
Jones, Caradoc 'Crag' 125, 460
Jones, Emlyn 269, 400, 416, 417, 418
Jones, Gareth 266, 460
Jones, J H Emlyn 416
Jopuno (5936m) 83
Joshi, Dhruv 325
Journey through the stereoscope from the 1850s to today (A) review 390
Jumbo Mountain (3399m) 286
Jumthul Phuk 83
Jungdung Kangri (6060m) 329
Jungfrau 277

K
K2 257-265, 365, 377, 378, 458, 460, 461
Kabru 241
Kaimuk Kangri (6952m) 314, 357
Kain, Conrad 286
Kaipo Wall 345
Kaltenbrunner, Gerlinde 376
Kamen Gyalmo 32-37, 354
Kande Huinchuli 41, 42
Kanehara, Keita 322
Kangchenjunga 75-90, 248, 333, 406, 408
Kang Yabat 329
Kanjiroba (6880m) 441
Kanjiroba Himal 41, 46

Kapadia, Harish 32, 36, 323, 331, 354
Karakoram 264, 313, 329, 330, 353, 384, 402
Karengjian 72
Karetai Peak 347
Karo, Silvo 372
Kauffman, Neil 319
Kawarani I 316
Kedar 11, 14, 16, 325
Kedarnath 323
Keenlyside, F H 271
Kekoo Naoroji Award 331, 448
Kelly, Brian 'Ned' 419
Kelly, Harry 449
Kemp, Dennis 252
Kennedy, Hayden 372
Kennedy, Michael 365
Kennedy, Steve 327
Kern, Cameron 321
Khanjaylak I (5424m) 358
Khan Tengri 359
Khhang Shiling (6360m) 327
Khyung Kangri (6183m) 331
Kichkidar (4370m) 285
Kilimanjaro 416, 447
King Edward Point 134
King Haakon Bay 136, 137, 139, 143, 428
Kirkpatrick, Andy 252
Kishtwar 19, 20, 22, 328, 329
Kizil Davan (5700m) 313, 315
Kleine Zinne 284
Knott, Paul 91, 351, 460
Koh-i-Bandaka 366
Kohl-Larsen Plateau 139, 140
Kokodag Dome (7137m) 313
Koktokay valley 313
Kolahoi (5425m) 403
Kongur 313
König Glacier 140, 141
Korzh, Boris 313, 358
KR II (6187m) 327
KR V (6258m) 327
Kranjc, Luka 291
Kruk, Jason 372
Kuchela Dhura (6250m) 324, 325
Kuen, Felix 379
Kulchintubulak Tower (5290m) 315

Kulha Kangri 72, 74
Kullu Makalu (6349m) 327
Kumaun 323
Kurtyka, Voytek 366, 389
Kyauk Khaung system 361
Kyrgyzstan 57, 64, 212, 214, 312, 358, 359, 360, 386
Kyuya, Fukada 199
Kyzyl Asker (5842m) 312

L
Lacedelli, Lino 257
Ladakh (area notes) 329
Ladies' Alpine Club 197, 198
Lagma (5796m) 36, 38, 354
Lama Angden (5868m) 77
Langpoche (5968m) 331
Langua-tai-Barfi (7011m) 355
Lapche Kang Range 311
Last Blue Mountain 430
Latok I 365
Laumann, Pablo 339
Lecomte, Elodie 321
Lei, Zhou 316
Le Mie Montagne 259
Lemon, Edward 360
Lennox, Gordon 304
Les Droites 293
Letters from Chamonix: stories and a novella, review 383
Lhokamburichi 79, 80, 82, 83
Lhotse 336
Liathach 309
Libecki, Mike 118
Lierenfeng (5362m) 319
Lim, David 315
Lindic, Luka 20, 292, 312
Link Sar (7041m) 356
Linth, Hans Conrad Escher von der 444
Little Konka (5928m) 319
Little Poobah (5481m) 57, 62, 358, 359
Liushen Tag (6535m) 313, 357
Lloyd, Emmeline Lewis 452
Lloyd, Hywel 456
Lloyd, R W 270
Lobuche East (6119m) 333

Lochmatter, J M 166
Lochnagar 301
Lolli, Alessandro 295
Long, Adele 452, 453
Longman, William 231
Longyala West (6000m) 315
Loocke, Koen Van 273, 463
Loppé, Gabriel 187, 363
Lorenzi, Davide 295
Lovatt, Jerry 454
Lowell, William 431
Luckett, Dr Richard 198
Lugula (6899m) 334
Lumba Sumba (5672m) 355
Lung Khor (6160m) 331
Lung Khor glacier 330
Lunn, A H 272
Lurking Tower 123
Lyskamm 48
Lyttle Peak 349

M
Maarof, Mohd Rozani bin 315
MacCarthy, Albert and Elizabeth 286
Macció, Sergio 107, 108
Macdonald, Reggie 454
Macfarlane, Paula 345
MacInnes, Hamish 177, 183, 184
MacIntyre, Alex 365-367
MacIntyre, Jean 369
Mackenzie, Dr Neil C W 421
Mackenzie, Reece 345
Mackintosh, Lee 349
MacLeod, Dave 300, 309
MacLeod, John 308
Maestri, Cesare 250, 370
Mahdi, Amir 259
Mahoney, Kevin 356
Maiandi 11, 16
Mainini, G 107, 108
Mainreachan Buttress 306
Makalu (8462m) 327, 333, 334
Malik, Spandan Kumar 327
Mallalieu, Joseph 353
Mallory, George 251, 387
Mana (7274m) 325

Manaslu 381
Manda II (6568m) 325
Manera, Ugo 148
Manson, Alan 368
Manual for the climber as athlete (A), review 389
Marcic, Nejc 312
Marguerite Spur 297
Marian Peak 345
Marliave, Christian de 126
Marshall, Robert 259, 260, 262, 264, 265
Martin, Ian 'Jock' 182
Marts, Steve 97
Mathews, William 168
Matipaganán (5170m) 107
Matterhorn, artwork: 1, 67, 111, 145, 159, 187, 207, 225, 255, 289, 363, 399; articles: 161-184; 194, 230, 236, 247, 277, 284, 443-445; in area notes: 293; in reviews 392
Matthews, William 451
Mattingley, Troy 345, 347
Maynadier, Mathieu 299
McCallum, Duncan 302
McGrath, Graham 305
McKinnon, Guy 345
McLean, Niall 345
McMahon Line 69, 71, 74
McNaught-Davis, Ian 181
McNaught, Elsie 192, 196
McPherson, Ursula 90
Meade, C F 270, 326
Mease, Jesse 313, 357
Measures, Richard 'Reg' 56, 345
Medcalf, David 418
Meiringen 273
Menlungtse 311
Mera Peak (6476m) 403
Mercier, Jeff 292
Mer de Glace 228, 238, 391, 392
Merkl, Willy 379
Messenger, Alex 161
Messini, Vittorio 319
Messner, Günther 379
Messner: My life at the limit, review 380
Messner, Reinhold 251, 370, 372, 380

Meyer, H 111
Meyer, Johann-Jakob 67
Middleton, Rob 64
Mighty Dur 347
Miller, Christopher 316
Millerioux, Hélias 299
Millgate, Michael 162
Mills Peak 345
Milner, Douglas 115
Minya Konka 317
Mitre Peak 345
Miyar valley 327
Moatti, Sébastien 312
Moffat, Gwen 450
Monaghan, Keith 90
Mont Blanc 147-157, 162, 191, 231, 245, 274-282, 292-299, 390
Mont Dolent 168
Monte Losetta (3054m) 453
Monte Nero (3344m) 295
Monte Rosa 236, 239, 284, 408
Mont Greuvetta 147-157
Mont Maudit 298
Mont Vert de Greuvetta 147-157
Monviso (Monte Viso) 168, 176, 451, 452, 453
Monypenny, James 329
Moorehead, Catherine 403, 442, 460
Moores, Paul 297
Moran, Martin 304, 391
Morgan, Jon 427
Morgan, Richard 425
Morrell, Bradley 43
Morris, Jaz 345
Morrison, Mike 329
Mortimer, Mike 432
Morton, Gus 313
Moulton, Hannah 64
Mount Abbe 91, 94, 97, 98, 100, 351
Mountains in my Heart, review 376
Mount Aspiring (3036m) 286, 345, 347, 348
Mount Bertha 91
Mount Burns 349
Mount Cook 286
Mount Crillon (3879m) 91, 92, 96, 97, 351
Mount Darwin 349

Mount Edith Cavell (3363m) 285, 286
Mount Everest Foundation (MEF) 17, 38, 56, 64, 100, 249, 350, 426
Mount Fairweather 96
Mount French 347
Mount Fuji 204
Mount Hicks 349
Mount Kenya 447
Mount Makere 347
Mount Meeson (2699m) 286
Mount Speight 349
Mount St Elias (5489m) 432
Mount Superior 251
Mount Suter 345, 346
Mount Tuhawaiki 347
Muchu Chhish 356
Mukherjee, Anindya 11, 75, 83, 84, 90, 325, 460
Mukherjee, Debabrata 326, 327, 331
Mullach nan Rathain 309
Mulvany, Stanley 345
Muni, Divyesh 329
Muratti, Glauco 340, 344
Murphy, Danny 347
Murray Snowfield 137
Murray, W H 270, 272
Mustang region 332
Muztagh Ata 310, 313
Myanmar 323, 361

N
Nagai, Tsuyoshi 74
Nakamura, Diego 342, 343
Nakamura, Tamotsu (Tom) 69, 74, 310, 461
Naka, Taichiro 349
Nam Tso: Kyizi (6206m) 73
Nanda Devi East (7434m) 325
Nanga Parbat 262, 265, 378, 379, 380, 381, 389
Nantai 203
Narsing (5825m) 83
Nath, Paresh Chandra 327
Navigator Range 349
Nazomi 349
Nedhuk 1 (5100m) 358

Negro Pabellón (6086m) 343
Nepal (area notes) 354
Nevado de Shicra (5150m?) 107
Nevado Pampash (5338m) 101, 107
Newman, Bernard 369, 461
New Zealand 47, 92, 286; area notes: 345
Nga Mokopuna 347
Ngapo Kangri 330
Nico Made (c4600m) 339
Nihon Hyakumeizan 203
Nilov, Sergei 312
Nisbet, Andy 301, 304-309, 327
Noel, John 247, 387
Norbu, Pemba (King Kong) 331
Nordenskjöld glacier 125, 128, 131
Nordenskjöld Peak 125, 135
Normand, Bruce 310-322, 357, 461
Norton, Christopher 387
Norton, Edward 387, 388
Norton, James Ryrie 326
Novak, Skip 126
Noyce, Wilf 249
Nyainqentanglha (Nyanchentanglha) 73, 74, 312

O
Oddo, Enzo 311
Odgsal I (6234m) 331
Odgsal II (6028m) 331
Odintsov, Alexander 389
Officers and Committee 2015 442
Olivares del Límite (6220m) 344
Olsen, Max 345
One Day as a Tiger, review 365
One Hand Peak (5100m) 90
One Hundred Mountains of Japan, review 199
Onodera, Kenji 322
Orco/Gran Paradiso 295
Orme, Zac 347
Otto, Jon 319

P
Paldor West (5500m) 403
Pandim (6691m) 83
Papert, Ines 309, 389

Parham, Felix 319
Parkin, Andy 329
Parnell, Ian 390
Parsons, Kieran 91, 97, 100, 345, 347, 349, 351
Pasaban, Edurne 376
Passauram 75, 76, 77, 79, 82, 83, 85, 87, 88, 90
Paternkofel 284
Paterson, Kris 182
Patey, Tom 397
Patrasi 39, 40, 42, 46
Payrola, Patricio 338
Peachey, Ian 64
Peacock, John DC 427
Peacock, Nigel 430
Peak After-You 47, 48, 50, 51, 52, 54
Peak Byeliy 312
Peak Fotheringham (4871m) 48
Peak Macmillan (5051m) 48, 56
Peak Vinton-Boot 47, 48, 56
Pelagic, Pelagic Australis 125, 127, 128, 130, 135
Peng, Wu 320
Pensilungpa 328
Pentecost, Allan 218, 461
Perotti, Livio 453
Perrin, Jim 331
Perry, Steve 304, 307, 308, 309
Pertusaria corallina 219
Peruffo, Alberto 81
Pesce, Korra 292, 297
Petit Dur 345, 347
Petrocelli, Adrián 340
Phelan, Caroline 452
Phormidium 218
Pickford, Lord Justice 286
Pico 7 de Ansilta (5780m) 339
Pico Bravo (6193m) 338
Pico Cichitti (6164m) 338
Pierse, Simon 234, 461
Pik Betelgeuse 56
Pik Byeliy ('Grand Poobah') 312, 360
Pik Currahee 212, 214
Pik Donstanski (4780m) 58, 59, 64
Pik Fotheringham (4871m) 56

Pik Kinmundy (4950m) 56
Pik Shchurovsky (4259m) 285
Pilley, Dorothy 189-198
Pilley, John 190
Pilling, Bill 97
Pinnacle Club 197, 198
Pinney, Mike 328
Piolet d'Or 389, 457, 461, 462
Pirámide Alejandro Lewis 338
Pissis (c6800m) 338
Plateau Peak (7300m) 330
Point Andrea (4566m) 48, 56
Pointe Alphonse Couttet (3660m) 154
Pointe Hélène 297
Pointe Marguerite 297
Pointe Whymper 297
Poire du Mulinet (2850m) 295
Pollinger, Georg 347
Pomiu 319, 320
Pontoriero, Pablo 342
Popes Nose 348
Porter, John 365, 397
Port Stanley 137, 143
Potala Shan 322
Poucher, Walter 249
Prentice, Tom 147-157, 295
Presanella Group 295
Preston, Jonathan 304, 305, 306
Prezelj, Marko 20, 312
Private diaries (The) and sketches of Edward Norton (Everest Revealed), review 387
Puchoz, Mario 264
Puma Yumco 74
Punta Clavarino (3260m) 295
Punte Gastaldi (3210m) 453
Purdy, Richard Little 162
Putha Hiunchuli (7246m) 334
Putnam, William (Bill) 431

Q
Qaqug(d)lugssuit 114, 123
Qiezi Feng (Aubergine Peak) 322
Qinghai 315
Qin Mountains 322
Qionglai Shan 319
Qizhi, Gu 321

Quebrada de Chorrillos 339
Quinag 305
Quincey, Duncan 353
Qungmo Kangri (7048m) 74

R
Raeburn, Harold 77, 79
Ramsden, Paul 19, 30, 31, 329, 353
Randall, Val 385
Ranimal Point 63
Ratel, Sébastien 321
Rébuffat, Gaston 397
Refuge Harbour 120
Reid, Bruce 427
Remarkables range 347
Rennard, Helen 305, 309
Revelations range 350
Rey, Guido 194
Richard Sale and Jochen Hemmleb 378
Richards, Ivor Armstrong 190, 194
Richardson, Simon 147, 295, 301, 304, 305, 461
Richards, Robin 413
Riffelberg 225, 444
Riis-Johannessen, Bjørn 136, 462
Rimo III 16, 353
Ritz, Anton 236
Roberts, Dave 127
Robertson, Guy 301, 302, 304, 307, 309
Roberts, Stephanie 434
Robinson, Doug 373
Roche, Clare 378
Rock Needles of Siniolchu 84-90
Rongdo valley 330
Rosita Bay 143
Rowland, Peter 455
Royal Air Force Mountain Rescue Team 415
Royal Geographical Society 165, 270, 350, 402, 429
Rudkin, Dave 309
Rupal Face 378, 389
Ruskin, John 159, 238, 239, 445
Russel Glacier 353
Russell, C A 284, 462
Ruyuebaojing 319
Rwenzori 221

S

Sagarmatha Pollution Control Committee 336
Sa'i Lhamo (6030m) 331
Salvaterra, Ermanno 371
Sam Ford Fjörd 123
Sánchez, Wenny 339, 341
Sangay Ri (6000m) 315
Sarikol (4160m) 285
Saser Kangri II 329
Sashindran, Gp Capt VK 330
Saunders, Victor 215, 329, 462
Scanu, Marcelo 338, 462
Schmiedt, Mauro 343
Scholz, Peter 379
Schuster, Lord 269
Scotia Sea 136
Scotland (area notes) 301
Scott, Doug 249, 252, 414
Scott Polar Research Institute 162
Sedgwick Museum 34
Seerdengpu 320, 322
Sella Foundation 168
Sella, Quintino 168-176, 294, 452
Sgurr an Fhidhleir 305
Shackleton 136, 137, 138, 141, 142, 143, 428
Shadbolt, Leslie 270
Shakawr (7076m) 355
Shaksgam Valley 313
Shaluli Shan 316
Shark's Fin (5086m) 321
Shepton, Bob 113, 115, 462
Sheridan, Guy 386
Sheridan Peak 131, 386
Sherpa, Lakpa 81, 83
Sherpa, Thendup 81, 82, 83, 90
Shicra Shicra nevados and valley 105
Shields, George 302
Shintani, Tadao 74
Shipton, Eric 313
Shirouma-dake 199
Shishapangma 312, 377
Shorrocks, Chris 427
Shroff, Cyrus 325
Shuangqiaogou 320
Shupka Kunchang glacier 330
Siguniang (6250m) 311, 319, 320

Sikkim 76, 79, 84, 87, 88, 90, 241, 324
Silver, Neil 305, 307
Silvestre, Ben 351
Simler, Rudolf Theodor 236
Simvu 75-89
Sim, Will 305
Single Cone 347
Siniolchu 75-90
Sisimiut 120
Sisne 42, 46
Skelton, Stephen 345
Ski Touring: a practical manual, review 393
Skov, Peter 200
Slioch 305
Small, Iain 304-307, 309
Smith, Albert 245
Smith, Ian 462
Smith, Rob 329
Smythe, Frank 247, 248, 249
Smythe, Tony 448
Somervell, Howard 387
Somnus 348
Southern Alps (New Zealand) 92, 286
Southern Japanese Alps 197
South Georgia 125-143, 386, 428
Spence, Kenny 302
Sperli, Johann Jakob 67
Spiers, James 347
Spillett, Richard 127, 128
Spiti 32, 37, 38, 354, 412
St Andrew's Bay 142
Steck, Ueli 389
Stephen, Leslie 279
Stevenson, David 383
Stitzinger, Luis 313
Stob a'Choire Mheadhoin 309
Stockham, Karen 189, 462
Stone, Tony 304
Storie, Chris 328
Straka, Jan 293
Straton, Isabella 452
Strazar, Luka 312
Stromness 136-143, 428
Studer, Gottlieb Samuel 236
Sulu Peak (6000m) 356
Sundt, Eilert 285

Sursun Ri (6535m) 312
Survey of India 38, 79
Sutton, Rob 300
Swanstrom, Paul 92
Swindin, Barbara 437, 439
Swindin, Les 437
Swiss Alpine Club 273
Swiss Foundation for Alpine Research 260
Syrett, John 368
Szu-Ting, Yi 322

T

Table Mountain (1087m) 285
Taiaroa 345
Tairraz, Joseph 231
Tai Shan 318
Tajikistan 358, 359
Talbot, Henry Fox 247
Talling, Peter 361
Talung glacier (Sikkim) 75-90
Talung nala (Spiti) 35, 354
Tancán 105
Tanggula Shan 315
Tangmor (5920m) 35-38
Tarlha Ri (6777m) 74
Tasilq Fjord 352
Tasman glacier 286
Taugwalder, Heini 181
Tavanini, Daniel 299, 319
Taxi to the Snow Line, review 386
Tees, Alan and Jimmy 90
Tejada-Flores, Lito 292
Telles, Marcelo 127
Temple, Philip 383
Te Puoho Basin 347
Terray, Lionel 370, 397
Thameserku (6623m) 334
Tharpu Chuli (Tent Peak) (5663m) 403
Theodule Pass 145, 166
Tholung Gompa-Kishong 84
Thomas, Hugh 55, 56
Thomas, Neil 55, 56
Thomas, Robin 304
Thompson, Pete 356
Thompson, Sam 313, 358
Thomson, Richard 347

Thornton, James 345
Tibawi, Rya 452
Tibet 22, 32, 33, 38, 69, 72, 74, 357; area notes 310, 334
Tien Shan 48, 50, 53, 56, 57, 312, 313, 358
Tilman, H W (Bill) 79, 203, 250
Tilting at Mountains, review 376
Tingchenkhang (6010m) 324
Todd, Chris 355
Tofana di Rozes 299
Tomé, J J 108
Tompkins, Jean 345
Tongshyong 75, 76, 77, 78, 81, 82, 89
Torre Blanca de Ectelion 342
Torres del Campanario 341, 342
Toshio, Fujishima 203
Tour Ronde 299
Town, John 313, 357
Toyoshima, Tadashi 77
Training for the New Alpinism, review 389
Treasures of the Alpine Club (exhibition) 455
Trillingerne 352
Trisul (7120 m) 324, 325
Tsurugi 202
Tuckett, Francis Fox 451, 454
Tuhawaiki 347
Tunnel Bluffs 345
Tupungato 344
Turner, Rich 347
Txibon, Jabi 338
Tyndall, John 207
Tyrol Shan 319
Tyson, John 440

U

Ulrich, Melchior 236
Umaram Kang 83
Unsworth, Walt 387
Unter Gabelhorn 443
Uren, Allan 345
Ushba 285
Uttarakhand 324
Uummannaq 113-116, 120, 122, 124

V

Valais 273, 274, 276, 282, 283, 293, 440

Val Ferret 147, 148, 152, 153, 157, 239
Valtournenche 293
Vanj Range in Pamirs 358
Vardy, Paul 355
Varengo, Freddy 348
Vass, Dave 347
Venables, Stephen 126, 245, 252
Venturelli, Giulia 298
Villaneuva, Sean 113, 123, 312
Vincent Islands 137
Vischer, Bas 312
Vogler, Romain 299
Volcán Bonete Chico (6759m) 338
Vritik, Pavel 293

W
Walker, Al 345
Walker Citadel 117, 118, 120, 124
Walker, Lucy 163, 194
Walker Spur 292
Walker, Susanna 358
Waller, Ivan 251
Wall, Ian 332, 463
Walmsley, John 435
Walton, Elijah 225, 445
Washburn, Bradford 91
Watson, Vera 365
Waugh, Colonel 78
Webb, Roger 304, 305
Wendenbaum, Evrard 312
Westcott, Tony 328
Westmacott, Mike 270
West, Miles and Laura 127
Weston, Walter 202
Wetterhorn 277
Wheatstone, Charles 228
Whillans, Don 250, 446
White, John Claude 84
White Mountains of New England 197
Whybrow, Barry 180
Whymper, Edward 161-167, 168-176, 181, 231, 236, 245-250, 297, 454
Wickens, Phil 136, 137, 143
Wickwire, James 97
Wilkens Peaks 140
Williams, Alfred J 234

Wills, Sir Alfred 387
Wilson, Ken 251
Wilson, Neil 305, 306
Wilson, Peter 345
Woodall, Chris 405
Worde Konggye (5725m) 71
Wright, Johnnie 182
Wynne-Jones, Dave 401, 453

X
Xanthoria elegans 222
Xiaofei, Zhu 322
Xinjiang 310, 311, 312, 313, 315, 357
Xuelian range 313, 358

Y
Yala (5820m) 317, 320
Yalaxianbo 69, 70, 74
Yaniro, Tony 389
Yarlung Tsangpo 69, 71, 74
Yearsley, Simon 10-17, 305, 307, 353
Yeend, Allan 435
Young, Annie Maria 190
Young, Geoffrey Winthrop 266
Yunqing, Liu 316
Yun, Ye 322

Z
Zamtu Chu 87
Zanskar 19, 20, 21, 22, 31, 327, 386; in area notes: 328
Zapiola, Facundo Juárez 338
Zawada, Andrzej 369
Zemu 77, 79, 81, 83, 85, 87, 90
Zermatt 67, 111, 161-168, 171-176, 180, 197, 229, 236, 277, 284
Zhiming, Wang 322
Zhixiong, Liu 320
Zholobenko, Aleksey 39, 463
Zhongli, Li 320
Zig-Zag pass 139
Zimmerman, Graham 350
Zmutt Ridge 293
Zumer, Martin 312
Zumthul Phuk 75-90

X

EXTREM

FOR THE HARSHEST CONDITIONS

Matterhorn calling.

150 years ago, Edward Whymper and his team made alpinism history by summiting the Matterhorn for the first time. To honor this incredible feat, Mammut and the Zermatt Mountain Guides illuminated the Hörnli Ridge to highlight the route of the historic first ascent. www.mammut.ch

MAMMUT
Absolute alpine.

SWISS TECHNOLOGY ✦

erdmannpeisker / Robert Bösch

Where there's
love there's pain.

MOUNTAIN
EQUIPMENT

mountain-equipment.co.uk

BEING BROADMINDED WIDENS HORIZONS

WHEN IT COMES TO INVESTMENT, SEE HOW WE'RE THINKING BEYOND THE OBVIOUS.

CALL HOWARD JENNER
INVESTMENT DIRECTOR

TEL. 020 7150 4167 OR VISIT
WWW.QUILTERCHEVIOT.COM

QUILTER CHEVIOT
INVESTMENT MANAGEMENT